MAMMON'S MUSIC

MAMMON'S MUSIC

*Literature and Economics
in the Age of
Milton*

BLAIR HOXBY

Yale University Press   New Haven & London

Published with assistance from the foundation established in memory of Oliver Baty Cunningham of the Class of 1917, Yale College.

Published with the assistance of the Frederick W. Hilles Publication Fund of Yale University.

Designed by James J. Johnson and set in Bembo Roman type by Tseng Information Systems, Inc.

Printed in the United States of America by Sheridan Books, Ann Arbor, Michigan.

Library of Congress Cataloging-in-Publication Data

Hoxby, Blair, 1966–
Mammon's music : literature and economics in the age of Milton / Blair Hoxby.
p. cm.
Includes bibliographical references and index.
ISBN 0-300-09378-0 (alk. paper)

1. Milton, John, 1608–1674—Knowledge—Economics.   2. Economics and literature—Great Britain—History—17th century.   3. Economics in literature.   4. Commerce in literature.
I. Title.
PR3592.E25 H69   2002
821'.4—dc21

2002002643

A catalogue record for this book is available from the British Library.

The paper in this book meets the guidelines for permanence and durability of the Committee on Production Guidelines for Book Longevity of the Council on Library Resources.

10 9 8 7 6 5 4 3 2 1

For
Caroline

Contents

Acknowledgments

Research for this book was generously supported by a Jacob J. Javits Fellowship and by several funds administered by Yale University: the Samuel and Ronnie Heyman Prize, the John Addison Porter Prize, a Whiting Fellowship in the Humanities, and a Richard J. Franke Interdisciplinary Fellowship in the Humanities. Its publication has been subsidized by the Elizabethan Club and by the Frederick W. Hilles Publication Fund, administered by the Whitney Humanities Center, Yale University.

For their expert assistance, I wish to thank the staffs of the Beinecke and British Art Center Libraries at Yale University; the Baker Business and Houghton Libraries at Harvard University; the Guildhall Library of the Corporation of London; the British Library; the Conway Library of the Courtauld Institute of Art; the Stichting Koninklijk te Amsterdam; the Amsterdams Historisch Museum; and the Rijksmuseum-Stichting. I also wish to thank Lara Heimert, Heidi Downey, and Kay Scheuer for overseeing the editing and production of this book.

This study has benefited from the comments of several anonymous referees and from the questions asked by audience members at Columbia, Princeton, the University of Michigan, the University of Southern California, the Medieval and Renaissance Colloquium at Yale, Yale School of Management, the Modern Language Association meetings, the Sixth International Milton Symposium, the Conference on John Milton, the Northeast Milton Seminar, and the *Sixteenth Century Journal* Conference, where I delivered portions of it as talks.

An earlier and shorter version of Chapter One appeared as "The Trade of Truth Advanced: *Areopagitica,* Economic Discourse, and Libertarian Reform," *Milton Studies* 36 (1988), ed. Albert C. Labriola: 177–202; © 1998 by University of Pittsburgh Press. Portions of Part Two appeared in "The Government of Trade: Commerce, Politics, and the Courtly Art of the Restoration," *ELH* 63 (1999): 561–627. An earlier version of Chapter Seven appeared as "At the Public Mill of the Philistines: *Samson Agonistes* and the Problem of Work after the Restoration," in *The Altering Eye: New Perspectives on Milton's "Samson Agonistes,"* ed. Mark R. Kelley and Joseph Wittreich (Newark: University of Delaware Press, 2002). I am grateful to these publishers for permission to incorporate that material here.

I owe an old debt to John Cary for guiding me through my first complete reading of Milton. During the course of this project, many colleagues at Yale and in the larger community of early modernists and Miltonists have offered me much-valued encouragement. Maija Jansson answered my questions about parliamentary records. Martine Julia van Ittersum patiently translated Dutch materials for me; the few such translations that appear in the book are hers. Leslie Brisman, Ruth Yeazell, Tyrus Miller, Laura King, and Lawrence Rainey read individual chapters. John Hollander and Lynne Greenberg commented on an entire version of the manuscript. Lawrence Manley, David Quint, Annabel Patterson, and John Rogers helped me shape this study from its inception as a prospectus, and they have been generous with their learning and judgment ever since, reading each chapter as it was produced. As a Calvinist, economist, and advocate of clarity, my wife, Caroline, has left her stamp on these pages in more than one way. But more than that, she helps me see every day that Odysseus's wish for Nausicaa (*Od.* 6.180–85) can be more than just fine words.

A Note on Conventions and Texts

Dates are given in old style, but years are assumed to begin on January 1. Unless otherwise stated, all books published before 1800 were printed in London. I have regularized the capitalization and punctuation of titles while retaining their original spelling.

Biblical quotations are from the Authorized (King James) version. Citations of classical sources, unless otherwise indicated, refer to editions in the Loeb Classical Library. In a few cases, I have made minor changes to the translations.

I cite the first editions of Milton's poetry: *A Maske Presented at Ludlow Castle* (1637), *Paradise Lost* (1667), and *Paradise Regaind. A Poem in IV Books. To Which is Added Samson Agonistes* (1671). These are reproduced in *John Milton's Complete Poetical Works in Photographic Facsimile with Critical Apparatus,* ed. Harris Francis Fletcher (Urbana: University of Illinois Press, 1943). I quote Milton's prose from *The Complete Prose Works of John Milton,* gen. ed. Don M. Wolfe, 8 vols. (New Haven: Yale University Press, 1953–82), henceforth abbreviated *CPW.*

I regularly use the following texts:

The Basic Works of Aristotle, ed. Richard McKeon (New York: Random House, 1941).

Sir William Davenant, *The Shorter Poems, and Songs from the Plays and Masques,* ed. A. M. Gibbs (Oxford: Clarendon Press, 1972).

Expans'd Hieroglypicks: A Critical Edition of Sir John Denham's "Coopers Hill," ed. Brendan O'Hehir (Berkeley: University of California Press, 1969).

The Works of John Dryden, ed. Edward Niles Hooker and H. T. Sweden-berg, Jr., 20 vols. (Berkeley: University of California Press, 1956–89).

The Poems and Letters of Andrew Marvell, ed. H. M. Margoliouth, 3d ed., rev. Pierre Leguois and E. E. Duncan Jones (Oxford: Clarendon Press, 1971).

The Works of Thomas Middleton, ed. A. H. Bullen, 8 vols. (London: John C. Nimmo, 1886).

Twickenham Edition of the Poems of Alexander Pope, gen. ed. John Butt, 6 vols. (New Haven: Yale University Press, 1939–61).

Introduction

In an age better known for its political, religious, and scientific revolutions, it may have been the commercial revolution of the seventeenth century that had the deepest effect on English culture and the literature it produced.[1] This book tells the story of what that revolution, spanning the decades from 1630 to 1700, meant both to the century's greatest poet and to the literary tradition in which he worked. I focus on texts produced from 1634 to the end of the Anglo-Dutch Wars in 1674, a period that coincides not only with the maturity of this study's central figure, Milton, but with the appearance of some of the century's most searching and contested inquiries into the meaning and uses of trade, the interdependence of the state and the economy, and the importance of labor. I contend that these inquiries made some of Milton's most compelling and creative thought possible, even as they engendered specters that would haunt the imagination of his late verse. In an effort to assess Milton's achievement with a measure of historical precision, I read his writings against texts written by his immediate contemporaries, including the Levellers, the Hartlib circle, Sir William Davenant, Edmund Waller, Sir John Denham, John Dryden, and Sir William Petty. I set my consideration of these, in turn, in the context of that longer period of economic transformation that stretched from the antimonopoly controversy of 1601 to the appearance of the final version of Bernard Mandeville's *Fable of the Bees* in 1724. I do so in order that I may describe more broadly how economic discourse made literary history swerve in the seventeenth century—how, by posing new moral and aesthetic problems for authors, it pressed them to inno-

vate formally and to reimagine such basic notions as self, community, and
empire.

When James I came to the throne in 1603, the vast majority of England's four million inhabitants lived in rural districts and worked the
land, and even tradesmen in medium-sized towns typically earned some
of their income from farming or wage labor on the land. Households consumed much of what they produced; they often worked the land on terms
that were determined by "custom," a continually renewed code of practice
that was the result of long-term negotiations between lords and tenants;
and to the extent that they participated in markets for labor, goods, and
capital, those markets were, in most cases, local rather than national. Although Elizabeth I had chartered the Spanish (1573–74), Eastland (1579),
Levant (1592), and East India (1600) Companies, England's major foreign
trade remained the sale of unfinished broadcloths to Northern Europe.[2]

James I's boldest commercial undertaking required him to suspend
the charter of the Merchant Adventurers, who had conducted that trade
since 1486; to ban the export of white cloths; and to entrust the dyeing,
dressing, and export of manufactured textiles to the King's Merchant Adventurers, a new group of projectors led by Sir William Cockayne.[3] The
year 1614 had been a record one for the traditional cloth trade, but the
Cockayne Project changed all that. Even when the projectors were permitted to ship white cloths, they proved incapable of doing so, and they
faced an even harder time selling the cloths that they did finish, for the
United Provinces banned their import. This trade stoppage was exacer-
bated by an international monetary crisis that was precipitated by the decision of several Continental monarchs to debase their currencies in an
effort to finance their war expenditures.[4] The economic catastrophe that
ensued has been compared to the Great Depression of the twentieth century, not only for its severity but for the foment of inquiry and analysis it generated. To be sure, Elizabethans like Sir Thomas Smith and Sir
Thomas Gresham had written insightfully about certain aspects of money
and trade, but the depression of the 1620s encouraged the production of
newly sophisticated economic treatises that had a profound influence on
English society.[5] They are the starting point of this book.

Thomas Mun, a merchant in the East India Company and a member of the Privy Council's subcommittee commissioned to gather evidence about the causes of the decay of trade and scarcity of coin, developed a conceptual model of the market in which the flow of goods and
the movement of prices and interest rates were interdependent and resistant to statutory regulation.[6] At the same time, Gerard de Malynes and

Edward Misselden debated the causes of the nation's shortage of coins. Contradicting Malynes's claim that the king could determine and enforce the value of his own coins and that merchants who sent coin abroad in order to profit from exchange were pursuing their own gain at the expense of the commonwealth, Misselden argued that currency exchange was just a kind of "*Commerce* exercised in money," one that gave merchants, not princes, the ultimate power to set the value of coins. He also denied Malynes's traditional distinction between the common wealth and private commodity. For "what else makes a Common-wealth," he asked in a question that would echo throughout the century, "but the private-wealth, if I may so say, of the members therof in the exercise of *Commerce . . . ?*"[7] Beginning with the aim of advocating isolated policies, Mun and Misselden took tentative steps toward developing a science of human behavior whose principles possessed not only the force and inevitability of natural laws but their resistance to moral judgment.

Although the trade and monetary crisis of the early 1620s did not last long into Charles I's reign, it remained apparent that England would not, in future, be able to rely on its trade in white cloths, which were in less and less demand. Whereas articulate opinion had once identified the commonwealth's interests with social harmony, it now identified them more closely with advances in national productivity. Landlords, whose relations with tenants were increasingly governed by the laws of property and contract rather than "custom," were permitted to undertake even suspect "improvements" like the enclosure of commons. Farmers were given a freer hand to dispose of their products to their own advantage on an agricultural market that was becoming more integrated and therefore less vulnerable to collusion and dearth. Manufacturers turned to innovative products like the New Draperies, which were not only dyed and finished but, just as important, lay outside the purview of the statutes and regulations that had accreted around the manufacture of traditional woollens since 1550. And merchants established new trades with the Mediterranean, Asia, Africa, and the Americas, which, if as yet insignificant in most cases, would combine to form great triangular trades after the Restoration.[8]

Because he chose to rule without Parliament from 1629, Charles I was particularly dependent on customs revenues from foreign trade, but even this could not finance the Crown. So he raised funds from impositions, ship money, royal grants of monopoly, and even, in 1640, his seizure of the gold that London merchants had deposited at the mint for safekeeping.[9] To Charles I's opponents, these and other unpopular acts were examples of arbitrary government. They not only cut at the power of Parliament and the liberties of the subject, they threatened the prosperity of the nation. For foreigners could not be expected to leave their capital in a nation where the king did not respect the property of his subjects, and his subjects were not likely to accrue property through hard work if they feared that it would be taxed away without their consent: they would grow dispirited.

When the Long Parliament sat in 1640, it consequently announced its intention to redress a range of grievances, including monopolies and unparliamentary taxes.[10] Because the system for controlling the press that the Crown had established began to crumble shortly after the assembly began to sit, a period of what Milton hailed as "free writing and free speaking" ensued.[11] This, the first of the century's two great publishing booms, lasted until the restoration of Charles II in 1660, despite the intervening efforts of Parliament to reestablish control over the press. Its effects were felt long afterwards.

Some of the tracts on trade that appeared during these years, such as Sir Ralph Maddison's *Great Britain's Remembrancer, Looking In and Out. Tending to the Increase of the Monies of the Commonwealth* (1640), hearkened back to arguments that had been advanced by Malynes as early as 1601. But others, like *Sir Thomas Roe His Speech in Parliament* (1640) and Henry Robinson's *England's Safety, in Trade's Encrease* (1641) argued that England's cloth trade could not be carried on in the old way. Rather than prop prices up, manufacturers and merchants would have to find new ways to "sell good cheap" now that other nations could make their own cloth.[12] England had to recognize that it was part of an increasingly integrated world market, so that the appearance, say, of West Indian cotton on the world market could deprive England of return goods from the Levant. That very integration meant that the export of treasure to the East Indies need not be bemoaned. Treasure was not to be accumulated unthinkingly, for exchange rates affected the price at which the nation could afford to sell its manufactures abroad; and the East India trade could, in any event, be integrated into what should become a more important part of the nation's commerce — the re-export trade.[13]

By the time Robinson wrote, he could consult a prior literature not just of statecraft, which recognized with Aristotle that "a state is often as much in want of money and of such devices for obtaining it as a household"; or of jurisprudence, which treated topics like prices, monopolies, and markets within the purview of commutative justice; but of what contemporaries called the study of *trade*.[14] The term *oeconomy* still referred, as it had for Aristotle, to the art of household management. The phrase *political oeconomy* would not be used in English to denote a discipline for another century. Until then, a range of topics that contemporaries perceived to be related—wealth, currency, the production and exchange of goods, patterns of saving and expenditure, methods of taxation, and population—were debated in tracts on "trade."[15] What I will frequently call "economic discourse"—the language and arguments that found their origin, if not their ultimate significance, in this literature of trade but that were not long confined to its narrow circuit—acquired cultural authority in part because it hailed from a *discipline* in the making. It would not be until the beginning of the eighteenth century that John Cary could declare complacently, "Trade has its principles as other sciences have," but even by the middle of the seventeenth century, the study of trade had its own past, its own developing lexicon, its own assumptions, and its own things to say about two concepts that lay at the heart of the period's religious, political, and scientific debates: *agency* and *organization*.[16] Economic discourse could place pressure on traditional categories of thought and established genres precisely because it was associated with a powerful new way of seeing and describing the world, one whose ramifications stretched far beyond narrow questions of commerce. Yet it is just as important to acknowledge that the literature of trade made progress only by borrowing diction, metaphors, and models from other disciplines and other discourses, including politics, medicine, and the physical sciences. Indeed, the unique conditions that obtained from 1640 to 1660—when individuals felt what it meant to be agents as never before, when the organization of church, state, the physical world, and the commercial realm all seemed to be up for grabs, and when all these issues could be debated in print—made it all the more likely that new lines of inquiry in one cultural field would be informed by those in others and would, in turn, make themselves felt in contemporary verse and prose.[17]

The economic thought that appeared in these auspicious conditions is remarkable for its range and diversity. Writers like Benjamin Worsley and Sir William Petty, both of whom dreamed, like Sir Francis Bacon, of mastering nature, could conceive of trade and industry as instruments of a statecraft that, in Petty's view, could be more perfectly conducted if only it were set on the sound basis of a "political arithmetic" whose object of study, the assets and organization of the nation, was conceived as a "political economy," or state-wide household. Troubled by underemployment in the realm, men like William Goffe could put forward plans that would make local communities the unit of organization for new enterprises in the fishing and hemp industries.[18] The Levellers, in sharp contrast, could make the liberty and property of individual householders the basis of their economic proposals. Not only did they seek to dismantle the monopoly privileges of the guilds, companies, and urban corporations; they argued,

by extension, that monopolies were as harmful when they took political
or religious form as when they took the form of exclusive trading privileges.[19] Most radically of all, Gerrard Winstanley could pronounce that
the king of righteousness would be free to rule in every heart only if the
earth were turned into a common treasury, prices were eliminated, and
the "crafty Art of buying and selling" were abandoned.[20]

It need hardly be said that Winstanley's proposals, some of which he
addressed to Oliver Cromwell, did not win wide assent; but in several
ways his writings are not as distinct from mainstream tracts on trade as
they might at first appear. Custom officers and company merchants also
invoked the authority of the Bible in their tracts, even if they preferred
to appeal to the precedent set by biblical figures like King Solomon when
advocating policies. A Puritan like Worsley, who served as Secretary to
the Commonwealth's Council of Trade, might even anticipate "the break-
ing forth, very shortly" of God's "Glorie" before proceeding, in rather
more mundane terms, to advise the English to learn from the commercial practices of the Dutch.[21] The religious beliefs of authors like Worsley,
Robinson, and Petty, who still figure in histories of economic thought,
were neither in conflict with nor irrelevant to their tracts on trade. Indeed, their faith may actually have helped them to conceive of trade's abstract operations. It is not a very long step from continuing revelation to
the elasticity of wealth, from the workings of providence to the invisible
course of trade. The inspiration for Petty's political arithmetic may even
have lain in scripture, for in claiming to reduce all to number, weight, and
measure, he asked readers to remember that God had "ordered all things
in measure and number and weight" (Wisd. of Sol. 11:20).[22]

If economic discourse derived some of its cultural authority from
trade's status as an emerging discipline, it acquired its urgency by dint of
its very permeability. It was a field of contestation whose terms and arguments might enter, or conversely be inflected by, religious or political
debates. In the pages that follow, I focus on concepts like *trade* and *labor* because their very pliancy made them more rhetorically charged and intel-
lectually suggestive than some other topics that also attracted considerable
attention, such as banking. That made them interesting to authors whose
foremost allegiance might be to a political or religious program rather
than an economic one.

In more general terms, economic discourse mattered to poets and
polemicists because it changed the language that they had at their disposal
by attaching new meanings to words and tropes. Take the word *commodity*.
To describe something as a commodity in the fifteenth and sixteenth centuries was to praise it and to affirm that it met your needs, that it was bene-

ficial to you. This is the sense in which some mid-seventeenth-century Puritans continued to apply the word to their schemes of reformation. But the frequency with which tradesmen applied the term of praise to their wares meant that it was natural for commercial writers to turn it into a neutral descriptor in their developing science. They applied it to any object of trade.[23] That meant that when Restoration poets praised London as the bank of world trade and imagined the world's "commodities" converging on the Thames, they were performing a complex verbal act — narrowing the application of the word to wares, invoking its technical sense as it was used in the literature of trade, yet at the same time reinvesting it with all the laudatory force of its root sense in order to contend that London *needed* to be at the center of the world's trade routes. In many cases when they used such economic diction, they were also signaling their allegiance to a poetic mode that was not allegorical or visionary but clear-sighted, precise, reasoned, and current. While the poets of the next century arguably wished to create a purged poetic diction, seventeenth-century poets were more often exhilarated than repelled by the polysemous language of trade.[24] Understandably so. For economic discourse relied on metaphors and analogies, posed basic questions of meaning and value, and faced — and in some cases even promised to solve — seemingly intractable problems of symbolization.

I should distinguish my interests and methods here at the outset from those of other critics who have written on literature and economics. Setting aside studies that employ economic vocabulary simply in order to redescribe familiar topics like desire and honor in terms of "libidinal economies" and "symbolic capital," we are left with analyses that may be described as materialist or semiological.[25] Relying on a master theory of economic development, materialist readings can treat authors as if they were the unwitting amanuenses of the large-scale developments, such as the transition from feudalism to capitalism, that Marxist theory would seem to dictate. While such readings need no longer assume that economic forces constitute a base that determines society's superstructure of politics, law, and religion, they still analyze economic events in Marxist terms that would be recognized by neither seventeenth-century Englishmen nor neoclassical economists — the two perspectives that I privilege over Marxist categories.[26] That language and money share problems of meaning, symbolization, and value has been the central contention of another body of semiological criticism.[27] The association between words and money is as old as Zeno, as Marc Shell has observed, and it remained current in seventeenth-century England.[28] That is why Michel Drayton claimed in a poem that the Goldsmiths presented to James I that Apollo was rightly the god of both poetry and minting.[29] My interpretive methods are compatible with semiological readings when they dwell on poetic moments like this, but I prefer to focus on economic topics *other* than money because they were of greater concern to Englishmen in the mid-seventeenth century and have attracted less commentary.

Taking as my starting point the issues that seemed important to contemporary observers (such as free trade, primacy in world trade, and the productive capacity of labor), I confine myself to literary texts in which authors quite directly address economic issues or avail themselves of economic reasoning. I thus refuse myself the license of Marc Shell's claim that because "all literary works are composed of tropic exchanges," they can all, regardless of content, "be analyzed in terms of economic form."[30] But precisely because I wish to argue that authors in the seventeenth century increasingly recognized that the public realm was an economic one and that economic logic had a centrifugal tendency to invade social and political relations hitherto governed by other principles, I have *not* refrained from reading texts like *Areopagitica* or *The Readie and Easie Way,* which register that change by applying economic reasoning to related problems in the public realm, such as the free circulation of ideas or the preservation of choice in the polity.

In focusing on texts that *represent* or that consciously *engage* economic subjects and forms of analysis, I aim to honor literature's mimetic and persuasive ambitions. The dissatisfaction of New Historicists with interpretive models that would make of literature either a simple reflection of its culture or a series of linguistic deferrals confined to the discursive domain has promoted "a reciprocal concern with the historicity of texts and the textuality of histories."[31] In exploring the "historical specificity, the social and material embedding" of all modes of writing and reading, however, New Historicists have tended to focus on texts that represent social relations only obliquely, as it were in spite of themselves.[32] Indeed, we might justly infer that the suitability of a text for New Historicist analysis is inversely proportional to its ostensible engagement with history. Having selected my texts according to quite different criteria, I assume that the developments I trace in seventeenth-century literature result at least in part from the conscious attempts of authors to register and respond to changes in the material conditions of their contemporaries, the political and economic forces to which they were subjected, the desires they felt, and the fears they conceived. That said, I have tried to remain alive to the ways in which representations of reality, even personal encounters with it, are inevitably mediated through prior representations. I have tried to remember, as well, that the reality that a text occludes or makes imaginable may be as important as the one it reflects.

New Historicists have reminded us that we can have no access to a genuine past unmediated by textual traces. All written remnants from the past, whether overtly imaginative or more simply intended to convey information, opinions, or commands are at once *texts* that require interpretation and *documents* whose production, promulgation or publication, and survival are the result of specific social forces and circumstances. Yet we cannot study the ways in which acts of representation invent or suppress reality unless we are willing to construct a historical account (however provisional) *against* which we propose to define the *fictiveness* of such representations. That is best done, I would argue, by reasserting a temporary and permeable division between the strongly complex poetry and prose that is the focus of this book and the other evidence that survives from the period (whether material, documentary, or discursive), which I use as the basis for a historical account whose value as a counterpoint to my close readings depends precisely on its adherence to evidence that is *not* drawn from overtly imaginative texts. Only through such a dialogue can we hope to analyze the processes by which imaginative literature is constituted by, and in turn helps to constitute, society. That such an approach privileges the literary seems to me entirely appropriate for a work that aspires to the name of historicist literary criticism, not historiography.

In practice, if not in theory, New Historicists tend to assume a provisional division between text and context much like the one I have just proposed. They often make other methodological assumptions, however, that I cannot accept. I do not assume (in keeping with a model adopted from structural anthropology) that literary texts, like any other products of their culture, share a single deep structure or mentality; much less do I assume that an entire society is produced by certain structures of domination, so that even forces of apparent opposition turn out to be mere "illusory epiphenomen[a] of conformity" and all efforts to write within a society's system of signs can be seen, finally, to be acts of complicity.[33] Both assumptions strike me as peculiarly unsuited to seventeenth-century England, especially when we stray far from the culture of the Court, for the society in question was increasingly pluralistic and decentralized, acutely aware of its own fractures along religious, political, geographical, and economic lines, vulnerable to two political revolutions, and increasingly permeable to foreign cultures as its trade and colonial relations expanded.

These theoretical demurrals have practical consequences for the pages that follow. I do not juxtapose literary texts with events or artifacts that bear no demonstrable relation to them except synchronicity and a perceived homology. Nor do I rely on exemplary anecdotes, for as soon as we dispense with the assumption that a society shares a single mentality, we must severely curtail all claims for the explanatory power of isolated incidents.[34] Instead, I focus on literary or topical allusions and on the more general engagement of literary works with particular strains of discourse that I define through their programmatic use of ideologically consequential arguments, tropes, or diction. Concurring with many of the methodological prescriptions of J. G. A. Pocock and Quentin Skinner, I limit the historical context in which I read texts by asking what contemporary events or strains of discourse these works seem either to invoke as their own context or to suppress with a bad conscience.[35] I believe this is the best way to honor literature's ambition and capacity to serve as an active mediator of culture.

While the authors who are the subject of this work could hardly have been alive to all their own cultural assumptions, or to the unintended consequences that their fictions would have for the society in which they lived, they were well aware that the new world of economic thought was itself the product of crisis and conflict within English society, and they recognized that few economic ideas were innocent of political or religious implications. By remaining alert to the circumstances in which authors wrote, I endeavor not only to recapture some of the complexity and contingency of economic life as it was experienced and recorded in the seventeenth century but also to show how individuals and groups (acting as deliberating agents) tried to influence that economic life, and how authors (working as conscious artists) made choices about representations that helped to shape their culture in discernible ways.[36] If, as Perry Anderson has said, one of the central problems of contemporary social theory is how structure and subject relate to one another in human history and society, then I have privileged the subject's ambivalent *experience* of his or her relationship with social structures—perceived as multiple, even contradictory in their imperatives—as they variously enable or disable his or her efforts at self-definition and determination.[37]

The very heterogeneity and dynamism that seventeenth-century Englishmen perceived in these social structures generated hope and profound anxiety by turns. Because that dynamism particularly interests me, my analysis is not so much synchronic as diachronic: I tell a *narrative* of Milton's personal career and of the century's more general literary engagement with the discourse of trade. I am aware that the coinvolvement of economic, political, and religious struggles in the seventeenth century will open any account of the period's economic controversies to the charge of being unidimensional—or conversely, unfocused—but far from discouraging the enterprise, that coinvolvement should make it the more urgent, for it only proves how powerfully suggestive the new world of economic thinking was to English society. That is why writers like Milton could not ignore it.

Milton's first engagement with the new economic discourse was a hostile one, staged in the debate on circulation between the Lady and Comus in *A Maske Presented at Ludlow Castle* (1634). It is all the more remarkable, then, to see how nearly Milton's views approach Comus's in the 1640s. That change is the subject of Part One, "Virtue, Commerce, Truth." I argue that *Areopagitica* (1644), like other pleadings for freedom of speech and liberty of conscience in the 1640s, is indebted to earlier defenses of free trade, which provided a model argument for the circulation of ideas and the consequent production of truth. For some reformers like those in the Hartlib circle, the contiguity between information and commodities suggested projects that endeavored to increase economic enfranchisement by disseminating information. Just as proponents of free speech learned from economic discourse, economic reformers learned, in turn, from arguments for the spread of truth. It may have been Milton's confidence in those arguments, I suggest in closing, that underwrote his defense of popular sovereignty from 1649 to 1651.

The creation of a new republic in the midst of the century's worst economic depression, together with the restoration of the king in the midst of another trade crisis, put tremendous pressure on politicians to articulate a theory of government's role in the economy. In "The Government of Trade," a part covering the years 1649–67, I describe the competing efforts of republicans and Royalists to align their respective governments with the cause of commercial expansion, a struggle that the Royalists eventually won. For Milton, it was a bitter turn, and he bemoaned "the vain and groundless apprehension of the people that nothing but kingship can restore trade."[38] Written as the cause of trade was being captured by the Royalists, his *Readie and Easie Way* is torn between clearing a space in the polity in which market forces can preserve a form of individual liberty and abandoning economic appeals as a rhetorical strategy because they have been captured by the opposition. Yet the Royalist victory carried its own price. In order to make their case convincing, Royalists had to present a revised ideal of kingship not only in the royal entry of 1661 but in the panegyrics that they published from Charles II's restoration to the appearance in print of Dryden's *Annus Mirabilis*.

One of their central claims was that force and commerce, Crown and

City, could coordinate their efforts and generate strength and wealth in a virtuous cycle. In Part Three, "Force, Commerce, and Empire," I examine the ways in which representations of trade, force, and geography intersect in *Annus Mirabilis* (1667), *Paradise Lost* (1667), Dryden's *Amboyna* (1673), and the tradition of topographic poetry that stretches from Sir John Denham's *Coopers Hill* (1642) to Alexander Pope's *Windsor Forest* (1713). For Dryden, the complementary relationship between force and commerce suggested by the Anglo-Dutch Wars provided an opportunity to renovate the epic tradition by revising epic *topoi* to accommodate the new realities of trade. In *Paradise Lost*—in which Satan is associated with grandiose mercantile ventures and imperial projects and Adam's vision from the Top of Speculation includes a disturbing panorama of global exploitation indebted to Luís Vaz de Camões's *Os Lusíadas*—the contiguity of trade and conquest is cast in a darker light, and the Restoration ideal of an empire of trade is subverted. In the other texts discussed in Part Three, we find authors turning to some of the figures that are important to *Annus Mirabilis* and *Paradise Lost*—from topographical visions to models of consensual but unequal relationships—in order to envision England's relationship with the periphery of its trade empire as one of power tempered by responsibility.

The close of *Paradise Lost* exhibits an overwhelming drive toward the individual, yet as *Samson Agonistes* (1671) recognizes, even so personal an activity as labor cannot be extracted from its social context. In Part Four, "The Meaning of Work," I read Milton's tragedy as a meditation on the consolations and temptations of labor after the Restoration, when some dissenters perceived the restored king as "an Egyptian taskmaster" and themselves as subjects who might be forced "to make brick without straw to build monuments of his rigour and our slavery."[39] If we may judge by some of the proposals advanced by Sir William Petty, their fears were not groundless. I argue that it is not just the brooding middle of Milton's dramatic poem that is troubled by the moral and political consequences of labor but its catastrophe, which I read in dialogue with the Restoration's politically inflected discourse of work, building, and production. Beyond yielding a fuller appreciation of the resonance that Samson's destruction of the Philistine theater must have had for contemporary readers, this approach should help us see why Milton refuses to reassure readers of a divine authority responsible for Samson's "rouzing motions." What is at stake is nothing less than the formative influence of economic principles and economic forces on the public sphere—an influence that Milton now conceives in very different terms than he did in *Areopagitica*.

Taken together, these chapters present a Milton who (contrary to received opinion) was neither indifferent to economic concerns nor incapable of understanding new economic theories. In fact, I argue that Milton could be more creative and radical in his use of economic principles than were some of his fellow republicans, even if they are better known for their emphasis on trade and productivity. But I hope these chapters, and in particular Chapters Five and Seven, will also convey how sensible Milton remained of the darker possibilities of economic intercourse and discipline. He well knew, for instance, that trade might become a tool of empire and that the state might be tempted to requisition the productive capacities of its citizens. Especially in his late verse, Milton seems peculiarly conscious both of the difficulty of imagining any system of economic relations that would be safe from such dangers and of the social and personal losses that would inevitably result from forgoing all commerce among men. I would argue, however, that if Milton's late exploration of economic problems leads him (and his readers) into paradoxes, contradictions, and ellipses, that is evidence less of his inability to follow the logic of economic reasoning—and here I trust that my analyses of some of Milton's earlier prose tracts will bear me out—than of his stubborn unwillingness to reconcile what cannot be reconciled, or deny what should not be denied, in the imagination of the heart.

Readers may well ask how this Milton squares with the advocate of political liberty and religious reform who is more familiar to them. While Milton's sensitivity to the demands of genre as a poet and his alertness to rhetorical opportunities as a pamphleteer must inevitably frustrate any attempt to distill a perfectly consistent system of settled convictions from his writings, readers cannot help but feel that certain preoccupations, ideas, and assumptions recur in his work with a regularity that may pass for coherence. It has been plausibly suggested that these habits of thought arise from two intellectual traditions. The first is an ancient ideal of freedom that informs both the *virtù* of Renaissance Italy's civic humanists and the Christian liberty of Northern Europe's Protestant humanists. The second is an evangelical, messianic strain of Puritanism whose English roots may be traced back to John Bale and John Fox.[40] We might refer to these in shorthand as Milton's *humanism* and his *millenarianism*. In what follows, I will periodically relate Milton's engagement with economic discourse to these more familiar aspects of his imagination not simply because the failure of that engagement to mimic the trajectory of his political and religious beliefs might otherwise cause puzzlement, but because I believe that Milton's profoundest contributions to political philosophy and free-will theology were in no small way owing to his sophisticated understanding of economic thought.

One of my larger ambitions in this book is to chart the growing conviction of Milton's contemporaries that the public realm was an economic one and that economic forces operated with an abstract inevitability that made them akin to natural forces and similarly resistant to moral analysis. As authors perceived the determinative role that economic forces could play in the fates of kings and states, as they became aware of the inextricable involvement of individuals in a network of economic relations, they accommodated literary traditions to this new construction of reality. The common vocabulary with which writers could articulate such insights became at once more varied and more precise as the century progressed, and their notions of what constituted the proper subject of epideictic, historical, and epic verse changed. By looking ahead to such figures as Bernard Mandeville and Daniel Defoe in my Conclusion, I hope to clarify that trajectory even in the literature of the mid-seventeenth century. Yet if many of the texts that I discuss were written in public modes or for public occasions, what was at stake when seventeenth-century authors made room in their texts for economic problems was not simply the nature of the public realm: what it meant to be, or to write about being, a man or woman could no longer be extricated from what it meant to be an economic agent or to be subject to economic forces. It may in fact be that shadowy interstice of economic force, representation, and selfhood that imaginative literature is uniquely suited to probe.

PART ONE

VIRTUE, COMMERCE, TRUTH

The young Milton first betrayed his cautious interest in the new economic reasoning of the 1620s in *A Maske Presented at Ludlow Castle* (1634). Having written one aristocratic entertainment for the dowager countess of Derby, a patron of reformist Protestant writers and the mother-in-law of John Egerton, earl of Bridgewater, Milton undertook two years later to produce a masque to celebrate the installation of the earl as Lord President of the Council of the Marches of Wales.[1]

Court masques had reached an apogee of scenic complexity and expense under Charles I and Henrietta Maria. They usually staged the union of Heroic Virtue with Divine Beauty or Love in a neoplatonic celebration of the royal marriage. By dancing in these masques, the king and his Catholic queen affirmed that spiritual truths must be embodied in spectacle and ritual, that political ideals must be identified with personal loyalties, and that they themselves could master the forces of misrule represented in the antimasques: unchecked passions, base or mutinous subjects, and foreign threats. Because they contained antimasques, these entertainments were not univocal. They provided a forum for covert critique of the Personal Rule (1629–40). But their primary purpose was certainly to strengthen it through mystification.[2]

Milton seems to have been familiar with the court masques of the Jacobean and Caroline court, which he could have read in printed form. He may have received more reports from his musical collaborator, Henry Lawes, and his performers, the Egerton children, who had danced in *Tempe Restored* (1632) and *Coelum Britannicum* (1634). What he produced is a reformed masque that gives greater scope to argument, prophecy, and song than to spectacle and that stresses virtue's ability to withstand trial rather than its power to effect a courtly resolution.[3] Milton's scenario begins with the children of the earl trying to make their way through the woods to their father's house, Ludlow Castle. The Lady is separated from her brothers, only to be waylaid, tempted, and threatened by Comus and his crew of bestial antimasquers. Although she withstands his advances and trumpets the power of her own prophetic speech to bring his "magick structures rear'd so high" toppling down on his head (line 797), she must rely on the intervention of her brothers and the aid of the nymph Sabrina, a figure of divine grace, to free her "insared chastity" (line 908).

Before she can be rid of Comus, however, the Lady is subjected to his arguments for the circulation of wealth and the consumption of the world's bounty.[4] It seems strange that the topic should arise, and it *is* strange. It would be difficult to imagine any subject less calculated to inflame the passions and secure the sexual favors of a fifteen-year-old virgin. But perhaps we should remember that as a representative of the king and the presiding member of an equity court, the Lord President of the Council of Marches did not simply impose fines for moral offenses and investigate crimes like the rape of Marjorie Evans—duties that, some critics have suggested, *A Maske* may obliquely commend; he also prevented illegal enclosures and suppressed the disturbances that they provoked, protected a local mining monopoly, and heard numerous private actions over debts and arrears in rent (which were due each year at Michaelmas, the date of the masque's performance).[5] Milton may have thought that the earl would be as interested in the exploitation of natural resources and the distribution of wealth as he was in sexual transgression. We can be sure that Milton was interested in Comus's arguments for the circulation of wealth not only because he includes them in the masque at the cost of dramatic probability but because, between the performance text of 1634 and the first edition of 1637, he restored a key passage from Comus's argument that had been cut for performance (lines 736–54).

Comus begins his seduction-by-economic-analogy by upbraiding the Lady for inverting the "cov'nants" of Nature's trust. Nature lent the Lady her "daintie limms" for "gentle usage, and soft delicacie." By refusing her limbs "refreshment after toile, ease after paine" and thus "scorning the unexempt condition" of her loan, says Comus, the Lady is dealing with Nature as an "ill borrower" would (lines 679–86). That Comus's language is reminiscent of Despair's effort to persuade Redcrosse to death in *The Faerie Queene* (1.9.40) may warn us that while Comus promises a death that will manifest itself as harmless sexual gratification (and perhaps a new life thereafter), what he is really proffering is the everlasting death that is sin. Yet the reappearance of such language also transfers some of the power of the Spenserian temptation to Milton's, where it is put to the service not of a theological but of an economic case.

Comus proceeds to bemoan the folly of men who listen to the Stoics' and Cynics' praise of "Abstinence":

> Wherefore did Nature powre her bounties forth
> With such a full and unwithdrawing hand,
> Covering the earth with odours, fruits, and flocks,
> Thronging the seas with spawne innumerable,
> But all to please, and sate the curious tast?
> And set to work millions of spinning worms,
> That in their green shops weave the smooth-hair'd silk
> To deck her Sons, and that no corner might
> Be vacant of her plentie, in her owne loyns
> She hutch'd th'all-worshipt ore, and precious gems
> To store her children with; if all the world
> Should in a pet of temperance feed on Pulse,
> Drink the clear streame, and nothing weare but Freize,
> Th'all-giver would be unthank't, would be unprais'd,
> Not halfe his riches known, and yet despis'd,
> And we should serve him as a grudging master,
> As a penurious niggard of his wealth,
> And live like Natures bastards, not her sons,
> Who would be quite surcharg'd with her own weight,
> And strangl'd with her wast fertilitie.

(lines 709–28)

Comus develops this vision of a superabundant Nature with imaginative rapture before drawing the lesson,

> Beauty is natures coine, must not be hoorded,
> But must be currant, and the good therof
> Consists in mutuall and partaken blisse,
> Vnsavourie in th'injoyment of it selfe.

(lines 738–41)

Comus is, in fact, playing the role of the conventional lover with such metaphors.[6] What will change his argument-by-analogy into something more, what will force us to consider its underlying assumptions, is the Lady's iconoclastic literalism, her striking response to the (economic) ve-hicle, rather than the (sexual) tenor, of the tempter's speech.

Comus's sexual and economic visions inform each other because the essential feature of both is their dynamism. The burden of his argument is to dissuade the Lady from hoarding at a moment of crisis and uncertainty. According to Comus, wealth, like pleasure, is not fixed but elastic. It is also abstract, no more to be identified with a hoard of coin than one's sexual assets are to be identified with a jealously guarded hymen. "Vnsavourie in th'injoyment of it selfe," coin is valued or "good" because it facilitates exchange and consumption in an indefatigable cycle of "mutuall and partaken blisse."

An emphasis on the circulation of trade and currency, coupled with a new insistence on conceiving the economy as a dynamic system of production, exchange, and consumption in which the wealth of a nation could not be easily equated with its stock of bullion are, as we noticed in the Introduction, the most striking features of the more innovative tracts on money and commerce that appeared in response to the monetary crisis and commercial depression of the early 1620s. Arguing against the defensive instinct of some in English government to retreat from foreign trade and discourage domestic consumption, writers like Thomas Mun stressed that production *and* consumption were required to turn the wheels of commerce. In his emphasis on the fluidity of currency markets, Edward Misselden began to make what would ultimately be an even more important claim: that economic laws were beyond the power of princes to control and therefore more akin to natural than to social laws.[7] Comus's argument derives part of its energy from such new, and newly sophisticated, arguments. The Lady seems to feel as much when she accuses Comus of attempting to "charme" her "judgement" by "obtruding false rules pranckt in reasons garbe" (lines 757–58). Comus's "rules," at once natural and economic, are deterministic rather than normative, with an explanatory force more akin to that of science than that of ethics.

With Comus's warning against serving God as a "grudging master" and in the process becoming a "penurious niggard of his wealth," it becomes clear that the key biblical authority for Comus's speech is the parable of the talents (Matt. 25:14–30), in which a master praises those servants who "traded" with the talents he gave them and casts into outer darkness the unprofitable servant who hid his talent in the earth. The parable glosses Comus's assertion that Nature has lent the Lady her body "for gentle usage" that might be repaid by generating new bodies from her own, a figure suggested by the discourse of usury, in which money's ability to beget more money when lent at interest was, following Aristotle, represented as "the breeding of money because the offspring resembles the parent."[8] Comus's assurance that his cordial julep will "restore all soone" may mean that it will help the Lady recover her strength, but it may also mean that if she drinks it, she will soon be in a position to restore the principal of her loan with another body (line 689).

The same parable motivates Comus's audacious allusion to Ovid's account of man's descent from a Golden Age to an Iron Age. Whereas in Ovid the gold in the earth's womb (*viscera*) was first extracted by men in an act of penetration occasioned by an excessive love of having (*amor habendi*) and figured as a rape (*Met.* 1.137–40), according to Comus the earth is really inviting the exploration of her every orifice by hutching gold in her loins. Comus has learned from the fate of the unprofitable servant: if digging into the earth and hiding money was wrong for him to do, then surely the reverse procedure must be right.

In his anticipated union with the Lady and in his description of mining in such sexual terms, production and consumption, effort and pleasure seem to converge. This is no accident, for the point of Comus's argument is that even consumption is beneficial because it makes room for production. Coins are valuable only when they are at work: it is their ability to work that justifies the payment of interest, and it is the generative power of such accommodations that makes it possible to consume and consume.

Even before Comus can make his speech in praise of consumption, however, the Lady complains about his abuse of her trust in terms that begin to transume his economic diction. She objects that he has betrayed her "credulous innocence" (line 696) through his "base forgerie" (line 697), an epithet that suggests counterfeiting and its accomplice, debasement. Since, as Erasmus had explained a century before, debasement was a means by which unscrupulous princes "[robbed] the people," it seems appropriate that Comus, as a figure of aristocratic greed and indulgence, should be associated, however obliquely, with such a form of fiscal oppression.[9] But the charge is even more directly appropriate because Comus is both other and less than he represents himself to be. The Lady's distrust of Comus and her annoyance at having acted upon false information are crucial not only to the masque's larger themes of faith, trial, and virginity but to its inset drama of economic models because belief is the sine qua non of what we now call the "multiplier effects" of the sort of dynamic economy that Comus celebrates—its ability to generate new wealth through a series of transactions. It is no accident that terms like *credit, trust, security, good will, assurance,* and *faith* enjoy such prominence in the economic lexicon.[10] The Lady, of course, has good reason *not* to credit Comus, but her own response to Comus's economic claims will make it clear that her reluctance is not simply the shamefastness of a fifteen-year-old girl. Like every sexual liaison, every loan—indeed, every economic transaction— is a leap of faith. But in a static economy in which the only problems are distributive and in which to consume is to exhaust one's store rather than to participate in a generative process, there is little call to take such a leap.

In what must be one of the most *un*dramatic moments of the masque because the Lady seems to forget what Comus is really after, she refutes the premises of his (economic) analogy:

> Impostor doe not charge most innocent nature,
> As if she would her children should be riotous
> With her abundance, she good cateresse
> Means her provision only to the good
> That live according to her sober laws,
> And holy dictate of spare Temperance:
> If every just man that now pines with want
> Had but a moderate, and beseeming share
> Of that which lewdly-pamper'd Luxurie
> Now heaps upon some few with vast excesse,
> Natures full blessings would be well-dispenc't
> In unsuperfluous even proportion,
> And she no whit encomber'd with her store,
> And then the giver would be better thank't,
> His praise due paid.
>
> (lines 761–75)

The Lady refuses Comus's "treasonous offer" to render an account of her stewardship at least in part because she recognizes that Comus is not her master. As Georgia Christopher has observed, she sounds as if she has been reading her Calvin: "[Let this] continually resound in our ears: 'Give an account of your stewardship' [Luke 16:2]. Let it also be remembered by whom this account is demanded; that it is by him who has so highly recommended abstinence, sobriety, frugality, and modesty."[11] Plato, Aristotle, and the Gospels all advised men to moderate or renounce their desires for wealth—a lesson that Milton never forgot, even if he countenanced the seemly enjoyment of fine things.[12]

But the Lady does not stand solely on the virtue of temperance. It is as if she answers with the Poverty of Thomas Carew's *Coelum Britannicum* (1634), "For mark how few they are that share the world" (line 603). Poor are the "numerous armies and swarming ants / That fight and toil" for those happy few (lines 604–5).[13] That a court masque can nod toward the armies of the poor should remind us of how boldly Comus overlooks them. He sees only worms spinning in green shops, whereas if he had looked just north of the Severn River, he would have seen human spinners who, still oppressed by the aftershocks of the recent trade depression, were living in a miserable estate. In Carew's masque, a nod does not issue in commiseration: Mercury simply decides that he "does not require the dull society" of Poverty's "necessitated temperance" (lines 659–60). In Milton's masque, in sharp contrast, the Lady asserts that what Comus describes as a problem of superabundance for some is really a problem of distributive justice and distributive efficiency in the larger society. She counters Comus's interpretation of the parable of the talents by reading it as an injunction to the wealthy to share some of what they have with the less fortunate. In doing so, she follows those moralists who, arguing against an oft-cited scriptural warrant for self-interested economic behavior—"Is it not lawful for me to do as I will with my own?" (Matt. 20:15)—reminded readers that they were but stewards of the Lord's riches. According to the Lady, both justice and efficiency demand better distribution, for not only do just men go without as it stands, but marginal goods are consumed by the wealthy in "lewdly-pampered Luxurie" when they might, in a transaction that would contribute more to society, stave off the hunger of those less fortunate. Against Comus's proffers of false love, the Lady sets the true Christian fraternity that should inflect commerce and charitable giving alike: Christ, Calvin said, would approve of "no other management of his blessings, than such as is connected to charity."[14] To be sure, the antimasques of entertainments performed for Charles I sometimes referred obliquely to the economic grievances of his subjects. "Several other *Projectors* were in like manner personated in this Antimasque," says Bulstrode Whitelocke of *The Triumph of Peace* (1634), "and it pleased the spectators the more, because by it an information was covertly given to the king, of the unfitness and ridiculousness of these projects against the law."[15] A speech like the Lady's seems to be of a completely different order, however, precisely because there is nothing oblique about it. It is easy to see why her social compassion and Milton's prophetic fire have appealed to critics like Christopher Hill.[16]

But it is just as important to recognize that the Lady's argument is predicated on the economy's being static rather than dynamic: distribution will be the sole important factor in an economy only if growth is not an important consideration. With the words "would" and "means," ascribed to Nature's purposes, the Lady shifts away from Comus's rhetoric of natural or economic law ("that's how it works") to moral categories of intent and ideal ("this is what was intended and how it ought to be"). Misselden and Mun had written of economic forces in terms of natural laws in part because they wanted policies to address what they saw as economic realities rather than social ideals and in part because they wished to emphasize that the appropriate response to an economic crisis like that of the early 1620s, one of whose chief characteristics was a shortage of coin, was not to withdraw from the economy and store one's capital, for that would simply deepen the depression. The Lady's instinct is quite the opposite: when threatened, she hoards.

If *A Maske* is Milton's first encounter with the claims of the new economic reasoning, we may conclude that it is an unconsummated one, for the overarching logic of the masque leaves little doubt that the Lady is right to hoard. I say *little* because in a plot development that critics have not always found easy to explain, the Lady's apparently virtuous abstinence nevertheless leaves her "in stonie fetters fixt, and motionlesse" (line 818). Some critics have suspected her of incontinent desires, and surely any account of her predicament must address the masque's preoccupation with sexuality.[17] Nonetheless, may not her situation, with her nerves "all chain'd up in alablaster" like a statue, her legs "root bound" like Daphne's (lines 659–61), also be the natural consequence of her inflexible notions of the economy and of sexuality alike?

It is certainly remarkable to see how nearly Milton converges on Comus's arguments for economic and sexual circulation in his tracts of the 1640s: the Lady's concern with abstention and distribution gives way to the pamphleteer's investigation of the processes of circulation, commerce, and generation; an ethic of sexual hoarding gives way to an ideal of chaste sexuality governed by dissoluble (and potentially multiple) marriage contracts. It is as if Milton had used Comus's arguments as a kind of thought experiment in which he might safely displace into the mouth of a tempter lines of reasoning that were as yet unthinkable in 1634. We shall have other reasons to recall the economic debate between Comus and the Lady— with its vision of a superabundant, and therefore threatening, nature that will reappear in *Paradise Lost*—but it is with the claims of circulation and commerce that my first chapter begins. By the time of *Areopagitica* (1644), the Lady's insistence that "none / But such as are good men can give good things" would no longer seem so absolute (lines 701–2).

The Trade of Truth Advanced

I t is no accident of history that a monopoly grant to a select group of printers elicited what may be the greatest apology for human liberty in the English language, Milton's *Areopagitica* (November 1644). While Milton's editors and critics have ably set his pamphlet in the context of the other tracts on freedom of speech and liberty of conscience that arose from the church government and licensing controversy of the 1640s, they have paid limited attention to Milton's knowledge of antimonopoly case law, to his use of contemporary arguments in favor of free trade, or to the expository burden of the commercial imagery in his tract.[1] That neglect has not only hindered our ability to chart the progress of Milton's economic thought between *A Maske* (1634) and his participation in the trade negotiations of the Commonwealth (1649–53); it has prevented us from fully understanding the very pleadings for expanded liberties amid which *Areopagitica* is usually situated. For, as we shall see, Milton's pamphlet is the crowning example of a tradition of legal commentary whose only *concept* of liberty was freedom from monopoly.

Milton was already thinking of intellectual exchange in terms of trade by 1642, when he published *The Reason of Church Government*. Recalling the parable of the talents, he reminded readers of their duty to improve the gifts entrusted to them. They must determine how best to "dispose and employ those summes of knowledge and illumination, which God hath sent [them] into this world to trade with," striving to bear themselves "uprightly" in their "spiritual factory" and to promote a "heavenly traffick" (*CPW* 1:801–02). Yet "having receiv'd amongst [their] allotted parcels certain pretious truths of such an orient lustre as no diamond can equall," they might find themselves kept from the market by powerful men who have an interest in suppressing what they have to sell. For "the great Marchants of this world fearing that this cours would soon discover, and disgrace the fals glitter of their deceitfull wares wherewith they abuse the people, like poor Indians with beads and glasses, practize by all meanes how they may suppresse the venting of such rarities" (*CPW* 1:801–02).

It is little wonder, then, that in responding to the Long Parliament's Licensing Order of June 14, 1643, Milton should again think of intellectual exchange in terms of trade. For the order used a grant of exclusive privileges to a select group of master printers to align the economic interest of the Stationers' Company with Parliament's aim of controlling the press: it erected an economic monopoly and imposed an intellectual restriction in a single measure. The Stationers themselves were granted rights of search and seizure so that in jealously guarding their monopoly against interloping printers and booksellers they might suppress unsanctioned printing. Milton felt the weight of their authority in August 1644, when they pursued him for the unlicensed publication of his divorce tracts.[2] In *Areopagitica,* Milton responded not just with a vindication of liberty in the face of oppression but with a model of intellectual exchange that, relying on the theories and arguments of free trade advocates, contended that men could best generate truth when they were left free to exercise their industry and employ their skill in producing, venting, and purchasing ideas in an open market. In short, he advanced a new ideal of the way the public sphere should operate.[3]

In this chapter, we shall also see that if free speech pamphlets like *Areopagitica* drew on the arguments of free trade advocates, they repaid their debt to economic thought. Justice demanded that the economic sphere be made more open and equitable, and free speech pamphlets suggested that one way that goal might be achieved was to make creative use of publicity and the free flow of information. Although Milton's direct involvement with such reforms was more limited than that of some other advocates of free speech like Henry Robinson and William Walwyn, the social resonance of *Areopagitica* and other free speech tracts in the economic realm is itself suggestive of how related some contemporaries thought the logic of economic and intellectual exchange really were. It is further evidence that Milton and like-minded reformers did not consider the economic analogies in their tracts and sermons mere flowers of rhetoric but vehicles for thinking systematically about the conditions of intellectual exchange that were likeliest to generate truth without bound.

In *Areopagitica,* Milton was able for the first time to reconcile his humanist and millenarian values with a subset of the century's new economic arguments and thus push beyond the tentative thought experiments of *A Maske*. Was it Milton's faith in the resulting model of intellectual exchange, I ask in closing, that underwrote his defense of popular sovereignty from 1649 to 1651?

The Case against Monopolies

Elizabeth I and her Stuart successors used their royal prerogative to grant patents of monopoly for manufactures not only to protect new industrial processes but to favor loyal courtiers and their clients with royal bounty.[4] Because patentees and chartered trading companies were willing to return a portion of their monopoly profits to the Crown in the form of taxes and loans, the monopoly system also provided an attractive form of extraparliamentary financing. By the end of Elizabeth's reign, however, the legal basis and economic effect of this unpopular system was already being controverted in the courts, in Parliament, and in print.

As Sir Robert Cecil observed in 1601, the "dispute" over monopolies drew "two great things in question; First the Princes power; Secondly the freedom of Englishmen." The queen, said Francis Bacon, had both an "enlarging" and a "restraining Power," either of which could be used to regulate or restrict trade and manufacturing, "for by her Prerogative she may first set at liberty things restrained in Statute Law or otherwise; and secondly, by her Prerogative she may restrain things which be at liberty." Yet even the queen's prerogative had a theoretical, if ill-defined, limit. "As I think it is no derogation to the Omnipotence of God to say he can do all but evil," said the lawyer Lawrence Hyde, "So I think it is no derogation to the Majesty or Person of the Queen to say the like in some proportion." Even if the queen granted letters patent, those grants could be deemed void if they violated divine law, deprived subjects of their native liberties, or were not for the good and avail of subjects generally.[5]

In the landmark case *Darcy v Allen* (1602), in which the courtier Edward Darcy pursued the haberdasher Thomas Allen for selling playing cards that Darcy had not manufactured, the defense successfully countered that Darcy's grant for the exclusive manufacture or importation of cards was void on just these grounds.[6] Arguing on behalf of Allen, the lawyer Nicholas Fuller asserted that "The ordinance of God is, that every man should live by labour, and that he that will not labour, let him not eat" (2 Thess. 3).[7] When the queen granted exclusive manufacturing privileges to just one subject, she prevented others from working in their calling. A "grant, ordinance, or law of any Christian king tending to prohibit some of his subjects" from laboring, Fuller said in Parliament when later summarizing the court's finding, was "unlawful" and "absurd" because it went "directly against the law of God, which saith six days thou shall labor; so the grant and prohibition of any king tending to prohibit any of his subjects to labor in his lawful calling or trade . . . when he knoweth no other . . . is contrary to the law of God and therefore . . . void."[8] The monopolist was *vir sanguinis,* or a man of blood, because, according to Deuteronomy 24:6, a man who took away another man's means of living took his life.[9] After explaining Fuller's claim in his *Institutes,* Sir Edward Coke pressed on to its logical conclusion: monopolists were "odious" because they were *viri sanguinis,* and "against these Inventers and Propounders of evill things, the holy Ghost hath spoken, *Inventores malorum, &c. digni sunt morte."*[10] They were, said Coke's Latin, worthy of death. The Leveller John Lilburne, who would later defend himself with the *Institutes* in hand, thought Coke's passage worth quoting in his own pamphlets.[11]

Fuller did not, however, rely solely on such arguments from divine law. Citing *Davenant v Hurdis* (1599), in which the Queen's Bench had adjudged that an ordinance of the Merchant Tailors requiring members to set out half their cloths to other members for dressing violated the twenty-ninth chapter of Magna Carta, Fuller argued that Darcy's monopoly similarly violated the Great Charter and took away what should have been the "surest" form of subjects' property, the "excellent skill in a trade" that they had acquired by their "industry."[12] The same charge had already been made in Parliament the prior year, when Richard Martin complained that patentees took "the fruits of our own Soil and the commodities of our own labour, which with the sweat of our brows even up to the knees in Mire and Dirt, we have laboured for."[13] To lay claim to other men's labors was to treat them like slaves; it was, said Fuller, "to make freemen bondmen."[14]

With the growing importance of foreign trade to the nation and the creation of powerful new corporations like the East India Company, a growing number of M.P.s, outport merchants, and domestic businessmen argued that despite consisting of more than one buyer, these companies acted as corporate monopolists and could thus be attacked on the grounds established by *Darcy v Allen.* The economic case against monopolies, which had been of secondary importance in Fuller's defense of Allen, was developed more fully by the opponents of the chartered companies because it was not so obvious that a privilege enjoyed by a company of men drove the public good into private hands and impinged on the native liberties of English subjects.[15] It therefore had to be shown that such charters did not benefit but harmed the commonwealth.

Invoking the traditional charge that monopolists were bloodsuckers—and perhaps responding to James I's reference to chartered companies as "the veins whereby wealth is imported into our estate"—company
opponents charged that such monopolies "like *Incubusses* doe suck the very
vitall spirits, and drive into one veine that masse of blood which should
cherish the whole body."[16] Insisting that "the more common and diffusive a good thing is, the better it is," they asserted that driving the public
into private hands, even when those hands were united in a company,
was unhealthy for the domestic body politic.[17] Even more important, they
argued that the growth of England's foreign trade was being stunted by
the restrictive policies of the Crown and chartered companies and that "if
the number of traders were enlarged, trade itself would be enlarged."[18]
Trade was not fixed, in other words, but elastic, and as long as the number of traders was restricted and their routes determined by a few legally
protected companies, its full pattern and extent would never emerge.

Such arguments put the chartered companies in a difficult position,
for they wished their own business activities to be relatively unfettered by
taxes, regulations, or currency manipulations that could impede the flow
of trade, yet they also insisted that their "politic Government, Laws, and
Orders" were the "root and spring" of their "incredible trade and traffic."
Trade that was thrown open to all Englishmen, they argued, would be
"dispersed, straggling, and promiscuous." They attacked interlopers as men
who "under pretence of liberty and free trade," possessing "neither skill
nor patience," had proved "disorderly and unskillful traders" who were
likely to subject the economy to unwelcome price and inventory shocks
through their incompetence and disorganization and who threatened to
diminish the reputation of English manufactures by producing or trading goods of inferior quality. It was imperative that trade be confined to
"well experimented merchants."[19]

Domestic businessmen such as clothiers and retailers who wished to
integrate trade into their other business activities rejected the company
merchants' claims to peculiar skill. They resented the ability of the companies, as monopoly buyers and sellers, to extract excess profits from them.
Any "mystery" to the Merchant Adventurers' trade was "well known,"
said one pamphlet, and the name *Adventurers* was an absurd misnomer,
"their hazard being so small, and the voyage so short." By associating the
"mysteries" of the companies not with the skills of the guilds but with
the ceremonies of the Catholic Church, Leveller pamphlets implied that
they were a superstition that would not withstand scrutiny, a mere instrument of despotic government. Skill was not something to be handed
down within a secret society of merchants, which would only enforce a

"servile kind of obedience," but something to be gained from rude experience of the market by "active and industrious spirits."[20] Far from guaran-
teeing quality, monopolies had the effect, as the Queen's Bench had recognized as early as *Davenant v Hurdis,* of driving quality down and prices
up.[21] The best way to make goods more plentiful and of superior quality
was to encourage the emulation of craftsmen who were left free to rival
one another.[22]

Fuller's claim that the Crown's monopoly patents infringed on the
liberties of freeborn subjects, while more difficult to demonstrate in the
case of corporate charters, was never abandoned. In 1604, for instance, Sir
Edwin Sandys's report from Parliament's Committee on Free Trade listed
"Natural right" as the foremost reason for the enlargement of trade:

> All free Subjects are born inheritable, as to their Land, so also to the
> free Exercise of their Industry, in those Trades whereto they apply them-
> selves, and whereby they are to live. Merchandize being the chief and
> richest of all other, and of greater Extent and Importance than all the
> rest, it is against the natural Right and Liberty of the Subjects of England
> to restrain it into the Hands of some few.[23]

In the free trade controversies of 1621–24, Sir Edward Coke affirmed that
"Freedome for trade was the ancient wisdome of the lawe," and in his
commentary on Magna Carta—whose publication was suppressed until
1642—he glossed the word *libertates* in chapter 29 of the charter by referring the reader to nothing but the monopoly cases *Davenant v Hurdis*
and *Darcy v Allen.*[24] This point did not escape the indefatigable Leveller
John Lilburne, who drew the attention of his readers to it.[25] According to
Coke's influential *Institutes,* then, to respect the liberties that a subject enjoyed by virtue of his membership in the commonwealth meant to leave
him free to labor. Conversely, "to barre any freeborn subject from the
exercise of his Invention and Industry" was, as a pamphlet attacking the
Merchant Adventurers charged, "to deprive him of part of his birth-right,
and that which God and Nature ordaynd for his subsistence; and not only
so, but it is to set a mark of strangeness, or rather, of a kinde of slavery
upon him in his own Countrey."[26] Because they set their faces against liberty, monopolists were likened to such tyrants as the Roman emperors,
the Catholic Church, the Habsburgs, and even the Beast of Revelation,
who "causeth all, both small and great, rich and poor, free and bond, to
receive a mark in their right hand, or in their foreheads: And that no man
might buy or sell, save he that had the mark, or the name of the beast, or
the number of his name" (Rev. 13:16–17).[27] Because exclusive manufacturing or trading privileges could take so

many different forms, politicians and jurists might defend one and attack another. What is important for our purposes is the series of questions that the opponents of monopolies posed. Was circulation essential to the vigor of trade and the commonwealth? How was skill acquired and transmitted? Would enlarging the number of traders actually enlarge trade itself? Was the exercise of one's industry and ingenuity a basic expression of liberty? The answers that advocates of free trade supplied to these questions could be used by extension to defend free speech and liberty of conscience.

Free Trade and Free Speech

Reformers of the 1640s were not the first to make the imaginative leap from trucking and trading in goods to exchanging ideas, for the contiguity between various kinds of commerce—economic, cultural, and spiritual—had long been celebrated in London's mayoral shows. In one of Thomas Middleton's pageants entitled *The Triumphs of Truth* (1613), for instance, the King of the Moors explained that his queen and their people had been won over by English merchants, "Whose Truth did with our spirit hold commèrce, / As their affairs with us." In another show, Middleton directed "commerce, adventure, and traffic," all habited like merchants, to present personified Knowledge to India, the "Queene of Merchandise."[28] But Sir Francis Bacon's ideal of a great instauration proved even more important to reformers who conceived of knowledge in terms of trade. Bacon had interpreted the text of Daniel 12:4—"Many shall run to and fro and knowledge shall be increased"—in light of contemporary strides in navigation and commerce and had believed that advances in science and religion would accompany them. In his *New Atlantis,* he had dubbed those who sought knowledge abroad "Merchants of Light," and engravings in both his *Instauratio Magna* (1620) and *Advancement of Learning* (1640) had featured Daniel 12:4 beneath a depiction of vessels of trade or discovery (fig. 1).[29] Millenarians like Milton's tutor at Cambridge, Joseph Mede, served as important conduits for these ideas to Puritan reformers. Bacon's essential insight into the contiguity of economic and intellectual exchange was further disseminated by the Hartlib circle in works like *Macaria* (1641), in which the Traveller says to the Scholar, "I conceive you trade in knowledge, and here is no place to traffick for it."[30]

It is not surprising, then, that some Puritan reformers committed to the ideals of free spiritual inquiring and continuing revelation made the imaginative leap from economic to spiritual commerce and found a suggestive model of intellectual exchange in the theories of the chartered

1. Title page of Sir Francis Bacon's *Instauratio Magna*. Vessels of trade or discovery promise to sail past the Pillars of Hercules. A Latin subscript cites Daniel 12:4: "many shall run to and fro and knowledge shall be increased." By permission of the Houghton Library, Harvard University.

companies' opponents, which stressed not only the benefits of free trade but the potential of wealth to be generated without bound. Since they were suspicious of claims that the Crown or even Parliament was skillful or disinterested enough to govern for the good of the people, these reformers were attracted to the idea that skill was dispersed widely and had to be exercised in commerce with other men, a form of intercourse that should ideally be an expression of community and freedom. In *property* they also found a right of ownership that subjects might assert not only to their lands and goods but to their invention, industry, and private convictions. In this claim they were preceded by Nicholas Fuller, who used his victory in *Darcy v Allen* to argue against the oath ex officio in the ecclesiastical courts, insisting in effect that subjects had a protected right to their thoughts, which, just like their skills or their property, they could not be compelled to yield without their consent.[31]

In a sermon entitled *The Pvrchase and Possession of the Truth,* which was not published until 1640, when he was already dead, the Puritan Jeremiah Dyke took as his key texts two biblical passages that held a special significance for the reformers in whom we are interested: Proverbs 23:23 and Matthew 13:45–46.[32] *"Buy the Truth, and sell it not,"* he enjoined, quoting Proverbs (p. 305). "Christians," said Dyke, "should be like Merchants" in "Marts and Fayres" seeking to buy the truth, a "commodity" that was "necessary and useful," "needful," "profitable," "gaineful," and "precious" (pp. 312–14, 319–22). They should look for the truth from their ministers, certainly, for "Sabbaths are the Market dayes, the publicke assemblies are the Market places, and the shoppes where this commodity is to bee bought," but they must also be willing to invest in books, for when Christians hear the words to the wise, *"Buy the truth,"* they should hear, *"Buy Bibles, buy good Bookes,* and . . . willingly bee at such charge for getting of the truth" (pp. 331, 349). A dearth of information about Dyke makes it hard to speak with certainty, but his admonitions were probably prompted by Charles I's attempts to control the pulpit and the printed word.[33] Whatever Dyke's original purpose, the publication of his sermon in 1640 supplied reformers like Thomas Hill with a language they could use effectively.

Educated at Emmanuel College, Cambridge, Hill would later prove committed to many of the educational reforms that had been advocated by Bacon and taken up by the Hartlib circle and Milton.[34] In an irony that we may wish to recall in later chapters—for the pupil would reject the Puritan and parliamentarian positions of the master with increasing vehemence—Hill was not only the rector of John Dryden's boyhood parish but his Master when the poet studied at Trinity College, Cambridge.[35] In

The Trade of Truth Advanced, a sermon that he preached to the House of Commons in 1642, Hill warned that "All the sons of wisdome, must be carefull to buy the Truth" (p. 3). While he recognized that the liberties Parliament had secured were largely those of person and estate, he wanted the assembly to establish analogous civil and spiritual liberties. "There are things in *Truth* well worth our *Buying,*" he said, "*first libertie of Truth,* that the *True Religion* may have free passage, and not be imprisoned in corners or clogged with difficulties" (p. 4). Suggesting that the skill and determination forged by the pressures of the marketplace were the same virtues needed to participate in the nation's civil and spiritual life, Hill enjoined all the subjects of the realm to demonstrate the "Wisdome," "Activity," and "Resolution" of a "Merchant or Factor" in searching for the truth (p. 25). Finally, he revealed how closely related he believed freedom of conscience and propriety over land and goods to be:

> Maintaine amongst us a free course of trading for eternall happinesse, set and keepe open those shops, such Pulpits, such mouthes, as any Prelaticall usurpations have, or would have, shut up. Secure to us not onely liberty of person and estate, but also liberty of Conscience from Church tyranny, that we be not pinched with ensnaring oathes, clogged with multiplyed subscriptions, or needlesse impositions. (p. 33)

More than a mere metaphor, Hill's "impositions" invoke Nicholas Fuller's case against monopolies, for Fuller had used *Darcy v Allen* not only to argue against the oath ex officio in ecclesiastical courts but to object to the Crown's impositions in a well-known speech to the Parliament of 1610.[36] In Fuller's expansive notion of a liberty free from any economic constraints or oppressions originating from the Crown, Hill found more than an analogue for his own spiritual ideal; he found his best legal argument for liberty of conscience.

Thomas Goodwin was likewise educated at Cambridge, enjoyed the friendship of prominent Puritan divines and politicians like John Cotton and Oliver Cromwell, and even served on a committee with Milton in 1650. Through members of his congregation like Samuel Moyer, an interloper merchant who served as a mediator between the political independents and the Levellers, he may have been exposed firsthand to arguments in favor of free trade. In a sermon on Colossians 1:26–27, Goodwin referred to Cambridge as a "mart of truth," to its instructors as "wholesale men," and to its divinity students as men who should "vent by retail in the country." He glossed Daniel 12:4 much as Bacon had: "That is, by doing as merchants do, travelling from place to place, comparing one with another, knowledge will be increased." Goodwin then enjoined his listeners,

"Therefore exchange, and truck one with another to that end." Appealing to the language of free trade, he warned, finally, against inhibiting speech or print: "Let the market stand open, take heed how you prohibit the truth to be sold in your markets; but let the world run and be glorified, and let wisdom cry all her wares."[37]

This, I would suggest, is the discursive context in which we should read *Areopagitica,* one in which apologies for liberty had left their mark on pleadings for free trade and in which those pleadings, in turn, had helped to define liberty under the law and to suggest, even to Puritan reformers more interested in free spiritual inquiring than in free trade per se, that liberty, whether spiritual, intellectual, or economic, could exist only where there were no monopolies.

The Long Parliament, Monopolies, and the Stationers' Company

The system for controlling the press that the Crown had established with the cooperation of the Stationers' Company, the King's Printer, and the university presses began to crumble shortly after the Long Parliament began to sit in 1640. While Parliament had exempted the Stationers from the porous Monopolies Act of 1624, the company's rights of search and seizure depended on a Marian charter, its Elizabethan confirmation, and two Star Chamber decrees, none of which carried much authority in a parliamentary world. The number of printers, the number of titles they printed, and the diversity of opinion they were setting in circulation were growing apace. The Stationers might complain that this expansion was "scandalous and enormous," but without the sanction of Parliament they were hesitant to move against printers and booksellers who were willing to challenge the legality of their searches. Meanwhile, Parliament was of two minds about pre-publication censorship. It was naturally tempted to take over the Crown's apparatus of social control. But it also felt an aversion to granting powers like search and seizure—with the threat they implied to law, liberty, and property—to a company of private men who had been accused of being monopolists.[38]

After all, the Long Parliament's popularity depended in part on its apparently firm stand against monopolies. In a petition of 1640, ten thousand citizens of London had listed monopolies among their foremost grievances, and the assembly's own members had not lagged behind in their denunciations of the "multitude of *Monopolies*" besetting the land.[39] Jesting bitterly about the number of everyday items that were patented, Sir John Culpeper had likened monopolists to "the *Frogs of* Egypt." They "have got-

The manner and forme how Projectors and Patentees have rode a Tylting, in a Parliament time.

FINIS.

2. The "riding" of a monopolist in a traditional rite of shame, from *A Dialogue or Accidental Discourse Betwixt Mr. Alderman Abell, and Richard Kilvert* (1641). By permission of the Houghton Library, Harvard University.

ten possession of our Dwellings," he had said, "and we have scarce a Room free from them: They sup in our *Cup,* they dip in our *Dish,* they sit by *our Fire,* we find them in the *Dye-fat, Wash-boul* and *Powdering tub;* . . . they have marked and sealed us from head to foot."[40] The Long Parliament had in fact matched its words with deeds in the case of some notorious projectors. Their investigation of William Abel and Richard Kilvert's patent for French and Spanish wines had led one pamphlet to rejoice that "in a Parliament time" projectors and patentees were put to shame (fig. 2).[41] But when another satire rejoiced that "damn'd *Monopolists*" were now "hid in holes and ke[pt] aloofe, / Being indeed not Parliamentall proofe," it spoke too soon.[42]

In the case of Abel and Kilvert, Parliament's taste for justice was quickened by its appetite for money. The assembly saw that it might fine away some of the project's obscene profits.[43] But in other cases, the assembly's distaste for patents and charters was assuaged by its growing recognition of their uses—particularly since, in a parliamentary world, exclusive trading privileges did not necessarily represent threatening extensions of the Crown's sovereign authority. In 1641–42, the Merchant Adventurers lent Parliament, rather than the Crown, £70,000, a favor that Parliament returned by upholding the company's privileges and allowing it to erect higher barriers to entry. Parliament likewise confirmed the Levant Company's privileges in March 1644. It even left intact the London Company of Soapmakers, perhaps the most detested monopoly in the land, because the company facilitated the collection of an excise tax on soap and its raw materials.[44] In short, what Robert Ashton has called a "*mariage de convenance* between big business and parliament" was being formed.[45]

Parliament now found itself in a position familiar to the Crown: in need of the sort of funds that monopolies and chartered companies could readily provide, eager to control the press, and resistant to the most radical calls for religious reform. So when Henry Parker petitioned Parliament to replace the Star Chamber Decree Concerning Printing (1637) with its own order and to reaffirm the exclusive privileges of the Stationers' Company, he could expect a receptive hearing, but he also had to be careful to word his plea with the controlling common law cases on monopolies in mind. Coke had summarized these in his report on "The Case of Monopolies" (*Darcy v Allen*) and in the second and third parts of the *Institutes*. He had pronounced that even corporate grants by charter could be monopolies "in effect" and thus work to the detriment not only of others who exercised the trade but of all subjects, for monopolies led to increased prices, diminished quality, and the impoverishment of displaced artificers.[46] Parker must have thought his task an easy one in comparison to his previous assignment, defending the role of the Vintners in Abel and Kilvert's unpopular wine project.[47] He contended that, because the Stationers' privileges were enjoyed by a considerable body of men, they did not qualify as an instance of a public good being driven into private hands. That the "Mystery and Art of Printing" was of "publike and great Importance" was not, as Sandys had said of foreign trade, a reason for throwing it open but a reason for regulating it. For it was not "meere Printing, but well ordered Printing" that was a public good. A regulated press would promote the "advancement of wholesome knowledge" through the "licensing of things profitable, and suppressing of things harmfull." It would also enrich "Printing and Printers" and ensure that they could support the poor of their company. A regulated press would be "beneficial to the state, and different in nature from the engrossing, or Monopolizing some other Commodities into the hands of a few, to the producing scarcity and dearth, amongst the generality."[48]

Parker was acutely aware that some vital commodities were thought to be too important to be monopolized. In the Commons debates in 1601, an exchange had turned on this principle for its humor: "Upon Reading of the Patents aforesaid, Mr. *Hackwell* of *Lincolns-Inn* stood up, and asked thus; Is not Bread there? Bread, quoth one, Bread, quoth another; this Voice seems strange quoth another; this Voice seems strange quoth a third: No, quoth Mr. *Hackwell,* if Order be not taken for these, Bread will be there before the next Parliament." [49] In defending Darcy's patent on playing cards in 1602, his counsel had stressed, on the other hand, that because cards were "not any merchandize, or thing concerning trade of any necessary use, but things of vanity, and the occasion of loss of time," it was in the queen's power to "take order for the moderate and convenient use of them." [50] Parker consequently spoke of books as if they were the same as playing cards: other than the Bible, they were "not of such generall use and necessity, as some staple Commodities are, which feed and cloath us . . . and many of them are rarities onely and usefull only to a very few, and of no necessity to any." Thus the Stationers' privileges could not "have the same effect, in order to the publike" as they might in the case of "other Commodities of more publike use and necessity." [51]

Disputing the evidence of inflated prices and inferior quality that Michael Sparke had compiled, Parker insisted that a regulated propriety of copies among Stationers would make "Books more plentifull and cheap," for there would be no excess production. It would, moreover, improve the quality of the books produced because booksellers facing a more certain market would be willing to undertake more ambitious publishing ventures. Without more certainty, "many Pieces of great worth and excellence" would be "strangled in the womb, or never conceived at all for the future." In short, the exclusive privileges of the Stationers would not have the effect that Coke said could be expected of any monopoly: inflated prices and diminished quality. [52]

Areopagitica: Letting Wisdom Cry All Her Wares

Areopagitica attacks Parker's petition even as it protests against the Licensing Order of 1643. Milton not only responds to arguments in favor of licensing advanced in the petition but omitted from Parliament's order, he responds to the petition's incidental imagery, seizing on Parker's ill-considered praise of the Inquisition's record of regulating the press and countering Parker's claim that without licensing worthy books will be strangled in the womb. Before the Inquisition, says Milton, "Books were ever as freely admitted into the World as any other birth; the issue of the brain was no more stifl'd then the issue of the womb: no envious Juno sate cros-leg'd over the nativity of any mans intellectual off spring" (*CPW* 2:505).

It was only "the fraud of some old patentees and monopolizers in the trade of book-selling" that led Parliament to reinstitute pre-publication censorship. "Under pretence of the poor in their Company not to be defrauded, and the just retaining of each man his severall copy, which God forbid should be gainsaid," the Stationers "brought divers glosing colours to the House, which were indeed but colours." The true end of their petition was nothing but to "exercise a superiority over their neighbours, men who doe not therefore labour in an honest profession to which learning is indetted, that they should be made other mens vassalls" (*CPW* 2:570). Milton thus revives the old complaints of the journeymen printers and of George Wither that the chief booksellers in the Stationers' Company petition for their privileges "vnder colour of relieuing the poore" but in reality make "the Printer, the Binder, and the Claspmaker" their slaves.[53] Milton's famous admonition, "as good almost kill a Man as kill a good Book" (*CPW* 2:492), and his extended imagery of book suppression as homicide are meant to identify the Stationers and licensors alike as *viri sanguinis*:

> We should be wary therefore what persecution we raise against the living labours of publick men, how we spill that season'd life of man perserv'd and stor'd up in Books; since we see a kinde of homicide may be thus committed, sometimes a martyrdome, and if it extend to the whole impression, a kinde of massacre, whereof the execution ends not in the slaying of an elementall life, but strikes at that ethereall and fift essence, the breath of reason it selfe, slaies an immortality rather than a life. (*CPW* 2:493)

Milton retraces the logic of Deuteronomy 24:6 as explicated by Fuller and Coke. He identifies books as the "living labours" of authors so that he may make his charge of monopoly clear: licensors and Stationers attack the labor of men and in doing so become figurative men of blood. Yet to assert that the intellectual labors of authors deserve to be protected under the law as surely as any tradesman's livelihood and that the reason of an author is dearer than his heart's-blood is a remarkable claim that goes beyond anything that Coke could have had in mind in his discussion of the monopolist as *vir sanguinis*.

George Wither had insisted before Milton that the writer must "enioy the benefit of some part of [his] owne labours," but Milton argues for an even more expansive notion of intellectual labor that comprises reading and writing—both of which must be safeguarded as surely as any labor in a worldly vocation.[54] Writers display "industry" and "diligence" when they dedicate themselves to "studious labours" like the "labour of book-writing"(*CPW* 2:489–90, 532). To *"seek for wisdom as for hidd'n treasures"* means to perform "the hardest labour in the deep mines of knowledge" (*CPW* 2:562). It entails both "incessant labour to cull out, and sort asunder" good from evil (*CPW* 2:514) and a willingness to contribute to the larger public project of building the Temple, "some cutting, some squaring the marble, others hewing the cedar" (*CPW* 2:555). As books and pamphlets are "publisht labours" and "writt'n labours," attacks on them may be seen as efforts to restrain men from undertaking their Godly duty to labor (*CPW* 2:493, 531). By insisting that reading and writing are labor, Milton asserts that to prevent any man from the exercise of his industry and invention would be to deprive him of his fundamental liberties as a Christian and a freeman. By extending the notion of labor into the realms of writing, reading, and thinking, Milton thus makes the ideal of liberty itself more capacious.[55]

Whereas Parker had argued that books were not of such "use and necessity" as many other commodities and could therefore be lawfully restrained into the hands of a few, Milton speaks not of books but of truth: "Truth and understanding are not such wares as to be monopoliz'd and traded in by tickets and statutes, and standards. We must not think to make a staple commodity of all the knowledge in the Land, to mark and license it like our broad cloath, and our wooll packs" (*CPW* 2:535–36). Milton's point is not that truth and understanding are not wares—for he later declares truth "our richest Marchandize" (*CPW* 2:548)—but that they are not wares to be monopolized. They are *vital* wares of public use and necessity whose production and exchange must not be driven into the hands of a few men.[56]

Whereas Parker had insisted that licensing would promote "the advancement of wholesome knowledge," Milton suggests that a free and open marketplace of ideas is the best way of ensuring that truth is enlarged and that men are diligent and ingenious in its production. The notion of a market informs even Milton's famous dictum "reason is but choosing" (*CPW* 2:527). By no means an obvious formulation, Milton's reduction of reason to the act of choosing goes beyond the Aristotelian judgment that "choice *involves* a rational principle and thought."[57] While the doctrine of free will is certainly at stake in Milton's statement, we cannot reduce it to just that, for Milton's habit of figuring reason as a process of choosing rather than intuiting or deducing truth differentiates his idea of reason from that of a Scotus or Aquinas. It is the reason of a consumer society, which can operate effectively only when men may choose freely and openly among ideas. In conditions of unrestricted exchange, men will, on the margin, choose truth over falsehood, and enlightenment will be enlarged. Because truth is a vital commodity, neither men's immediate choices nor their long-term success as they search for truth may be put on a plane with their efforts, say, to find Seville oranges at market, but the process of reasoning does, in Milton's formulation, bear a marked resemblance to buying at market.

Ideas that ring true will be taken up and passed on by more and more men while those that ring false will lose favor and drop out of the market. Not only does this model avoid the untenable claim that any group of intellectuals or counselors has a corner on the truth (CPW 2:521), it also makes it unnecessary to make extravagant claims about the good will and discernment of common Englishmen. Although Milton calls the Licensing Order "an undervaluing and vilifying of the whole Nation" (CPW 2:535), he only needs to assume that Englishmen, like investors in joint-stock companies, are not systematically misguided or perverse; they may make many random errors on either side of the truth without impeding the market-wide advancement of truth. The analogy of the market also rescues Milton from the specter of pure subjectivity, since the consensus of free thinking men over time, like the valuation of stock on an exchange, approaches the ideal of an objective and disembodied judgment. In other words, the market is a means by which imperfect men may, in the long term, approximate, if never really attain, the wisdom of God. Just as important, it offers a way to keep control of evaluation and distribution out of the hands of corrupt men and corrupting institutions—whom Milton's fellow reformers routinely denounced as monopolists. Richard Overton complained in this spirit that "the inhancing and ingrossing all Interpretations, Preachings, and Discipline" in the hands of the clergy was "a meere Monopole of the Spirit, worse then the Monopole of Soap," while his fellow Leveller John Lilburne never tired of denouncing men in positions of settled power as "Prerogative-Monopolizing arbitrary-men."[58]

Milton's text is persuasive because it seems to enact the open model of discourse that it propounds. In other words, it abounds with the contradictions that have interested readers like Christopher Kendrick and Stanley Fish in large part because it makes itself into a forum of competing subtexts, a process that begins with the pamphlet's title.[59] However appropriate the *Areopagitic Discourse* is as a rhetorical model for Milton's tract, its tenor is directly opposed to Milton's: Isocrates wanted to expand the authority of the Court of Areopagus over education and the censorship of manners. But the title also recalls Paul's sermon at Areopagus, where "all the Athenians, and strangers which were there, spent their time in nothing else, but either to tell or to hear some new thing." When Paul finished, some men mocked him, others wished to hear him speak on another occasion, and still others "clave unto him, and believed." Acts 17:18–34, which recounts Paul's experience, is, then, a story of truth's progress in an open forum, however incremental that progress may be. Our sense that Milton's title contains competing subtexts is affirmed when we read his catalog of customs and opinions concerned with the restriction of speech or print. After the exordium, Milton discusses the laws of the Athenians, Spartans, and Romans. While he concludes that no ancient state practiced pre-publication licensing, he does not suppress seemingly damaging precedents of speech being restricted in other ways: authors like Protagoras, Archilochus, and Naevius were banished or imprisoned; works condemned for atheism, blasphemy, or libel were suppressed; and some comedies were banned from the stage (*CPW* 2:494–500). Licensing itself, however, must be seen as one of the innovations that the Christian emperors and the Church employed to achieve a repressive control over their subjects (*CPW* 2:500–507).

His history lesson complete, Milton consults authorities. While most of those he cites support his case, he does not suppress evidence from Solomon, Plato, the Ephesians, and even some of the primitive doctors of the Church that would seem, at least on first glance, to undermine his position (*CPW* 2:508, 510, 514, 522). Responding to Milton's inclusion of so many precedents that either contradict one another or can be reconciled only by drawing nice distinctions, Ernest Sirluck writes: "The 'authority' of one primitive father is opposed to that of another in such a way as to prevent either from being decisive, and hence the way is cleared for submitting the issue to the test of reason alone."[60] While Sirluck's insight is an essential one, it would be odd for a pamphlet devoted to the importance of a public sphere inundated with competing texts to appeal to reason alone. I think we can better describe Milton's method by saying that it creates the illusion of a free marketplace of ideas operating within *Areopagitica* itself. We do not sense that Milton's position is patently clear or indisputable, for truth and falsehood are as difficult to sort out as Psyche's seeds, but his position does seem to emerge from a plethora of views as the best. We feel as if we have been "fast reading, trying all things, assenting to the force of reason and convincement." We experience Milton's dictum "opinion in good men is but knowledge in the making" (*CPW* 2:554).

True and original ideas are so hard to come by—"revolutions of ages doe not oft recover the losse of a rejected truth, for the want of which whole Nations fare the worse" (CPW 2:493)—that their production and circulation must be allowed to proceed unencumbered. For only then may they be properly tested and valued by the market. By adopting and transvaluing the epithet *promiscuous*, which company merchants had often used to stigmatize unregulated trade, Milton suggests the extreme importance that he attaches to such a state of intellectual free trade, in which books may be "promiscuously read" (CPW 2:517). His later comparison of licensing to a trade embargo reinforces that emphasis on circulation: "the incredible losse, and detriment that this plot of licensing puts us to, more then if som enemy at sea should stop up all our hav'ns and ports, and creeks, it hinders and retards the importation of our richest Marchandize, Truth" (CPW 2:548). Although Thomas Goodwin would ask in similar terms, "If every truth be thus precious, is it not an impoverishment of the kingdom to hinder the traffic of any?," Milton's reference to havens, ports, and even creeks suggests more strongly that truth runs in the same elastic, responsive, ultimately irrepressible patterns as trade.[61]

Exploiting the metaphor of bodily circulation that free trade pamphlets sometimes employed, Milton later says that it is a sign of London's vigor that despite being "beseig'd and blockt about, her navigable river infested" by Royalist forces, her "blood is fresh, the spirits pure and vigorous" enough to supply not just the vital organs but the rational faculties (CPW 2:556–57). While Milton means most simply that Londoners have not only managed to sustain themselves physically but have continued to publish, his differentiation between the circulation required for the vital organs and that needed for the rational faculties also suggests that if circulation is important in matters of trade, the free flow of ideas is even more crucial to generating the intellectual equivalent of wealth, truth. This is just one of several passages that evince Milton's basic assumption that the natural state of the public sphere is one of flux; he also warns, for instance, that as licensing attempts to control some corruptions, others will "break in faster at other dores which cannot be shut" (CPW 2:537). Hard experience in the economic realm had taught Englishmen by the 1640s that circulation was natural, that borders were permeable, and that policies that tried to controvert the flow of currency or commodities would be circumvented. For Milton, not fluidity but constriction, stagnation, and congealment pose a threat to the public sphere (CPW 2:543, 545, 562, 564): the waters of truth must flow "in a perpetual progression" (CPW 2:543).[62]

In asserting that the flow of truth breaks the "triple ice" that can cling about men's hearts (CPW 2:568), Milton suggests that a free marketplace of ideas will change the nature not only of the public sphere but of the

individuals participating in it. Milton invests traditionally suspect qualities like flexibility and opportunism with a striking positive valence. His
is a nation "acute to invent, suttle and sinewy to discours," "so pliant
and so prone to seek after knowledge" (CPW 2:551, 554). He asserts that
"our knowledge thrives by exercise, as well as our limbs and complexion"
(CPW 2:543), and he lionizes the psychic mobility and unceasing vigi-
lance that are forced on men by market relations. In a free market, even
fending off erroneous opinions is improving.

Milton develops this idea most fully in his striking description of a
lazy parochial minister who cobbles together his sermons with "a little
book-craft" from the received ideas neatly arranged and digested in
widely sold topic folios, breviaries, interlinearies, "and other loitering
gear" (CPW 2:546). Milton insists on the similarity of these books to the
clothing, shoes, and other "vendible ware of all sorts ready made" sold
in London's commercial precincts (CPW 2:546–47). His imagery shocks
readers into seeing that even religious discourse is already thoroughly im-
plicated in the market. The problem is not that ideas are packaged and
sold as wares but that the market in which they are sold is dysfunctional.
If the lazy parochial minister could not depend on the protectionism
of licensors, a "bold book" might "now and then issue forth" and force
the minister to become more alert and diligent when expounding and
defending his ideas. His flock would find themselves "better instructed,
better exercis'd and disciplin'd" (CPW 2:547). That is Milton's personal,
moral argument for a free marketplace of ideas. It makes better men, men
who are responsible, quick-witted, and imaginative.

It may seem curious, then, that Milton subjects an imaginary man of
business to some of his sharpest moral criticism.[63] Preaching against the
excesses of the reformation a century before, Roger Edgeworth, who believed that ministers should attend to religion and merchants to trade,
each using his God-given skills in his own calling and deferring to the
expertise of the other, had complained, "I haue knowen manye in this
towne, that studienge diuinitie, hath kylled a marchaunt, and some of
other occupations by theyr busy labours in the scriptures, hath shut vp the
shoppe windowes, faine to take Sainctuary."[64] For Edgeworth, tradesmen
who meddled too much with scripture were neglecting their proper occupations and undermining the divinely ordained authority of the Church.
Milton, in contrast, is bothered by the tradesman who remains "in the
shop trading all day without his religion"(CPW 2:545).

Milton's tradesman seems directly opposed to contemporary descriptions of the shopkeepers who agitated for reformation in the early 1640s.
London's merchants and tradesmen went on strike in 1642 to protest the
king's actions, and they closed their shops when presenting petitions. A

witness recounted that tradesmen agitating for the earl of Strafford's execution "threatened that after Wednesday they will shut their shops, and
never rest from petitioning, till not only the Lieutenant's matter, but also
all things else that concern a Reformation be fully perfected."[65] The willingness of London's retailers to close their shops was, then, a sign of their
political and religious commitment. Thus, while Milton may have agreed
with John Millar's later assertion that "a constant attention to professional
objects" made "the superior orders of mercantile people . . . quick-sighted
in discerning their common interest, and, at all times, indefatigable in
pursuing it," his discussion of the tradesman shows that he was troubled
by a point that was not as important to Millar: while the constant attention to professional objects may make a man independent, resourceful,
and fierce in defense of his liberty, it may also lead him to construe his
interests too narrowly.[66] The business of getting may dull his religious and
civic spirit. "A wealthy man addicted to his pleasure and to his profits"
may find "Religion to be a traffick so entangl'd, and of so many piddling
accounts, that of all mysteries he cannot skill to keep a stock going upon
that trade." Used to thinking of labor as something that can be contracted
out, he may resolve "to give over toyling, and to find himself out som
factor, to whose care and credit he may commit the whole managing of
his religious affairs" (*CPW* 2:544).

We arrive at a crux. *Areopagitica* rests on the assumption that men can
be improved by market relations, and it implicitly urges them to be enterprisers in *all* aspects of the public sphere. The tradesman's mistake is not
just that he privileges his trade over his religion but that he treats his
economic, civic, and spiritual lives as if they were "dividual moveable[s]"
when they are not (*CPW* 2:544). When ministers commit the same fault
in reverse by shunning economic toil, they too draw Milton's fire. Milton
is not ashamed to defend mechanic preachers who (like Jesus, Paul, and
some early reformers) were bred up among trades.[67] But how is one to
ensure that participation in one market will make men enterprisers in all
markets? If the tradesman's decision to hire a factor for his religion springs
from a native sloth, that is to be regretted. But there is a darker possibility.
By narrowing the scope of a tradesman's actions, the economy's demand
for the division of labor might actually impair his ability, as Adam Smith
later acknowledged, to think and act as a citizen and moral agent.[68] With
the figure of the tradesman, Milton similarly confronts the possibility that
energy expended in one sphere of human flourishing—economic, political, or spiritual—may not, after all, translate into the others. We shall have
reason to recall this passage in the next chapter, when the English people,
seemingly consulting their profits and their pleasures, invite the king and
his bishops to return as their political and spiritual factors.

In *Areopagitica,* however, Milton still feels that the market harbors much greater dangers than its power to lull shopkeepers into complacency, dangers that are most apparent when he writes about truth's place in history. Like Bacon and many Puritan reformers, Milton believes that truth is acting in the sort of tragicomedy suggested by the pairing of Genesis, which records a lost state of innocence and wisdom, with the prophetic books of the Bible, which assert that an age of bliss and enlightenment will return.[69] In places, Bacon says that "Time is like a river, which has brought down to us things light and puffed up, while those which are weighty and solid have sunk." But when rapt by his vision of a great instauration, he intones the reverse, saying humbly that his insights are the product of time rather than wit and eagerly anticipating the age of progressive invention and discovery envisioned by Daniel.[70] Milton's seemingly contradictory statements about truth follow the same pattern. On the one hand, he says that Typhon and his conspirators dismembered Truth and scattered the pieces, which implies that Truth used to be more complete than it is now (*CPW* 2:549). On the other hand, he says that building truth is like fitting together Truth's body or constructing Solomon's Temple: progress is possible and the goal is clear.

Bacon and Milton differ sharply, however, in the way they account for knowledge's past failure and its future success. For Bacon, truth's expansion or contraction is a matter of experimental and discursive method. He asked James I (without success) to fund the compilation of a vast natural and experimental history because his instinct was to centralize scientific investigation; saying that "the materials on which the intellect has to work are so widely spread that one must employ factors and merchants to go every where in search of them and bring them in," he implied that the best way "to establish and extend the dominion of the human race itself over the universe" was to establish a trade in knowledge between periphery and center that bears a striking resemblance to the ideal of an empire of trade—focused on a single entrepôt—that we will consider in subsequent chapters.[71] Less convinced by that model than many contemporary Puritan intellectuals were, Milton believed that the crucial determinant of whether truth would expand or contract was not a method of investigation or exposition, much less a matter of royal backing, but the free flow of ideas. While Bacon is likely to blame the poor state of truth on the wayward judgment of the vulgar masses, Milton blames it on Typhon and his conspirators—on the willful distortion of powerful men who can restrain the marketplace of ideas. He asks, "who ever knew Truth put to the wors, in a free and open encounter" (*CPW* 2:561), but his account of history makes it clear that truth has rarely if ever been given a free and open field since the Incarnation. Indeed, the Koran's sway in the Ottoman Empire proves how readily tyrannies may suppress the vent of truth (*CPW* 2:548). The link between absolutism and poverty, which M.P.s had asserted to Charles I's detriment in 1642, had its analogue in the intellectual realm, and Milton could easily suggest that just as absolutism tended to limit the production of wealth because it interfered with the natural course of trade, tyrannical interference in the traffic of ideas would inhibit the generation of truth.[72] Markets, not methods, lie at the heart of Milton's vision in *Areopagitica*.

Like William Walwyn and Henry Robinson before him, Milton cites 1 Thessalonians 5:21 in arguing that common men have the ability to tell true from false: "Prove all things; hold fast that which is good" (*CPW* 2:511–12).[73] But as we have seen, Milton was already, in 1642, acutely aware of the power of "the great Marchants of this world" to "suppresse the venting" of rare truths.[74] These merchants have skills of their own that are antithetical to the skills valued by Hill, Goodwin, and free trade apologists, and it is those skills that Milton renounces at the end of his tract: "of these *Sophisms* and *Elenchs* of marchandize I skill not" (*CPW* 2:570). It is precisely Milton's respect for the power of Typhon and his crew that leads him to redirect his attention from the vulnerable commoner proving all things (in the first part of the tract) to a heroic personification, Truth (at the end). Truth's martial contest with falsehood makes it seem as if she can fend for herself. Milton's recourse to personification may be in part a natural response to the difficulties of representing the countless transactions of an open marketplace of ideas. Truth's sword has the additional recommendation of making the civil power of the magistrate, often represented by a sword, seem redundant. But I think the most important reason for Milton's recourse to personification is that it diverts attention away from the abilities and inabilities of the common men who will have to discern what is true before they can hold fast to it—and toward the abstract processes of the market. If Milton begins *Areopagitica* with a rousing apology for the moral import of personal trial, he ends by putting his faith not in men but in a system of commerce and exchange. He puts his faith in the market. But it is a freer market than any the world has ever seen, and he knows it.

Invention, Publicity, and Prosperity

Although Milton's ideal of intellectual exchange was suggested by an economic analogue, a truly free and open economic sphere was just as notional. For reformers like the Levellers, it therefore seemed natural to wage a war on *all* the monopolies, actual and metaphorical, in English society. A year after *Areopagitica* appeared, John Lilburne launched a three-pronged attack on "the patent of ingrossing the Preaching of the Word" by those "grand Monopolizers" the clergy, "The Patent of *Merchant Adventurers,* who have ingrossed into their hands the sole trade of all woollen commodities," and a "third *Monopoly* . . . that insufferable, unjust, and tyrannical Monopoly of Printing, whereby a great company . . . are invested with an Arbitrary unlimmited *Power,* even by a generall Ordinance of Parliament."[75] The Levellers were not alone in seeking to expand religious, economic, and political liberties simultaneously. What I wish to consider in this section, however, is a specific subset of proposed reforms that used the principles of publicity and information flow in order to make the economic realm more open and equitable. It is important to recognize that there was a flip side of the relationship between free speech arguments and economic discourse, first, because it clarifies how coherent the ideal of a public sphere in which autonomous individuals could trade freely and openly in ideas, services, and commodities really was, and, second, because it serves as further proof that an important group of reformers thought of exchange, whether intellectual or material, in terms of systems governed by basic laws.

Company merchants had long recognized that certain kinds of knowledge were essential to commercial success. While they might publish works like Lewes Roberts's *The Merchants Map of Commerce* (1638), a virtual encyclopedia of useful commercial facts that evinced their appreciation of the importance of information to success in the market, they also depended heavily on exclusive access to information as a barrier to entry. The regulations of the Merchant Adventurers actually codified the practice by insisting that transactions remain secret and that retailers, nonmembers, and foreigners be denied access to letters, accounts, and warehouses. The Levant and East India Companies were so adept at using the private exchange of market information, collusive stinting, price setting, and family-based capital arrangements to exclude competition that they were able to maintain an effective monopoly on the eastern trades without insisting upon the more formal and visible barriers to entry—such as high membership fees—that the Merchant Adventurers so staunchly defended.[76] This habit of harboring information led to a reputation for secrecy among monopolists and chartered company merchants. Free trade pamphlets and popular verse referred to their "clandestine wayes," their habit of blinding "the peoples eyes" like "*Egyptian* flies," and their "cozening secrets and underhand dealings in the pursuance of their patent."[77] Theirs was the sort of communication "privily from house to house" that Milton had warned in *Areopagitica* was "more dangerous" than open publication by named authors (*CPW* 2:548).

Recognizing that one way to unveil these privy communications was to follow the money, some pamphleteers printed minutes that exposed not just the companies' gratuities to influential men but the votes of their membership to falsify their account books in order to hide such payments.[78] The premise that publication would promote openness, and that openness would inhibit the conniving of interest groups and enable the public to mobilize against named malefactors or practices underlay the similar demand of some reformers that the government keep full and open financial accounts and report to the people, as if subjects were members of a joint-stock enterprise, the commonwealth.[79] Well aware that any government would almost inevitably impose upon the people unless restrained by appropriate checks, Milton included a similar provision in *The Readie and Easie Way* for "inspectors deputed for satisfaction of the people" to monitor how public revenues were "imploid."[80]

If publicity could be used to limit economic injustices, the exchange of information and ideas, together with the dissemination of knowledge, also held out the more positive promise of making the economy more expansive. Troubled by the secular stagnation of the cloth trade and a loss of skilled labor to the United Provinces, economic writers were becoming convinced that England's future prosperity would depend on a diversification of trade and industry, the attraction of skilled labor, and the creation of a larger, less centralized merchant community that could expand beyond traditional trading centers, where organized buyers were currently able to collude to beat down prices.[81] If invention, innovation, and skill were what England's economy needed, then restrictions on the flow of ideas and information could be seen as a real threat to the advancement of trade. Most of the Hartlib circle claimed as much at one time or another, but for our purposes, it is of particular interest that John Hall seemed to think the logic of *Areopagitica* could be extended to reach such conclusions. Styling his *Humble Motion to the Parliament of England Concerning the Advancement of Learning and Reformation of the Universities* (1649) an *"Aereopagitick"* and reworking some of *Areopagitica*'s most memorable images, Hall expressed his faith that eliminating "that hatefull gagg of licensing which silences so many Truths," reforming the universities, and establishing better libraries and museums would promote the "dispersing" and "augmentation" of knowledge, which would, in turn, contribute to economic advancement and enfranchisement. "What better way to your profit," he asked Parliament, "then to command abundance of fruitfull wits, which shall every day bud forth with some invention, serviceable to the necessities of the poore, or the graver magnificence of the rich?"[82] If Hall's reading of Milton was partial, it was not misguided, for Milton anticipated some of the pamphlet's ideas and (as we shall see in the next chapter) would adopt others.

While a text like Hall's evinced the belief that an open public sphere characterized by intellectual exchange, invention, and experimentation would contribute to England's prosperity, a more radical attempt to put the ideal of freely flowing information to work in the economic sphere was promoted by John Dury and Samuel Hartlib.[83] Realizing that information and personal association were scarce commodities and that their democratization could spread economic enfranchisement, they proposed that an Office of Public Addresses be established to facilitate "Accommodations" and "Communications" of all kinds. Explicitly modeled on the Royal Exchange, which already served as a clearing house for information, with different pillars serving as meeting sites for merchants specializing in different trades, Hartlib's information exchange would match industrialists with inventors, merchants with capitalists, laborers with employers, and even husbands with wives, thus making opportunities for profit available to those who were "in the dark" about "what good things are extant in private, or publickly attainable for Vse" or who lacked the wherewithal to "encounter readily and certainly with them."[84] Wenceslaus Hollar's engraving of native and foreign merchants exchanging information and making deals in the courtyard of the Royal Exchange (fig. 3) may suggest something of what Hartlib had in mind. The free speech advocate and economic theorist Henry Robinson actually advertised an office based on Hartlib's proposals, which, besides being promoted as "the only Course for poor people to get speedy employment, and to keep others from approaching poverty, for want of Employment," held the more general ambition of multiplying trade and promoting navigation by making directions and advice widely available.[85]

Milton and the Hartlib circle certainly influenced one another's ideas about free speech, education, and economic reform through personal association, correspondence, and publications.[86] We know that Hartlib considered Milton the author of "many good books" and "a great traveller and full of projects and inventions" and that Milton reciprocated Hartlib's good opinion, wrote Of Education (June 1644) as a letter to him, and probably even helped to fund one of the projects for which Hartlib sought a subscription.[87] But I do not wish to claim that Areopagitica directly precipitated Hartlib's Office of Public Addresses. Its seeds may already be found in Michel de Montaigne's Les Essais, in Théophraste Renaudot's Bureau d'Adresse, and in Gabriel Plattes's Macaria.[88]

I do think, however, that such an attempt to institutionalize the insight that information could be traded just like a commodity clarifies

3. Wenceslaus Hollar's engraving of *The Royal Exchange* (1644). Men wearing the costumes of various countries converse in groups, while a woman sells broadsides. BL shelf mark P1306. By permission of the British Library.

the extent to which reformers in the 1640s not only recognized the contiguity between the exchange of ideas, services, and commodities but thought in terms of the systems of production and exchange that would be most likely to generate wealth (in some cases) and truth (in others). What was needed was a free way of trading. That is why Sir Cheney Culpeper urged Hartlib to persevere with his office in the face of opposition from "monopolyzinge Corporations." He insisted that "the monopoly of trade" would "proue as great greeuance (when rightly vnderstoode) as any in this kingdome whatsoeuer, nexte vnto that monopoly of Power which the King claimes." Once that "great monopoly" was down, they would be able to dismantle "the monopoly of trade[,] the monopoly of Equity, . . . & the monopoly of matters of conscience & scripture (a very notable monopoly) . . . and thus," he predicted in a prophetic strain, "will Babilon tumble, tumble, tumble."[89] Like the Levellers, Culpeper had found that where there was evidence of oppression or inequitable distribution, whether political, economic, or religious, the problem could often be analyzed in terms of monopoly power. We have already noticed that in

Areopagitica Milton shifts the reader's attention from the vulnerable commoner proving all things (at the beginning) to a heroic personification of Truth (at the end). Such a shift, I suggested, implies that Milton finally puts his faith not so much in individual men as in a system of commerce and exchange. We can think of his marketplace of ideas as just one of the Revolution's various experimental social systems that were meant to be productive despite the frailties of common men and the more insidious designs of uncommon ones. Yet we lose sight of *Areopagitica*'s moral design if we forget that Milton's goal was not to eliminate the need for good men by establishing good laws so much as to initiate a virtuous cycle in which the right system of commerce and exchange would not only advance truth but improve those who participated in it, making them less "ignorant . . . , brutish, formall, and slavish" (*CPW* 2:559). To say this is to register the remarkable distance that Milton had traversed since writing *A Maske,* which, in pitting the Lady's virtue and the iconoclastic power of her speech against the tempter's arguments for commerce and consumption, set humanist and millenarian values against a series of economic arguments revealed to be nothing but "false rules pranckt in reasons garbe" (line 758).

In the 1640s, Milton, the Hartlib circle, the Levellers, and some moderate reformers like Hill and Goodwin all believed that just as knowledge could be harbored to exclude competition and maintain market position, it could also be made available to promote enfranchisement, invention, and reformation. We cannot fully understand their thought until we recognize its coinvolvement with the literature of trade. Nor can we assume that religious and political reformers took what inspiration they could from economic analogies, then refused to repay the debt. On the contrary, many of them followed the logic of their beliefs about intellectual exchange back into the economic sphere. Their religious, political, and economic reforms were calculated to reinforce one another and to create a public sphere in which autonomous individuals might freely exercise their skill and diligence in the vent and purchase of ideas, services, and commodities. *Homo economicus* might have shortcomings that Milton would later have occasion to rue, but all these reformers, including Milton, knew that any reformation that ignored him would not be universal.

Jus Populi and the Workings of the Market: Milton's Regicide Tracts and Defenses of the English People

While some of Milton's fellow free speech advocates were devoting themselves to the economic projects we have just been considering, Milton was making his most important contribution to the restoration of ancient liberty with his regicide tracts, *The Tenure of Kings and Magistrates* (February 13, 1649) and *Eikonoklastes* (October 6, 1649), and his defenses of the newly established republic, his Latin *Defence of the English People* (February 24, 1651) and *Second Defence of the English People* (May 30, 1654). Much as a theory that exchanging information should generate truth could provide a basis for the economic reforms of free speech advocates, it permitted Milton, I submit, to defend a minority's violent revolution in the name of the people. Yet we shall also see that just as Milton harbored misgivings that a tradesman might well choose to treat his civic, spiritual, and economic lives as "dividuall moveable[s]," he was beginning to ask himself what would be the result if his faith in the improving effects of open markets proved unwarranted.

In his political tracts of 1649–54, Milton advances three broad claims: (1) that when a king is not checked by the people, he becomes a tyrant and his subjects become slaves; (2) that the contract between a king and his subjects is a matter of civil law and must be considered dissoluble; and (3) that freeborn men can and should govern themselves in a free state.

Milton's first two contentions sit happily with *Areopagitica*. Just as he attacks the Stationers, licensors, and churchmen in *Areopagitica* for seeking economic and intellectual monopolies that will enable them to turn freemen into bondmen—and associates these oppressions, in turn, with tunnage and poundage, ship-money, and cote and conduct—he denounces "Monopolies," "Cote, Conduct, and Ship money," and other infringements on the right to hold property and to engage in trade in *Eikonoklastes* (*CPW* 2:545, 559; 3:353). Milton does so because he sees the restraint of trade as a favorite device of arbitrary government: just as monopolists act like tyrants when they deprive other subjects of their natural economic rights, tyrants aspire to be monopolists by seeking exclusive control of rights and powers that ought naturally to be dispersed. Milton would have known Aristotle's story of the tyrant Dionysius's confrontation with his alter-ego, a monopolist. The tyrant exiled the monopolist precisely because the man "had discovered a way of making money that was injurious to his own interests": Syracuse was not big enough for the two of them because they were, essentially, striving to occupy the same position of power in relation to their fellow men.[90]

Milton's claim that the true basis of government is a provisional contract that is established when freeborn men covenant to be ruled by some power is also consistent with the model of social relations that he advances in *Areopagitica*. In his divorce tracts (1643–45), Milton had, in what seems a surprising step for the author of *A Maske*, represented marriage as a desacralized relationship governed by a dissoluble contract and, like all

other civil affairs, assigned to the jurisdiction of the secondary laws of nature. No longer content with the Lady's ideal of stoic self-mastery, Milton
had reconceived autonomy in more social terms as the power to enter and
dissolve contracts and thus, potentially, to circulate sexually. The divorce
tracts show a dawning awareness of the potential for decentralized forms
of organization to depend on freely undertaken "dealings" between men
and women, an awareness that becomes far more pronounced in *Areopagitica*. As Milton's opponents recognized, it was but a short step from these
notions of natural law and social contract to the revolutionary claims of
The Tenure of Kings.[91] If, as Milton maintained in his *Doctrine and Discipline
of Divorce* (1644), divorce was a "pure moral *economical* Law" (*CPW* 2:317–
18), and if, as he held in *Tenure,* any people who professed themselves to be
a "free Nation" must not want "that power, which is the root and sourse
of all liberty, to dispose and *oeconomize* in the Land which God hath giv'n
them, as Maisters of Family in thir own house and free inheritance" (*CPW*
3:236–37), then the people should be able to withdraw their support not
only from a tyrant but from a king. They should in effect be permitted
to divorce him.[92] In thus denying any but provisional sovereignty to the
king, Milton asserts what Henry Parker had earlier called *jus populi.*

While the right of the people need not be translated into an extreme
form of popular sovereignty, Milton does seem receptive to a democratic
model in his regicide tracts and *A Defence* (1651). He not only defends the
"popular heat" of the elections for the Long Parliament; he also champions,
more abstractly, "the liberty and right of free born Men, to be govern'd as
seems to them best." Even when it is charged that his model of kingship
is no different from popular rule except that "'in the one case there are
sole leaders and in the other several,'" he stands firm: "What if there were
no other difference," he asks, "would that injure the state?"[93] Although
it is not hard to imagine the author of *Areopagitica* preferring to place his
trust in the people rather than in a monopolist of power like a king, it is
unsettling to find him defending a regicide undertaken by a minority of
Englishmen against the wishes of the majority and, however equivocally,
endorsing a principle of popular sovereignty.

This apparent contradiction may be resolved if we refer back to *Areopagitica*'s account of the past suppression of truth. While in his regicide
tracts, Milton calls the decision of Englishmen to subject themselves to
a king sometime in the distant past a sign that they were "slaves within
doors" who had chosen to ratify their interior servility with a "public
State conformably govern'd," he cannot "willingly ascribe" such "dejection and debasement in the mind of the people" to the "natural disposition
of an Englishman" (*CPW* 3:190, 344). Instead, he emphasizes the debilitat-

ing effects of tyranny once it is established. In the spirit of Thomas Johnson's complaint that monopolies "bring the hearts of the people" to "servility," Milton blames the "dejection and debasement" of the people on the "Prelats and thir fellow-teachers . . . whose Pulpit stuff . . . hath been the Doctrin and perpetual infusion of servility" and whose persuasive power depends on their having brought "Religion to a kinde of trading monopoly" (CPW 3:344, 348–49).[94] "Their sins were taught them under the monarchy, like the Israelites in Egypt," Milton says of the English people in A Defence (1651), "and have not been immediately unlearned in the desert" (CPW 4:386–87). The Levellers offered a similar account of English history in which the corruption of public institutions by monopolies—a process whose origins could be traced back to the Norman Conquest—had dispirited English subjects.[95]

Milton's conviction that the opinions of Englishmen are the result of a state of deprivation in which they were denied the free exercise of their liberty presumably makes him willing to argue for opinions shared by so few of his countrymen, while his trust that a free marketplace of ideas will improve the men who participate in it makes him ready to place a bet on a majority who, as yet, do not agree with him on key matters of policy. He can argue against the immediate will of the people in his regicide tracts, while at the same moment defending "the liberty and right of free born Men, to be govern'd as seems to them best," only by believing that his fellow countrymen have been oppressed by political, religious, and economic tyranny, and that once the marketplace of ideas is opened, once men are no longer prevented from exercising their virtue through active participation in the market, the church, and the polity, they will develop "uninthrall'd" judgments, listen to the "Instruction" that he is willing to "bestow on them," begin working toward a new consensus, and grow into their liberty (CPW 3:206, 346, 194). Milton knows that "among mortal men" Truth "is alwaies in her progress" (CPW 3:256). The model of intellectual exchange advanced in Areopagitica thus emerges as the missing link between his advocacy of a radical, sectarian position and his initial desire to endorse a principle of popular sovereignty.

Milton's claim in Tenure that the success of his own party implies a sanction "next under immediat Revelation" and his willingness to speak of King Charles's judges in Eikonoklastes in the same breath as the saints at the Last Judgment may remind us that in these heady days Milton felt, despite momentary misgivings, that his humanism, his millenarianism, and his faith in free trade were all pointing to the same conclusions (CPW 3:194, 597). In the future, he would be forced to make painful choices among these intellectual allegiances. Indeed, as early as A Defence (1651), he was already considering the more disturbing possibility that even given world enough and time, the English people might prefer to submit themselves once again to a king. "If a majority in Parliament prefer enslavement and putting the commonwealth up for sale," he asked, "is it not right for a minority to prevent it if they can and preserve their freedom?" (*CPW* 4:457). We shall see Milton confront this troubling question in the next chapter and arrive at an answer that would forever unsettle the complementary relationship between the humanist, millenarian, and economic strains of his thought that he managed to achieve in the 1640s.

PART TWO

THE GOVERNMENT
OF TRADE

When Dryden satirized Slingsby Bethel for his part in the Exclusion Crisis, he recalled the economic case that the old Commonwealthman had made for the Rump Parliament. "His business was, by Writing, to Persuade," he wrote in *Absalom and Achitophel* (1681), "That Kings were Useless, and a Clog to Trade" (lines 614–15). As critics have noticed, Dryden had taken every care in *Annus Mirabilis* (1667) to suggest that Charles II was anything but useless and that London's ambition of becoming the entrepôt of world trade would be realized only by showing "passive aptness" to Stuart rule (line 564).[1]

That Dryden was in all probability named poet laureate for the service that *Annus Mirabilis* did the Crown and could later muster such animus against Bethel for expounding the virtues of trading republics should alert us to the high political stakes that were riding on the symbolic alignment of Charles II's monarchy with the cause of trade. Writing in 1674, the Anglican Royalist John Evelyn saw that alignment as an important event in English history. While it was usual, he claimed, for "illustrious Nations" to esteem "the gain by Traffick and Commerce incompatible with *Nobless*" in their early stages of development, the ancients had eventually discarded that "ill-understood Reproach." Now, more perfectly than any previous monarch, Charles II had cultivated an ideal of noblesse that was compatible with merchandising, and when trade was so honored by kings, "dignified by their Example, and defended by their Power," it rose to "its Ascendent."[2]

Evelyn implied that matters had been different under the early Stuarts, and in support of his view he might have cited Sir Francis Bacon. "For merchandising," Bacon complained in a letter of advice to James I, "it is true it was ever by the kings of this realm despised, as a thing ignoble and indign for a king."[3]

From the metaphor of theophanic advent that structured James I's royal entry of 1604 to the neoplatonic conflation of personal virtue and public benefit that resolved many Caroline masques, the early Stuart monarchy was supported by fictions of kingship that could not readily accommodate the values of economic reformers. Renaissance courtesy literature held that the Court should stand as a model for the realm, yet if it prized conspicuous expenditure, gift-exchange, and patronage rather than savings, merchandising, and investment, if it celebrated the thaumaturgic effect of the royal presence rather than the power of calculation and industry, it could hardly serve as a mirror for merchants.

To be sure, the early Stuarts' courtly entertainments did leave some room for exchange and reflection between sovereign and merchant. While the tableaux of James I's entry said little about the commercial conditions that a new Golden Age could be expected to bring England, the fact that the Italian and Dutch merchants sponsored arches bore witness to the importance of foreign trade to the Crown's finances. We also know, for instance, that Ben Jonson devised two entertainments to celebrate the economic projects of courtiers in the presence of James I and that, as we have already seen, the gentlemen of the Inns of Court had James Shirley include monopolists among the antimasquers of *The Triumph of Peace* (1634) so that Charles I might be made to see the "unfitness and ridiculousness of these projects against the law."[4]

Yet such moments were rarities in the artistic culture of the early Stuart Court, and their vision did not, in any event, meet John Evelyn's requirement that the king be seen to dignify trade by his example and defend it by his power. While it would be inaccurate to interpret the reigns of the early Stuarts as a steady march toward revolution hastened by their failure to comprehend where England's economic future lay, we shall be interested primarily in the way the Commonwealth and the restored monarchy defined themselves in *relation* to the early Stuarts, and for polemicists on *both* sides it often proved useful to represent them as having been unresponsive to the prophets of commercial change. In 1641, Lewes Roberts advised Charles I to take merchants as counselors, back ventures with loans from the public treasury, and study to become "a Lover of trade and traffike" because the nation would take its impression from his character, but neither the king nor his poets managed to reconceive their ideal of the monarchy in a way that could square with Charles I's financial dependence on trade or project an economic vision whose scope and coherence approached that of London's contemporary mayoral pageants.[5] John Pym placed trade grievances second only to religion among the causes of the king's undoing.[6]

In stark contrast, Charles Stuart was greeted upon his return by numerous panegyrics that remarked on the state of trade and looked for its improvement under the restored monarchy. His royal entry of 1661 marked as sharp a departure from early Stuart precedents: dividing its attention equally between economics and politics, it presented a fully developed vision of the Crown's new role in the advancement of trade. That change is the subject of this part. I ask what events motivated it, how Milton resisted it, and how court poets and artists made room in their art for it.

These representations of trade merit our attention because they mark a turning point in England's literary and cultural history—a moment when the attributes of monarchy, the concept of empire, and notions of what constituted a fit subject for courtly and urbane verse were made to accommodate the growing importance of commerce to England. Not only did they establish a panegyric tradition in which Dryden's *Annus Mirabilis* participates; they also persuaded Milton to contemplate the dark underbelly of trade. While we shall be much concerned with poets and artists other than Milton in this part, it is against the artistic ground that they created at the Restoration that we shall read *Paradise Lost* in the next.

CHAPTER TWO

Republican Experiments, Royalist Responses

The trade depression that was just beginning when Oliver Cromwell died in 1658 made economic grievances central to the political struggle that culminated in the Restoration. As republicans aggressively promoted the Commonwealth's record of trade and advanced a strong economic case against monarchy, Royalists, for their part, realized that taxes and trade grievances might be used to oust the Rump just as they had been used to undermine Charles I. In the midst of this struggle, Milton produced his only version of what a more perfect commonwealth might look like. I argue in this chapter that, in an innovative attempt to preserve Christian liberty by clearing a space for market forces in the polity, he advocated a federalist model that was informed by contemporary arrangements in the United Provinces and the American colonies. Understanding how integral an economic agenda is to *The Readie and Easie Way* (1660) does not simply permit us to see that its proposals are more coherent and more creative than critics have recognized, it also helps us to understand why the tract's famous renunciation of the claims of trade in its peroration is not merely a rhetorical dismissal of arguments that could no longer serve the cause of the republic, but the record of a deeper intellectual crisis that left its mark on *Paradise Lost*. Treating the initiatives of the Commonwealth and Protectorate largely in retrospect, as they were remembered and debated after the death of Cromwell and before the return of Charles II, this chapter should help us get a purchase on the Royalist representations of trade that are the subject of the next. For it was as contested memories that the Commonwealth and Protectorate governments of trade made their force felt after the Restoration. But in order to understand the strength of the Rumpers' case in 1659—and the extent of Charles II's subsequent borrowings—we must first turn back to the Commonwealth itself.

An Iron Parliament, a Trading Parliament

The new Commonwealth was formed in the midst of the century's worst trade depression as the nation tried to recover from three years of disastrous harvests and intensified competition from the Dutch. It was as a protest against such dire conditions that the Diggers established their ten experimental agrarian and communist colonies from 1649 to 1650. The new government's response was entirely different. Far from rejecting "the thieving Art of buying and selling the Earth with her fruits to one another," it applied itself to the advancement of trade with unexampled determination.[1] In power now were many of the same Puritans, political independents, and colonial merchants who had impugned the policies of the early Stuarts by reminiscing about the Golden Age of Elizabethan maritime supremacy and harping on the ascendancy of the Dutch.[2] Of course, the break with the Stuart past was not as crisp as some of the new men liked to imply. For instance, a scheme to colonize Madagascar, which Prince Rupert and Lord Arundel both championed in the late 1630s, and which the poet Sir William Davenant and the painter Sir Antony van Dyck both commemorated (fig. 4), lay behind a similar plan advanced by Maurice Thompson, one of the colonial interloping merchants to whom the Commonwealth entrusted extensive duties. As was the case in all the century's Parliaments, landed members far outnumbered merchants. But there can be no doubt about the importance that the new government attached to trade. It is suggested by a letter to the Senate of Hamburg that Milton translated and probably helped to compose:[3]

> Of what necessity & advantage to the generall State of humane society a free & full & mutuall commerce is, carryes with it soe great an evidence as none can be ignorant of, who are at all conversant in civill affaires. And Wee cannot alsoe but know the profit & emolument that accrues to this Commonwealth thereby and our special obligation and Interest to promote and further the same. (*CPW* 5:491)

The Rump accordingly established a Council of Trade, devoted 20 percent of its budget to the navy, and modeled many of its commercial initiatives on the Dutch example.[4]

The turn away from the Habsburgs, whose court the early Stuarts had

4. Antony van Dyck, *Thomas Howard, 2d Earl of Arundel, with Alethia, Countess of Arundel* (c. 1639). Both figures point to Madagascar, which the earl proposed to colonize. The earl rests his hand on the globe with an easy command. By kind permission of His Grace the Duke of Norfolk. Photograph: Photographic Survey, Courtauld Institute of Art.

admired, entailed a reconceptualization of power in economic terms. As Benjamin Worsley, the secretary of the Council of Trade, wrote:

> It hath been a thing for many years generally received, That the Design of *Spain* . . . is, to get the Universal Monarchie of Christendom. Nor is it a thing less true (how little soever observed) that our Neighbors [the *Dutch*] . . . have, likewise for som years, aimed to laie a foundation to themselves for ingrossing the Universal Trade not onely of Christendom, but indeed, of the greater part of the known world; that so they might poiz the Affairs of any other State about them, and make their own Considerable, if not by the Largeness of their Countrie; yet, however, by the Greatness of their Wealth; and by their potencie at Sea, in strength and multitude of Shipping.[5]

Worsley thought that England could follow no better precedent than the United Provinces'.[6] "Though *Holland* seem to get the start of Us," wrote the army preacher Hugh Peter, "yet wee may so follow as to stand at length upon their shoulders, and so see further."[7] Rather than tailor its commercial policies to meet its fiscal needs, as the early Stuarts had done, the Rump raised taxes in order to provide naval support for merchant convoys.[8] Francis Osborne could contrast such expenditures by the new republic with the "*vast Treasure* mouldereed away in *Masques* and other effeminate *vanities*" by the early Stuarts.[9] Some observers believed that a close working relationship between the government and English merchants was finally being achieved. The Venetian ambassador reported that England's trade was "now improved by the protection it receives from parliament, the government of the commonwealth and that of its trade being exercised by the same individuals."[10]

The young republic's relations with the Dutch were complicated by divisions within the United Provinces.[11] While Amsterdam was trying to resist the Prince of Orange's efforts to become "absolute Monarch of all the United Netherlands" and to interfere on behalf of his brother-in-law Charles II in England, the Orangists in the States General were determined not to recognize the Commonwealth.[12] When William II died suddenly of smallpox, however, the States of Holland decided to assume the powers that he had wielded as Stadholder, and the Dutch General Assembly adopted a soundly Protestant religious policy. In England, republicans like Marchamont Nedham and Oliver St. John began floating the idea of a strict political union with the United Provinces; at least initially, the prospect appears to have been welcomed by both classical republicans and apocalyptic opponents of monarchy. So shortly after Milton published his *Defence of the People of England* (February 24, 1651), the Council of State sent Walter Strickland and Oliver St. John (a patron of Samuel Hartlib) on a special mission to treat with the Dutch. The ambassadors found, however, that the Dutch were still more politically divided than they had supposed. Although Holland, Utrecht, and Zeeland supported a union of some sort with the Commonwealth, Orangist sentiment proved too strong in some provinces, and negotiations broke down. The English ambassadors concluded with bitter disappointment that the Dutch were not interested in anything more than a trading alliance.

Rather than pursue these commercial negotiations or accept the Council of Trade's plan to create free ports, the Rump Parliament, in what appears to have been an act of retaliation against the United Provinces, passed the Navigation Act of 1651, which, in holding that all goods carried into British territories must be transported in ships from Britain or their place of origin, sought to promote the English ship-building industry and to cut into the Dutch carrying trade—at the cost and inconvenience, it must be said, of many English merchants who relied on Dutch shipping.[13] In a statement to the Dutch ambassadors that Milton put into Latin, the Rump defended the act by explaining that it had "thought it necessary to arouse this nation by every just and due means to an interest in naviga-

tion and the increase of our commerce in the seas" (*CPW* 5:567).[14] The
Navigation Act marked a real and symbolic turning point in the history
of England's commercial regulation. With it, writes Charles Wilson, "we
have arrived at a fully fashioned conception of economic policy in an
essentially national form." Its dynamic was no longer the restraint of greed
or exploitation in the name of Christian justice, says Wilson, "it was the
welfare of Leviathan."[15]

That change is apparent in Marchamont Nedham's 1652 translation of
a work that was first written for Charles I, John Selden's *Mare Clausum*
(1634), a refutation of Hugo Grotius's *Mare Liberum* (Leiden, 1609). The
engraved frontispiece of the new edition, titled *Of Dominion, or Ownership
of the Sea,* depicts Neptune addressing a figure who, resembling Minerva,
seems to embody both force and wisdom. The engraving identifies her as
"Angliæ Respub.," or the republic of England (fig. 5). In the accompanying
verses, Neptune addresses her more simply as "great STATE!" (stanzas 1,
6). The awkward fact that Selden's case for the nation's "Sea-Dominion"
is "by descent maintain'd," and therefore presupposes a hereditary monarchy, prompts the verses to exclaim that such dominion "may as well bee
gain'd / By new acquests" (stanza 5). Because such an expansionist program
must depend on the support of the nation's citizens, whether as sailors
or merchants or mere tax-payers, it is natural that Nedham should seek
a wider readership in English. The verses seem conscious of the fact that
some members of the Rump's constituency, such as millenarians and Protestant imperialists, may still desire an assault on Spain's holdings in the
western hemisphere, but they strive to present that ambition as outdated
and to redirect the attention of the nation's citizens to a new source of
wealth and power (control of the seas) and a new threat to the security
of the state (the Dutch):

> Thy great endeavors to encreas
> The Marine power, do confess
>   thou act'st som great design.
> Which had Seventh *Henrie* don, before
> *Columbus* lanch'd from Spanish shore,
>   the *Indies* had been thine.
> Yet do thy Seas those Indian Mines excell
> In riches far: the *Belgians* know it well.
>
>   (stanza 3)

To Selden's case for English dominion of the seas, Nedham adjoins the
legal case that the Venetian republic had made for its own dominion of
the seas. "If little Venice bring's alone / Such waves to her subjection,"

5. Frontispiece of Marchamont Nedham's 1652 translation of John Selden's *Mare Clausum* (1634). Personified as a woman, the new republic asserts her mastery of the sea. By permission of Houghton Library, Harvard University.

ask the verses, why shouldn't Britannia "rule as Ladie o're all seas" (stanza 5)? That Nedham imagines such rule will depend not on an assertion of legal rights but on learning from the Dutch is made apparent by a discussion of the Dutch economy that Nedham and John Bradshaw add to Selden's work (pp. 486–500). By making it its business to advance trade through national policy—and thus to "dilate" the "power" of England beyond "Narrow Seas" that were "too straight" for the "capacious heart" of the nation (stanza 6)—the Rump threw down a gauntlet that Charles II would eventually be forced to pick up.

In the meantime, however, the Commonwealth's relations with the Dutch deteriorated into war.[16] Few Englishmen could have imagined that the war would profit England in the short term. Many classical republicans, members of the Hartlib circle like Benjamin Worsley, and merchants were, however, willing to bear its obvious costs in the short term in order to enhance the power and maintain the commercial viability of the Commonwealth in the longer term. If the aggressive, monopolistic trading practices of the Dutch were left unchecked, they feared, England might be altogether shut out of important long-distance trades. It was to such emulous rivalry that the great Dutch poet Joost van den Vondel assigned the blame for the war: "De hoop van London vischt een net vol Amsterdammen" [London hopes for a catch full of Amsterdam].[17] But there was also an even more radical faction of Englishmen who believed that the Dutch deserved to be attacked precisely because, in setting their own economic interests above union with their Protestant neighbors, they had shown themselves to be servants of Mammon, even agents of the Beast. To such apocalyptic Protestants it seemed only fitting that the United Provinces should be laid waste, for had not that been the punishment of another great trading city, Tyre, when it "said against Jerusalem" (Ezek. 26:2)?[18]

Because it had strengthened its own navy and the Dutch had disbanded much of theirs before the war, the Commonwealth held the upper hand. The Rump had already vindicated the long-standing English belief in the utility of sea power by forcing open all Spanish and Portuguese trading territories on favorable terms.[19] Now it shook the States-General to their foundations. The war was certainly hard on some English merchants, but because the Commonwealth won the major battles of the North Sea and took more than 1,200 Dutch prizes, it enjoyed much broader support than Cromwell's Western Design ever would. By dissolving the Rump on the eve of a resounding victory over its arch-rivals in trade, Oliver Cromwell unleashed a wave of millenarian excitement, as apocalyptic Protestants hailed yet another revolution of the Lord, but he also prepared the way in the longer term for the Rump's retrospective glorification.[20] Within two years, some members of the Protectoral Parliament would remember the Rump as "an Iron Parliament, a Trading Parliament."[21]

The World's Mistake in Oliver Cromwell

For a brief time after the dissolution of the Rump on April 20, 1653, its successor, the Nominated Assembly, waged war against the United Provinces with equal vigor. Based loosely on the Sanhedrin of ancient Israel, this assembly of godly men was thickly populated with apocalyptic Protestants who were eager to pursue an aggressive foreign policy and who considered the Netherlands a worldly and tyrannical power that must be swept away as by the waves of the sea. It was precisely their fear of such thinking that persuaded a group of the assembly's more moderate members to resign its sovereign power on December 12, 1653.[22]

When, four days later, Oliver Cromwell assumed the powers of Lord Protector, he could at last end a war of which he had never approved. Despite having served on the Committee of Trade and Plantations in the 1640s, he placed a premium on political considerations when he negotiated the peace. He insisted on the exclusion of the Prince of Orange from office, but he pressed for no commercial concessions. Most of the money that the Dutch paid in reparations to the English East India Company he kept for the government, leaving it up to the competing East India Companies to work out whether the English or the Dutch were to control the Moluccas (or Spice Islands of the Malay archipelago). He did not even make sure that Pula Run, which had been adjudged to the English, was handed over. Nor did he support the wish of English merchants to be allowed to trade directly with Antwerp without paying dues to the Dutch at the mouth of the Scheldt.[23]

England's success in a war against the world's premier trading republic nevertheless encouraged some poets to hail the Lord Protector as the leader of a commercial power in the making. In an imitation of *Coopers Hill* written for Cromwell's visit to Oxford in 1654, William Godolphin anticipated the day when England would be the center of world trade:[24]

> Far now our Ships their Canvas Wings shall stretch,
> And the World's Wealth to richer *England* fetch,
> Till greater Treasures over-spread our Coast,
> Than *Tagus* or *Pactolus* Sands can boast.
> With this Design our busy Vessels range

About, to make our Isle the World's Exchange.
Others in times of Brass and Iron live,
Naught but our Pines the Golden Age can give:
Which fell'd, bear better Fruit than when they stood
The branching Glories of the fruitful Wood.
        No foreign Navy shall impede their Course,
Circling the Globe with uncontroled Force.
While, with the Sun, they round the World, their Might
Becomes as Universal as his Light.

(lines 17–30)

Godolphin hails the navigation of the seas in keels of pine not, as Ovid would have it, as a symptom of the greed and insolence that destroyed the Golden Age (*Met.* 1.130–34), but as the means to create a new Golden Age that will be defined by an abundance of gold and a flurry of trade, not by their absence. The powers of dispersion and concentration, which had thus far persuaded some reformers to think of the progress of God's truth in terms of trade, are here celebrated as the means of establishing a temporal empire whose only resemblance to the millennial kingdom will be its resistless spread. While Godolphin's phrase "their Might / Becomes as Universal as his Light" asks to be read strictly as a reference to the sun's diffused illumination, it derives an unsettling energy from the more startling idea that the light whose universality these ships will emulate may be God's.

In his panegyric of the same year, Edmund Waller similarly hails the Lord Protector for turning England into a "seat of empire" whose power can be projected as far as "swelling sails upon the globe may go" (lines 15, 20):

Lords of the world's great waste, the ocean, we
Whole forests send to reign upon the sea.

(lines 41–42)

In Waller's poem, the traditional figure of the microcosm recommends itself as a figure naturally suited to an entrepôt of world trade:

Our little world, the image of the great,
Like that, amidst the boundless ocean set,
Of her own growth hath all that Nature craves,
And all that's rare, as tribute from the waves.

(lines 49–52)

To control trade is to intervene late in the production process, to enjoy the fruits of others' labors:

> The taste of hot Arabia's spice we know,
> Free from the scorching sun that makes it grow;
> Without the worm, in Persian silks we shine;
> And, without planting, drink of every vine.
>
> To dig for wealth we weary not our limbs;
> Gold, though the heaviest metal, hither swims;
> Ours is the harvest where the Indians mow;
> We plough the deep, and reap what others sow.
>
> (lines 57–64)

Waller's lines could serve as a gloss on Cicero's apothegm: *qui mare teneat, eum necesse esse rerum potiri* [he who is master of the sea must be master of everything] (*Ad Attic.*, bk. 10, letter 8). "The wealth of both Indies," Bacon had concluded after citing such ancient authority, "seems in great part but an accessary to the command of the seas."[25] Waller's poem is certainly a paean that celebrates England's naval hegemony, but with its emphasis on reaping what others have sown not purely through force so much as through shipping, it may also celebrate another variety of coercion, the market power enjoyed by the monopolist. For as Hobbes had rightly asserted three years before, a monopolist who intervenes at any stage from production to sale should be able to extract profits from the entire process: if England could control the world's shipping, it really could profit from all the world's labors.[26] In thus appropriating the terms of the Rump's program of naval and commercial expansion in order to celebrate and consolidate the rule of a single man, Waller anticipated the co-optation that Royalists would manage at the Restoration. His poem was out of step, however, with the direction in which the Protectorate was moving.

Whether in terms of praise or blame, the Protectorate would be described in the next few years as devoted to building through acquisition an empire of dominion, not one of trade.[27] While members of the landed gentry in Parliament had not only supported but helped formulate the commercial and imperial policies of the Rump, the declining influence of the small core of merchants and economic theorists with whom some of them had worked in close cooperation during the Commonwealth could not but make its effect felt in the policies of the Protectorate.[28] Although Godolphin and Waller could hardly have known it in 1654, the Lord Protector was determined to pursue a Protestant foreign policy whose ambitions were quite different from those implied in their panegyrics. Through his friend Cornelius Vermuyden, he proposed a perpetual alliance with the Dutch—for which he was prepared to abrogate the popular Navigation Act and give the Dutch free fishing rights in English waters. In return for a declaration of war against Spain, he was even prepared to surrender all of England's holdings in the East Indies, to let the Dutch retain Brazil, and to accept nothing in return but the remaining western holdings of the Dutch. He hoped to partition the Spanish and Portuguese Empires with the Dutch, of course, but his plan jeopardized the immediate interests of established merchants.[29]

Under the early Stuarts, some of the very merchants and landed gentry who played a key role in the Commonwealth's program of naval and commercial expansion had supported plans for an anti-Spanish Western Design. Steven Pincus holds that Cromwell supported the revival of the plan because he still genuinely believed that the alliance between the pope and the king of Spain posed the greatest foreign threat to England and to Protestantism.[30] Cromwell also claimed that the English fleet must be employed and that sending it to the Indies might yield gold. But there was something nostalgic about the entire enterprise. It was already clear to many other Englishmen that the United Provinces and not Spain now posed the greatest politico-economic threat to England. Thus while we should not underestimate the number of Englishmen who were willing to support a successful Protestant foreign policy, they could not be expected, once English forces suffered serious setbacks, to sustain a war effort that could not be justified in terms of any immediate peril. The Anglo-Spanish War that broke out as a direct result of Cromwell's Western Design cut English traders off from their largest market (Spain) and allowed the Dutch to take control of it. By contemporary estimates, the conflict cost England 1,200 ships.[31]

A refutation of Waller's panegyric of 1654, which was probably written by the republican Lucy Hutchinson in 1658, indicts Cromwell as a king in all but name.[32] Whereas Waller's poem celebrates England's ascendancy over the Dutch (lines 101–08), Hutchinson's faults Cromwell first for failing to press home the Commonwealth's advantage against the United Provinces (lines 101–08), then for launching an ill-conceived assault on Spain whose cost in blood and treasure—tallied up in lines that cancel out Waller's catalog of the world's goods converging on England— is seen to consume all the wealth that was at Cromwell's command when he assumed the reins of power:

II

Hee being made in his Vsurped Raigne
Lord of the Worlds great Wast the Ocean
The enclosed Isle with sadd Exactions greiues
And forreigne Lands more troubles then Releiues.

12

Angells and wee haue one prerogative
That none can at Our happy Seates arrive
Yet hence the quiet Nations he Invades
And barrs the oppressed Natives straingers aides.

13

Our little world with blessings doth abound
A pleasant heauiness a fruitfull ground
Of her owne growth hath all that nature craues
And all that's rare as Tribute from the Waues.

14

Whence the Vsurper doth his Treasures raise
And greuious Imposts upon all things layes.
Yet none what the Ocean or the Earth Supplies
Can his ambitious greedy thoughts suffice.

15

Not choicest Aromatiques nor Rich Wine
Nor bright Silkes which our Scorned fetters line
Can comfort the vnwilling Slaues that be
Cheated of their more pretious Liberty.

16

Whils't free born English sent to other Soyles
Are there kill'd vp with Sicknesse and vaine Toyles
To augment his Highs. Treasure and his Name
Not satisfi'd with any Wealth or Fame.

(lines 41–64)

Hutchinson's poem is instructive because it comprises the criticisms that republicans and Royalists alike would make of Cromwell's record on trade. Even years after the Restoration, and for the same reasons, Bethel would look back on the Protectorate as *The World's Mistake in Oliver Cromwell* (1668). Hutchinson's poem also establishes a standard of criticism that Charles II's panegyrists would not be able to ignore: her Cromwell is a greedy and ambitious man motivated by outmoded, aristocratic ideas of wealth and honor conceived narrowly in terms of gold and military glory, one who underestimates what might be achieved by promoting the liberty and industry of Englishmen. He is just the sort of ruler that, many monarchists would later conclude, a king could no longer afford to be. When they later came to search for a courtly idiom in which to praise the ideal of an empire of trade, Royalist panegyrists found that Waller's vision of the world's luxuries converging on England would, on the other hand, suit. Indeed, Waller's poem probably incited Hutchinson's ire not only because it praised Cromwell but because it praised him in verse fit for a king.

When Cromwell died in 1658, turning over the reins of government to his son Richard, the country was in debt, overburdened with taxes, and on the brink of another trade depression. While the costly war with Spain precipitated a stop of trade that hit overseas merchants especially hard, the depression was worsened by several harvest failures that increased the real cost of living, diminished the capacity of the middling sort and the laboring poor to buy nonessential goods, and thus caused unemployment and an increase of subsistence migration in England. The great man was not without his elegists and biographers, but in contrast to the terms of praise with which he had been hailed in 1654, he was remembered in death as a general, a prudent governor, and a man of faith, not as a patron of trade.[33] Although each successive regime would be undermined by its failure to achieve a satisfactory constitutional and religious settlement, we should not underestimate the destabilizing influence of the depression that was just getting under way at his death. Every bid for power in the final months of the Interregnum was defended on the basis of the need to improve trade.

Trading Republic or Mercantile King?

When the want of money forced Richard Cromwell to assemble a Parliament in January 1659, republican M.P.s took his father Oliver to task for dashing England's chance at commercial hegemony. Drawing an invidious comparison between England's current plight and its thriving condition when the Rump was dissolved, Sir Arthur Haselrig exclaimed: "We see what a confusion we are in. We have not prospered. Our army at Jamaica prospered not. The trade and glory of the nation are much diminished." He recalled how differently matters had stood in 1653: "I appeal to all, if the nation, that had been blasted and torn, began not exceedingly to flourish. At the end of four years, scarce a sight to be seen that we had had a war. Trade flourished; the City of London grew rich; we were the most potent by sea that was ever known in England." In the same vein, Thomas Scot lamented: "We never bid fairer for being masters of the whole world."[34] Slingsby Bethel continued to make such claims even after the Restoration.[35] If the memories of former Rumpers were selective, they were not groundless, and when a military coup forced Richard to dissolve his Parliament in April, petitions suggested that the Rump's old members might bring greater experience to the nation's problems of trade and diplomacy. When the Rump was actually reassembled in May, one writer averred that trade had flourished under the Commonwealth as it had not under the kings of England.[36] Another said that if "the Glory and Top of their Great Advice" had been followed by enforcing the Navigation Act, "*England* had been the most happy, and most rich People this day upon the face of the whole Earth: they had been the Ware-house of the World."[37]

The Rump's record seemed so strong in part because a tradition of thought stretching back some decades had prepared observers to see trade flourish in a free state. In 1610 the common-law lawyer Thomas Hedley could say, for instance, that just as free states consisting of citizens secure in their property produced more valorous soldiers, so too would they produce more virtuous merchants than could absolutist states, whose subjects showed "little care or industry to get that which they [could] not keep and so [grew] both poor and base minded."[38] While Hedley thought the English constitution could support, indeed required, both the liberty of the subject and the sovereignty of the king, many courtiers and merchants, even those who depended on royal charters, went further and held up the trading republics of Venice and the United Provinces as model commercial societies.[39] The economic hardships of 1649–50 and 1659–60 gave a satiric edge to Thomas Hobbes's assertion that "the city of London and other great towns of trade, having in admiration the great prosperity of the Low Countries after they had revolted from their monarch, the King of Spain, were inclined to think that the like change of government here, would to them produce the like prosperity."[40] Yet in 1649, republicans really had made such bald claims—and asked Milton to translate them into Latin.[41] Even as the restored Rump struggled unsuccessfully to arrest the vicious cycle of debt, war expenditure, and depression that the Protectorate had bequeathed it, it declared confidently in 1660 that trade and navigation were "encouraged and promoted" by republics but "stinted and restrained" by monarchies. In the following month, as he secured the readmission of the M.P.s who had been excluded by Pride's Purge, General Monck likewise gave Parliament his opinion that the interests of London were "the Bulwark of Parliaments" and that London's interests lay "in a Commonwealth," for only then could London become "the Metropolis and Bank of Trade for all Christendom, whereunto God and Nature hath fitted them above all others."[42] We may wonder whether Monck was expressing himself candidly, since his actions were bringing the Restoration ever closer, but his speech suggests how strong the imaginative link between republicanism and trade really was.

If the Rump's hardening secularism had helped to precipitate its dissolution by an army eager for religious reform in 1653, it invigorated and perpetuated the Commonwealth's trade policies as an example and

a shame to the monarchy in 1660.[43] Because it had been willing to fight
Protestant republicans in a conflict whose stakes could easily be described
in commercial terms, and because its greatest spokesmen in 1659 and 1660
were secular republicans like Haselrig, Scot, and Bethel, the Rump's program remained a model for naval and commercial policies motivated by
national interest rather than political or religious ideology. The initial dependence of the Rump's program on the intellectual and political support
of millenarians and Protestant imperialists was suppressed in the accounts
of men like Bethel.

As the depression deepened in 1659, Royalists began to think that if
the only real grievances of citizens were taxes and other obstacles to their
private gain (as Hobbes claimed), then these might smooth the way for
Charles Stuart's return as surely as they had precipitated his father's exit.[44]
Royalist pamphleteers scored their first real success with interest-based arguments. The discord of the Revolution had proven that Englishmen did
not cleave to a single notion of the public interest or the highest good.
Neither could be invoked without reference to private interests and lesser
goods. Yet it was precisely these lesser goods—like low taxes, secure property, and peaceful trade—that might serve as the basis of settlement. On
these subjects, revolutionaries and Royalists, nonconformists and Anglicans could understand each other.

One of the most important attempts to organize overlapping private
interests as a basis of settlement appeared in July 1659. Rather than appeal to a mystical ideal of kingship, The Interest of England Stated promised
political and religious stability, limited taxation, a return to normal economic activities, and a revival of the nation's "languishing and almost dead
trade" (p. 4). It argued that the king's return "and this onely will advance
trade" (p. 9). It closed by asking its readers to "remember these two plain
truths, that they are English men, and so consider the good of the Nation;
and then that they are Men, and so pursue their own" (p. 16). The Interest
of England Stated implied that it was willing to have kingship stand or fall
on the basis of its demonstrable, concrete benefits to the nation and its
subjects. In Interest Will Not Lie (August 17, 1659), Marchamont Nedham
adduced opposing arguments from interest. More important than the specific claims of these pamphlets, however, was their professed willingness
to advance or obstruct the king's cause according to his usefulness as an
instrument of settlement, not his personal claims.

The army's forceful dissolution of the Rump on October 13, 1659,
opened the way for more strident Royalist claims that only the king's return could reestablish the peaceful routines of material life, claims that
George Wither attempted to refute by rehearsing the economic misdeeds

of the early Stuarts. Wither himself realized, however, that "our *present sufferings*" caused most men to forget their misfortunes under the monarchy.[45] Their short memory permitted John Evelyn, in his *Apology for the Royalist Party* (October 27, 1659), to condemn the taxes of Interregnum governments and promise that the "Merchant will be secure, Trades immediately recover" with the king's return.[46] A printed letter directed to the nobility and gentry of Scotland made the same promise.[47] A conviction that the very turmoil of the Revolution was the great hindrance to trade made some reconsider whether the goal, say, of ecclesiastical reformation had been worth the disruption to commerce. A broadside published by London's "apprentices" lamented: "We are very sensible what Inconveniences Innovations bring with them, we shrewdly conjecture that the cry of *No Bishops* hath been sadly echoed with the complaint of *No Trade*."[48] These were the weeks when, painfully aware of the "crimes" of his own party, yet in greater dread of what a restored monarch might do, Milton made his final bid to save the republic by formulating the proposals that he would include in *The Readie and Easie Way to Establish a Free Commonwealth,* his only account of what a more perfect republic might look like.[49] The intent of pamphlets like the self-described *Recital of the Ruins Overrunning the People and Their Trades; with an Opportune Advice to Return to Obedience to Their Kings, under Whom They Ever Flourished* was quite the reverse;[50] it was less to defend Charles I's economic record than to persuade citizens that prosperity could be reclaimed only by a return to old ways—and thus to promote what Milton called that "vain and groundless apprehension that nothing but kingship can restore trade" (*CPW* 7:385–86). It is remarkable that, even as he worked in haste to mount an opposition to such Royalist apologists for commerce, Milton could conceive a radical vision of the polity as a political economy in which institutional arrangements and market forces might work in tandem.

The Readie and Easie Way: Trade, Federalism, and Christian Liberty on the Eve of the Restoration

Written in a mood of retrenchment rather than expansion and liberation, *The Readie and Easie Way* (February 23–29, 1660) has never been considered one of Milton's most sympathetic works, yet lying as it does at the threshold between the Interregnum and the Restoration, between Milton's prose and his major poems, it naturally demands a privileged position in any account of his thought. In that capacity, it has most often been made to yield two unhappy lessons: that Milton was no political economist and that his thought took an authoritarian turn toward the end of the republic. Indeed, Arthur Barker has interpreted Milton's proposals as little more than a grab for power that would sacrifice "liberty to gain the truth which ought to be free."[51]

I would contend, quite to the contrary, that as a work of political economy, *The Readie and Easie Way* is more coherent and creative, more important in the history of ideas, than even Milton's most generous readers have recognized. By allowing for a centralized government with authority over certain matters of state even as he devolved most legislative and judicial powers to the counties, Milton proposed a federal system of government that, in distinguishing between the few powers that ought to be granted to the central and highest authority in the land and the many that ought to be reserved for local jurisdictions, sought to discriminate between functions that naturally required a uniform national policy enforced by a central authority and those that could accommodate, even flourish because of, local diversity and competition. When deciding which powers ought to be granted to the central government and which could be reserved for the counties, Milton could simply improve upon the contemporary practices of the United Provinces. But in order to get a better idea of how the forces of mobility and selection might operate on "many Commonwealths under one sovrantie" (*CPW* 7:385), he had to look farther abroad, to the Puritan colonies of New England. At the heart of Milton's federalism, I would argue, lies an innovative attempt to put market forces to work in the polity. By neglecting the tract's economic content, critics have not only slighted important evidence of Milton's economic convictions, they have, more crucially, failed to appreciate the dynamic aspect of his federalism, which would clear a space in the polity for market forces to preserve the possibility of individual liberty. In making this case, I propose to reappraise two aspects of Milton's tract that have elicited attacks, expressions of sympathy, and appeals to circumstance, but few if any endorsements: its refusal to supply the blueprint for a Puritan utopia and its embarrassing readiness to oppose the claims of popular sovereignty.

Milton first outlined his proposals in the interim between the expulsion of the Rump in October 1659 and its reassembly that December. Yet by the time the first edition of *The Readie and Easie Way* appeared in February 1660, the conservative and moderate M.P.s who had originally been excluded by the purge of the Presbyterians in 1648 had been readmitted to the Rump, and the long-standing discursive link between republicanism and the advancement of trade had finally been reversed. In its internal contradictions, *The Readie and Easie Way* inscribes some of these changes in the political logic of economic arguments. In order to make sense of the tract's conflicting ideas about the proper relationship of the economic and political spheres, I wish, therefore, to distinguish Milton's basic proposals, which he outlined earlier in *A Letter to a Friend* and *Proposalls of Certaine Expedients,* from the persuasive rhetoric introduced in the tract itself. I turn to that rhetoric in the second part of my analysis.

Writing in straitened political circumstances, Milton must have thought of a few of his proposals as desperate expedients, not the basis of an ideal society.[52] We could, for instance, understand the opposed tendencies of his treatise — vesting a Grand Council with perpetual authority over matters of state while decentralizing other legislative and judicial powers — as an attempt to remove the specific hindrances that he thought had impeded the Rump's progress: its frequent "interruptions" (by the army or by calls for new elections) and its inability to achieve a national consensus on legal and religious reforms. Milton's scheme would preclude the former and make the latter unnecessary. Yet if the political crises of the Interregnum pushed Milton to contrive an instrument of government that was blunt in some ways, his proposals nevertheless delineated a politico-economic system that was consistent in many other ways with his experience and values.

Milton's scheme would have endowed the Grand Council and its smaller deliberative committee, the Council of State, with the authority to direct the army and navy, raise and manage public revenues, coin money, and oversee foreign commerce (*CPW* 7:329, 337, 368, 433). As Secretary of Foreign Languages for the Commonwealth (1649–53), Milton had learned what an important part of government business the maintenance of commercial relations could be. Precisely because critics have assumed that Milton's interest in economics was minimal, they have tended to overlook the letters on trade that he helped to compose or translate. These were directed to Hamburg, Portugal, Spain, Denmark, Sweden, Tuscany, North Africa, and the United Provinces.[53] Through his work in the negotiations that preceded the First Anglo-Dutch War, Milton would have learned that although the Dutch States-General and Council of State theoretically lacked the authority to direct foreign commerce, the practical requirements of modern commerce had led them to assume such powers de facto.[54] Through his work for the Commonwealth, Milton discovered not only how essential to the viability of the republic was its international trade but how necessary it was to negotiate with foreign powers from a position of strength, both economic and military: among his personal papers, he kept a full record of the East India Company's losses to the Dutch (*CPW* 5:600). The vulnerability that the United Provinces had shown to the intense pressure of a conflict like the First Anglo-Dutch War may have led Milton to distinguish his own federation from such a confederacy.[55] Under his proposals, Milton says, England would comprise "not many sovranties in one Commonwealth"—like the Dutch republic, in which each province theoretically retained sovereignty—"but many Commonwealths under one sovrantie" (*CPW* 7:385). Indeed, the Dutch republic was able to pursue its commercial objectives and survive such tests as its war against the Commonwealth only because, despite being a "confederacy in form and theory," it verged on a "federal state in substance and practice."[56] The *Federalist Papers* would later affirm that the protection of commerce and fisheries, together with the negotiation of commercial agreements from a position of strength, should be among the chief duties of a strong central government.[57]

Unwarranted as it may have been, George Starkey's complaint that, in taking the Dutch republic as his model, Milton embraced a society for whom riches were the "only standard of advancement" should nevertheless remind us that if Milton did not believe that riches were the measure of a society's progress, he did recognize them as a legitimate aspiration for a republic.[58] In chastising the Commonwealth for failing to build "another Rome in the west" after laying the foundation "gallantly," Milton even draws an unfavorable comparison with the United Provinces, which, despite being "inferiour in all outward advantages"—as England's economic writers never tired of pointing out in comparing the nations' ports, wool, and arable land—were now "settl'd in all the happie injoiments of a potent and flourishing Republick" (*CPW* 7:357). It was precisely that three-faceted character of the United Provinces, as a military power, trading nation, and republic, that the Rump had sought to emulate. When Milton claims that with the Grand Council sitting in perpetuity, "ther can be no cause alleag'd why peace, justice, plentiful trade and all prosperitie should not therupon ensue throughout the whole land" (*CPW* 7:374), he is not throwing out a vague hope but envisioning what republicans like Sir Arthur Haselrig and Thomas Scot claimed the Rump had been on the brink of achieving in 1653 when it was dissolved by Cromwell.

If Milton saw the need for a strong national government in the provision of certain public goods, he nevertheless called for a system that was decentralized in other respects. We know that before writing his proposals, Milton received a letter from Moses Wall recommending a series of economic reforms advocated by members of the Hartlib circle. Some, like a national fishery, were conceived as state-sponsored industries. Others, like the division of waste commons, would leave the land's development up to the individuals who received it. While Milton's *Pro-*

posalls of Certaine Expedients made it clear that he considered such schemes "of a second consideration" to the immediate establishment of a secure republican government, those initiatives that he does mention in the various versions of his proposals—like "the just division of wast Commons, whereby the nation would become much more industrious, rich & populous" (*CPW* 7:338) or the erection of schools for the people "at thir own choice," which would make "the whole nation more industrious, more ingenuous at home, more potent, more honourable abroad" (*CPW* 7:384)—consistently assumed that the wealth and power of the nation could best be promoted through enhanced opportunities, personal initiatives, and individual choices, not state planning. There had long been a tension between economic reformers like Benjamin Worsley, who valued reform primarily as a means of state-building, and those like the Levellers, who valued it as a way to increase opportunity and enfranchisement. Some members of the Hartlib circle, like Henry Robinson, seemed at times like burros unable to choose between two bales of hay. But as David Quint has argued, Milton's vision was consistently at odds with the statists'—whether Royalist or republican.[59] Although explicitly directed against the return of kingship, Milton's quotation of Proverbs 6:6–8 could have been applied as readily to republicans who wished to marshal England's inhabitants as economic resources rather than teach them to be economic agents: "*Go to the Ant, thou sluggard, saith Solomon, consider her waies, and be wise; which having no prince, ruler, or lord, provides her meat in the summer, and gathers her food in the harvest*" (*CPW* 7:362).

For Milton, it was precisely the diffusion of autonomy that should differentiate a truly republican economy from a monarchical one. Royalist arguments from interest had increasingly stressed that since the Crown's finances now depended on customs from trade and since it was through commercial power that one state compelled compliance from another, it was in the king's rational interest to promote the wealth of the nation. Milton could hardly deny such arguments in toto, but he made a saving distinction. To proposals like the dissemination of education, he says, "a free Commonwealth will easily assent . . . for of all governments a Commonwealth aims most to make the people flourishing, vertuous, noble, and high spirited" (*CPW* 7:384). In the second edition of his tract, Milton amplified his point with an image of bodily invigoration: erecting schools at the people's choice would communicate "the natural heat of government and culture more distributively to all extreme parts, which now lie numm and neglected" (*CPW* 7:460).[60] But monarchs can "never permitt" the creation of an educated citizenry, for they want only to "make the people, wealthy indeed perhaps and wel-fleec't for thir own shearing, and for the supply of regal prodigalitie; but otherwise softest, basest, vitiousest, servilest, easiest to be kept under; and not only in fleece, but in minde also sheepishist" (CPW 7:384).[61] Even in *Areopagitica,* in his portrait of the shopkeeper who made his religion a "dividuall movable" so that he might remain "in the shop trading all day" without it, Milton had recognized that an exclusive concern with the market could make men less than complete (CPW 2:544–45). That was a paradox, since the ingenuity, industry, and decision required by the market also promised to encourage analogous political and religious virtues. In *The Readie and Easie Way,* Milton was faced with the prospect of a Crown that might actively encourage its citizens to abandon their agency and become cogs in a wheel.

I have suggested that Milton's federalism may have been an attempt to solve the problems of factionalism, tumult, and abuse of trust in the national government, for where there had been discord at the national level during the Interregnum, there frequently had been consensus within counties. As a student of Aristotle and Machiavelli, Milton would have anticipated that the size of a political unit might make a difference to its concord.[62] Aristotle held that friendship, which could be sustained only in communities of moderate size, was "the greatest good of states" and a "preservative" against "revolutions." The population of a state could not be expanded without limit because "if the citizens of a state are to judge and to distribute offices according to merit, then they must know each other's characters; where they do not possess this knowledge, both the election to offices and the decision of lawsuits will go wrong. When the population is very large they are manifestly settled at haphazard."[63] In different terms, Machiavelli also held that the quiet and unity of a state, which must be accomplished by the domination of a few, could be maintained only when the population of a state was, like Venice's, restricted.[64]

The elaborate balloting system that Milton proposes for selection of the nation's General Assembly shows that Venice was one of the models that he had in mind when he wrote his tract, but his federalism amounts to more than just an effort to establish political units that will not be unwieldy; it embodies his continued commitment to the ideals of trial, toleration, and self-determination.[65] While Milton's scheme yokes the local jurisdictions to the central government more tightly, in specific respects, than did the Dutch republic's system of government, Milton pointedly omits to confer on his Grand Council some powers that the States-General had de facto assumed, such as the direction of church affairs.[66] He even goes so far as to devolve legislative powers to the counties, a proposal that surpasses any of the Levellers' demands for local courts and locally chosen magistrates (*CPW* 7:383).[67] It was not Milton's willingness to invest the Grand Council with perpetual authority that struck George Starkey with horror as much as his eagerness to protect English counties from "any *Commanding,* or *Prohibiting,* or any way *Coercive Power,*" thus making them as *"Autocraticall"* as Dutch towns.[68]

Rather than centralized planning, Milton's system prizes experimentation. It aims to make Englishmen not just "free" citizens who are governed by a representative assembly chosen by a majority but reasoning ones who will be forced to make deliberative choices about the ways and means of government. By allowing a majority to choose one course for all, national democratic elections would foreclose options that might be kept open by permitting counties to diverge from one another.[69] While governments could be more or less intrusive and communities more or less homogenous, they could never refrain entirely from impinging on individuals with tender consciences, for if nothing else, they had to make corporate choices about taxes and expenditures. That even such corporate choices could rankle some radicals is suggested by Roger Williams's call, in a pamphlet that Milton almost certainly knew, for "a true and absolute *Soul freedom* to all the people of the Land impartially, so that no person be forced to *pray* nor *pay,* otherwise than as his Soul believeth and consenteth."[70] Individual liberty could be preserved only by the atomization of society into smaller units whose citizens, like the members of independent churches, had some freedom to select among alternatives and, if necessary, separate from the polity into which they were born. I would suggest that this basic insight lies behind Milton's proposals.

It also lay behind the proliferation of Puritan congregations in New England—despite the determined opposition of the General Court of the Massachusetts Bay Colony. Developments in New England were of great interest to English Independents. Hugh Peter was said to have exasperated the Commonwealth's committee on the reform of the law because he talked so often of the practices of New England. Milton would have received much of his information about the new colonies from Roger Williams, with whom he traded ideas and language lessons from 1651 to 1654.[71] We may fairly assume that Williams told Milton of the new settlements that had been established in Connecticut and Rhode Island and supported by settlers who had migrated from Plymouth, Salem, or Massachusetts Bay for reasons of conscience or economic opportunity.[72]

Under *The Readie and Easie Way*'s scheme, the political map of England would begin to look more like that of New England. It would come to resemble a marketplace in which mobile subjects could express their preferences not so much by casting ballots as by voting with their feet.[73]

To be sure, most people, prey to the tyranny of custom or constrained by circumstance, would show no inclination to move. But the preservation of constant alternatives would allow a more meaningful form of self-determination for educated citizens of moderate means than would the right of the majority to pick a new government for all on a regular basis.

I think critics have been right to observe a decline of Milton's confidence in the ideal of popular sovereignty from the high point in his tracts of 1649–51. His faith in the ability of common men to try all things and hold fast to the good must likewise have decayed. But we should recall that if Milton's faith in the multitudes had suffered, so too had his reliance on government. Milton sensed that any government, even a republican one, had an innate drive to aggrandize itself and abuse the public trust. He had warned against it publicly in his *Second Defence of the English People* and bemoaned it privately in his digression on the Long Parliament in *The History of Britain (CPW* 4:681; 5:443, 445, 449). He was less worried about the state's ability to gather resources than about making its management of public revenues accountable to "inspectors deputed for satisfaction of the people" (*CPW* 7:433).

In permitting variation among county governments, Milton's proposed scheme places them in competition. The idea that governments could and should compete for citizens had been suggested by economic writers like Henry Robinson who were distressed by the exodus of skilled workers to the United Provinces and who wished to attract them back to England.[74] It would be acted upon by the Harvard graduate and former republican Sir George Downing as soon as he started to steer the economic policies of the Restoration government. He not only attempted to recruit individuals with valuable skills by promising them government support for their operations, he tried to institute an act of General Naturalization that would make all Protestants "be as natural borne subjects."[75] Especially during the Third Anglo-Dutch War, when the French threatened to overrun Flanders and Holland, English diplomats would attempt to persuade entire Dutch towns to relocate to England, where they might live under a more desirable government than France's and where their capital and skills might promote the economic growth of the island.[76] I would not claim that Milton is so explicit about his reasons for favoring such autonomous counties, but I would suggest that he was worried about government's capacity to erode individual liberty, that he was unceasingly suspicious of men in office who pretended to have a monopoly on the truth, and that both the economic writings of the Hartlib circle and the experience of Puritans in the new world had prepared him to think about governments in terms of experiment, self-selection, and competition. Unlike a true democracy, Milton's system would enable an individual to resist the judgment of the majority, for the majority's choice would not clear the market of all other alternatives; unlike a perfect autocracy, it would permit competition among "commonwealths" to discipline the governments themselves.

While I would endorse Austin Woolrych's assertion that "the challenges of the next half-century were to confirm the need for a dynamic rather than a static concept of the function of government," I must contest his conclusion that "Milton's concept was so essentially static as to reflect more his reading of classical authors than his limited experience of actual government in the service of the Council of State" (*CPW* 7:187). Quite to the contrary, dynamism lies at the heart of Milton's system. It would be surprising if it were otherwise. To this day New England retains stronger town governments and more numerous jurisdictions than any other region in the United States, for the region was taking its stamp from the Puritans even as Milton wrote, and its institutional arrangements still show the effect of the Puritans' reliance on the forces of mobility and self-selection to achieve conformity *within* communities even as they tolerated divergence *between* communities.[77] When seen in this light, Milton's refusal to provide the blueprint for a Puritan utopia is no mere failure of nerve or imagination; it is the product of his recognition that any system of government must be able to accommodate divergent preferences. Allowing counties to coexist side by side while pursuing divergent policies may provide a more meaningful set of alternatives for citizens than any single government, subject to regular elections tipped one way or the other by a block of swing voters, possibly could.

A federal system would do more, however, than simply permit citizens to agree to disagree. It would provide scope for innovation, for the spread of ideas, for the reformation of less successful counties according to the model of more successful ones. Thus, when James Holstun asserts that Milton sees the state "as the embodiment or expression of a preexistent virtue, not as a pedagogical and disciplinary mechanism for the production of virtuous citizens" like most Puritan utopias, he mistakes the absence of a *centralized* mechanism of pedagogy and discipline for a complete absence of such forces in the commonwealth.[78] Milton's federalism does hold out the hope that, like those whom Milton pictures in *Areopagitica* searching for the sundered pieces of Truth, going "up and down gathering up limb by limb still as they could find them" (*CPW* 2:549),

England's citizens might set their disjointed counties side by side, keeping what was valuable and discarding what was not, until they had assembled a more perfect body politic.

Clearing a space in the polity for market-like forces to preserve the possibility of Christian liberty, Milton put economic principles to work in what was in many ways a defensive project. That very defensiveness has made *The Readie and Easie Way* less appealing to most readers than works like *Areopagitica,* but in some circumstances a rout averted is a victory, especially since preserving diversity and competition meant maintaining the hope of progress in the future. Of course, as an exercise in persuasive rhetoric, Milton's pamphlet had slight chance of being embraced by a populace frustrated with the chaos of 1659–60. The English people had had quite enough of paper constitutions. Besides, Milton's proposals were opposed to that deeper, structural movement (apparent in both the Commonwealth's and the restored monarchy's policies) toward the creation of what is sometimes called the "modern state," with its centralized government, established bureaucracy, high taxation, and powerful war machine, all supported by commercial growth.[79] These are presumably the developments over the next half-century that Woolrych thinks the bookish Milton did not foresee (*CPW* 7:187). But I would counter that Milton did see the potential for such developments even in the policies of the Commonwealth and the theories of statists like Worsley: his proposals constitute a powerful theoretical attempt to find a better way.

With a system of institutions and laws that had grown gradually through accretion and a government whose powers had become more and more centralized under the Tudors and Stuarts, England could not provide the right setting for such a system. But across the Atlantic, where the problem for federalists was how to *create* a central government rather than how to limit it, something very like it did evolve. Before we dismiss Milton's system as a "crazy structure," it is worth noting that in assigning the responsibility for directing the armed services, raising and managing public revenues, coining money, managing foreign commerce, and adjudicating intercounty legal disputes (and nothing more) to a central government, Milton made a division of powers that was sanctioned in its details by neither the theory nor the practice of contemporary English or Dutch government but that has been confirmed to the last item by modern theorists of federalism.

While the organization of Milton's proposed commonwealth invited market forces to operate in the political sphere, the more crucial issue in the mind of the public in 1660, as we have already seen, was the simpler question: Who would provide the better national government for trade, the king or the restored Rump Parliament? In this context, Milton bemoaned the people's "vain and groundless apprehension, that nothing but kingship can restore trade" (*CPW* 7:385–86). Repeating arguments that Marchamont Nedham had made six months before, he warned that a restored king would be certain to keep the people "narrowly watch'd" and "low"; indeed, Nedham had warned that Charles Stuart would check London's prosperity in order to limit the City's power to overthrow him (*CPW* 7:378).[80] "Besides this," Milton continued, in an effort to dispel the popular hope that Charles would reduce taxes, "a new royal-revenue must be found; which being wholly dissipated or bought by private persons, or assign'd for service don, and especially to the Armie, cannot be recovered without a general confusion to men's estates, or a heavy imposition on all men's purses" (*CPW* 7:378).[81]

To objections like these against the king's return, Milton added his arguments for the Commonwealth. Although it was certainly a plea of divine sanction for the republic, Milton's warning that the people should be mindful of "the frequent plagues and pestilences" that had wasted London under the monarchy but had not been "felt since" was also a reminder of one of the Interregnum's real economic blessings, for the plague epidemics that had struck under the early Stuarts had not only led foreign ports to impose trade embargoes for fear of infection, they had killed working-age males in disproportionate numbers, thus depleting the labor pool and causing economic shocks (*CPW* 7:386). To this Milton added what had always been the strongest argument of republicans, the empirical observation "that trade flourishes no where more, then in the free Commonwealths of *Italie, Germanie,* and the Low Countreys" (*CPW* 7:386). The "potent and flourishing" United Provinces could thus serve not only as an indictment of the Commonwealth's failures but as a measure of its promise.

The Censure of the Rota upon Mr. Milton's Book complained that Milton always fought with the "flat" of his hand like a rhetorician, not with a "Logical fist."[82] I have argued that Milton's proposals outline a political system that is more coherent than is often supposed—even in the economic terms that Milton has been thought to repudiate in the tract. I must admit, though, that in his peroration—written after the purged members of Parliament had returned to their seats and the Royalists had succeeded in making the trade depression their issue—Milton turned back on himself. While he showed himself perfectly capable of adducing the economic arguments of republicans, his rhetorical instincts seem to have told him that economic grievances could no longer be used as a rallying

cry for the Good Old Cause. The same appeal to material calculation that
Francis Osborne had once used to persuade Englishmen to comply with
the newly formed republic could now be used to quite opposite effect.[83]

The tradesmen for whom Milton had reserved such kind words in August (when defending the morally salutary effect that working in a trade
would have on ministers bereft of state support) thus found themselves
on the wrong end of a fulsome moral denunciation:[84]

> yet if trade be grown so craving and importunate through the profuse
> living of tradesmen that nothing can support it, but the luxurious ex-
> penses of a nation upon trifles and superfluities, so as if the people gen-
> erally should betake themselves to frugalitie, it might prove a danger-
> ous matter, least tradesmen should mutinie for want of trading, and that
> therefor we must forego and set to sale religion, libertie, honour, safetie,
> all concernments divine or human to keep up trading. . . . (CPW 7:386)

It is one thing to rank economic considerations below religious and political ones. It is another to eschew the sort of forward-looking economic
reasoning of which Milton had shown himself capable for an older moral
rhetoric that dismissed import goods as luxuries and disregarded the in-
convenient point that a healthy economy required a dynamic of consumption and production. Having explored the half-truths of Comus's
speech on circulation with increasing interest in the 1640s—evolving an
ideal of free and upright commerce among men and vigorous circulation
within the public sphere—Milton tried to find his way back, at the moment of crisis, to the purity of the Lady's doctrine of abstention. Precisely
because economic principles are so integral to Milton's proposals for the
polity, we must understand this renunciation of the claims of trade not
merely as a parting shot at tradesmen for withdrawing their support from
the Good Old Cause but as the record of a deep intellectual crisis that
would have consequences for *Paradise Lost*.

It is worth observing, however, that even such a sophisticated economist as David Hume, writing as late as 1752 but still mindful of the classical
accounts of republican virtue that had inspired many Commonwealthmen, could discuss with interest a scenario that sounds much like the one
that Milton proposed:

> Could we convert a city into a kind of fortified camp, and infuse into
> each breast so martial a genius, and such a passion for public good, as to
> make every one willing to undergo the greatest hardships for the sake of
> the public; these affections might now, as in ancient times, prove alone a
> sufficient spur to industry, and support the community. It would then be
> advantageous, as in camps, to banish all arts and luxury; and, by restric-

tions on equipage and tables, make the provisions and forage last longer than if the army were loaded with a number of superfluous retainers.

In his darker moments, Milton may have entertained the notion that what Hume proceeded to assert was true:

> But as these principles are too disinterested and too difficult to support, it is requisite to govern men by other passions, and animate them with a spirit of avarice and industry, art and luxury. The camp is, in this case, loaded with a superfluous retinue; but the provisions flow in proportionately larger. The harmony of the whole is still supported; and the natural bent of the mind being more complied with, individuals, as well as the public, find their account in the observance of those maxims.[85]

To admit what Hume contended, however, would mean not only accepting that most men are unregenerate and then accommodating political forms to them—as Milton was prepared to do—but deliberately reinforcing and directing their baser passions so that they might become the predictable and stable basis for a society whose ultimate standards would be concord, strength, and prosperity, not the cultivation of Christian liberty.

Milton issued his pained lament at a time when the ability of economic considerations to foreclose certain civic and religious options was just becoming more widely accepted. If, unlike some later authors, he would not allow that the impetus of anonymous market forces could absolve individuals of ethical responsibility for the courses they followed, he did see—and in this way continued to evince a real imaginative engagement with economic problems—the constraints that seemingly free and uncoercive contractual relations could impose, once aggregated into market forces, on the moral life of individuals. Defying what he had learned from his service for the Commonwealth (that a new civil and religious order could remain viable only as long as it had a strong commercial basis), Milton imagined the English people treating their economic, civil, and spiritual lives as "dividual movable[s]"—and selling their civil and spiritual autonomy for the hope of a better economic life. What Leslie Brisman has said of *Paradise Lost*—that one choice for all time is succeeded by many choices in time—is played out here in reverse, with the nation's many choices during the Interregnum being interrupted suddenly by a timeless choice among spheres of human experience.[86] The virtues of the marketplace that Milton valorized in *Areopagitica*—pliancy, responsiveness, and acuity—now seemed to be encouraging the return of a chosen people to Egypt "because they falsly imagind that they then livd in more plenty and prosperitie" (*CPW* 7:387). Even the climatic theory

that Milton adduced as a possible explanation of the English people's inability to hold to a political course seemed to entail such a paradox. After
all, the "uncertain and unfaithful ways" attributed to islanders by the likes
of Plato and Jean Bodin were associated with their excellence in sea traffic and commerce as well.[87] Thus, the traits that made the English people
peculiarly susceptible to the folly of recalling the king in a fit of frustration
and disillusionment—and therefore made a perpetual senate needful—
were the very characteristics that would enable them to make Milton's
system of federalism function effectively.

The contradictions in Milton's tract could not, finally, be reconciled.
On the one hand, he tried to clear a space for civil and religious liberty
in his proposals by letting market forces penetrate the political sphere
—leaving room for experiment, divergent preferences, and the diffused
discipline of competition—yet on the other hand, he saw that trade was
the people's rallying cry back to Egypt. It was perhaps the most painful
paradox to date in Milton's intellectual struggle to differentiate between
economic relations that could promote and preserve Christian liberty and
those that would enslave and corrupt the spirit.

CHAPTER THREE

The King of Trade

I f Royalists eventually succeeded in making an acceptance of old political and religious forms seem like a necessary precondition for the return of prosperity, they too paid a price. In order to make their case persuasive, Royalist polemicists and panegyrists alike were compelled to promise that a restored king would take a personal interest in trade and evince such traditionally civic virtues as care and industry. There were, of course, Royalists who were as nostalgic for an uncommercial past as Milton showed himself to be at the end of *The Readie and Easie Way* and who tried to find their way back to it by means of an occulted language of kingship and miracle. But they could no more erase the lessons of the Interregnum than could Milton. The monarchy that returned in 1660 could not be the same as it had been in 1649: it would have to be a government of and *for* trade.

The earl of Clarendon recalled that when Charles II returned to England, he accordingly manifested a "very great desire to improve the general traffick and trade in the kingdom," conferred "with the most active merchants," and "offered all that he could contribute to the advancement thereof."[1] Poets responded to, and perhaps encouraged, such demonstrations in panegyrics that in turn influenced the symbolic program of Charles II's royal entry of 1661. From the entertainment of the East India Company to its triumphal arches, the entry articulated an ideal of the Court's relationship to the City and their cooperative role in advancing trade. It also announced Charles II's determination to fulfill the promise of the Rump's government of trade and to surpass the commercial empire of the Dutch. Sir William Davenant's *Poem to the Kings Most Sacred Majesty* (1663) is not just the culmination of this Royalist program, it is also, I submit, one of the century's most striking meditations on the processes of trade and the meaning of empire and, therefore, deserves to be recognized as a strong poem. It is the imaginative achievement that this chapter sets against Milton's *Readie and Easie Way*.

Both Indies Brought Home with the Court

Because Charles recognized the strength of the economic case that had been mounted against monarchy, he coopted the Rump's ideology of naval and commercial expansionism. Having declared all acts made during the Interregnum null, he and the Convention Parliament set about making the Rump's trade initiatives their own through a program of almost obsessive legislative imitation. They created their own Council of Trade based on instructions drafted by Benjamin Worsley, the secretary of the Rump's Council of Trade. The symbolic import of the action was not lost on John Evelyn. In the panegyric that he presented to the king on the day of his inauguration (April 23, 1661), Evelyn said that the king's "industry in erecting a *Counsel of Trade*" had not only fulfilled his promise to "propose some useful things" that would render the nation "opulent, splendid and flourishing," it had made good his pretense to universal sovereignty by showing that not only his birth and title but his "Princely care," evinced in his creation of the Council, recommended him.[2] Even more telling, the Convention Parliament passed a revised version of the Rump's most famous piece of commercial legislation, the Navigation Act of 1651.

Even as Charles II styled himself in his public acts as a lover of trade and traffic, many of the public entertainments that were mounted by— and to a large extent *for*—the merchant elite of London reinforced that image.[3] For instance, the entertainments given to General Monck at the Vintners and Clothworkers Halls celebrated the part that the general had played in reviving the City's commerce and trade by helping to restore the king. In the Lord Mayor's Show of 1660, the figure Oceanus enjoined the Lord Mayor, as a "Royal Substitute," to "Imploy" his "Interest" so that "Trade may now encrease," while Peace, addressing the king himself, prophesied that "Trade long since dead reviv'd, shall be again / By th'Vertual Influence of your Sovereign."[4] The king's presence at the show was itself a gesture of solicitude to the City's beleaguered tradesmen. Charles II would be the first monarch to attend the City's inaugural shows and feasts regularly, thus making an implied commitment to abet the commercial ambitions expressed in the City's entertainments.

Poets responded to Charles II's self-presentation. An anonymous panegyrist would declare a year later that "the Seamans Art, and his great end,
Commerce" were the king's delight.[5]

The frequency with which panegyrics to Charles II excoriated the
taxes of the Interregnum and anticipated the revival of trade under the
restored monarchy seems remarkable when we remember that explicit attempts to align the monarchy with trade had been absent not only from
the well-known verse panegyrics of Samuel Daniel, Ben Jonson, Michael
Drayton, William Drummond, Edmund Waller, and Abraham Cowley to
the early Stuarts but also from the minor English panegyrics collected in
anthologies for the Stuart progresses to and from Scotland in 1617, 1633,
and 1641.[6] At the Restoration, in contrast, both the encomiastic verse of
broadsides and the more ambitious panegyrics of men like John Crouch,
John Evelyn, Thomas Higgons, Thomas Mayhew, and Edmund Waller
celebrated the king as, among other things, an instrument of trade's revival.[7] Waller, for instance, looked forward to the return of "the city's trade,
and country's easy life" with the king, while Crouch professed to see

> The City now long squeez'd and wire drawn, made
>   *The Citadel,* and *Mart of Europe-trade;*
> The Ship-wrackt Merchants in full *Change* resort,
>   Conceive both *Indies* brought home with the *Court.*[8]

We have seen that General Monck cited London's interest in becoming
"the Metropolis and Bank of Trade for all Christendom" as a reason for
Parliament's choosing a commonwealth over a monarchy. In contrast,
Crouch's panegyric sought to align London's interest with the king's restoration. In all these poems, the tempered arguments from interest that
Royalist pamphleteers had published before the Restoration continued
to exert an influence. While it was traditional in such verse panegyrics
to praise rulers conditionally and to uphold the example of rulers who
had allowed their wills to be confined by the law and the consent of the
people, it was a literary innovation to praise the king for his practical application to economic problems and the material improvements he would
achieve. Such praise sought to meet the standard set both by the economic
success of the Dutch republic (which economic writers attributed not to
any natural advantage but to "the manner of their Care, and of the Government that is among them, and the meer vigilancie over Trade, that is
observed by them") and by the interest-based arguments of 1659 and 1660
(to which Waller explicitly alluded when he praised Charles II for having
been able to "divide such ravell'd interests" peacefully).[9]

A Character of Charles the Second (April 30, 1660), written by one of

Charles's courtiers, had already admitted that there could be a disconti-
nuity between the private virtues of a king and the benefits that he conferred on the public: "and if it be granted that His MAJESTY does possess
these Illustrious Qualities, yet if he wants the Nature to produce them by
Practise, they may serve his Flatterers for *Panegyrics,* but they will be of
little benefit to his People; therefore it is necessary to evince his *Industry,* to confirm the Character of an accomplish'd Prince" (p. 6). Similarly,
Clarendon worried that because "the king was not yet the master of the
kingdom . . . there was in no conjuncture more need, that the virtue and
wisdom and industry of a prince should be evident . . . in application of
his mind to the government of his affairs."[10] Such statements contradicted
the logic of Charles I's entertainments, in which the private virtues of the
king and queen seemed to communicate benefits naturally to the public.
The panegyrics of writers like Arthur Brett, Evelyn, and Waller suggest
that they, in contrast, felt compelled to show Charles II applying himself
to the practical concerns of his subjects. Brett imagined Charles walking
about the "Royal Change," conversing about "high things," whether they
concerned trade or religion, Asia or Africa.[11] We have already seen that
Evelyn praised the king's industry and care in establishing a Council of
Trade. Such compliments were to become an important element of Restoration panegyrics. In his envoi "To the King" in *Instructions to a Painter*
(1666), Waller likewise praised Charles's "care,"

> Which keeps you waking to secure our peace,
> The nation's glory, and our trade's increase;
> You for these ends, whole days in council sit,
> And the diversions of your youth forget.
>
> (lines 318–22)

Although they were not entirely excluded from the tradition, neither care
nor industry was among the important virtues commended in humanist
mirrors for princes, and they almost never appeared in those parts of the
early Stuarts' entries or masques that were meant to teach the prince by
presenting and praising virtues.[12] Spenser's *Faerie Queene* even set a rival
precedent that understood care as a vice, not a virtue: Care is one of the
guardians of Mammon's Cave (2.7.25), and in contrast with the sleep-
lessness that Waller adduces as a symptom of Charles's solicitude for his
subjects, there is nothing praiseworthy about the sleepless night that Sir
Scudamour spends, in an episode closely related to Guyon's descent into
Mammon's Cave, in the Smithy of Care (4.5.28–46).

On the other hand, London's mayoral pageants had long accorded a
central position to care and industry in their moral scheme. Care was

often commended to the mayor when the procession finally stopped at
his house. In 1619, for example, Love enjoined the Lord Mayor, "O, thank
'em in thy justice, in thy care"; then after equating the mayor with care
and the City with love in lines that invoked "care" three more times, Love
bid the Lord Mayor to be "according to your morning vows, / A careful
husband to a loving spouse," the City. So too in the pageant of 1617, Industry pronounced, "I know this is my time and place." Referring thus to
the installation of the Lord Mayor and the City (and implicitly contrast-
ing *this* time and place with the coronation of the king and Westminster),
Industry explained:

> For Industry is the life-blood of praise:
> To rise without me, is to steal to glory.[13]

In mounting an economic case for monarchy before the Restoration, Royalists subjoined responsibilities to the office of king that had more often
fallen within the purview of City magistrates, and in doing so, they established new expectations that encouraged poets to praise the virtues of a
Lord Mayor in the king.

It was Waller who most successfully made concessions to this ideal of
practical kingship without sacrificing the more traditional attributes of
majesty that some other Restoration panegyrists eagerly revived. In *On
St. James's Park, as Lately Improved by His Majesty* (1661), Waller presents a
king who, while sacrificing the "pleasures of his youth" to "public care"
and banishing all "private passion" from his mind (lines 111–14), can nevertheless rule an empire and restore trade by taking counsel with himself
in a park:

> Here, free from court compliances he walks,
> And with himself, his best adviser, talks;
> How peaceful olive may his temples shade,
> For mending laws, and for restoring trade.
>
> (lines 115–18)

Waller's poem extricates the ideal of commercial expansion from its usual
urban ethos and reconciles it to an aristocratic ideal of retirement: a garden, not a market or exchange, lies at the center of England's trade empire, and the task of advancing trade, as of improving other aspects of the
realm, comes to resemble that of laying out a park.

In the envoi of *Instructions to a Painter,* on the other hand, Waller praises
the king for sitting in councils of trade and taking an interest in ordnance
and ships. Then with a closing conceit that recalls Claudian's prophecy
of military and commercial empire in his *Panegyric on the Third Consul-*

ship of the Emperor Honorius—and that replays Sir Scudamour's descent into
the Smithy of Care only to redeem it—he demonstrates what condescen-
sion these activities imply: Charles II is like Jupiter descending into "Vulcan's smoky cave" in order to inspect the nuts and bolts, in this case the
Cyclopes' thunderbolts, of empire (line 20).[14] Waller's alignment of trade
with pleasure in the first poem and with arms in the second is a response
to changing circumstances: *On St. James's Park* was written in 1661 in the
aftermath of Cromwell's unpopular war with Spain, whereas *Instructions*
is a product of the Second Anglo-Dutch War (1664–67), a conflict with
which the king and his program of commercial expansion were closely
associated. Yet as we shall see in our consideration of Charles's royal entry,
both of Waller's imaginative solutions to the problem of making trade
and traffic worthy of a king—celebrating it as a wellspring of opulence
or as a source of power—were already current in 1661.

Charles II's Royal Entry and the Trade of Ophir

On February 9, 1661, Charles informed London's city fathers of his desire to process along the traditional route from the Tower of London to
Whitehall.[15] He instructed Clarendon that after all the innovations of the
previous decade, the ceremonies should conform to ancient precedents.[16]
Yet while the entry's Augustan theme recalled the ceremonial advent of
Stuart rule with James I's entry of 1604, it also rejected as misguided both
the Commonwealth's emulation of republican Rome and Oliver Cromwell's rival presentation of himself as a second Augustus. It stressed the
obvious parallel between Augustus's imposition of one-man rule after the
civil wars of Rome and Charles II's restoration of order, and most significant for our purposes, it celebrated Imperial Rome as a commercial
achievement in a way that James I's entry had not. Rather than suppress
the economic themes in the verse of Virgil and Claudian as Renaissance
humanists had often done, it applied them to current economic concerns: the trade depression, taxation, and London's ambition to become
the world's entrepôt. By thus characterizing Imperial Rome as a commercial empire, it disengaged the Rump's popular ideal of mercantile expansion from its republican context, and—reaching behind the Rump to a
prior originary moment, much as Evelyn would invoke a classical precedent for Charles II's ideal of mercantile *noblesse*—it made a claim to *authority* for the royal program through supposed *priority*. Yet if Charles II's
entry co-opted the Rump's ideal by translating it into a courtly idiom,
with the entertainment of the East India Company it also allowed civic
ritual to impinge on courtly spectacle, thus making modes of expression

that had previously been used by some commercial interests to check the extension of sovereign authority seem less oppositional.

The "Poetical part" of the coronation festivities, "consisting in Speeches, Emblemes, Mottoes, and Inscriptions," was entrusted to John Ogilby.[17] As an experienced master of revels, theater director, and classicist who had dedicated his translations of Virgil to Royalists during the Interregnum, Ogilby was a natural choice to produce a neoclassical royal procession, but he also understood the commercial aspirations of London's merchant classes. His first investment as a poor youth had been in a lottery for the advancement of the Virginia Company; he probably knew Benjamin Worsley before Worsley became secretary of the Rump's Council of Trade; and as the "king's cosmographer and geographic printer," he would later publish descriptive atlases based on information collected from Dutch trading companies. He chose Sir Balthazar Gerbier to design the triumphal arches for the entry.[18] Gerbier was in some ways an improbable choice. Although he had served Sir George Villiers and Charles I and had even arranged for his friend Pieter Paul Rubens to paint Whitehall's Banqueting House, he had also served the Rump with equal diligence. Indeed, he was even suspected (on grounds that now seem uncertain) to have penned a character assassination of the Stuarts that was published in 1651.[19] On the other hand, it would have been hard for Ogilby to find anyone better able to express the Rump's ideology of naval and commercial expansionism in a triumphal arch fit for a king. Himself a native Zeelander, Gerbier had been a tireless advocate, in both the English and French Courts, of financial, trade, and industrial reforms that were largely inspired by Dutch practices. He had advised the Rump's Council of Trade, warned it of the Dutch primacy in world trade, and conducted secret negotiations for the Rump in Holland. Frustrated with the Protectorate's indifference to his plans, he had embarked on an ill-fated mining venture to Guiana under the auspices of the Dutch West India Company and the States-General shortly before the Restoration. Even if Gerbier was innocent of writing *The None-Such Charles* (1651), his service to the Rump was a black mark on his career, and his contributions to the entry had to remain anonymous. The Restoration regime was, however, practical enough to borrow from the Commonwealth and the Protectorate not only policies but personnel.

The royal procession paused at five major sites: (1) an arch expounding monarchy's triumph over rebellion, (2) an entertainment at East India House, (3) an arch extolling monarchy's contribution to England's naval and mercantile empire, (4) an arch celebrating concord, with its political and economic blessings, (5) and an arch anticipating the return of plenty with the end of civil and foreign war. Because I wish to focus on the entry's economic agenda, I shall bypass its musical interludes, say little about its political themes, and concentrate instead on the East India Company's entertainment and the entry's second arch. The themes of the first arch were political and ecclesiastical, while the allegorical schemes of the final arches were less elaborate than those of the first two.

Commencing at the Tower of London, Charles proceeded to the first arch in Leaden-Hall Street. He then continued on to East India House, which lay on the same street.[20] While it was not unusual for foreign merchants to present a tableau in a royal entry, this appears to have been the first time that an English monarch stopped at a merchant house. Here the East India Company expressed its "dutiful Affections to His Majesty" (*Rel.*, p. 9). It certainly had an incentive to do so, for while the company had finally been granted a charter by Oliver Cromwell in 1657, it had judged it best to suppress the document at the Restoration, and it had not yet secured a royal charter in its place.

The speaking roles of the East India Company's entertainment were played by the sons of Sir Richard Ford.[21] Ford had abetted Royalist forces from his self-imposed exile in Rotterdam in the 1640s before returning to London in the 1650s, where, in his own words to Clarendon, he had been "among the most active of those that contrived and actuated the City's interest to be instrumental to his Majesty's blessed Restoration."[22] His reward was a post at Court. He was one of five newly elected aldermen in 1661 who had served, or were shortly to serve, on the Committee of the East India Company.[23] He would become one of the most powerful merchants in Restoration London, with high-ranking positions in the Merchant Adventurers and Africa and East India Companies, all of whom must have valued his access to the Lord Chancellor and the king.

Ford's sons appeared dressed as Indians and attended by *"Black-Moors."* One of them knelt before the king's horse to present him with a "full fraught Caravan / Of Perfect Loyalty," while the other, mounted on a camel, brought out "Jewels, Spices, and Silks, to be scattered among the Spectators" (*Rel.*, p. 9). While it was usual for the company sponsoring a Lord Mayor's Show to distribute samples of its goods—thus symbolizing, with a liberal gesture, the civic benefits of the countless mercantile transactions that the company performed each year—the East India Company's show of munificence is striking not only because it appears to have been the first of its kind in a royal entry but because the company doing it was not one of London's livery companies, who sponsored the Lord Mayor's Show each year, but a powerful upstart that had yet to be accorded a prominent role in the City's tradition-bound ceremonies, despite the fact that, since the 1620s, many of the City's aldermen and mayors had held leadership positions in the company.

The East India Company was careful to explain its gesture, which might be interpreted as an intrusion of civic ritual into courtly ceremony, in complimentary terms already established by Restoration panegyrics.[24] It could gladly part with its duly cataloged "Glorious Trifles of the East" because in his own person Charles had "brought / Home all the Wealth, that can be found, or thought." The company figured its own business as a "Nest / Of Spicy Trade" that, after being scorched in the same flames of civil war that consumed Charles I, had happily given rise to the phoenix Charles II (*Rel.*, p. 10). However indirectly, the metaphor turned the East India Company into the instrument of Charles Stuart's restoration.

If the East India Company made a discreet claim to the king's political gratitude, it granted the king a far more explicit and laudable role in the restoration of trade. Its verse announced themes that would be articulated by the second arch:

> For You have outdone *Solomon,* and made
> Provision for more than *Ophir* Trade;
> Among Your first of unexpected Cares
> Enlarg'd our Charter, and dispeld our Fears
> Of the encrouching *Holland's* Rival Force.
> Nor can we doubt, but by the bounteous Source
> Of Your Successful Right, not only We,
> But all the Merchants of the Realm shall see
> This *Empory* the *Magazine* of All
> That's Rich, from Phoebus Rising to his Fall;
> And Your imperial *Title* be the same
> In Deed, which *Spain's* proud Crown vaunts but in Name.
>
> (*Rel.*, p. 10)

Responding to James I's fondness for Solomon as a type of kingly wisdom, and working on behalf of the East India Company, Samuel Purchas had tried to remind the king that Solomon was also an exemplary patron of trade.[25] Henry Parker, that staunch advocate of parliamentary supremacy and Secretary for the Merchant Adventurers in Hamburg, had likewise held up Solomon as "the most Majesticall of all Kings that ever raigned" and "the most ample adventurer that ever traffickt," who "had not been so great a Prince, if he had not been so ample a Merchant."[26] Thus the East India Company was asserting that Charles II surpassed the ideal against which his own father and grandfather had been tested and found wanting. But by implying that Charles was able to see more deeply into economic matters than Solomon, the company also suggested that economic wisdom was not timeless. According to 1 Kings and 1 and 2 Chronicles, Solomon sent ships to Ophir—thought by some commentators to lie at Soffala, Chersonese, or the mouth of the Indus, all in the company's trading territory—whence they returned with gold. The East India Company depended on the opposite procedure; it exported bullion in order to pay for the luxury goods it imported. Because the bullion in the country was considered a measure of wealth, and because debasements of foreign currencies could lead to national shortages of specie, the exportation of bullion was generally illegal. It was by far the most controversial aspect of the East India trade. Yet Charles's reconstituted Council of Trade had recommended in 1660 that the company be allowed to export bullion.[27] This, then, was the *more* than Ophir trade that the verse credited Charles with the insight to patronize. With such an enlarged charter, the company would now be able to compete with "encrouching *Holland's* Rival Force." This wise decision, the verse suggested, was just one concrete example of the new (and thus "unexpected") royal care that would enable London to become the magazine of "all that's rich." As the entrepôt of the world, London would be at the center of a trading empire whose periphery would know no bounds, east or west. Through trade, Charles II would truly become the universal monarch that the Habsburgs had only aspired to become through dominion. A week after it presented this interlude to the king, the East India Company received its royal charter.[28]

From East India House, Charles proceeded to the second arch, which was erected in Cornhill (fig. 6). Proximity to the Exchange made this the natural location for an entertainment with commercial themes. Surmounting the pediment of the arch, Atlas supported a globe on which, in turn, was balanced a ship. On the entablature below, two hemispheres flanked the motto *unus non sufficit* [one does not suffice]. A central panel depicted Charles I showing the young Prince Charles the pride of his fleet, the *Sovereign of the Sea*. On either side of this panel stood live figures playing the Four Continents; they held regional products in one hand and in the other "Escutcheons, and Pendants, bearing the Arms of the *Companies* trading into those parts" (*Ent.*, p. 67). Some of these features, and in particular the motto, must have been suggested by one of Pieter Paul Rubens's arches for the Habsburg entry into Antwerp in 1635.[29] But by changing Rubens's motto from *polus non sufficit unus* [one pole does not suffice] to the briefer *unus non sufficit*, Gerbier was able to unite the two sides of his arch in a series of thematic pairs: by setting the Tower of London opposite the Exchange and Mars opposite Neptune, the arch could suggest that Crown and City, force and commerce were codependent (fig. 7). Here too, *unus*

6. The naval and commercial arch in Charles II's royal entry of 1661, designed by Sir Balthazar Gerbier. Wenceslaus Hollar's engraving of it appears in John Ogilby's *Entertainment* (1662). Beinecke Rare Book and Manuscript Library, Yale University.

non sufficit. The panels' inscriptions suggested that if the Crown's responsibility was security, the City's was the production of wealth. *Clauduntur
belli portae* associated the Tower with the Temple of Janus and signified
the cessation of civil and foreign war with Charles's restoration. Beneath
the Exchange, a motto from Virgil's georgic description of the commonwealth of bees—*generis lapsi sarcire ruinas*—extolled, in Ogilby's account,
the "Industry of *Bees,* never discouraged by their Losses" (*Ent.,* p. 66). The
inscription between these mottoes, which hailed Charles II as the master
of the sea and winds, was adapted, as Ronald Knowles has noticed, from
the panegyric to the Emperor Honorius to which we have already seen
Waller allude.[30] Its position between Tower and Exchange suggested that
the prophecy of commercial empire with which Claudian's poem concluded might result from the synthesis of Crown and City:

> *vobis Rubra dabunt pretiosas aequora conchas,*
> *Indus ebur, ramos Panchaia, vellera Seres.*
> [To you the Red Sea shall give precious shells, India her ivory,
>   Panchaia perfumes, and China silk.][31]

Dramatic interludes reinforced the arch's synthesis of force and commerce, Crown and City. On one side of the street, sailors standing on the
deck of a ship professed their loyalty to the Crown and their readiness
to extend England's control of the seas. On the other side of the street,
holding a ship and crowned with London Bridge, Father Thames asserted
that Charles II's "blest Return!" had enabled the City to renew its import-
export trade and had "restor'd" London "to all the Wealth remotest Lands
afford" (*Ent.,* p. 104).

With some reason, Ronald Knowles has stressed Rubens's influence
on the arches that Gerbier devised, for the architecture of Gerbier's initial arches does resemble the Arch of the Cardinal Infante Ferdinand that
Rubens designed for the Habsburg entry into Antwerp in 1635. But Rubens's arches on commercial themes were of little direct use to Gerbier.
These opposed the wealth of Spain, derived from mines worked by slaves
(fig. 8), with the poverty of Antwerp, a trading city ruined by the restrictive measures of the Habsburgs (fig. 9).[32] The commemorative volume of
the festival drove the point home by quoting Lodovico Guicciardini's rap-
turous sixteenth-century description of Antwerp as the most celebrated
emporium of Europe only to lament, laconically, *sed haec fuêre* [but these
are things of the past].[33] Gerbier did not especially wish to associate the
Stuarts with the Habsburgs: since the Treaty of the Pyrenees (1659), the
Habsburgs were no longer a force of empire, and the ruinous effect of
their rule over Antwerp could be too readily seen as an object lesson in

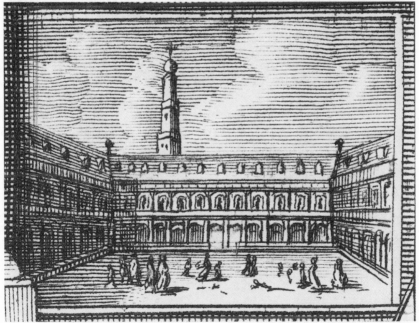

7. Details of the naval and commercial arch as it appears in Ogilby's *Entertainment* (1662). *Above,* The Tower. *Below,* The Exchange. The arch suggests that Tower and Exchange, Crown and City, force and commerce must work in tandem. Beinecke Rare Book and Manuscript Library, Yale University.

8. Arch designed by Pieter Paul Rubens for the Habsburg entry into Antwerp in 1635. The rich mines of Mt. Potosoi, worked by slave labor, generate wealth for Spain. From Jean Gaspard Gavaerts, *Pompa Introitus* (Antwerp, 1642). Beinecke Rare Book and Manuscript Library, Yale University.

9. In another arch for the Habsburg entry, Antwerp is shown languishing beneath Spain's oppressive trade restrictions: the Scheldt River nods with exhaustion, and Mercury abandons the city. From Jean Gaspard Gavaerts, *Pompa Introitus* (Antwerp, 1642). Beinecke Rare Book and Manuscript Library, Yale University.

the incompatibility of a strong monarchy with commercial prosperity. Gerbier looked, instead, to the United Provinces, the greatest trading power in the world, England's model and its chief competitor.

The most important sources for the iconography of Gerbier's second arch were the arch of the Dutch merchants in James I's entry of 1604 and Amsterdam's new Town Hall. Gerbier was well acquainted with the latter, for in an architectural treatise of the following year he displayed a knowledge not only of the hall but of the preliminary models for it.[34] Yet to my knowledge, the influences of the Dutch merchants' arch and Amsterdam's new Town Hall have alike gone unnoticed.

Like Gerbier's arch, that of the Dutch merchants in 1604 had also been erected in Cornhill, near the Exchange. Presumably in deference to the royal image that James I wanted to project, the Dutch had portrayed the king surrounded by military and political iconography on the front of their arch, but they had depicted *themselves* in economic terms on the back—in painted tableaux that won the admiration of Thomas Dekker, even if they left James himself cold.[35] Over the central portal, a large panel had represented their fishing and shipping industries, while paired smaller panels had depicted (to one side) Amsterdam's Bourse and the Dutch toiling at their husbandry and (to the other side) their Mart and the Dutch working in various industries like weaving.

With a naval vessel flanked by depictions of the Tower and the Exchange, Gerbier's arch bore such a schematic resemblance to the Dutch arch that we can read it as a response made the more pointed by the subsequent rivalry between the two nations. Against the Dutch fishing and shipping industries, England could pit its navy, which would be able to enforce the Navigation Acts and the sale of fishing licenses.[36] An inscription proclaimed Charles II the judge of whether the seas were free or closed. By countering the Dutch Mart and Bourse with the paired Tower and Royal Exchange, Gerbier invoked the common belief, which had been encouraged by the Rump's success against the Dutch, that England's strength *and* wealth would outlast the *sheer* wealth of the Dutch. The Dutch merchants had erected their arch before the relatively amicable trade in cloth between England and the Low Countries had been superseded by the antagonistic struggles between the English and Dutch East India Companies. The exclusion of foreign merchants from the entry of 1661 and the prominent role of the English East India Company speak volumes about the increasingly nationalistic edge that foreign commerce had since assumed.

It is not surprising, then, that Gerbier should also respond to what even the Dutch understood to be their proudest assertion of primacy in world trade: Amsterdam's new Town Hall. Begun in earnest with the Peace of Münster in 1648, the new Town Hall was the product of the wealth that flowed into the city (and away from London) after the Dutch made peace with Spain (fig. 10). The medal that commemorated its inauguration in 1655 featured Mercury, the god of commerce, hovering above the new Town Hall (on the obverse), while (on the reverse) the Argo returned to the port of Amsterdam. Beneath the ship—part ancient trireme, part Dutch *fluit*—a legend from Valerius Flaccus's *Argonautica* (1.169) declared: *pelagus quantos aperimus in usus!* [to what great profits we open the sea] (fig. 11).

10. Jacob van der Ulft, *The Square of the Dam at Amsterdam* (1659). The Town Hall dominates the west side of the square. To the right is the Weigh House. Behind that is the Nieuwe Kerk, just north of which Johannes Blaeu produced his atlases. Giraudon / Art Resource, N.Y.

Yet Gerbier and Ogilby did not respond to the Town Hall simply because the Dutch were England's fiercest trade competitors. They responded to it because its architect, Jacob van Campen, had already discovered how to expound an essentially burgher and republican ideology of trade in a scheme whose architectural and decorative components drew on Italian classicism, French and English Court architecture, and even Rubens's designs for the Habsburg entry of 1635. Van Campen's decorative scheme was probably the most sustained exposition of mercantile ideals in the language of emblem, allegory, and classical allusion extant anywhere in the world. In designing a town hall that could rival the splendor of foreign courts and impress visiting diplomats, van Campen had established an architectural and iconographic vocabulary that could negotiate the middle space between Europe's courts and Amsterdam's city magistrates. The building's Citizens' Hall is a case in point. Just as Marcus Gheeraerts

11. Medal commemorating the inauguration of Amsterdam's new Town Hall, by Jurriaan Pooll, 1655. *Left,* Obverse: the inaugural procession crosses the Dam with Mercury (god of commerce) and Amphion (builder of Thebes) looking on. Legend: "sapientia quondam fuit haec" [wisdom once did these things]. *Right,* Reverse: the Argo sails home. Legend: "pelagus quantos aperimus in usus!" [to what great profits we open up the sea]. Amsterdams Historisch Museum.

the Younger had painted Elizabeth I atop the world, van Campen allowed Amsterdam's burghers to stride across both hemispheres of the globe (figs. 12–14). But whereas the territories depicted in the Ditchley portrait of Elizabeth are drawn out of scale, the maps of the Citizens' Hall reflect the new precision made possible by advances in the (land) measurement of longitude in the 1650s. Rather than being pressed under foot in a static image of sovereign authority, they were crossed as individual citizens of a trading republic transacted their business. Symbols of power, they were also tools of empire, for they could be used to plan business ventures or naval campaigns.

    We can conceive of the Town Hall as the meeting point of two cultures whose convergence was described by Sir William Temple. In the early Renaissance, said Temple, only "Free states and cities" concerned themselves with trade, while kingdoms and principalities took to war. The former initially revered the latter as merchants would noblemen and gentlemen, but as they acquired wealth and power through "Industry and Parsimony," they began to "carry it like Gentlemen"; conversely, the "Gentlemen" among Europe's states, impoverished by their penchant for war and luxury, ceased to despise the concerns of the free states and began to "take a fancy of falling to Trade."[37] In showing the United Provinces

12. Marcus Gheeraerts the Younger, *Elizabeth I*. The "Ditchley" portrait
(c. 1592). Elizabeth adopts a stance of sovereignty atop the globe. By courtesy
of the National Portrait Gallery, London.

how they could "carry it like gentlemen," van Campen had thus inadver-
tently formed a language in which the English Court could articulate its
monarchical revision of an ideology of trade associated with the English
and Dutch republics—all without departing from the sort of international
neoclassical vocabulary that the early Stuarts had also employed.

The ship and Atlas figure that surmounted Gerbier's arch were visual
quotations from the finial of the Town Hall's cupola, which is not illus-
trated here but was likewise in the form of a ship, and its west pediment,

13. The Citizens' Hall of Amsterdam's Town Hall, looking toward the Magistrates' Hall. Atlas, supporting the globe, overlooks a floor with the two hemispheres of the world. By courtesy of the Stichting Koninklijk Paleis te Amsterdam.

which was surmounted by Atlas supporting the world (fig. 15). Gerbier's triangular composition beneath Atlas—the Stuarts with a ship, flanked by the Four Continents holding offerings—more loosely revised the frieze of the west pediment's tympanum, in which Lady Amsterdam sat in front of a ship, flanked by representatives of the four continents presenting offerings to her (fig. 16). Finally, the arch's two hemispheres, with the

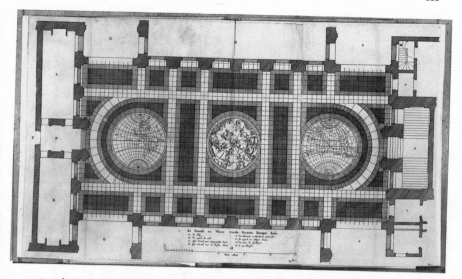

14. Jacob Vennekool's depiction of the floor of the Citizens' Hall in Jacob van Campen, *Afbeelding van 't Stadt Huys van Amsterdam* (Amsterdam, 1661). The northern sky is flanked by the world's hemispheres, suggesting the complementary relationship between astronomy and navigation, science and commerce. Rijksmuseum-Stichting Amsterdam.

motto *unus non sufficit,* responded not only to the similar motto on one of Rubens's Habsburg arches but to the vast maps of the eastern and western hemispheres featured on the floor of the Citizens' Hall beneath another statue of Atlas supporting the globe (again, see figs. 13 and 14). Gerbier must have crossed that floor in 1660 in order to be deposed in the Magistrates' Court about the mutiny that had cut short his venture to Guiana. In his poem on the Restoration, John Crouch had accounted for London's shifting political allegiance in terms of its desperate efforts to stay even with Amsterdam: "Twas time to *King* it, when thy purse and fame / Lore'd to th' Imperious *Bank of Amsterdam.*"[38] By mirroring the Town Hall's declaration of world trade primacy in his own triumphal arch, Gerbier suggested that London's citizens had been right to pin their hopes of rivaling Amsterdam on the king's restoration.

If Gerbier's arch issued a silent challenge to the Dutch, it also sought to consolidate Charles II's domestic political support. Since the Dutch had denied the Rump's legal claim to sovereignty of the seas because the English case had always been based on rights accorded to English kings (not the nation), Charles II's claim to the same right was more than just a challenge to foreign powers; it was a reminder to his subjects that kingship was

15. West pediment of Amsterdam's Town Hall, designed by Jacob van Campen and sculpted by Artus Quellinus de Oude. *Above*, Atlas supports the globe. *Below*, Lady Amsterdam accepts the tribute of the Four Continents. She sits

16. Artus Quellinus de Oude's terra cotta model for the tympanum of the Amsterdam Town Hall. Rijksmuseum-Stichting Amsterdam.

inextricable from the English constitution. In proclaiming that one hemisphere did not suffice, Gerbier's arch was again addressing English subjects as much as foreign powers. It implicitly criticized Cromwell's willingness to offer the Dutch all of England's holdings in the east—proof of his willingness to sacrifice the interests of trade in return for amity with his Protestant neighbors. It furthermore promised that the royal eye, which had once neglected the western hemisphere, would henceforth look east *and* west.

But if England was going to build an empire in the west, it would have to do so largely through the efforts of English merchants and planters. Rubens's *Arcus Monetalis* (fig. 8) had applied the *Georgics'* most famous celebration of industry to the toil of slaves: *labor omnia vicit improbus* [labor vanquished all things, unrelenting labor] (1.145–46). We have seen that Ogilby preferred to recall the spontaneous industry of the *Georgics'* bees. He drove home Virgil's comparison between bees and merchants by rendering *genus* as "nation" and *fori* as "Exchange" when he translated the passage in his *Entertainment:*[39]

> How much by Fortune they exhausted are,
> So much they strive the Ruins to repair
> Of their fal'n Nation, and they fill th'*Exchange,*
> Adorning with the choicest Flow'rs their Grange.
>
> (*Ent.*, p. 66)

Besides conveying an appreciation of the industry of England's merchants, did this allusion to the *Georgics* hold any other meaning for the entry's spectators? While the inscription's "Ruins" might recall the trade depression of 1659–60, readers of the *Georgics* would have known that they referred, more precisely, to the beekeeper's exactions. By the Restoration, taking honey from the bees was an established metaphor for taxation. The motto, then, may have condemned the ruinous taxes of Cromwell. We will see that at least one observer, Samuel Pordage, read it that way.

It might also have been intended as an assurance that, like Virgil's more solicitous beekeeper, the king recognized his private interest in sustaining merchants. As his former tutor, the duke of Newcastle, had advised Charles in a letter of 1660: "It is the merchant that only brings honey to the hive. . . . Therefore your Majesty will be pleased to keep up the merchant that can only fill your kingdom with riches, and so consequently enrich your Majesty; for if your kingdom be poor, where can your Majesty have it?"[40]

The last arches were less elaborate than the first two, but their inscriptions and interludes reinforced the gentler and more celebratory aspects of the entry's political and economic themes. Songs at the third arch, dedicated to Concord, celebrated Charles II's role as an instrument of settlement: because of him, "Proud Interests" no longer engaged one another, and herdsmen, farmers, and merchants could concentrate their "whole Endeavours" on their businesses. It was peace and concord, the songs declared, that would make London's streets shine with wealth and bring her "Ships freight with Spice, and Golden Ore" (*Ent.*, pp. 135–36). The last arch, dedicated to Plenty, stressed that the precondition of "glitt'ring Plenty" was the end of civil and foreign war (*Ent.*, p. 165).

The appearance of Bacchus on the final arch dedicated to Plenty, together with the wine that was flowing in the streets, should remind us that if Charles II's entry appropriated the Rump's program of naval and commercial expansion, it also revived the theophanic fictions that Milton had found so offensive in past entries. In *The Readie and Easie Way,* Milton had warned that a restored king would have to be "ador'd like a Demigod" with "masks and revels . . . on the publick revenue" and would "pageant himself up and down in progress among the perpetual bowings and cringings of an abject people, on either side deifying and adoring him who for the most part deserves none of this by any good done to the people" (*CPW* 7:360–61). Although Restoration panegyrists did feel pressed to show what *good* the king had done for the people, they did not always retreat from scenes of luxury. In *On St. James's Park,* Waller wrote that "The sea, which always served his empire, now / Pays tribute to our Prince's pleasure too" (lines 7–8). A reference to the park's new canal, the lines also posited an alternative to the ideal of outwardly projected force and self-imposed frugality that classical republicans had upheld. We have already seen that with the trade grievances of 1660 finally working against him, Milton had bemoaned the fact that trade was growing "so craving and importunate through the profuse living of tradesmen that nothing can support it, but the luxurious expenses of a nation upon trifles or superfluities, so as if the people should betake themselves generally to frugalitie, it might prove a dangerous matter" (*CPW* 7:386). The increasing recognition among economic writers that consumption was as vital to a dynamic economy as production lay behind Milton's frustration, for Royalists found the theoretical insight especially welcome. They could use it to reinterpret the aristocratic indulgence of conspicuous consumption as an economic service. Even as they opposed Puritan restraint and dramatized the return of a Golden Age, then, the images of indulgence that concluded Charles II's entry valorized an economic activity that had been little-celebrated in London's mayoral pageants and that could, therefore, be recognized as a distinct contribution of the Court: consumption. According to such logic, the king was not "the great cypher" that Milton had made him out to be even when he was just "eating and drinking of excessive dainties" (*CPW* 7:360–61).

We are fortunate to have a contemporary restatement of the entertainment's economic themes. In his poem on the coronation of Charles II (1661), Samuel Pordage offered a reading of the second arch in particular:

> The Merchant fears no Foes, but angry skies,
> His ships flie home with wealth not made a prize:
> The wealthy Cit'zen plies his gainful Trade,
> And fears no Tax, as when the tyrant sway'd:
> The Citie rich holds up her head on high,
> And with her ships sucks both the *Indies* dry:
> Thus by their stately Arches they would shew,
> All by the blessing comes of having you.[41]

Omitting only the virtuous cycle of consumption and production suggested by the entry's other images of indulgence, Pordage's lines on the second arch neatly encapsulate the joint project of Crown and City: the productive coordination of force and commerce, a universal empire of trade comprising both hemispheres, and legitimate taxation. But from the standpoint of this book, the most important lesson that Pordage drew was his last: that the City's dearest aspirations could be fulfilled only through the monarch.

The King's Design: Sidney, Davenant, Dryden

However reassuring Charles II's royal entry may have been to London's trading interests, the early 1660s brought hardships that could not be easily dispelled by the Crown's gestures of good will. English merchants were losing ships to Algerian and Venetian privateers in the Mediterranean. They could not recoup the Spanish markets lost to the Dutch during the

recent Anglo-Spanish War. They saw the United Provinces making spectacular gains in the East Indies, and they could only wonder what would
be the issue of Louis XIV's plan to form a French East India Company.
The Crown was forced to impose new taxes to pay old debts, but it could
not even keep its current expenditures within the bounds of its revenues.
A French visitor to London reported that the multitudes complained "of
the neglect of the interest of Trade, of the mispending of the Treasure,
of the oppressions of the Court, and of the decrease of our glory at Sea"
since "the times of the Rump."[42]

If Paula Backscheider is right that the City pageants of 1662, with their
increasingly didactic emphasis on the importance of the sea to the nation's
prosperity, betray a mounting tension between the City and the Crown,
they do so not by turning against Charles II's program of naval and commercial expansion but by reproaching him with it.[43] With its play on the
meanings of "magazine" as a *repository of merchandise* or a *storehouse of artillery,* the speech addressed to the king in the Lord Mayor's Show of 1662,
for instance, could be read as a strong restatement of the naval and commercial arch's pairing of Exchange and Tower: "Whil'st we employ our
Magazines for you, / And you to us have *yours* commited too!"[44] Londoners who complained that the king "care[d] for nothing, attending only to
his hunting, his lusts and other amusements," wanted him to pay more
attention to magazines of both sorts.[45]

Such discontent no doubt gave old Commonwealthmen the heart to
reaffirm the traditional links between a republican form of government
and flourishing trade. Algernon Sidney, who had served as a member of
the Commonwealth's Council of State and returned with the rest of the
Rump Parliament after the fall of the Protectorate, revived such familiar
arguments. Writing from exile in the United Provinces, where he could
observe the strength of Dutch trade first hand, he let the Royalists condemn themselves from their own mouths. In a series of dialogues between courtiers, he imagined what a seasoned courtier might admit if
he were speaking in confidence. Free to put aside all pretense, Philalethes confides that it is actually in "the king's interest to destroy trade. For
there is no keeping a people low while that continues which increases
their number, riches, and strength." One need only consider how deso-
late Antwerp, Ghent, and Bruges became "by loss of trade," he continues,
and how powerful and flourishing Carthage and Amsterdam became by
plenty of traffic to understand what a force to be reckoned with trade
really is. Both the Venetians and the duke of Florence know that much.
That is why the commonwealth seeks to promote trade, while Cosimo
de Medici, "following the politic maxims of a prince," has "by destroying

trade . . . weakened the spirited commonwealth's men of Florence." With foreign treaties, monopoly grants, and taxes at his command, confides Philalethes, Charles II has ample means to ruin his merchants. It might seem that he risks diminishing his revenues that way, but princes have found that it is better to be master of a poor people and all they have than to contend with wealthy subjects who are fierce in defense of their liberty and property. For "princes are never so rich as when their subjects are poor." If the king actually sought "the people's good," he would "make the people's yoke easy, take off burdens, not invent and lay on many more, increase trade, not destroy it," but then virtue, and what is worse, religion, would flourish, and all the "delights and interests" of the court party would be destroyed.[46] The manuscript circulation of Sidney's *Court Maxims* was presumably limited. But Charles must have known that similar criticisms were circulating among dissident groups in exile and that they might quite easily exploit the discontent of merchants at home.

Thomas Sprat, historian of the Royal Society, tried to counter such criticisms. The glories of the Rump should not really be "given to the Riches and Interest of *Scott, Haselrig,* or *Vane*" but to the confiscated "Treasures of the *King,* and the *Royal Party.*" It was furthermore "the publique and the cheerfull voice of all *Englishmen,* that are ingag'd in Traffick, that there have been farr more incouragements for Merchants, and more vigorous attempts for the advancement of Commerce, within these four years and a half, then in many ages before." The king was, in fact, at the center of a grand "Designe, which will infallibly make the *English* the Masters of the Trade of the World; and that is the bringing in of our *Gentry,* and *Nobility,* to contribute towards it." At the center of Charles's design, according to Sprat, were the Royal Africa Company's plans to establish a heavily militarized trade with Guinea. The king, his family, and numerous members of the Privy Council invested in the company, which took the motto *Regio floret patrocinio commercium, commercioque Regnum* [commerce flourishes with royal protection, and the kingdom with commerce]. Like the Rump and unlike the early Stuarts, Charles provided naval support for the company in its struggles with the Dutch. His brother James even took over as the company's governor in 1664. As Sprat saw it, Charles was taking the advice that Lewes Roberts had given his father. He was becoming a mirror for merchants, for he made "the Arts of Commerce and Navigation" not just his "business and his interest, but his very delight and recreation."[47]

It is in the context of Charles's continuing struggle to legitimize his position at the center of an empire of trade that we should understand panegyrics from the mid 1660s like Sir William Davenant's *Poem to the Kings Most Sacred Majesty* (1663), in which the poet praises a range of the new king's policies, from his enforcement of religious conformity to his program for the advancement of trade. Like many other panegyrics, Davenant's celebrates the plenty that the Restoration brought ("In Fields we Harvests find, in Cities Wealth" [line 231]) and anticipates more ("No Prince e're brought so much, or promis'd more" [line 236]). And like Waller's encomia, Davenant's poem attempts to align Charles II with an ideal of productive kingship that is not stripped of all majesty. Invoking a traditional justification of sovereign authority, Davenant says that kings represent God on earth, but he adds that they have "chang'd his Image whom they represent." Unlike God, they have to work "hard" and "long," "to the stretch of thought forever bent," and they can preserve what they have wrought only with "pains or thought" (lines 349–54). Like the Charles of many Restoration panegyrics, Davenant's Charles evinces *care* (lines 77–80, 341, 405).

He will distinguish himself, however, not only by his application but by the tasks he sets himself, which will not be dictated by the outmoded value system of a warrior aristocracy. He will not attempt to perpetuate his name by erecting the sort of costly monuments on which Louis XIV is wasting his "solid Treasure" (line 281). Nor will he make "Levies" in order "to exercise his Valor, or his Pride" in beating "little peremptory" towns into submission at a cost that exceeds their worth (lines 329–38). "Whilst other Kings, in taking Towns, displease / Their Subjects," Davenant avers, "*You,* for yours, take all the Seas" (lines 339–40). This model of productive kingship and limitless commercial empire resembles the ideal advanced in *Of a Free Trade* (1648), where, in a long passage that I mentioned in analyzing the East India Company's interlude, Henry Parker champions the "mercatorian" Solomon over Alexander the Great because "whilest the cruell depredations of war impoverish, dispeople and by horrid devastations root up, and so shrinke (as it were) great Empires into small Provinces: Merchandise on the other side beautifies, inriches, impowers little States, and so alters their naturall dimensions, that they seem to swell, as it were, into spacious Empires" (p. 34).

If Davenant's poem seeks to differentiate Charles II from other kings and his trade empire from empires of dominion, it also attempts, like Waller's *On St. James's Park,* to free the king's program of naval and commercial expansionism from its natural association with the municipal government and civic ceremonies of London, which had provided the most important source of support and expression for such a program before the Restoration. In the context of 1663, we may see this as, on the one hand, an attempt to relieve the pressure that London was applying to the Crown in the name of trade and, on the other, an attempt to placate the fears that England's smaller towns had of being swallowed up by the metropolis. Adopting Ogilby's rather unusual figure of fleets as cities of the sea, Davenant uses it to different effect:[48]

> Great Monsters, Cities, over-grown with Pow'r,
> Do Neighb'ring Towns by hungry Trade devour.
> *You* Cities build which not destructive be;
> Ships grown to Fleets are Cities of the Sea.
>
> (lines 297–300)

Whereas Ogilby had used this image in Charles II's entry to suggest the special stake that London held in the country's trade and to celebrate the City's global reach, Davenant employs it to keep London in its place. There is, of course, something less than candid about Davenant's effort to give credit for England's foreign trade to the Crown, but his claim that Charles II's policies will be productive rather than destructive, presumably because smaller towns will flourish by supplying the fleet, is also meant to instruct the king even as it praises him.

It is perhaps no accident that Davenant's son Charles (1656–1714) would grow up to be one of the more important economic theorists of the late seventeenth century, for more than any other panegyrist Sir William evinces an interest in trade for trade's sake in this poem.[49] He even transforms a dry principle like Henry Robinson's *capital begets trade which begets ships* into a living metaphor in which ships are lovers and trade their form of intercourse:[50]

> And Ships by Trade each other still improve
> More fruitfully than Sexes do by love.
>
> (lines 301–02)

In an effort to express trade's elusive flexibility and range, Davenant turns to the mind for his comparisons. After writing near the poem's opening that "dexterity of Thought" could bring Fancy "All scater'd Forms collected till she spie / A *single* Map of all *Diversity*" (lines 49, 51–52), he later describes trade in language suggesting that it can make its own map of the world's diversity:

> Ships, which to farthest distances are sent,
> Are so concern'd their numbers to augment,
> That they by nought but Number can dispence
> The vital heat of Trade, Intelligence.
> By pow'r of Number they themselves disperse

> For a Collection, through the Universe,
> Of all the *Freights* which ev'ry Country yields
> From *work* of Cities or from *growth* of Fields.
> They grow to be a *Squadron,* then they meet
> In a free *Road,* and make a friendly *Fleet;*
> Where patience, as her hardest trial, finds
> How much they can indure who wait on Winds.
> From thence (suppli'd at length with sev'ral Gales)
> Each to her proper *Course* does spread her Sails.
>
> (lines 303–16)

The ships disperse by power of number because there is strength in convoys and power in accounting: the calculation of supply and demand, cost and profit, speed and orientation directs them around the world. Yet the passage's abstract diction makes its full meaning seem elusive, an effect that results, I think, from Davenant's desire to suggest the unrepresentability of economic processes that are too diffuse and involved to particularize.

The poem's complex repetition of words like *disperse, collect, number,* and *dispense* in different passages generates the implicit proposition that it takes imagination to see the real possibilities in a trade empire, a mental mobility and adaptability that find an emblem, in turn, in the perfect elasticity of trade. "*Nature* has nothing made more unconfin'd / Than your strong Island, but your mighty Mind" (lines 265–66), writes Davenant, and it is that probity that will enable Charles II to obtain "that *Neptune's* pow'r which Poets did but feign" (line 276). Davenant's poem thus argues that for Charles II to reconceive the role of king and the exercise of power in economic terms is a substantial imaginative achievement.

But it also makes an equally strong claim for the poet's daring refiguration of the artistic imagination as a faculty of dispersion, collection, and dispensation as irreducible and imponderable as trade — a refiguration that Margaret Cavendish likewise undertook in a poem of about the same date.[51] In Davenant's panegyric, the most important "pow'r of Number" directing the poem's ships is, after all, the poet's number, or meter, and just as the circulation of Charles's fleets will earn him fame, so the printed copies of Davenant's poem will "ev'ry where *disperse*" that fame by the power of number (line 526). Because in doing so his verse will be acting like a fleet of trading vessels, Davenant can hardly resist reviving Dante and Ariosto's figure of the poem as ship (lines 37–42, 413–16, 507–09). In this figure, too, Charles and Davenant converge, for like the ships of lines 313–14, both king and courtier had to exercise patience as they waited for the winds of fortune to change during the Interregnum. By permitting a larger order to emerge unforced from an elusive network of verbal connections, even the poem's form seems to simulate the processes of trade: it is ordered by an invisible hand.

The imaginative strength of Davenant's poem has been lost on critics in our century. It shares with *The Readie and Easie Way* the dubious distinction of being dismissed even by normally sympathetic readers as "cumbersome and incoherent."[52] Perhaps in redefining familiar ideas in terms of economic processes—the polity in Milton's case, monarchy and the poetic imagination in Davenant's—both writers arrive at conceptions that seem awkward because unfamiliar. I suspect, however, that there is an even deeper incompatibility between their own projects and the nature of representation. The language of poetry "naturally falls in with the language of power," said William Hazlitt; it "puts the individual before the species, the one above the infinite, might before right."[53] In contrast, Milton's tract and Davenant's poem celebrate process and seek (even as they affirm a sovereign authority at the center of their imagined nations) to represent power not as something fixed and concentrated but as something diffused and dynamic and therefore liberating rather than oppressive.

It is interesting to note that Charles Davenant—the son of Sir William and elder brother of the boy whom Milton tutored—would later espouse an international vision that in its positive valuation of dispersion resembles his father's poem and in its emphasis on a multiplicity of commonwealths bears an important resemblance to Milton's tract.[54] He argues that universal rulers, in bringing all commerce to focus upon their centers of government, tend to destroy trade and virtue alike. It is better that there be multiple centers of religion, liberty, power, and trade so that the earth's limited stock of virtue and commerce might not be concentrated in one place. If dispersed, its multiple possessors will nourish one another. For these reasons, a plurality of trading commonwealths is to be preferred, he argues, to a single emporium of world government.[55] To the extent that Sir William's panegyric shows any affinities with Milton's tract or with this strain of his son's thought, it may be said to fall outside the mainstream of Royalist panegyric, which sought to consolidate the power of the monarchy by depicting it as the center of a universal monarchy of trade in the making.

Dryden's *Annus Mirabilis* (1667), which appeared in the final year of the Second Anglo-Dutch War, might more properly be named the culmination of that tradition. In the next chapter, I shall offer a more extended consideration of Dryden's poem as an epic of trade, but here I would like more briefly to point to its participation in the panegyric tradition that we have been examining.

After its great opening stanzas, which establish the Dutch primacy in world trade as the premise for the poem's action (lines 1–36), *Annus Mirabilis* introduces Charles II applying himself to the problem:

> This saw our King; and long within his breast
> His pensive counsels ballanc'd too and fro;
> He griev'd the Land he freed should be oppress'd,
> And he less for it then Usurpers do.

> (lines 37–40)

By thus depicting the king jealously watching "the wealth of all the world" as it flows to the Dutch (line 7), taking counsel with himself for the advancement of English trade, and determining to live up to the legacy of the Interregnum's "Usurpers," Dryden introduces key themes that the poem will develop. He later portrays Charles II as a "careful Monarch" who not only surveys "the charge" of the war "with careful eyes" but who shows his solicitude for the nation's security and trade's increase by inspecting the navy's ordnance (lines 593, 549; cf. lines 1043–50). Wishing to depict Charles II as a productive king, Dryden also turns, like Davenant, to the analogy of a creative God: "God and Kings work, when they their work survey, / And passive aptness in all subjects find" (lines 563–64). While Dryden blurs Davenant's distinction between a God who produces unlaboriously and kings who can create only by applying themselves, he recognizes that the comparison can depict observing, thinking, and directing as regal forms of *work*. In Dryden's case, this barely submerged claim that in confronting the Dutch, building an empire founded on commerce, and helping to reconstruct the metropolis that is destined to be its entrepôt, the king is engaged in a great labor is reinforced by the poem's prolific allusions to the *Georgics*. But Charles's efforts are just half of a cooperative venture. Dryden's comparison of Londoners as they refit England's naval vessels to bees repairing their honeycombs (lines 573–96; cf. lines 909–12) reminds us that Charles's entry had celebrated the City's contribution to a joint program of naval and commercial expansion in just such terms: *generis lapsi sarcire ruinas.*

Just as Charles II's entry could be understood only against the ground provided by the Rump and the Dutch, Dryden's poem everywhere evinces its awareness that power has shifted from the Habsburgs to the United Provinces and France and that this war is a repeat performance (lines 1–36, 197–98). And yet, just as Charles's entry sought to authorize the royal program by invoking Imperial Rome as its origin, Dryden's poem traces the genealogy of England's trade empire back to the Tiber, "Where Coin & first Commerce" initially arose (line 632). By prophesying that London will receive the East's tribute of incense and the West's of gold and so become a "fam'd Emporium," Dryden finally reaffirms the Royalist claim that London's dearest ambition can come only of the blessing of having a king (lines 1169–1216). *Annus Mirabilis* may thus be seen to share key features with many of the other works we have been considering in this chapter. Far from merely versifying "mercantilist" notions when he wrote the poem, Dryden was contributing to a young, contested, but coherent tradition of courtly art that had helped make a republican issue the king's.

But whereas Waller and Davenant had both searched for ways to disengage the ideal of a commercial empire from its long civic context, Dryden, writing in the midst of a costly war that could not be funded without the good will of the City, reaffirms the cooperative union of Crown and City that Charles's royal entry of 1661 propounded. Not only does he dedicate *Annus Mirabilis* "To the metropolis of Great Britain, the most Renowned and Late flourishing City of London"; he applies terms from the Royalist discourse of martyrdom, generally reserved for Charles I and his phoenix son, to the burned City, which is like "a *Phoenix* in her ashes" and "a great Emblem of the suffering Deity." It is the City's, not the monarchy's, "restoration" that *Annus Mirabilis* prophesies.[56] Dryden's preface thus launches a larger pattern of interlegitimation between City and Crown (completed by the imputation of civic virtues to the king) that is one of the poem's essential features and key political strategies.[57] However much Charles and his poets might dream of disentangling the Crown from the City, the expense of modern government would not permit it. Indeed, the bond between the Crown and certain City interests would become an increasingly strong one as Charles's reign progressed. Sir Josiah Child and the East India Company would not only supply Charles with £322,000 during the course of his reign; in the interest of maintaining their exclusive trading privileges, they would support the Stuart monarchy even in the darkest years before the Glorious Revolution, when it became increasingly clear that the Stuarts were attempting to establish a more absolute monarchy.[58] To Milton, as we shall see in the next part, that was nothing short of a devil's bargain.

PART THREE

FORCE, COMMERCE, AND EMPIRE

For much of the century, the commercial realm had served as a suggestive alternative to more coercive modes of social and political organization. Writing in 1643, Richard Mather had distinguished between natural relations like those between a parent and child, violent relations like those between conquerors and captives, and voluntary relations, of which the most obvious example was the "covenant or agreement" between "Partners in Trade (2 *Chron.* 20.35, 36, 37)." Applying that model of voluntary covenanting to the relations between husbands and wives, princes and subjects, and ministers and their congregations, Mather contributed to the reformist ideal that was the subject of Chapter One.[1] We have also seen that even for more conservative men who saw a continuing utility in traditional forms of social organization—the guilds and urban institutions celebrated in London's mayoral pageants, the regulated companies defended by Henry Parker, the restored monarchy hailed by Sir William Davenant—the centrifugal force of economic logic, its tendency to invade social and political relations hitherto governed by other principles, held the promise of another kind of liberty. If that liberty was not so egalitarian, it still prized accommodation and production over conflict and destruction. In this spirit, Simon Ford, chaplain to the restored king, depicted the development of commerce after the Fall as a peaceful solution to the problem of scarcity, a social arrangement that had evolved only gradually from more violent and direct solutions: *"Force"* gave way to *"Compact"* and "that which we commonly call *Merchandise*" was born.[2]

Yet at least since Bacon and Ralegh, statists had emphasized that sea power could extend the scope of English commerce and that wealth was the sinews of war. In the terms of Mather's taxonomy, trade relations could be violent rather than voluntary: that made force and commerce not substitutes but complements for each other. This was nowhere more evident than in the East Indies, where the Dutch derived their commercial rights by title of war and where the English, impressed with the success of the Dutch, operated on the principle that the natives were "best treated with the swoord in one hand and the caducean," or Mercury's heraldic staff, "in the other" because fear was a surer and stronger passion on which to base a trading relationship than love.[3] We saw in Part Two that by pursuing the logic of this dark premise more doggedly than any English government before it, the Rump not only won a reputation for championing the cause of English commerce but forced Charles II to live up to that example by reimagining his empire in terms of trade rather than dominion. His royal entry suggested that such an empire could be achieved only through the coordinated exertions of Crown and City, force and commerce. The charter that he granted the East India Company a week after that entry supported the company's right to make "Peace or War" with non-Christians in its trading territory purely in the interest of profit.[4]

In the next three chapters, I propose to read a group of texts that, for all their generic differences and their divergent interests, share a deep concern about the relationship of force to commerce and turn to an overlapping set of literary traditions and *topoi* in order to examine it. At the heart of Part Three lie my readings of two poems that appeared in 1667 near the close of the Second Anglo-Dutch War: *Annus Mirabilis* and *Paradise Lost*. They may be read profitably against each other in this context because they both engage the Restoration regime's ideology of trade and because it is partly by way of their strikingly opposed representations of force and commerce that they ask to be read in, and understood against, the heroic tradition. Because what was at stake in the relationship between force and commerce was how England should conceive of its neighbors and the world around it, we shall see that questions of relationship and topography link *Annus Mirabilis* and *Paradise Lost* in surprising ways to Dryden's *Amboyna* (1673) and to the tradition of topographic verse that extends from Denham's *Coopers Hill* (1642) to Pope's *Windsor Forest* (1713). That tradition is important, I argue, because trade's natural resistance to modes of representation like narrative—it is abstract, impersonal, routine—encouraged poets writing about commerce to think in terms of charts, maps, and panoramas.

CHAPTER FOUR

Royalist Topography and the Epic of Trade

O ne of the chief architects of England's commercial policy after the Restoration was Sir George Downing, a graduate of Harvard who had served under the Protectorate.[1] Downing worked tirelessly to improve England's systems of government financing, banking, and overseas trade on the model of Dutch practices. He expected his progress to be slow, however, in part because of the conviction of men like the earl of Clarendon that such economic reforms were suited to a "commonwealth, but not at all agreeable to a monarchy," and he feared, in the meantime, that the United Provinces would be able to establish its primacy in world trade with an unassailable permanency.[2] Downing therefore resisted signing any comprehensive trade treaties with the United Provinces and instead tried to exact concessions from his Dutch opposite, Johan de Witt, through the threat of force. Although Downing knew that England had little chance of forcing the hand of the United Provinces at the margins of the globe, he believed that England's commanding position on the North Sea would allow it to cause sufficient disruption to Amsterdam's entrepôt trade to make it worthwhile for the Dutch to make limited trade concessions. This theory found its way into Edmund Waller's couplet on the duke of York in his *Instructions to a Painter:*

> While his tall ships in the barred channel stand,
> He grasps the Indies in his armed hand.

(lines 27–28)

For Downing, the threat of force in the North Sea was just one card in a poker game whose stakes were, as Waller suggested, holdings in the East

and West Indies. Downing appears to have had no desire to go to war—
and indeed professed himself satisfied with the progress of negotiations
shortly before the Second Anglo-Dutch War broke out—but his incessant
pressure on de Witt, and de Witt's firm resistance, helped lay the ground
for open conflict.

Burdened by the legacy of the Rump, some members of the Court
party were more anxious to spark another war with the Dutch. They
found a natural vehicle for their designs in the Royal Africa Company,
which displaced the English East India Company from the west coast of
Africa, where it had been trading in harmony with the Dutch. A trade
slump in Europe coupled with a boom in sugar exports from the West
Indies and a consequently greater demand for slave labor made the west
coast of Africa of great interest to both the Dutch and the English. Rather
than seek a foothold in unoccupied sections of Africa or buy a trading en-
clave at Fredericksburg from the Dutch (as Downing wished it to do), the
Royal Africa Company commissioned Sir Robert Holmes to dislodge the
Dutch from the Guinea coast, using ships lent by Charles II.[3] The duke
of York, who was by then the Director of the Africa Company, was eager
to provoke a war because he had dreams of distinguishing himself as a
naval commander and of increasing the share of world trade on which
the Crown would be able to impose nonparliamentary custom taxes. He
promptly expanded the scope of the conflict by sending Holmes across the
Atlantic to seize New Amsterdam (now named New York in his honor).
Thenceforth, Charles II no longer concealed his connivance in the company's campaign of aggression.

A committee of the House of Commons established to investigate the
problems of the woollen industry had its brief expanded to include the
"generall decay of trade," and merchants were encouraged to bring in their
complaints against the Dutch. Thanks in part to the skillful maneuvers of
Thomas Clifford (who was working in the interests of the duke of York),
the Commons subsequently resolved to assist the king in outright war
because, together with the damage done to English merchants by Dutch
traders, "the Several and Respective Wrongs, Dishonours, and Indignities
done to his Majesty by the Subjects of the *United Provinces,* by Invading
his Rights in *India, Africa,* and Elsewhere" were the greatest impediments
to England's foreign trade.[4] The supply Parliament voted for the war was
the greatest that had ever been granted an English monarch.

A heightened awareness of how much the conflict's image as "the
merchants' war" was actually influenced by propaganda from the Court
has led some historians to deemphasize the contribution that trade rivalry
made to the war's outbreak.[5] While it is true that few merchants expected
a war to bring anything but losses in the short term and that some of

the war's prime movers, such as the duke of York, were not actuated by any simple profit motive, the patterns of English and Dutch trade did set the two countries naturally at odds with each other, and there were valid arguments for the use of force in the interest of England's long-term position in trade.[6] For our purposes, in any case, *appearances* and *perceptions* are of the essence. When Dryden recalled hearing the sound of the English and Dutch fleets engaging out to sea on a summer's day "wherein the two most mighty and best appointed Fleets which any age had ever seen, disputed the command of the greater half of the Globe, the commerce of Nations, and the riches of the Universe," his view might have been tinged by his Royalist politics, but it would nevertheless have sounded unexceptionable to a frequenter of coffee houses.[7]

With the Second Anglo-Dutch War, efforts to articulate what was in the public's interest and what could be expected of an able government were increasingly expressed in terms of trade supremacy and fiscal responsibility, while the information that was required for such public debates was often supplied by the financial markets rather than the Crown or Parliament. For instance, fluctuations in maritime insurance rates and in the price of the Dutch East India Company's stock came to be seen as offering more honest assessments of naval engagements than official government reports. Observers watched the conflict with interest because it promised to test the theory that if England was at a disadvantage in commerce (because republics encouraged more individual initiative and industry), it should have the advantage in war (because monarchies possessed strong command structures and aristocrats motivated by honor, not profit). By sailing up the Medway to burn the English fleet in 1667, the Dutch disproved that theory with dramatic flair, but what put the Dutch in a position to strike such a blow in the first place was not their navy so much as their superior credit system, which enabled them to outspend England two to one while putting less pressure on their economy: with its reliance on great ships and the depredations of privateers, modern naval war was a contest of financial resources and logistics more than men.[8] In contrast with its Dutch counterpart, the English administration had embarrassing difficulty not only raising money but accounting for the funds' whereabouts. In the satirical responses to Waller's *Instructions to a Painter*—two of which had probably appeared before Dryden published *Annus Mirabilis*—the administration's violation of public trust and mismanagement of the war are often represented, for this reason, by its dissipation of public funds.[9] The convergence of force and commerce, policy and finance, the public trust and private interests that had seemed so promising at the beginning of the war would begin to seem more distressing by the end.

It is against this backdrop that I wish to consider Dryden's *Annus Mira-*

bilis (1667), the greatest poem to emerge from a conflict that generated a surprising quantity of verse and prose.[10] In the previous chapter, we saw that in lauding Charles II's naval and commercial policies, *Annus Mirabilis* marks the culmination of a tradition of Royalist panegyric that sought to align the monarchy with the cause of trade. In this chapter, I propose to read the poem—whose action is motivated by commercial rivalry and resolved by a prophecy of London's primacy in world trade—as an epic that begins and ends with trade. While Dryden's prefatory prose and notes show that Virgil and Lucan were much on his mind as he wrote *Annus Mirabilis,* he also learned from his contemporaries, especially those whom he credited with formulating the new poetic style of the age: Sir William Davenant, Sir John Denham, and Edmund Waller.[11]

Entrepôts and Trade Wars: The Example of Denham and Waller

We saw in the last chapter that Davenant's panegyric of 1663 influenced *Annus Mirabilis.* From Denham's *Coopers Hill* (1642), a poem whose local descriptions provide occasions for what Samuel Johnson described as "historical retrospection or incidental meditation," Dryden learned how effective it could be to represent the rest of the world converging on an entrepôt while allowing the natural rhythm of the tides—and of the verse itself—to stand as metonyms for the repetitive processes of trade, which are seen to share with nature and poetry alike some of the formal aspects of rule or law.[12]

According to Denham's poem, the Thames is notable not for its golden sands but for the industry it supports and the trade it attracts—what some contemporaries would have called its "above ground mines":

> And though his clearer sand no golden veynes,
> Like *Tagus* and *Pactolus* streames containes,
> His genuine, and less guilty wealth t'explore,
> Search not his bottome, but behold his shore.
>   (The "A" Text, Draft 3, lines 191–94)

Unlike "profuse Kings," the river does not take back the wealth it gives (line 198). Instead, it establishes a flourishing peace at home before venturing abroad to enrich its own people:

> As a wise King first settles fruitfull peace
> In his owne Realmes, and with their rich increase
> Seekes warre abroad, and then in triumph brings
> The spoyles of Kingdomes, and the Crownes of Kings:

> So Thames to *London* doth at first present
> Those tributes, which the neighbouring countries sent;
> But at this second visit from the East,
> Spices he brings, and treasures from the West;
> Findes wealth where 'tis, and gives it where it wants,
> Cities in Desarts, woods in Cities plants,
> Rounds the whole Globe, and with his flying towers
> Brings home to us, and makes both Indies ours:
> So that to us no thing, no place is strange
> Whilst thy faire bosome is the worlds Exchange.
>
> (The "A" Text, Draft 3, lines 205–18)

While the Thames's association with a whole system of tributaries suggests its role in domestic trade, the regular ebb and flow of its tidal estuary also mimics the movement of goods as they are imported and exported. Although Denham's simile comparing the natural realm to the political may say no more than that the river facilitates all the transactions necessary to create a strong domestic economy that can participate in foreign trade, we may also wonder whether, given the aggressive political creed of the first half of the simile (in which peace generates prosperity, and prosperity is increased through war), an analogous act of violent dispossession underlies the Thames's return with the spices of the East and the treasures of the West. The use that poets celebrating England's involvement in the Anglo-Dutch Wars made of it certainly suggests that the passage lends itself to such an interpretation.[13] Denham's countervailing appreciation of an entrepôt's likeness to a bosom—both sustaining and vulnerable, able to supply wants even as it makes the strange seem familiar—did not hinder them from turning his topographic vision into an emblem of commercial power sustained by naval force. That Denham himself did not endorse such an interpretation of his text may be suggested by his elimination of the bellicose image of kings seeking spoils abroad from the edition that he issued in 1668 at the end of the Second Anglo-Dutch War. In a manuscript insertion in his own copy of the 1668 edition, Denham added six more lines whose significance is ambiguous:

> Rome only conquered halfe the world, but trade
> One commonwealth of that and her hath made
> And though the sunn his beame extends to all
> Yet to his neighbour sheds most liberall
> Least God and Nature partiall should appeare
> Commerse makes everything grow everywhere.
>
> (The "B" Text, Draft 4, inserted after line 188)

On first reading, Denham's lines seem to propound the notion that trade has the power to create a more extensive empire than Rome; in this light, they may be seen as an effort to bring the more Caroline expression of Denham's earlier edition into conformity with the Restoration's increasing emphasis on commerce as a force of empire sanctioned by the example of Imperial Rome. But the lines may also be read as a celebration of the ability of trade to make a *commonwealth* of a world that was once divided by empire. Starting in the fourth century, writers had periodically suggested that the dispersal of the world's commodities was a providential blessing meant to promote the community of mankind through commerce.[14] The appeal of that idea seems to have started growing in the late seventeenth century until it culminated, as Albert Hirschman has demonstrated, in Montesquieu's notion of *le doux commerce*.[15] Is it, rather, this gentler vision of commerce that Denham inserted into his own poem? The ambiguity of his lines could well serve as a gloss on Part Three of this book. For we shall see that Dryden, Milton, and Pope all confront such alternative visions in their own verse.

Other writers like Waller looked to the tradition of heroic rather than topographic poetry in their efforts to represent the Anglo-Dutch War in verse. But even Waller, in his *Instructions to a Painter* (1665), a poem that describes scenes as if in preparation for their being rendered on canvas, thinks first in terms of geography. "Draw the whole world," he instructs the painter, "expecting who should reign, / After this combat, o'er the conquered main" (lines 5–6). At issue, among other things, is whether the seas are closed, as the English claim, or free, as the Dutch insist. Much as the royal entry of Charles II declared the English king master of the winds and seas as a majestic way of asserting his right to require fishing licenses of the Dutch, Waller instructs the painter to make the duke of York, Admiral of the Fleet, "bestride the ocean, and mankind / Ask his consent to use the sea and wind" (lines 25–26). The Dutch, who are "greedy mariners, out of whose way / Diffusive Nature" has been able to lay "no region," are unwilling, however, to submit (lines 69–70). So "Europe and Africa, from either shore," must watch as "Spectators" and "hear our cannon roar" (lines 61–62).

This is not a war that is fought solely in set-piece battles, for both sides are intent on capturing or destroying the merchant vessels of the enemy. The Dutch are like "hungry wolves"—a traditional emblem of avarice— "greedy of their prey" (line 23). But the English are just as hungry when they find Dutch "merchants left a wealthy prey" (line 40). Whereas the Spanish prosecuted a land war in the Netherlands in their effort to build an empire of dominion, and were consequently able to press only "single towns," the English fleet, ranging the seas and disrupting the United Provinces' trade with the rest of the world, is able to invest "all their provinces at once," "And, in a month, ruin their traffic more / Than that long war could in an age before" (lines 73–76). Their aim is not just to win a point of honor by making the Dutch once again strike their sails to English vessels, it is to take over the trade routes of the United Provinces: "Deserted by the Dutch, let nations know, / We can our own and their great business do" (lines 51–52).

Contemporary observers were much struck by the almost apocalyptic fire power that the fleets were able to direct at each other when they did finally meet in the battle off Lowestoft, and Waller is no exception. "Ingenious to their ruin," he says, "every age / Improves the arts and instruments of rage" (lines 237–38). In modern naval warfare, "Iron and lead" are "from the earth's dark entrails torn" so that "wretched mortals" may hurl "their mother's bowels at their foes" (lines 233–36). Waller's image, with its allusion to one of the crimes that brought the Golden Age to a close (*Met.* 1.137–40), seems to invoke a *topos* of Renaissance epics: the lament over the invention of gunpowder, which had made feats of martial heroism like those of Achilles impossible. But Waller is past complaining. It is a given that unlike Achilles, who dared not enter a field where "no bullets flew" until he had received Vulcan's shield and arms, Waller's "bolder hero" must simply stand exposed, "Defensive arms laid by as useless here" (lines 129, 131, 133). His courage amounts to standing calmly amid the accidents of war. At night "burning ships the banished sun supply, / And no light shines but that by which men die" (lines 121–22). When "flame invades the powder-rooms" of the Dutch vessels, "Their guns shoot bullets, and their vessels men" (lines 255–56). Waller's descriptions are, I think, self-consciously cold and precious precisely because there is something unnatural about such deaths. One observer recorded the melancholy sight of bodies floating in the sea the morning after such an engagement: having been impressed on their way home from church services, the men were still dressed in their Sunday best.

But Waller ultimately succeeds in containing much of what is strange about the Second Anglo-Dutch War in familiar idioms. If naval warfare will not permit the duke of York to be an Achilles, there is still a place in the navy for an admiral possessing precisely the sorts of virtues that van Dyck was wont to impute to his noble sitters. By telling the painter to "make the proud sails swell" not so much with the "wind" as with the hero's "extraction, and his glorious mind," Waller cleverly imposes on himself a challenge reserved for painters: without actually having to do so, he purports to express the inner resource of his subject by means of an external element of the composition, the swelling sails (lines 19–20). But Waller's lines also suggest that the virtuous example of the duke *is* the wind that swells the sails of the entire fleet. Blood and virtue *do* tell even in these times.

Waller's poem commences, then, by insisting that there is a continuing role for the character of a nobleman in the modern state, and it ends, despite its detour into the themes of commerce and modern warfare, by assuring readers that the Anglo-Dutch War is really still a contest of empire whose terms should be familiar to them. It can be likened to the battle of Actium, in which Roman fleets engaged "for the empire of the world they knew." It is simply more impressive because the English and Dutch are now contending "for the Old . . . and for the New" (lines 115–16). In a poem that purports to be giving instructions to a painter, Waller's final comparison of Charles II to the young Augustus after the battle of Actium is particularly felicitous (lines 299–308), for it alludes to what is already an ecphrasis in the *Aeneid,* Virgil's description of the shield of Aeneas (*Aen.* 8.720–28). Thus all that may seem strange or unheroic about a war that must be funded by supplies voted by the Commons and fought at the far reaches of the globe over scattered trading forts is finally authorized by *the* image of western empire, Augustus's receipt of tribute from the defeated peoples of the world.

Samuel Johnson remarked that "new arts are long in the world before poets describe them, for they borrow every thing from their predecessors, and commonly derive very little from nature or from life."[16] Waller's poem certainly does reflect *some* of the novelty of the Second Anglo-Dutch War, but Dryden would use the occasion of a trade war to test the conventions of heroic verse with more determination.

Annus Mirabilis and the Ideal of a Trade Empire

Perhaps the assured transparency of *Annus Mirabilis*'s verse has persuaded critics that close textual analysis would be otiose, for although they have long recognized that commerce is one of the poem's preoccupations, they have said little about the way the poem actually *represents* trade. They have proceeded as if Dryden were merely versifying mercantilist doctrine rather than innovating within a poetic tradition.[17] I propose to correct that tendency by considering how the coinvolvement of force and commerce, first celebrated in Charles II's royal entry of 1661 and now instantiated in the Second Anglo-Dutch War, enabled Dryden not only to heroize commerce by collapsing the distinction between trade and war

but to renovate the traditions of epic verse by redefining the forces involved and the prizes at stake in economic terms. That meant that Dryden
had to reimagine empire in terms of trade rather than dominion, a task
that he accomplished by structuring his poem around a series of topographic visions.

The opening stanzas of *Annus Mirabilis* show Dryden initiating these
projects:

> In thriving Arts long time had *Holland* grown,
>   Crouching at home, and cruel when abroad:
> Scarce leaving us the means to claim our own.
>   Our king they courted, & our Merchants aw'd.
>   2.
> Trade, which like bloud should circularly flow,
>   Stop'd in their Channels, found its freedom lost:
> Thither the wealth of all the world did go,
>   And seem'd but shipwrack'd on so base a Coast.
>   3.
> For them alone the Heav'ns had kindly heat,
>   In Eastern Quarries ripening precious Dew:
> For them the *Idumæan* Balm did sweat,
>   And in hot *Ceilon* Spicy Forrests grew.
>   4.
> The Sun but seem'd the Lab'rer of their Year;
>   Each wexing Moon suppli'd her watry store,
> To swell those Tides, which from the Line did bear
>   Their brim-full Vessels to the *Belg'an* shore.
>   5.
> Thus mighty in her Ships, stood *Carthage* long,
>   And swept the riches of the world from far;
> Yet stoop'd to *Rome,* less wealthy, but more strong:
>   And this may prove our second Punick War.
>   6.
> What peace can be where both to one pretend?
>   (But they more diligent, and we more strong)
> Or if a peace, it soon must have an end
>   For they would grow too pow'rful were it long.
>   (lines 1–24)

With its anti-acquisitive ethos, the tradition of Virgilian epic inherited
by Dryden disapproved of the love of having and discounted the power
of wealth in human affairs.[18] In contrast, Dryden announces with his first
words—which according to convention should define the scope of an
epic's action—that not *arms and a man* but *the thriving arts* will be his sub-

ject.[19] In a poem comprising the two basic theses of the epic tradition, a quest and a strife, the thriving arts will emerge as the key to both.[20] They are not just another category to be added to the *Aeneid*'s distinction between sculpture, oratory, and astronomy (at which other cultures will excel) and the arts of empire (at which Rome will excel): they *are*, in large measure, the new arts of empire (*Aen.* 6.847–53). Dryden's "thriving arts" recuperate members of Virgil's first category—like astronomy—as effective instruments of empire even as they reimagine what it means to subjugate peoples and impose peace through *economic* laws. Holland has literally "grown" in the thriving arts because the United Provinces were the prime example of trade's ability to alter "the naturall dimensions" of "little States" so that, as Henry Parker phrased it, "they seem to swell, as it were into spacious Empires."[21] By the end of the fourth stanza, they seem to have extended their reach out to the sun and moon.

Dryden's opening vision owes something to Waller's *Of a War with Spain, and Fight at Sea* and to its ultimate source, Eumolpus's epic fragment in the *Satyricon,* but Dryden tries to define a variety of control based on trade, not dominion.[22] The first stanza asserts that as practiced by the Dutch, the thriving arts involve both awing merchants and courting kings. The judicial murder of representatives of the English East India Company on the island of Amboyna in 1623 (an event to which we will return in Chapter Six) provided the most famous instance of both, for not only had the Dutch tortured and executed several English merchants, they had reportedly bribed James I £20,000 not to press the case of his own countrymen.[23] Amboyna was just the most notorious instance of what one pamphlet called a *List of XXVII Barbarous and Bloody Cruelties and Murthers, Massacres and Base Treacheries of the Hollanders against England and English Men.*[24] This charge of cruelty and bribery is transformed, in the second stanza, into what amounts to a charge of being monopolists of world trade. Using the image of bodily circulation, that suggestive figure that had already done considerable service in domestic debates between the anticompany coalition and the chartered companies, Dryden levels a charge at the Dutch that differs little from *A Discourse Consisting of Motives*'s complaint against company merchants in 1645: that as monopolists they "drive into one vein that masse of blood which should cherish the whole body" (p. 4). Accusations such as William Cooper's (that the Dutch sought "a monopoly of trade which they make their interest") or Clarendon's (that they showed "an immoderate desire to engross the whole traffic of the universe") were common complaints by the Second Anglo-Dutch War, especially among those Anglican Royalists who were its staunchest advocates.[25] Although the Dutch owed their primacy in world trade in no small measure to the superior efficiency of their shipping and credit arrangements, it is also true, as we shall see later, that they were ruthless in the pursuit of monopoly power and engaged in any number of practices that were anticompetitive.

Even as Dryden makes what sounds like a moral and legal case against the Dutch, however, a grammatical shift away from the Dutch as actors in the second stanza—now economic abstractions or natural processes are the agents—begins to suggest that if the Dutch have harnessed the power of economic forces, they may have done so not through any simple act of violence or usurpation but through diligence and an understanding of the laws that govern the action of such forces. After all, they neither possess nor have exclusive access to the sun or moon.

If the first six lines present a legal *case* against the Dutch—one form that an epic *causa* can take—the fifth and sixth stanzas supply a more neutral account of the war's *cause*. For if Rome ultimately prevailed over Carthage, it precipitated each of the Punic Wars with a deliberate act of aggression. Such ambiguities are in the best tradition of the Virgilian epic, which, by supplying multiple *causae,* draws attention to alternative accounts that might be given of the same events and that the epic's "official" ideology only half suppresses.

Dryden's staunch refusal to recede from the world of politico-economic forces to any of the ultimate causes sanctioned by the Virgilian tradition—such as the intervention of the gods—is, in contrast, an innovation that reflects his desire to redefine the Virgilian ideal of empire in the terms suggested by the Restoration regime's program of commercial expansion, a program that, while sometimes joined unconvincingly to fictions of kingship's mystical power, was more often presented as self-consciously modern and free of pretense.[26] In order to achieve a tone of demystifying analysis appropriate to his project, Dryden omits the most vatic and archaic features of an epic *principium*—the *invocatio* ("sing, goddess") and *professio* ("I sing")—while retaining the more impersonal and objective *exordium* ("Behold two nations then" [line 25]) and *ianua narrandi* ("This saw our king" [line 37]). Much as Simone Weil has said of the *Iliad,* "the true hero, the true subject, the center" of *Annus Mirabilis* will emerge as "force. Force employed by man, force that enslaves man, force before which man's flesh shrinks away."[27] Writing of a war whose stakes and staggering costs were measured in trade routes and currency more than land and bodies, Dryden is concerned to redefine the forces that matter, however, in economic terms.

That redefinition not only allows Dryden to achieve a measure of originality in the epic tradition, it also permits him to make commerce a heroic subject by erasing the distinction between trade and war. He shows himself most determined to make his point in his account of the pursuit and destruction of a Dutch fleet returning from India, a passage that critics since Samuel Johnson have regretted as a lapse of taste:

24.
And now approach'd their Fleet from *India,* fraught
       With all the riches of the rising Sun:
And precious Sand from Southern Climates brought,
       (The fatal Regions where the War begun.)
25.
Like Hunted *Castors,* conscious of their store,
       Their way-laid wealth to *Norway*'s coasts they bring:
There first the North's cold bosome Spices bore,
       And Winter brooded on the Eastern Spring.
26.
By the rich scent we found our perfum'd prey,
       Which flanck'd with Rocks did close in covert lie:
And round about their murdering Canon lay,
       At once to threaten and invite the eye.
27.
Fiercer than Canon, and then Rocks more hard,
       The *English* undertake th' unequal War:
Seven Ships alone, by which the Port is barr'd,
       Besiege the *Indies,* and all *Denmark* dare.
28.
These fight like Husbands, but like Lovers those:
       These fain would keep, and those more fain enjoy:
And to such height their frantick passion grows,
       That what both love, both hazard to destroy.
29.
Amidst whole heaps of Spices lights a Ball,
       And now their Odours arm'd against them flie:
Some preciously by shatter'd Porc'lain fall,
       And some by Aromatick splinters die.

                                                      (lines 93–116)

Johnson was surely right that the passage seems contrived, that the horrors of war might be treated with greater decorum by being treated with greater simplicity.[28] I would suggest, however, that Dryden's verse strains to differentiate itself from the epic tradition.

     If you are caught in a Virgilian epic, it is a bad idea to carry booty about with you, for you are likely to provide the epic's anti-acquisitive ethos with an opportunity to confront and dispatch its demonic other.[29]

Since it is one of Dryden's many fictions that the English are honorable and the Dutch acquisitive, this scene may at first seem to lend itself to a similar reading. Yet Dryden's figures insist that what motivates the English here is not honor but the love of having. Aware that the stag is the traditional quarry of epic heroes, Dryden instead compares the Dutch to beavers, industrious animals trapped for their sacs, not hunted for sport, the image of war. The myth that castors would emasculate themselves in order to escape with their lives may have appealed to Dryden's desire to slight the courage and virility of the Dutch, but it also suggests that what the English are after is not blood so much as commodities, the perfume into which the sacs of beavers were made. Dryden's comparison of the disputants to lovers and husbands struggling over a woman likewise emphasizes that this is a struggle of possession in which the object is not *really* a Helen or a Lavinia but a convoy of luxury goods.

Whereas in the classical epic—and particularly in the *Iliad*—fighting is about *being,* about expressing a heroic identity, in this confrontation fighting is really about *having.* The emphasis shifts from *having* to *being* only in death, when the Dutch, reduced to bodies bristling with aromatic splinters and porcelain shards, become indistinguishable from their merchandise. The image gives new meaning to the "beautiful corpse" of epic tradition. Far from being a freak of fancy, it must have appealed to Dryden's judgment as a reader, for it is the only thing, besides the opening of his poem, that he lifted from *Of a War with Spain,* where, in much the same spirit, Waller had described the Spanish:

> Spice and gums about them melting fry,
> And, phoenix-like, in that rich nest they die.
>
> (lines 83–84)

In a war in which what was remarkable was the trade at stake, not the number of men killed, Dryden's poem must derive its magnificence from an expenditure of wealth. With this baroque image, Dryden erases the distinction between trade and war. That he is willing to risk mingling the sublime and ridiculous in doing so suggests how central to his plan the passage is.

Elsewhere, in more felicitous passages, Dryden structures his poem around a series of chartlike descriptions that I will refer to as topographic visions. His opening stanzas constitute the first of these visions, which not only privilege space over time but serve as repositories of place names.[30] In using local descriptions to imagine England's wider commercial engagement with the world, Dryden learned something from *Coopers Hill,* but what makes his visions particularly chartlike, I think, is the prominence they accord to forces such as ships, the tides, and the winds, which, possessed of speed and direction, seem to give shape to the globe like so many vectors. Dryden's visions do not strive to evoke the spirit of a place by marrying description to lore, as do many chorographical poems. They are interested in the highly schematic view of the world that is yielded when commerce becomes the primary agent of mapping.

I would suggest that Dryden's visions may, in fact, have been informed by the Dutch sea atlases that were becoming so popular throughout Europe at mid-century. If, for instance, we consider the opening pages of Arnold Colom's sea atlas of 1655 with Dryden's opening stanzas in mind (lines 1–20), we find (1) a map of the two hemispheres, (2) a view of Amsterdam, its port crowded with ships, and (3) a navigational chart of the North Sea, with rhumb lines converging from every direction on Amsterdam (figs. 17–19). In sequence, the plates so much as say, "Thither the wealth of all the world did go" (line 7).

In the "Digression Concerning Shipping and Navigation," Dryden imagines how London might become such an entrepôt:

162.
The Ebbs of Tydes, and their mysterious flow,
    We, as Arts Elements shall understand:
And as by Line upon the Ocean go,
    Whose paths shall be familiar as the Land.
163.
Instructed ships shall sail to quick Commerce;
    By which remotest Regions are alli'd:
Which makes one City of the Universe,
    Where some may gain, and all may be suppli'd.
164.
Then, we upon our Globes last verge shall go,
    And view the Ocean leaning on the sky:
From thence our rolling Neighbours we shall know,
    And on the Lunar world securely pry.

(lines 645–56)

By referring to these ships as "instructed," Dryden suggests that they are intelligent and autonomous; he thus captures a sense of the impersonality of commercial forces expressed by Davenant's phrase, "by pow'r of Number they themselves disperse." The importance of these stanzas to the development of *Annus Mirabilis* depends, however, on their presenting an imaginary reversal of the poem's opening. In a gloss to which Samuel Johnson objected, Dryden explains that the English ships are "instructed"

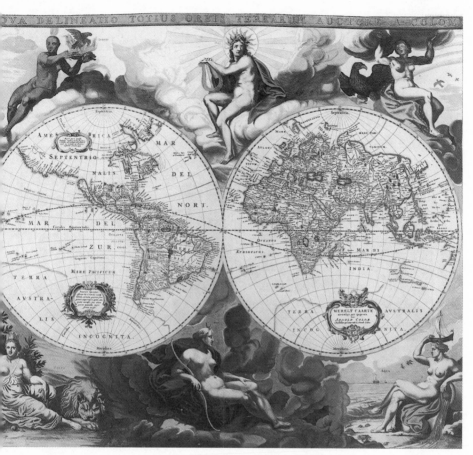

17. The first map in Arnold Colom's *Zee Atlas* (1655), depicting the two hemispheres of the globe. Beinecke Rare Book and Manuscript Library, Yale University.

by a more exact knowledge of longitudes than they now possess. They thus sail as directly and certainly as the rhumb lines on contemporary sea atlases suggested they should be able to do, if only they could ascertain their position precisely (again, see fig. 19). The magnitude of this ambition is suggested by the passage in Job that it recalls, in which God asks of the earth, "who hath stretched the line upon it?" (38:5). Although the word "Line" refers to the equator in the poem's opening (line 15) and to longitude and latitude here, the fantasy of mastering the globe, the obsession with being served by the tides, the talk of the moon bring the

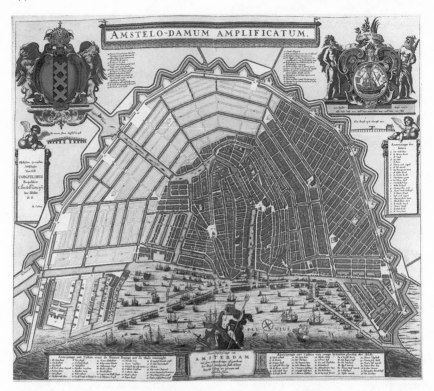

18. The second map in Arnold Colom's *Zee Atlas,* depicting the port of Amsterdam. *Bottom center,* Neptune is surrounded by navigational instruments. Beinecke Rare Book and Manuscript Library, Yale University.

two passages together. This is, in fact, the second time that Dryden has imagined such a reversal of the Dutch sovereignty over sun and moon, for he has already alluded to Joshua 10:12–14, in which the sun and the moon are held still for three days in order that the chosen people might defeat the Amorites (lines 469–72). But here Dryden presents the hope of a secular reversal wrought by science rather than by a national covenant with God. At the naval and commercial arch in Charles II's royal entry of 1661, the king had been presented with personifications not of the virtues (as precedent dictated) but of arithmetic, geometry, astronomy, and navigation.[31] An empire of trade required a knowledge of, and mastery over, the heavenly bodies and the tides.

Dryden revises the opening vision of his poem yet again in his description of Sir Robert Holmes's surprise raid on some one hundred and seventy Dutch merchant ships that were anchored off the coast of Hol-

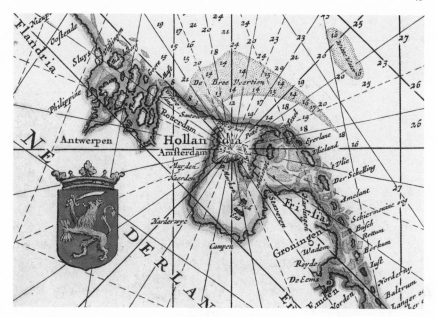

19. Detail of the third map in Arnold Colom's *Zee Atlas,* depicting the North Sea. Rhumb lines converge on the port of Amsterdam. Beinecke Rare Book and Manuscript Library, Yale University.

land, near the isle Vly (shown in fig. 19). Because only two warships stood between the English and the richly laden vessels, Holmes succeeded, as the enthusiasm of Dryden's stanzas would suggest, in burning the vast majority of them:

204.

Nor was this all: in Ports and Roads remote,
  Destructive Fires among whole Fleets we send:
Triumphant flames upon the water flote,
  And out-bound ships at home their voyage end.

205.

Those various Squadrons, variously design'd,
  Each vessel fraighted with a several load:
Each Squadron waiting for a several wind,
  All find but one, to burn them in the Road.

206.

Some bound for *Guinny,* golden sand to find,
  Bore all the gawds the simple Natives wear:
Some for the pride of *Turkish* Courts design'd,
  For folded *Turbans* finest *Holland* bear.

207.
Some *English* Wool, vex'd in a *Belgian* Loom,
    And into Cloth of spungy softness made:
Did into *France* or colder *Denmark* doom,
    To ruine with worse ware our staple Trade.
208.
Our greedy Sea-men rummage every hold,
    Smile on the booty of each wealthier Chest:
And, as the Priests who with their gods make bold,
    Take what they like, and sacrifice the rest.

                          (lines 813–32)

As must any cartographer or surveyor, Dryden defines the places that matter in the world, and he does so in terms of trade: entrepôts and centers
of production articulate the globe, and they, in turn, are differentiated
from one another in terms of the products they manufacture, finish, or
consume.

While the *OED* and the poem's editors tell us that the "Roads" of
line 813 are "sheltered piece[s] of water near the shore where vessels may
lie at anchor in safety," the word also suggests that while the English can
only *imagine* a time when improvements in navigation will allow them to
negotiate an ocean "whose paths shall be familiar as the Land" (line 648),
the Dutch, with their goods prepared for "Ports and Roads remote," are already in possession of such mastery. That the idea of spanning the sea with
roads was a particularly resonant image of power for the celebrators of
a sea-borne empire is suggested by the claim with which the personified
Thames had hailed Charles II in his royal entry of 1661:

> You are our *Neptune,* every Port, and Bay
> Your Chambers: the whole Sea is Your High-way.[32]

Annus Mirabilis may suggest that the Thames spoke prematurely in 1661,
but it endorses the ambition.

In Dryden's description of Holmes's raid, however, the same network
of routes that seemed capable of sustaining such an inexorable flow of
products inward toward Amsterdam in the poem's opening stanzas now
emerges as a means by which the English may engineer a destructive reversal of the process. This was the paradoxical character of an entrepôt that
Denham had understood: in order for it to be a source of power, it also
had to be a bosom of the world's exchange. The very openness and extent
of the Dutch trading economy, with its complex interconnections and responsive capital flows, meant that any blow struck against its vulnerable
bosom would damage the whole.[33] In Dryden's stanzas, the English are

accordingly able to make their fury felt all the way to the margins of the globe simply by burning the Dutch ships "in the Road," or sheltered water near the Vly. With this mastery through violence of the sea paths that the Dutch have built through commerce, the English come to resemble their antagonists, whom Waller's *Instructions to a Painter* had labeled

> Those greedy mariners, out of whose way
> Diffusive Nature could no region lay.
>
> (lines 69–70)

As the final event before *Annus Mirabilis*'s transition to the account of the Fire of London, this act of centrifugal destruction prepares the way for the poem's closing prophecy, which imaginatively repairs the damage done by Dutch economic competition and by the Great Fire itself.

In the poem's final stanzas, London receives hourly suitors to her "fam'd Emporium," while the English ship of state, in its efforts to overcome the Dutch and assume their position of primacy in world trade, is imagined as a merchant vessel successfully rounding the Cape of Good Hope:

> 297.
> Now, like a Maiden Queen, she will behold,
>   From her high Turrets, hourly Sutors come:
> The East with Incense, and the West with Gold,
>   Will stand, like Suppliants, to receive her doom.
> 298.
> The silver *Thames,* her own domestick Floud,
>   Shall bear her Vessels, like a sweeping Train;
> And often wind (as of his Mistress proud)
>   With longing eyes to meet her face again.
> 299.
> The wealthy *Tagus,* and the wealthier *Rhine,*
>   The glory of their Towns no more shall boast:
> The *Sein,* That would with *Belgian* Rivers joyn,
>   Shall find her lustre stain'd, and Traffick lost.
> 300.
> The vent'rous Merchant, who design'd more far,
>   And touches on our hospitable shore:
> Charm'd with the splendour of this Northern Star,
>   Shall here unlade him, and depart no more.
> 301.
> Our pow'rfull Navy shall no longer meet,
>   The wealth of *France* or *Holland* to invade:
> The beauty of this Town, without a Fleet,
>   From all the world shall vindicate her Trade.

302.

And, while this fam'd Emporium we prepare,
    The *British* Ocean shall such triumphs boast,
That those that now disdain our Trade to share,
    Shall rob like Pyrats on our wealthy Coast.

303.

Already we have conquer'd half the War,
    And the less dang'rous part is left behind:
Our trouble now is but to make them dare,
    And not so great to vanquish as to find.

304.

Thus to the Eastern wealth through storms we go;
    But now, the Cape once doubled, fear no more:
A constant Trade-wind will securely blow,
    And gently lay us on the Spicy shore.

(lines 1185–1216)

By freeing him from the necessity of narrating one exemplary voyage—such as Jason's quest for the golden fleece—as a synecdoche for all mercantile ventures, Dryden's topographic visions permit him to do justice to the very qualities that normally make commerce resistant to narrative: it is abstract, impersonal, routine. Yet I hope it will also be apparent by now that Dryden is able to impart a narrative impetus to his poem by presenting a *series* of visions that, when read in sequence, tell the story of London's displacement of Amsterdam as the entrepôt of world trade. That displacement can occur only in prospect, yet it may be precisely in using an epic prophecy to celebrate not a people or a dynasty (the more usual subjects of such prophecies) but a trade empire defined by its monarch and its major trading metropolis that Dryden's poem most clearly registers the important transformation of England's public sphere, and therefore of its public poetry, that was marked by Charles II's royal entry of 1661.

Epic antagonists are never so prone to seem indistinguishable as when they are locked in mortal combat. Once the struggle is over, however, and London has replaced Amsterdam as an imagined entrepôt of world trade, Dryden attempts to reassert the moral distinction between the two nations that his first stanza posited (before his fifth and sixth dismissed it). He does so by mystifying the actual trade relations that would exist if London did become such an entrepôt. The coercive power that Amsterdam had enjoyed over the circulation of trade is figured as the entrancing power of a woman now that it is imputed to London. London's *charm* persuades merchants to unload commodities as *tribute* rather than as goods to be exchanged and sold. Her very status as a "maiden" seems to deny the intercourse that is a natural part of any trading economy.[34] Such a vision is consistent with the neofeudal mythology favored by the Court and City earlier in the century, and in turning to it, Dryden may be attempting to make the novel project of the Restoration Crown seem, in the end, less strange. Yet his closing stanzas also insist on London's real resemblance to Amsterdam. London is not a capital seat of kings but an "Emporium" like the Amsterdam of contemporary maps.[35] Thus it is fitting that London should assume the role in which Dutch artists frequently depicted Lady Amsterdam, the object of London's emulous desire, and accept tribute from the Four Continents (figs. 15, 16, 27).

Dryden was not deceiving himself when he said in his letter to Sir Robert Howard that he had taken Virgil as his "Master in this Poem" (*Works* 1:55). In his effort to speak for a people, to tell their story as if it were inevitable, to instruct a prince even as he praises him, to uphold the value of work and the work of ruling, and to prophesy a lasting peace, Dryden writes in the spirit of his master. But for a trading nation like Restoration England, the building of a city could no longer be the reward of long wandering: it could only be a preparation for new quests. That is why Dryden's final stanza turns the ship of state into a merchant vessel rounding the Cape of Good Hope and heading toward the East Indies. Dryden could not have identified the national destiny with the joint program of the Crown and chartered trading companies more firmly.

CHAPTER FIVE

Speculation in Paradise

By invoking the Muses' "aid to my adventrous Song" (1.13), Milton announces that one subject of his epic will be Satan's "bold adventure to discover wide / That dismal world, if any Clime perhaps / Might yield them easier habitation" (2.571–73).[1] David Quint has provided a striking account of the mytho-poetic function played by the association of Satan's design with trade.[2] My object is to define the historical and ideological impetus *behind* it so that I may ask what development in Milton's politico-economic thought it implies. Setting himself a similar task, David Armitage argues that the poem evinces Milton's opposition to the Machiavellian ideal of a republic for expansion, an opposition that stemmed from Milton's belief that the Lord Protector's failed Western Design brought the republic toppling down.[3] While I concur that *Paradise Lost* subjects expansionist commercial policies to scrutiny, I argue that Milton's more immediate target is the Restoration regime's ideology of trade.

Not only did this program pose a continuing threat to Milton's values both at home and abroad, it possessed a symbolic coherence and appeal, thanks to the efforts of authors like Waller, Davenant, and Dryden, that invited a sustained response from a strong imagination like Milton's. Relying on Thomas Ellwood's belated claim to have read *Paradise Lost* in manuscript in August 1665, critics have not asked whether the poem might be responding to *Annus Mirabilis,* which appeared in January 1667, about four months before Milton turned his manuscript over to the printer and eight or ten months before it appeared in print.[4] That both poets were familiar with the symbolic program that had been used to support the Restoration regime's ideology of trade is sufficient motivation to ask whether the poems may be read instructively against each other. Yet even if we accept Ellwood's word that *Paradise Lost* was substantially complete by August 1665, his account hardly precludes the possibility of later additions or revisions. While the points of convergence between *Annus Mirabilis* and *Paradise Lost* that we shall encounter might well have been produced by two poets responding in opposed ways to the same symbolic program, I propose that we entertain a simpler explanation: that, at least in some of their telling details, they constitute a direct response on Milton's part to Dryden's poem. Certainly, when Milton added his note on the verse of his epic to the edition of 1674, he had the author of *Annus Mirabilis,* a series of heroic dramas in rhyme, and the essay *Of Dramatick Poesie* squarely in mind as his poetic and political foil, chief proponent of that "troublesom and modern bondage of Rimeing" from which he had recovered the "ancient liberty" of the heroic poem. We saw in Chapter One that for many of the reformers with whom Milton had allied himself in the 1640s, the cry of "ancient liberties" was a plea to be "free of" the commonwealth of which they were members, with all the economic and political liberties that were implied by such a notion of "freedom." It was, among other things, a protest against the tyrannous union of the Crown and the chartered companies that Dryden had celebrated in *Annus Mirabilis.* When, in turn, Dryden transformed *Paradise Lost* into the operatic *State of Innocence* (1674), he proved to be as astute and hostile a reader of Milton's political and commercial themes as, I am suggesting, Milton had been of his.

Beginning with Milton's representation of Satan's "enterprise," I point to some hitherto unnoticed ways in which the poem engages the contemporary discourse of trade empire. I argue that, much like Dryden, Milton investigates the literary consequences of the codependence of force and commerce in the Restoration regime's ideology of trade—though with strikingly different results. I also suggest that some of the poem's apparent indecision about how to represent Satan—as sovereign, soldier, or merchant—may reproduce contradictions endemic in the Royalist program. At the heart of my reading is Adam's vision from the Top of Speculation in Book 10 of the 1667 edition (Book 11 of the second edition). This passage, which may be read profitably against the topographic visions of trade discussed elsewhere in Part Three, has been relatively neglected by critics interested in the themes of commerce and empire in *Paradise Lost;* yet it represents the clearest expression of what Milton feared from the expansionist commercial policies of the Restoration regime. In closing, I argue that, as opposed to *Annus Mirabilis*'s vision of an England whose strength will win it new trade (and with it, new wealth and yet more power), the final books of *Paradise Lost* present human history as an unprogressive alternation of luxury and violence. This is a dark view of economic intercourse, and we shall have to ask if any room remains for Milton's more optimistic and revolutionary belief in the capacity for economic forces to preserve Christian liberty and secular choice even as they discipline saints and citizens.

Satan's Enterprise

Paradise Lost's strife plot—which recounts first a great battle in heaven, then a guerrilla action conducted on the margins of God's empire and closely linked to merchandising—seems to reproduce the Restoration conclusion that England must leave Continental land wars behind and conduct its operations by sea, on the margins of the globe, with trade, not dominion, at stake. Only once do the rebelling angels fight for "Honour, Dominion, Glorie, and renowne" (6.422)—motivations associated with the outmoded ideals of a warrior aristocracy. "Our better part remains," as Satan concludes after the expulsion from heaven, "To work in close design, by fraud or guile / What force effected not" (1.645–47). Thus in the counsel in hell, as the fallen angels debate what to do next, live peacefully to themselves or renew the assault, Beelzebub asks, "What sit we then projecting Peace and Warr?" (2.329). As a middle course, he proposes "Some easier enterprize" conducted in "another World, the happy seat / Of som new Race call'd *Man*" (2.345, 347–48).

As Beelzebub pleads "his devilish Counsel" (2.379), he displays all the diligent concern that Restoration panegyrists had taught readers to expect of the new monarch who sat patiently in councils of trade:

> deep on his Front engraven
> Deliberation sat and publick care;
> And Princely counsel in his face yet shon,
> Majestick though in ruin; sage he stood
> With *Atlantean* shoulders fit to bear
> The weight of mightiest Monarchies.
>
> (2.302–7)

The passage is peppered with the Royalist vocabulary of praise that imputed the virtues of public care and deliberation to Charles II and associated these with his patronage of England's trade empire, a project that was symbolically countenanced by Atlas, grandfather of Mercury, the god of commerce.[5] The object of this "bold design" is to "mingle and involve" earth with hell (2.386, 384) and, by uniting them into "one Realm, one Continent / Of easie thorough-fare" (9/10.392–93), to found a "nether Empire" in "emulation opposite to Heav'n" (2.296, 298). Built by neither pure conquest nor sheer industry (the alternatives represented by the rejected advice of Moloch and Mammon), this is a far-flung empire whose "high Capital" (1.756) is divided from its distant possessions by a vast space compared to the sea.[6]

If Satan's design is hatched in an "infernal Court" (1.792) and authorized by monarchical virtues like Beelzebub's, it is supported by the city.[7] As they gather in preparation for the council of Book 2, the fiends are compared to bees flying to and fro among flowers and conferring on state affairs "on the smoothed Plank, / The suburb of their Straw-built Citadel" (1.772–73). The erection of the citadel is the first major step in the fiends' efforts to found a nether empire. It is in the city that they anxiously await news of Satan's voyage,

> reduc't in careful Watch
> Round thir Metropolis, and now expecting
> Each hour their great adventurer from the search
> Of Forrein Worlds.
>
> (9/10.438–41)

Since the flying Satan has been compared to a fleet returning from "*Bengala,* or the Iles / Of *Ternate* and *Tidore,* whence Merchants bring / Thir spicie Drugs" (2.638–40) and to "them who saile / Beyond the *Cape of Hope,* and now are past / *Mozambic*" (4.159–61), the fallen angels appear like merchants or investors awaiting "th'account" of one of the East India Company's voyages (9/10.501). Like the bees celebrated in Charles II's royal entry, they are laboring to repair the ruins of their race (*generis lapsi sarcire ruinas*). They must believe they have succeeded when the archfiend tells them that they

> Now possess,
> As Lords, a spacious World, to our native Heaven
> Little inferiour, by my adventure hard
> With peril great achiev'd.
>
> (9/10.466–69)

When we consider that Joshua Sylvester's *Bartas His Devine Weekes and Works* (1605) cites the natural example of bees in describing how quickly men might colonize the world, the darker implications of Milton's earlier bee simile hit home.[8] The sudden metamorphosis of the fiends into serpents (9/10.504–17), which recalls an earlier transformation after the

simile of the bees in Book 1, deflates any such plans. Perhaps, as he professed to the City of London in his preface to *Annus Mirabilis,* Dryden
was unable to imagine how Providence, once deeply engaged, could resolve "the ruine of that people at home, which it has blessed abroad with
such successes" (*Works* 1:49), but Milton had no such difficulty. The metamorphosis of the fallen angels underlines how immeasurable would be
the labor required to repair the ruins of *their* race. Milton's plot line thus
neatly defies those Restoration panegyrics that first hailed Charles II's return as an occasion for the restoration of trade and later celebrated the
simultaneous rebuilding of London and fight for a commercial empire as
the chief examples of the power, industry, and cooperation of the Court
and City.

It is fitting that, as a deceitful rhetorician modeled partly on Odysseus, Satan should admit to no mercantile motive when striking up an
alliance with Night and Chaos—"Yours be th'advantage all, mine the revenge" (2.987)—yet should boast of the trivial price for which he has just
purchased a spacious new world when he reports to his backers in the
metropolis. Satan is a liar and the father of lies. I sense, however, that the
contradictions that may be found not only in Satan's stories but in the literary models to which he seems to conform at any given moment (Satan
is a young epic warrior as he volunteers to undertake the enterprise proposed by Beelzebub, an East India merchant shortly thereafter) cannot be
reduced to his mastery of appearances.[9] Like Charles II, Satan is a new
monarch in a provisional regime. His powers are poorly defined, and he
is committed to an enterprise that is better defined by what it is *not* than
by what it is.

It is not the act of open war called for by that hot-headed warrior
Moloch. Nor is it the sort of industry enjoined by Mammon, who sounds
for all the world as if he has just been reading English accounts of how
certain provinces in the Netherlands—determined to live "Free, and to
none accountable, preferring / Hard liberty before the easie yoke / Of
servile Pomp" (2.255–57)—revolted from Spain, and, despite the opposition of the Habsburg Empire and a dearth of natural resources, built a
great empire through work, not conquest:[10]

> Our greatness will appear
> Then most conspicuous, when great things of small,
> Useful of hurtful, prosperous of adverse
> We can create, and in what place so e'er
> Thrive under evil, and work ease out of pain
> Through labour and endurance.
>
> (2.257–62)

Writing of the Dutch during the First Anglo-Dutch War, the Independent divine John Goodwin had described just such a scene of exhortation in a hymn: "*Mammon* their God inflam'd their zeale / And set them all on fire."[11] The empire that Milton's Mammon wishes to found is even described as

> this nether Empire, which might rise
> By pollicy, and long process of time,
> In emulation opposite to Heav'n.
>
> (2.296–98)

That the "nether empire" of Mammon might be equated with the trading empire of the Netherlands did not escape Dryden, who, in his operatic version of *Paradise Lost,* pitted Satan and the "States-General of Hell" against the "Universal Monarchy" of God.[12]

Neither open war nor sheer industry, Satan's bold enterprise lacks its own terms; therefore it must waver between the courses recommended by Moloch and Mammon. This is one of the reasons that Satan wavers between warrior and merchant, sovereign and commoner.[13] We saw in Chapter Three that Restoration celebrations of England's trade empire showed their own tendency to shuttle uncomfortably back and forth between discourses of sovereignty and trade, majesty and industry, because they were syntheses of two longer established discourses, that of the Court and that of the City. The need for England at once to distinguish itself from the United Provinces as a monarchy rather than a republic and yet to identify with them as model traders promoted a similar oscillation. In constructing Satan from rival discourses, and having him occasionally resemble a Dutch merchant more than the archfiend himself might appreciate, Milton unmasks the contradictions in the Royalist symbolic program.[14]

These contradictions are just the symptoms of a deeper structural problem: Satan is excluded from any positive role in providence. Because he can have no identity that signifies, he suffers an identity crisis. Clearly, this is a subject that demands discussion in the sort of theological and psychological terms that would divert us from our subject, but I would like to suggest that the erratic and at times irrational behavior of the aristocrats who tried to participate in Charles II's plan to master the world's trade—as they wavered between the prospects of glory and gain, of military honor and commercial success in their conduct toward the Dutch, as they rubbed shoulders with more experienced merchants whom they were not used to treating as equals, as they tried to define a role for themselves in a society undergoing deep structural changes—may have offered an example nearer home of how trying it could be for an aristocrat raised with one ideal of martial honor to adapt to changing circumstances and undertake an enterprise as ambiguous as Satan's.[15] It may have presented a secular analogue for Satan's impossible theological position.

If Satan's ambiguous enterprise, or "great design," were really intended as a precise reference to the Protectorate's religiously motivated Western Design as David Armitage suggests, it would be odd for Milton implicitly to assign blame for it to the Court, City, and chartered companies, none of whom had been enthusiastic about Cromwell's Protestant foreign policy. The phrase "great design" is better understood more generally in the context of Charles II's efforts to appropriate the terms of the Rump's ideology of naval and commercial expansion, for before the Western Design was launched, the word "design" had been applied to London's efforts to become the world's bank of trade, and after the Restoration it was again used to describe Charles II's efforts to establish an empire of trade.[16] Although Milton's verse and prose arguments repeatedly refer to earth as "a new World" or "this new World," Eden itself is associated with virtually all the destinations of Europe's long-distance trades—including the Levant, Cathay, India, East India, the Canary Islands, North Africa, and the Americas—making it clear that Satan's is far more than a *western* design.[17]

Eden contains all that is best in the world, including the sort of commodities that Dryden had imagined Amsterdam (and eventually London) attracting from distant lands.[18] It has "Brooks, / Rowling on Orient Pearl and sands of Gold," as well as "Groves whose rich Trees wept odorous Gumms and Balme" (4.237–38, 248). Readers of *Annus Mirabilis* might suspect that it even has precious gems beneath its surface, for the sun directs his "fervid Raies to warme / Earths inmost womb"—"more warmth than *Adam* needs," perhaps, but just what is wanted to ripen precious dew in eastern quarries (*PL* 5.301–02; cf. *AM,* lines 9–10). It was a commonplace of mercantile literature that commerce was necessary to help repair the ruins of the Fall, that it made everything grow everywhere, but in Eden everything already grows in one place without the intervention of commerce. When gathering a meal for Adam and Raphael, Eve has at her disposal:

> Whatever Earth all-bearing Mother yeilds
> In *India* East or West, or middle shoare
> In *Pontus* or the *Punic* Coast, or where
> *Alcinous* reign'd, fruit of all kindes, in coate,
> Rough, or smooth rin'd, or bearded husk, or shell
> She gathers, Tribute large.
>
> (5.338–43)

I would submit that Milton's first readers would have been incapable of reading such descriptions without noticing their incongruous indebtedness to the Restoration language of trade empire, with its celebration of the tribute brought to London from both the Indies, East and West. If, as Alastair Fowler notes, Punic figs were best known for the threat to Rome they symbolized in one of Plutarch's anecdotes about the elder Cato, then there may even be a dark reminder of the wars being fought between England and the United Provinces, whose struggle for control of commerce poets had often compared to the Punic Wars.[19] Milton not only forces upon the consciousness of the reader the painful irony of writing about an unfallen world with language that is indeed fallen, he reverses the procedure by which poets like Dryden had elevated, and endowed with scriptural significance, England's ambition to build a trade empire. As Satan sees "in narrow room Natures whole wealth" (4.207), and thus mentally converts the blessed seat of unfallen man into little more than a warehouse in an entrepôt, the drive of many contemporary poems and paintings to map the world in terms of its products, to catalog its commodities and display such infinite riches in a little room, is revealed as profoundly fallen (fig. 20).

In the last chapter, we saw that with the commencement of the Second Anglo-Dutch War, another strategy of poets like Dryden who wished to celebrate the codependence of force and commerce, already propounded in Charles II's entry of 1661, was deliberately to collapse the distinction between war and trade, martial valor and mercantile calculation.[20] The distinction is likewise collapsed in *Paradise Lost*. Satan appears not only as a general, soldier, scout, and voyager but also as a mere raider bent on spreading havoc, spoil, and ruin. He even appears as a hunter. The epic's heroic ideal is roomy enough to accommodate all these activities, but when Satan appears as a merchant and trifler he passes farther along the continuum from war to trade than the Virgilian tradition will sanction. The very aspects of trade war that Dryden had celebrated as the points of convergence between force and commerce—destruction without the hope of gain, gain through the violence of the hunt—are simply evidence of how far Satan is from being either a martial hero or a productive trader.

In his Interregnum tracts, Milton had prized the processes of trade initially because they promised to generate truth and wealth through the free, open, and fully informed exchange of ideas and goods, and later because they might sustain Christian liberty by preserving choice. It need hardly be said that dealings like Satan's with Eve are not what Milton had in mind. They are not open, nor is the information that the two parties possess symmetrical. It does not help Eve any that Satan sets up the only

20. Jan van Kessell II with the assistance of Erasmus Quellinus, *America,* from the series *The Four Continents* (1664–66). The central panel, featuring the natural wonders of Brazil in a narrow room, is surrounded by sixteen small scenes (not shown). Bayerische Staatsgemäldesammlungen, Alte Pinakotek, Munich.

shop in Eden. He is one of "the great Marchants of this world" who brings "deceitfull wares" with which he plans to "abuse" Adam and Eve "like poor Indians with beads and glasses"—the more so because, like the figurative merchants in the Anglican Church of whom Milton complained in 1642, he is selling not goods so much as false doctrine.[21] Satan embraces this view of himself when, with all the satisfaction of a colonist who has trifled with Indians, he gives "th'account / Of my performance" to the fallen angels (9/10.501–02). He reports that "by fraud," with no greater penalty than a bruise, he was able to "purchase" an entire world, "and the more to increase / Your wonder, with an Apple" (9/10.485, 500, 486–87).[22] Far from preserving choice, Satan's deal is meant to foreclose it.

Satan's bold adventure is no more productive than it is honest. Whereas some Restoration panegyrists had associated Charles II's creation of a trade empire and diffusion of the "vital heat of Trade" with God's primal act of creation, Satan and Beelzebub seem to realize that such creation is beyond them.[23] Beelzebub dismisses Mammon's plan for building a "nether Empire" from scratch, through sheer industry, as "Hatching vain Empires" (2.378), a pale imitation of God's creation of his own empire, when

> on the watrie calme
> His brooding wings the Spirit of God outspred,
> And vital vertue infus'd, and vital warmth
> Throughout the fluid Mass.
>
> (7.234–37)

Satan admits the purely destructive nature of his enterprise when he glories in the prospect of marring in a day what God created in six (8/9. 135–43). Although Sin thinks of her father as a conqueror, not a vandal, she too notices his uncreativeness: "thy vertue hath won / What thy hands builded not" (9/10.372–73).

Satan's enterprise mars not only material goods but liberty. Proceeding against his better feelings on grounds of "necessitie, / The Tyrants plea" (4.393–94), he ensnares Eve by using an apple as "bait" (9/10.551), a technique that associates Satan with the tyrant Nimrod, hunter of men. That Satan's design has really been all about the spread of tyranny and death is finally confirmed when he deputizes Sin and Death, placing them in command of man: "Him first make sure your thrall, and lastly kill" (9/10.402). Satan's adventure thus emerges as a diabolic inversion of the ideal of free and open commerce among men—a commerce intended to circumvent the forces of tyranny through publicity—that Milton had propounded in his prose tracts.

While Milton had entertained hopes that the processes of trade might help to build and sustain a republic that could support his ideal of Christian liberty, he had never been willing to identify the good of the nation exclusively with that of foreign trade. Indeed, on the eve of the Restoration, he had registered his dismay that considerations of trade should overwhelm all those of "religion, libertie, honour, safetie, all concernments divine or human."[24] It seems natural, therefore, that Milton should resist the closing image of *Annus Mirabilis,* which depicts the ship of state rounding the Cape of Good Hope after the storms of war and thus seeks to identify the national destiny with the joint commercial project of Crown and City. Milton applies the same image to Satan as he nears the blessed seat of man:

> As when to them who saile
> Beyond the *Cape of Hope,* and now are past
> *Mozambic,* off at Sea North-East windes blow
> *Sabean* Odours from the spicie shoare

> Of *Arabie* the blest, with such delay
> Well pleas'd they slack thir course, and many a League
> Cheard with the grateful smell old Ocean smiles.
>
> (4.159–65)

We shall see that even Milton's late and much diminished hope that market forces might at least resist the extension of centralized authority gives way in *Paradise Lost* to an apprehension that commerce may extend the sway of empire.

Adam's Cartographic Vision

The semantic strategies that we have seen Milton use in his description of Eden should prepare us to read Adam's vision from the Top of Speculation with some attention to the vocabulary it employs.[25] In Book 10 of the first edition (Book 11 of the second), Adam submits himself to the hand of heaven and follows Michael. What initially appears to be the first vision — "It was a hill / Of Paradise the highest" (10/11.377–78) — will, in fact, be the central vantage point of a panorama that encompasses an entire hemisphere of the earth. As such, it recalls similar visions in Deuteronomy and in Luís de Camões's *Os Lusíadas*.[26]

A tradition of biblical commentary interpreted the Promised Land that Moses beheld from the mountain not as territory to be usurped but as a glimpse of the afterlife.[27] Later in *Paradise Lost,* Milton in fact invokes that tradition when he has Michael explain that Moses, being but a minister of law, will not lead his people into Canaan; that office will be reserved for

> *Joshua* whom the Gentiles *Jesus* call,
> His Name and Office bearing, who shall quell
> The adversarie Serpent, and bring back
> Through the worlds wilderness long wanderd man
> Safe to eternal Paradise of rest.
>
> (10.1202–06/12.310–14)

By comparing Joshua's conquest of the Amorites to the English defeat of the Dutch in the initial engagements of the Second Anglo-Dutch War, Dryden had, on the other hand, proven that the Old Testament's more literal story of tribal expansion and displacement had not been irretrievably buried. He had not only implied that England's promised land was the Dutch sea-borne empire, he had suggested that his own closing vision of London as the entrepôt of world trade was a secular antitype of Moses' prospect from the hill, a prospect that in the Old Testament and *Annus*

Mirabilis alike is permitted only after the sorrows of the pestilence. Both interpretations of Moses' vision seem to offer themselves as keys to understanding what Adam sees; this is just one instance of Milton's more general reliance in this passage on the reader's experience of duplicity and misprision to generate meaning.

Especially in the first edition of *Paradise Lost,* when this passage fell in the tenth and final book of the epic, its relationship to Vasco da Gama's vision in the tenth and final book of *Os Lusíadas* would have been plain.[28] Whereas da Gama was shown a prospect of Portugal's destined empire from a beautiful hill, "Making them think old Paradise was *That*" (*Lusiad,* 10.77), Adam looks out from a hill of Paradise itself,

> from whose top
> The Hemisphere of Earth in cleerest Ken
> Stretcht out to amplest reach of prospect lay.
>
> (10/11.378–80)

The view itself is deferred, as Milton introduces the story from the Synoptic Gospels that is most closely related to the vision of Moses:

> Not higher that Hill nor wider looking round,
> Whereon for different cause the Tempter set
> Our second *Adam* in the Wilderness,
> To show him all Earths Kingdomes and thir Glory.
>
> (10/11.381–84)

In *Paradise Regained,* Jesus sees not only rivers and pastures but "Huge Cities and high-tower'd, that well might seem / The seats of mightiest Monarchs" (3.261–62). With its use of words like *or* and *might* and its dependence on negative formulations like *nor . . . not,* the vision in *Paradise Lost* seems to be couched in language that is even more provisional than that of the temptation of the kingdoms in *Paradise Regained,* yet its catalog of names is nothing if not definite. It continues,

> His Eye might there command wherever stood
> City of old or modern Fame, the Seat
> Of mightiest Empire, from the destind Walls
> Of *Cambalu,* seat of *Cathaian Can*
> And *Sarmarchand* by *Oxus, Temirs* Throne,
> To *Pacquin* of *Sinæan* Kings, and thence
> To *Agra* and *Lahor* of great *Mogul*
> Down to the golden *Chersonese,* or where
> The *Persian* in *Ecbatan* sate, or since
> In *Hispahan,* or where the *Russian Ksar*

> In *Mosco,* or the sultan in *Bizance,*
> *Turchestan*-born; nor could his eye not ken
> Th'Empire of *Negus* to his utmost Port
> *Ercoco* and the less Maritine Kings
> *Mombaza,* and *Quiloa,* and *Melind,*
> And *Sofala* thought *Ophir,* to the Realme
> Of *Congo,* and *Angola* fardest South;
> Or thence from *Niger* Flood to *Atlas* Mount
> The Kingdoms of *Almansor, Fez* and *Sus,*
> *Marocco* and *Algiers,* and *Tremisen.*
>
> (10/11.385–404)

Whose eye this is—Jesus' or Adam's—is unclear for some twenty lines, so that its inflection, whether satanic or godly, is equally indeterminate. This uncertainty extends to the vision itself. Is the eye beholding cities or an abstract expanse of territory that is articulated only by the *names* of places, which will later be built? Before adducing this passage as evidence of Milton's "hypertrophy of the auditory imagination at the expense of the visual," T. S. Eliot should, perhaps, have examined contemporary sea atlases, where he would have found Milton's catalog of names—"*Mombaza,* and *Quiloa,* and *Melind,*" for instance, "And *Sofala* thought *Ophir,* to the realm / Of *Congo,* and *Angola* fardest south"—succeeding one another in bold print as the eye skips across the page (fig. 21).[29] We know, in fact, that Milton asked his young friend Pieter Heimbach to report to him in 1656 about the price and accuracy of the atlases published by the Dutch cartographic houses of Blaeu and Jansen.[30]

Adam's views of Asia and Africa correspond closely to the usual division of the East Indies in Dutch atlases. Some like Jansen's featured Africa and India on one page and India and the Moluccas (or Spice Islands) on the facing page (fig. 22).[31] Others divided the region into two separate maps, with the eastern coast of Africa lying near the center of the first and Chersonese (in the Malay Peninsula) near the center of the latter (figs. 23–24). By placing "*Sofola* thought *Ophir*" and the "golden *Chersonese*" in the central, or fifth position of his first two catalogs, Milton is faithful to their central geographic position on such maps. His catalog of names has a *visual* exhilaration that Eliot did not feel, but the thrill is not in the concrete particular; it is in the synoptic and abstract. Milton's catalog has the appeal of a chart rather than a painting. In suggesting that Adam looks out from the hill only to see something like a map, Milton's verse may retain some of the quality of Camões's account, in which da Gama likewise ascends a hill only to examine a crystal model of the heavenly spheres and terrestrial globe.[32]

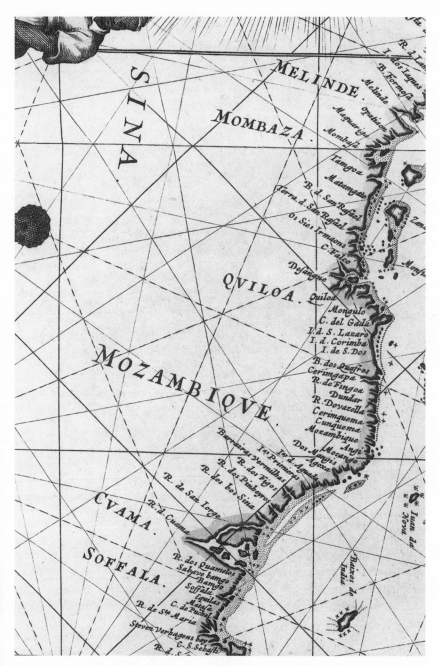

21. The east coast of Africa, a detail from Pieter Goos's *De zee-atlas* (1666).
Place names from Milton's catalog—"*Mombaza,* and *Quiloa,* and *Melind,*/ And
Sofala thought *Ophir*"—catch the eye. Beinecke Rare Book and Manuscript
Library, Yale University.

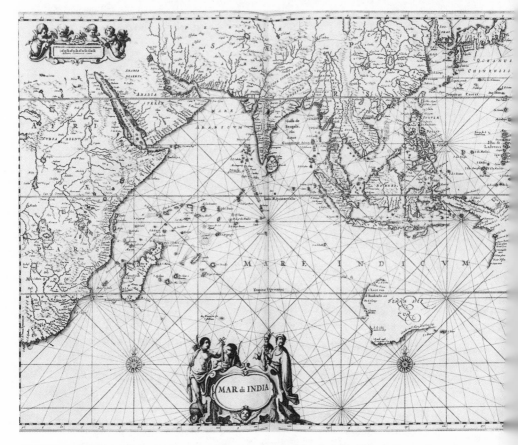

22. Map of the Indian Sea from Jansen's *Grand Atlas* (1652). Jansen's was one of the two atlases that Milton asked his friend Pieter Heimbach to investigate buying. BL shelf mark 9 TAB.5. By permission of the British Library.

The true location of the biblical Ophir, whence Solomon imported gold for the construction of his Temple, was a matter of conjecture. Milton informs us that Sofala was one candidate for the honor.[33] Camões, in the passage that Milton takes as his model, tells us that Chersonese was another:

> That *this* was Chersonese till that divorce
> And from the wealthy *mines,* that *there* remain,
>   The *Epithete* of Golden had annext:
>   *Some* thinke it was the Ophyr in the *Text.*

(10.124)

Milton's arrangement thus accords a special prominence, or what Fowler calls a "secret sovereignty," to Ophir. This implicitly places King Solomon and his trade with Ophir at the center of the poem's panoramas of Africa and Asia.[34]

What Fowler does not consider is the shifting and contested meaning of Solomon's example in contemporary discourse. We have seen mercantile writers stress the "mercatorian" nature of Solomon's kingship in an effort to find a biblical exemplar of the sort of king they wished Charles II to become, and we have likewise seen the East India Company obligingly praise the king for patronizing their "more than Ophir trade."[35] In doing so, the East India Company stressed the literal meaning of Solomon's involvement in long-term trade and subordinated the long-standing interpretation of the gold of Ophir as wise sovereignty or the unseen sovereignty of Christ. By writing "Sofala *thought* Ophir," Milton, as in the case of his more famous "thus they relate, / Erring" (1.746–47), suggests that the *true* Ophir may not be found at Sofala or any other port of call.

It is not until the viewer looks "On *Europe* thence, and where *Rome* was to sway / The World" (10/11.405–06), however, that the darker aspects of empire are made perfectly explicit. This may be ancient Rome, but it may also be the Catholic Church and Habsburg Empire, or even England, with its Catholic queen and its penchant for styling itself Rome to Holland's Carthage. It is this Rome that seems to cast its shadow across the Americas:

> in Spirit perhaps he also saw
> Rich *Mexico* the seat of *Montezume,*
> And *Cusco* in *Peru,* the richer seat
> Of *Atabalipa,* and yet unspoil'd
> *Guiana,* whose great Citie *Geryons* Sons
> Call *El Dorado.*
>
> (10/11.406–11)

The Americas are themselves not innocent of empire, yet there is a note of pathos here as lesser empires fall to greater and a shadow descends over "yet unspoil'd / *Guiana.*" This "yet" has a double temporal sense, for in the time of Adam or Jesus it would not yet have been spied by Europeans, but even in 1667 it remained relatively intact. Although Guiana had thus far been the object of Sir Walter Ralegh's ambitions more than the victim of his enterprises, England had just ceded its claims there to the United Provinces as part of the settlement of the Second Anglo-Dutch War, and the Dutch, at least, had shown themselves well capable of making their pres-

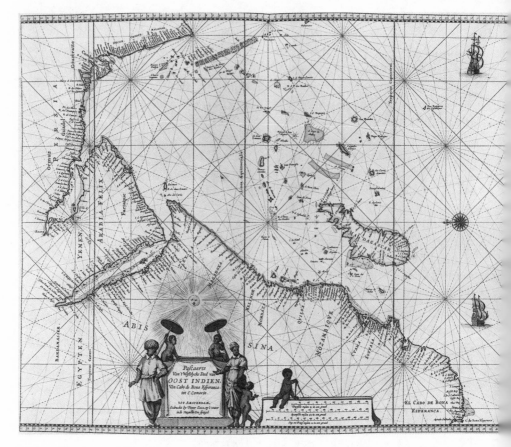

23. Map of the western portion of the East Indies, from Pieter Goos's *De zee-atlas* (1666). Beinecke Rare Book and Manuscript Library, Yale University.

ence felt in Brazil. The frontispiece of Pieter Goos's sea atlas of 1666 had featured English and Dutch ships in combat, as if the maps that followed would detail what was at stake (fig. 25), and I think Milton's language here generates a similarly desperate sense that the entire globe really *is* at stake, that a commercial empire, whether Dutch or English, may foreclose on the last inaccessible reaches of the globe. By the time the second edition of *Paradise Lost* appeared in 1674, members of polite society were symbolically playing for the world with packs of "geographical" playing cards (fig. 26).

North America above Mexico is palpably absent from the panorama. Because this is not simply a geographical vision but a vision of empires, that omission could be explained away by the absence of any empire in the

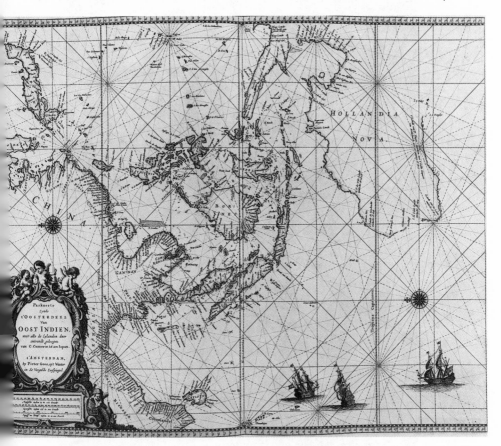

24. Map of the eastern portion of the East Indies, from Pieter Goos's *De zee-atlas* (1666). Beinecke Rare Book and Manuscript Library, Yale University.

more temperate regions of North America whose fame and sway could match the others in the catalog, but I think we are also meant to ask, anxiously, how long that will be the case. The Bay Colonies were at the heart of the Restoration Crown's plans to harness England's dissenting religious colonies to the motherland. Indeed, the earl of Sandwich had already advocated leveling them. Although Boston was deemed too strong to be subjugated that way, the Crown was able to pursue its objectives indirectly. It boxed the Bay Colonies inside more cooperative jurisdictions (including the newly captured New Amsterdam, now New York). It required, through legislation like the Navigation Acts, that the Bay Colonies direct virtually all their trade through English ports. And it saw to it that some of New England's richest trades, such as naval supplies,

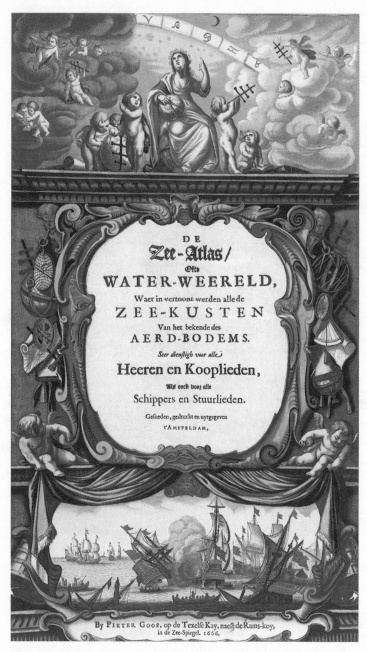

25. Title page of Pieter Goos's *De zee-atlas* (1666). Dutch and English ships engage near the Texel during the Second Anglo-Dutch War. The title page implies that the maps that follow will detail what is at stake in the war. Beinecke Rare Book and Manuscript Library, Yale University.

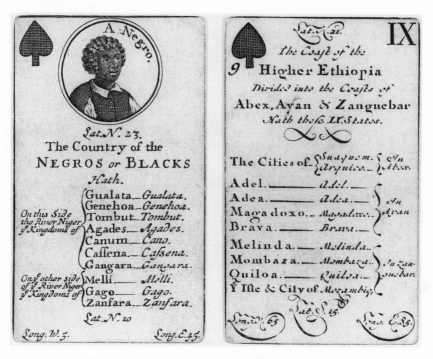

26. Playing cards from a pack known in later editions as "Geographical Cards." First sold in 1672 by Henry Brome. Guildhall Library, Corporation of London.

were controlled by men with contacts at Court. Such stratagems were slowly but surely pulling the dissenting religious colony into London's orbit.[36]

In *The Readie and Easie Way,* Milton had attempted to disrupt the progress of sovereignty by creating in blueprint a multiplicity of jurisdictions even within England, permitting them to vary from one another, and in so doing, unleashing the processes of experimentation, choice, and competition to check the trespasses of which he knew governments to be capable. Here we see the possibility that commercial energies projected abroad may erase difference. The poem's very description of the mount as the Top of Speculation—the closest it arrives to a name—reinforces that sense, for the word *speculation* was just taking on its economic meaning as prospective investment: the *OED*'s first recorded use in that sense is by John Evelyn in 1666. We sense that there may be no little commonwealths left in the greater sovereignty, that a secular empire may become all in all. Adam sees all this in a single hemisphere, yet Charles II's entry had insisted that *unus non sufficit.* The enormous ambition of such a claim was breathtaking.[37]

In *Os Lusíadas,* da Gama had been vouchsafed his vision of empire by grace:

> The Supreme Wisdome hath vouchsaf'd thee, *Knight,*
> The grace to see with thy corporeall Eyes
> What the *vain Science,* what the *erring Light,*
> Of miserable *Man* cannot comprize.
>
> (10.76)

Adam, too, has ascended in the visions of God. But with the caesura at line 411, Milton catches us up:

> but to nobler sights
> *Michael* from *Adams* eyes the Filme remov'd
> Which that false Fruit that promis'd clearer sight
> Had bred; then purged with Euphrasie and Rue
> The visual Nerve, for he had much to see;
> And from the Well of Life three drops instill'd.
> So deep the power of these Ingredients pierc'd,
> Even to the inmost seat of mental sight,
> That *Adam* now enforc't to close his eyes,
> Sunk down and all his spirits became intranst.
>
> (10/11.411–20)

What Camões had represented as a vision of grace is here revealed as a fallen prospect. This is the second such deflationary moment in quick succession, for even while he was preparing to lead Adam up the mount, Michael had remarked:

> All th'Earth he gave thee to possess and rule,
> No despicable gift; surmise not then
> His presence to these narrow bounds confin'd
> Of Paradise or *Eden:* this had been
> Perhaps thy Capital Seate, from whence had spred
> All generations, and had hither come
> From all the ends of th'Earth, to celebrate
> And reverence thee thir great Progenitor.
>
> (10/11.339–46)

All this was simply an opportunity for Michael to observe:

> But this præeminence thou hast lost, brought down
> To dwell on eeven ground now with thy Sons.
>
> (10/11.347–48)

Paradise Lost does entertain and even privilege something like the Royalist vision of an empire that could unify center and periphery, its capital seat planted firmly in an otherwise dynamic realm of outward expansion and inward flow—just as it applies the terms of Virgilian epic to the unfolding of God's plan—but it rejects such a vision as unsuited to the postlapserian world, where to refuse to "dwell on eeven ground now with thy Sons" is to be like the tyrant Nimrod, who rises "of proud ambitious heart" and, "not content / With fair equalitie, fraternal state," arrogates "Dominion undeserv'd / Over his brethren" (10.917–20/12.25–28).

The turn to nobler sights on the Top of Speculation is also a generic signal. Whereas the narration of the nymphs gives way to da Gama's culminating topographical vision in *Os Lusíadas,* that order is reversed in *Paradise Lost.* Adam's panoramic view gives way to the drama of Cain and Abel, a story not of empire, but of individual relationships with God. Here is a different variety of stock-taking and a different form of verse. This is just the first of two generic shifts—the second is from dramatic spectacle to relation (10.900–903/12.8–11)—and in each case, Milton deliberately eschews immediacy. Eve's instruction will depend on yet another layer of mediation, Adam's voice (10.1489–91/12.597–99). Many readers, beginning with Dryden and Addison, have expressed disappointment with the epic's final turn from vision to narration, and I think Camões's progression from narrative to vision really *is* more satisfying. But perhaps it is that very feeling of disappointed vision that Milton wishes us to interrogate.[38]

It may only be from this point in the epic that we can truly understand in retrospect why Raphael answers Adam's inquiries about the heavenly bodies as he does in Book 7/8. "To ask or search I blame thee not, for Heav'n / Is as the Book of God before thee set" says Raphael (7.703–04/8.66–67), but (and this comes after an intervening discussion of astronomy), "Dream not of other Worlds, what Creatures there / Live, in what state, condition or degree" (7.812–13/8.175–76). Among its other models, the passage is patterned on an incident in Torquato Tasso's *Gerusalemme Liberata,* when Carlo asks the personified Fortuna whether he may set foot on one of the Fortunate Isles and view their people and their customs.[39] She answers:

> —Ben degna in vero
> la domanda è di te, ma che poss'io,
> s'egli osta inviolabile e severo
> il decreto de' Cieli al bel desio?
> ch'ancor vòlto non è lo spazio intero

ch'al grande scoprimento ha fisso Dio,
né lece a voi da l'oceàn profondo
recar vera notizia al vostro mondo.

$(15.39)^{40}$

["In truth the request is well worthy of you; but what can I do, if Heaven's decree inviolable and severe is opposed to your noble desire? for not yet is the whole span of time accomplished that God has set for the great discovery; nor is it permitted you to bring back from the Ocean deeps true notice to your world."]

The echo is painful because by the time Milton is writing—less than a hundred years after the appearance of Tasso's poem—that span of time has almost expired: in contemporary Dutch sea atlases, only a few sections of Australia's coast line, for instance, were left blank, and these shrank with the appearance of revised editions throughout the century.

Although it might be objected that Raphael's "other worlds" refers strictly to heavenly bodies, not other worlds on the earth, such a reading occludes the links between earthly and heavenly discovery that cartographers, poets, and merchants alike felt in the mid-seventeenth century. An increasing sense of the finitude of the earth, together with a conviction that the same techniques of mapping, digesting, and printing might be applied to the heavens, prompted the publication of heavenly atlases like Johannes Hevelius's *Selenographia* (Leiden, 1647), whose charts of the moon manifested the same penchant for domesticating new lands with familiar place names that European settlers in the Americas had already betrayed. For a poetic analogue, we need look no further than Thomas Traherne, who transferred the language of discovery and trade to other worlds in the 1660s:

> Within the Regions of the Air,
> Compass'd about with Hev'ns fair,
> Great Tracts of Land there may be found
> Enricht with Fields and fertil Ground;
> Where many num'rous Hosts,
> In those far distant Coasts,
> For other great and glorious Ends,
> Inhabit, my yet unknown Friends.[41]

The widespread conviction that astronomical data and not a sea-worthy chronometer held the key to ascertaining longitude at sea was yet another factor that encouraged artists and poets to think of earthly and heavenly discovery in dialogue: in van Campen's design for the Amsterdam Town Hall, the earth's hemispheres were divided by a chart of the northern con-

stellations (fig. 14), and, as we have already seen, Dryden imagined the
United Provinces' mastery of the globe as extending out to, and in some
way depending on, the sun and moon. I would contend that, when we
bear this context and the poem's careful balancing of astronomical and
navigational imagery in mind, Raphael's speech naturally seems to apply
not just to heavenly discoveries but to voyages of trade and exploration
in this world.

Because Raphael's warning echoes Carlo and Fortuna's exchange by
the Fortunate Isles, it asks to be read in conjunction with the yet earlier
passage in Book 3, when Satan surveys the world from the primum mobile, and then plunges down

> Amongst innumerable Starrs, that shon
> Stars distant, but nigh hand seemd other Worlds,
> Or other Worlds they seemd, or happy Iles,
> Like those *Hesperian* Gardens fam'd of old,
> Fortunate Fields, and Groves and flourie Vales,
> Thrice happy Iles, but who dwelt happy there
> He stayd not to enquire.
>
> (3.565–71)

When Satan does stop to inquire after the inhabitants of our world, he
does so with all the system and care of a surveyor, following the earth's
rivers and seas in circuits north to south, then east to west:

> Sea he had searcht and Land
> From *Eden* over *Pontus,* and the Poole
> *Mæotis,* up beyond the river *Ob;*
> Downward as farr Antarctic; and in length
> West from *Orontes* to the Ocean barr'd
> At *Darien,* thence to the land where flowes
> *Ganges* and *Indus:* thus the Orb he roam'd
> With narrow search; and with inspection deep
> Consider'd every Creature.
>
> (8/9.76–84)

Is it encounters like this one that Raphael wants to preclude? Milton's
revolutionary arguments, from *Areopagitica* to *The Readie and Easie Way,*
had presupposed that commerce among men was, on the margin, productive. How deeply Milton must have questioned his own premises to
place that warning in the angel's mouth! In the next book, Sin and Death
undertake the "Adventrous work" of founding a "path" across Chaos to
ease the passage of the infernal host "for intercourse / Or transmigra-
tion, as thir lot shall lead" (9/10.255, 256, 260–61). Dryden's dream that

the oceans might be crossed with roads and paths is thus pursued to its hellish conclusion.

Luxury, Violence, and the Course of History

Critics have noticed that when Adam's topographic vision shifts to dramatic spectacle on the Top of Speculation, the story of man's early assertion of dominion over the earth is a reprise of the fiend's activities in Books 1 and 2.[42] Cain founds a city; the sons of Lamech invent the arts of music and forging; and the descendants of Seth (whom Josephus credited with the invention of physics and astronomy) couple with the daughters of Cain, producing "Giants of mightie Bone, and bould emprise," tyrants who threaten war against others (10.638/11.642).[43] Like Restoration panegyrists, Milton represents city-building and the mastery of the fusile and scientific arts as complementary parts of a unified program devoted to empire, but he then reveals its terrible cost: "Concours in Arms," "Carcasses" on bloody fields, "Sword-Law," bringing "home spoils with infinite / Man-slaughter," nations subdued as "rich prey" (10.637, 650, 668, 688–89, 789/11.641, 654, 672, 692–93, 793).[44] The spoils of such wars can bring little good to the victors because, as Adam concludes, "I see / Peace to corrupt no less then Warr to waste" (10.779–80/11.783–84). In place of the virtuous cycle of force and commerce posited by Dryden, in which force can generate wealth and wealth will bring with it new power, Michael presents only a nonprogressive alternation of violence and luxury. Still speaking to Adam of the men before the flood, Michael informs him:

> Those whom last thou sawst
> In triumph and luxurious wealth, are they
> First seen in acts of prowess eminent
> And great exploits, but of true vertue void;
> Who having spilt much blood, and don much waste
> Subduing Nations, and achievd thereby
> Fame in the World, high titles, and rich prey,
> Shall change thir course to pleasure, ease, and sloth,
> Surfet, and lust, till wantonness and pride
> Raise out of friendship hostile deeds in Peace.
> The conquerd also, and enslav'd by Warr
> Shall with thir freedom lost all vertu loose
> And feare of God, from whom thir pietie feign'd
> In sharp contest of Battel found no aide

> Against invaders; therefore cool'd in zeal
> Thenceforth shall practice how to live secure,
> Worldlie or dissolute, on what thir Lords
> Shall leave them to enjoy; for th'Earth shall bear
> More than anough, that temperance may be tri'd.
>
> (10.783–801/11.787–805)

The men Adam sees "in acts of prowess eminent / And great exploits" are the "giants" described in Genesis 6:4, "mighty men which were of old, men of renown." One tradition of biblical commentary—provoked by the puzzling survival of the earth after the deluge despite God's threat that he would destroy it (Gen. 6:13)—held that God had simply destroyed the *fertility* of the earth. The obvious inference was that in the time of Noah the earth had produced the sort of abundance of which only a race of men mighty in their carnal appetites could properly dispose.[45] In Michael's account, the tyranny of these giants is just one form of an intemperance that finds more general expression in acts of violence and luxury alike, which emerge as alternative but equally deleterious forms of consumption. Michael's account can thus stand as a scriptural refutation of the two economic arches of Charles II's royal entry of 1661, the first espousing the economic uses of force, the second, with its Bacchic theme, celebrating not only the Garden of Plenty but the Court's luxuriant consumption of that plenty as a contribution to the economy.[46]

The passage sounds not just like a versification of Genesis but like an attack on the members of Milton's party who had accommodated themselves too readily to the new order of things. While in the first couple of years after the Restoration, officials in the Bay Colonies had spoken openly of their hope that the Crown would shortly be overthrown again, the commercial incentives and regulations that emanated from London had gradually pulled even such a staunchly anti-Stuart satellite into the Crown's orbit: too many New Englanders were practicing "how to live secure, / Worldlie or dissolute, on what thir Lords / Shall leave them to enjoy" (10.798–800/11.802–04), and the process of accommodation and assimilation could only have been more rapid in the capital itself. In the Restoration world of long-distance trade, Comus's superabundant nature reemerges and, far from being rejected as a false representation, is accepted as too true. When plenty rather than scarcity is the real threat, the crucial moral response will not be the redistribution that the Lady advocated but the abstention that she practiced—a private, not a social response.

The poem's final drive to the personal is relentless. As Michael enjoins Adam in closing:

> This having learnt, thou hast attaind the summe
> Of wisdom; hope no higher, though all the Starrs
> Thou knewst by name, and all th'Ethereal Powers,
> All secrets of the deep, all Natures works,
> Or works of God in Heav'n, Air, Earth, or Sea,
> And all the riches of this World enjoydst,
> And all the rule, one Empire.
>
> (10.1467–72/12.575–81)

The dream that scientific knowledge might promote the prosperity of the nation, which might in turn help England encompass the globe in a single empire of trade—all that is disregarded for faith, virtue, patience, temperance, and love (10.1473–77, 12.581–85).[47] Michael's admonition comes near the end of a poem that is, among other things, a meditation on the fragility of communion and communication, both so susceptible to misvaluation, misinterpretation, false report.

To the extent that a logic of loss and redemption obtains in the epic's account of the Fall, its terms lie outside history and beyond the ken of political arithmetic. Only with the descent of Adam and Eve onto the subjected plain does the poem look forward to a field of action in which the rules of the marketplace promise to operate. The pathos of this closing prospect—

> The World was all before them, where to choose
> Thir place of rest, and Providence thir guide:
> They hand in hand with wandring steps and slow,
> Through *Eden* took thir solitarie way
>
> (10.1537–40/12.646–49)

—depends, in part, on our recognition that Adam and Eve are entering the world we know, where the choices they face will be as numberless as their steps. The poem finally elevates our first parents to the status of *representative* man and woman precisely by sending them *down* into a common world of small things and minor choices, of the domestic arrangements still familiar to us from Dutch genre paintings, the novel, our own lives.[48] Here, Adam learns, he may "by small" accomplish "great things" (10.1457–58/12.566–67).

The very familiarity of this world may persuade us to forget that the poem's consolatory emphasis on a "paradise within" is also a historically conditioned response to the Restoration, a means of empowering and liberating individuals alienated from the national community.[49] For those nonconformists who resisted the fierce threats and fair proposals that Anglican Royalists made in an attempt at once to unify England's trade empire and to curb religious dissent, such an inner paradise permitted them to follow their "worldly business with a heavenly mind, as a citizen of heaven, and pilgrim on earth."[50] No vision of empire but an inner light, an intuition of what it meant to trade and merchandize "in the Seed of God," similarly led George Fox to formulate a set of practical business principles for Quakers that, by attaching an exultant spiritual significance to plain dealing, prepared them to make a disproportionate contribution to England's commercial and industrial revolutions.[51]

I would submit that even though *Paradise Lost*'s engagement with the theme of trade is largely negative, even though it expends more energy attacking the Restoration regime's ideal of a commercial empire and reconsidering some of the more optimistic assumptions of *Areopagitica* and *The Readie and Easie Way* than it does in presenting a set of positive prescriptions for trade, the values and habits of thought that underlie its very rejection of the claims of institution and place, its enlarged sense of human liberty, and its profoundly *abstract* and *mobile* conception of the individual and the community alike may have done more to promote the expansion of English trade, the growth of the English economy, and the development of abstract economic analysis than did the more overt imperialist ambitions of the Court and its poets. What has come to be known as the "English model" among economists is defined, after all, not in terms of any specific pattern of trade but in terms of the contracts, transparent pricing, trust, credit, and faith it somehow manages to support.[52] Milton himself must have suspected how easily the personal powers of a paradise within could be transformed into a different sort of individual initiative and accountability, for his language insists that from Adam's "by small / Accomplishing great things" (10.1457–58/12.566–67) to Mammon's creating "great things of small" (2.258) there is scarcely a slip.

CHAPTER SIX

From Amboyna
to Windsor Forest

I have thus far stressed the efforts of Royalist poets to secure a place
for the Crown in England's commercial future by asserting the complementary relationship between force and commerce in their program of trade. We have also seen that in representing Adam and Eve as
natives defrauded of their territory and their lives by a merchant adventurer working in the name of empire, *Paradise Lost* submits that Restoration program to a withering analysis. Had we leisure to consider the
Painter poems that Andrew Marvell and others produced in response to
Waller's *Instructions to a Painter,* we would find that the gap between the
Royalists' rhetoric of trade and the administration's mismanagement of
the Second Anglo-Dutch War encouraged a rather different attempt to
evolve a stance of loyal opposition through satire, one that saw the inter-
penetration of the political and economic spheres exemplified in the war
less as an ideal convergence of interests than as a dangerous erasure of
saving distinctions. Here I wish to return, however, to the monarchical
ideal of a trade empire. For despite its evident brutality and aggressive-
ness, despite its antipathy to the reformist conception of commerce that
men like Milton began formulating in the 1640s, this conception had its
own ways of acknowledging some of the costs and responsibilities that
achieving primacy in world trade might bring. In this chapter, I consider
two such acknowledgments, the first written by Dryden on the eve of the
Third Anglo-Dutch War, the second written by Pope in celebration of the
Peace of Utrecht, which ended England's involvement in the protracted
Wars of the Spanish Succession.

From the Triple Alliance to the Third Anglo-Dutch War

In the aftermath of the Second Anglo-Dutch War, England and the United Provinces put aside their differences and joined with Denmark to form a Triple Alliance that was intended to check the expansion of France. Louis XIV's territorial ambitions in the Spanish Netherlands and Colbert's aggressive trade and naval policies, which entailed prohibitive tariffs on imported goods, were a grievance to both England and the United Provinces. This alliance had the support not only of courtiers like Sir William Temple, who played an important role in forging it, but of opposition politicians and dissenters, who found France's absolutist government, its Catholicism, and its protectionist trade policies threatening.[1] Slingsby Bethel affirmed that it was in the "Foreign Interest of *England*" to hold "firm to their present tripple League, and in that especially to *Holland*" because England and Holland were of "one and the same Religion" and because the "greatness" of Dutch trade was no adequate excuse for ruining the United Provinces. Their success depended on "Industry, and Ingenuity," not on "unjust dealings, exactions, and falseness." If other countries were deprived of "the example and emulation of their Trade," those countries would simply become "lazy and weary of commerce." The "world" could afford "matter enough to satisfie both" England and the United Provinces.[2] Such a claim was more credible in 1671 than it might have been fifty years earlier because the English East India Company felt less resentful about its poor access to the Moluccas (or Spice Islands) now that it was driving a successful business on the Indian peninsula in goods such as calicoes. The House of Commons duly voted money for the Triple Alliance in its session of 1670–71.

Little did it know that the king had already secretly committed himself to join France in a war of aggression against the United Provinces. In the Dutch republic he saw a threat to monarchy. In an alliance with France, on the other hand, he saw an opportunity to establish a more absolutist monarchy by eliminating his own dependence on parliamentary financing. He was willing to prepare for England's Catholicization and to abet Louis XIV's plans to seize some of the provinces of the Netherlands in return for a French subsidy and the expectation that, in wresting some trade away from the Dutch, he might increase his own customs revenues. Because he was aware that a war against the Dutch might provoke the opposition of dissenters, he timed his Declaration of Indulgence to coincide with its commencement. The war had been underway for ten months before he even sought the assistance of Parliament. By that time, Louis XIV's troops were in the heart of Dutch territory, and Holland and Zeeland had evaded capture only by flooding their own lands.[3]

England, however, had yet to win a naval victory, and money would be needed from Parliament to finance the expensive naval campaign. During the debate on supply, Secretary of State Henry Coventry justified the abandonment of the Triple Alliance in simple terms: "We have found the danger of being against the King of *France,* therefore we joined with him."[4] The new Lord Chancellor, the first earl of Shaftesbury, emphasized England's traditional rivalry with the United Provinces: "a War was absolutely necessary and unavoidable," he said, because the United Provinces were "the common Enemies to all Monarchies, and I may say, especially to ours, their only Competitor for Trade and Power at Sea, and who only stand in their Way to an Universal Empire." He even claimed that because Parliament had voted a supply for the last Anglo-Dutch War, it had implicitly called for this one. "But you judged aright, that at any Rate *delenda est Carthago,* that Government was to be brought down; and therefore the King may well say to you, 'Tis your War. He took His Measures from you, and they were just and right ones; he expects a suitable Assistance."[5]

What Shaftesbury strove to do in Parliament, Dryden tried to accomplish on stage. It was probably Thomas Clifford (whom we saw skillfully building parliamentary support for the Second Anglo-Dutch War), who suggested that Dryden write *Amboyna, or the Cruelties of the Dutch to the English Merchants.* Not only is the play dedicated to Clifford; we know that as Lord Treasurer he saw to it that Dryden was paid his usual salary despite the notorious Stop of the Exchequer in 1672, by which the Crown "found" the money to carry on its war. Such an arbitrary assault on the property of bankers, which might be compared to Charles I's seizure of the mint in 1640, together with the growing suspicion that Charles II may have had secret dealings with Louis XIV, made public relations efforts like Dryden's that much more necessary. It seems most likely that the play was staged during the parliamentary session in which Shaftesbury delivered his famous address, but we can date its first performance with certainty only between June 1672 and May 1673. Its text was sold, appropriately enough, at the New Exchange.[6]

Force, Contract, and Consent in Dryden's *Amboyna*

Far from confining itself to the Dutch "massacre" of English factors on Amboyna in 1623, Dryden's play stages three parallel inquiries into the dealings of the English and Dutch East India Companies—and into their relations, in turn, with the natives of the Malay archipelago. In expository

dialogue, the play's first four acts supply considerable historical information about the Portuguese, Dutch, and English claims to the Malay archipelago and about the operational details of their trade there. Thus we learn
that the Dutch raised the price of pepper once they wrested the trade from
the Portuguese (1.1.10–14); that they have forced the English East India
Company to accept only £80,000 in compensation for £500,000 worth
of damage done in just one year (1.1.28–31); and that, according to a recent treaty of 1619, they are supposed to be dividing the trade of the East
Indies with England, taking two-thirds for themselves and leaving one-
third to the English (1.1.62–65). The Dutch have abused the terms of that
treaty, we hear, by forestalling English shipments to Europe when favorable market conditions prevail and by charging the English (through false
accounting) for more than one-third of the expenses incurred in establishing and supplying mutual trading bases, thus making it impossible for
the English to compete with the Dutch in terms of cost (1.1.66–71).

What's more—and the argument frankly runs counter to the idea
that the Dutch are succeeding in subsidizing their trade through the English, unless we assume that both companies are losing money—the Dutch
method of trade is so costly that it can be supported only through monopoly pricing. It is costly not because Dutch shipping is inefficient—
indeed, the play admits to the superiority of the Dutch merchant fleet
(2.1.352–62, 391–93)—but because it depends on a method of business that
approaches military conquest (1.1.72–76). The account on which Dryden
based his more compressed explication of this problem may serve as an
interpretive key for the entire play:

> the Neatherlanders, from the beginning of their trade in the Indies not
> contented with the ordinary course of a fair and free commerce, inuaded
> diuers Islands, took some Forts, built others, and laboured nothing more,
> than the conquests of Countries, and the acquiring of new dominion.
> By which reason, as they were accordingly prouided of shipping, soul-
> diers, and all warlike prouision, as also of places of Rendeuous vpon the
> shore, and thereby enabled to wrong the English as well as others: so the
> cost and charges of their shipping, Forts, and souldiers, imployed vpon
> these designes, rose to such an height, as was not to bee maintained by
> the trade they had in those parts . . . vnlesse they vtterly draue the English
> out . . . ; thereby to haue the whole and sole traffick of the commodities
> of the Indies in these parts of Europe, in their owne hands; and so to
> make the price at their pleasure, sufficient to maintain & promote their
> conquests, and withall to yeeld them an ample benefit of their trading.[7]

Most of what the Dutch do in the play—from almost tripling the price of
pepper in Europe to torturing and executing their English competition

on the island of Amboyna—may be seen as the logical extension of their designs to achieve economic domination through force, a policy whose crushing costs make that domination all the more indispensable. The English Captain Towerson may observe to the Dutch Governor that "This Ile yields Spice enough for both; and *Europe,* Ports, and Chapmen, where to vend them" (1.1.215–17)—a claim reiterated by critics of the Third Anglo-Dutch War—but the Dutch account books, with their record of investment in a trade predicated on force, dictate otherwise.[8] The play's settled conviction that things could not really have worked themselves out in any other way, once the Dutch began conducting their trade in such a manner, accounts for the tone of tragic inevitability that is not entirely undermined by the work's evident sensationalism.[9]

The two love plots that Dryden introduces do more than draw a line between the Dutch and the English, between a culture (on the one hand) that follows interest as its only guide and puts a price on everything including love and one (on the other) that clings to the romance of the priceless and honors the nobility of hopeless sacrifice.[10] They also provide an additional vehicle for the play's economic inquiries.

In the first of these plots, the English Captain Towerson is betrothed to a native Amboyner named Ysibanda. His unwelcome and undeserving rival is the loutish son of the Dutch Governor, Harman Junior. Towerson's prior claims on Ysibanda's affection parallel England's precedence over the Dutch in its trade with her island. The English "were first discoverers of the Isle, first Traded hither, and show'd us the way" admits the Dutch merchant Van Herring, whose name alludes to another economic controversy between England and the United Provinces, the herring fisheries off the coast of England and Scotland (1.1.60–61). *Amboyna* repeatedly equates sexual relations with commercial ones. In comparing the relationship of England with Amboyna more specifically to a marriage, Dryden turns to a figure often applied to the bond between the English king and his subjects. By thus representing the relationship between England and native Amboyners as a contractual one predicated on affection and consent, Dryden reiterates the claims of authorities like Robert Codrington, who, writing of the period just before the massacre of Amboyna, said that the natives preferred the English to the Dutch,

> for the *English* aimed at nothing more, then a lawful and competent profit by Commerce and Traffick with the Natives, and the *Dutch;* And though in some places the *English* had erected some Forts, and setled some Strength, yet it was not by any Force or Violence, nor against the good will of the People of the Country, but with their own good liking,

and consent, for the better security of their Trade, and upon the voluntary submission of the Natives to the Obedience and Sovereignty of the
Crown of *England,* in which submission the Antient Laws and Liberties
of the said Natives, and all their own Immunities were comprehended,
and reserved.[11]

With phrases like "good will" and "good liking, and consent," Codrington thus depicted the relationship between the English and natives as
one of "voluntary submission," a process refigured in Towerson's court-
ship and marriage of Ysibanda, a story that, if it emphasizes the value of
a bond freely undertaken from affection, also naturalizes the submission
of a native people to a European as the yielding of the weaker sex to the
stronger in a union that is, crucially, indissoluble.

Although Towerson marries Ysibanda, he is executed before he can
consummate his relationship with her; his sexual frustration serves as a
transparent figure for England's thwarted commercial ambitions on the
island. Ysibanda's brutal rape at the hands of Harman Junior, on the other
hand, represents both the immoral directness of Dutch methods and their
dire costs. Harmon Junior's compatriot, the Fiscal (or treasurer), may attempt to justify the violation —

> Pray what makes any thing a sin but Law; and, What Law is there here
> against it? Is not your Father Chief? Will he condemn you for a petty
> Rape? She an *Amboyner,* and what's less, now Marry'd to an *Englishman:*
> Come, if there be a Hell, 'tis but for those that sin in *Europe,* not for us
> in *Asia;* Heathens have no Hell. (4.4.52–58)

—but the moral distinction between Europeans and the natives of Amboyna is defined more credibly by Ysibanda when she implores Towerson to "fly this detested Isle, where horrid Ills so black and fatal dwell,
as *Indians* cou'd not guess, till *Europe* taught" (4.5.15–17). Ysibanda, who
announces her intention to commit suicide, will pay for that lesson with
her life. Her fate suggests that, contrary to the settled conviction of many
East India traders, fear is not a surer and a sounder basis on which to base
trade relations than love.

Yet the play's other romantic interest forces us to ask what that love
should look like. In contrast to the rivalry between Captain Towerson and
Harman Junior for the absolute possession of Ysibanda—which results in
the annihilation of all three—this ancillary plot shows the English merchant Beamont and the Dutch Fiscal sharing the favors of a third man's
wife, Julia, in the happy knowledge that, as the Fiscal says in a virtual
quotation of Towerson's earlier remarks to the Dutch Governor, "Oh Sir,

in these Commodities, here's enough for both, here's Mace for you and Nutmegg for me in the same Fruit" (2.1.285–87). That this *ménage à trois* presents an alternative model of Dutch and English relations in the East Indies is made perfectly explicit when Julia says, "If my *English* Lover *Beamont,* my *Dutch* Love the *Fiscall,* and my *Spanish* Husband, were Painted in a piece with me amongst 'em, they wou'd make a Pretty Emblem of the two Nations, that Cuckold his Catholick Majesty in his *Indies*" (2.1.226–30). A secret conference between the Dutchman and the Spaniard thus reminds us that the Dutch treated secretly with the Spanish for their East Indian holdings: "Yonder's my Master, and my *Dutch* Servant, how lovingly they talk in private; if I did not know my Don's temper to be monstrously jealous, I shou'd think, they were driving a secret Bargain for my Body" (2.1.220–23). Similarly, Beamont will refer jestingly to the 1619 trade agreement between the Dutch and the English when he finds Julia in the Fiscal's arms: "Now, Mr. *Fiscall,* you are the happy Man with the Ladies, and have got the precedence of Traffick here too; you've the *Indies* in your Arms, yet I hope a poor *English* Man may come in for a third part of the Merchandise" (2.1.281–84). Julia, in turn, is confident that her "Husband's Plantation's like to thrive betwixt" the attentions of the two merchants (2.1.288). Such bawdry emphasizes the equation between commercial relations and sexual relations that is established more subtly in the love plot of Towerson, Ysibanda, and Harman Junior. The Julia plot asks whether the relationship between the Dutch and the English must degenerate into the domestic tragedy of the Ysibanda plot. May it not be a city comedy instead?

That would mean treating the Indies less as a peerless jewel than as a city madam. In the contrast between Ysibanda's virginity and Julia's sexuality—the former a fragile asset, the latter enjoyed in its use—we find the debate between Comus and the Lady about the true nature of wealth repeated; we also find an instance of *Amboyna*'s thematic inquiry into the relationship of names to things, an inquiry that, if it frequently reveals the duplicity and depravity of the Dutch, also suggests, at times, that being over-particular about names can make one lose sight of the more basic accommodations and gratifications that an economy of trade is best suited to supply. In the play's overarching logic, however, the Fiscal's eventual effort to eliminate Beamont along with Julia's husband and all the other Englishmen on the island suggests that the English are only deluding themselves if they think the Dutch are happy to share and share alike. This is certainly the lesson that Towerson wishes his employers to learn from his own death: "give to my brave Employers of the *East India* Company, the last remembrance of my faithful service; tell 'em I Seal that Service with my Blood; and dying, wish to all their Factories, and all the famous Merchants of our Isle, that Wealth their gen'rous Industry deserves; but dare not hope it with *Dutch* partnership" (5.1.399–403). It may be, however, that in failing to see that his arguments about personal contentment and the plenitude of the East India trade might be readily applied to Ysibanda, Towerson is guilty of idealization. Indeed, it may be precisely this fault that qualifies Towerson not just as a man sinned against but as a tragic hero—admirable, yes, but rather too good for this world. If this is so, then Dryden's secondary love plot indicts not only Towerson but Dryden himself for turning the East Indies into an idea, a point of honor, something to fight over rather than to use. Such a reading is true, I believe, to the play's divided conscience, which, after faulting the Dutch for making interest their God, urges the English to put aside their own religious scruples and follow their interest. This is the counterplot that resists the play's powerful drive from the wrongs done Ysibanda, to the injuries done the English merchants, to the epilogue's final incitement to war.

The pace of that movement becomes breakneck in the fifth act as the English merchants on the island are tortured and executed. The actual events that serve as the basis of Dryden's final scene may be briefly related. They were set under way when a sentry suspected that a Japanese soldier working for the Dutch might be a spy because he had been asking too many questions about the fort's defenses. Plied with leading questions about the English while he was subjected to torture, the Japanese soldier confessed to being part of a conspiracy to take control of the fort. Other Japanese yielded similar stories under torture. On the strength of this evidence, the Dutch gathered up the English on the island, who likewise confessed to a plot under torture or threats of torture. Eventually, four Englishmen were released because they could prove that they were elsewhere on the day when the plot was supposedly hatched; four Englishmen and two Japanese were pardoned; and ten English merchants, nine Japanese soldiers, and a Portuguese slave captain were decapitated. Whether these proceedings constituted a cynical attempt on the part of the Dutch East India Company to eliminate their economic competition under cover of law, a tragic overreaction to unfounded suspicions, or a swift response to a genuine threat will probably never be known. But the English East India Company insisted, in plausible arguments that are given to Captain Towerson in the play, that, according to their treaty with the Dutch, the governor had no authority to judge English subjects, that the confessions of the English merchants had been extracted under torture, and that it was simply not credible that a few unarmed men would conspire to raid a fort that was not only manned by four hundred Dutch merchants and soldiers but supported by two more forts elsewhere on the island.[12]

In *Amboyna*, all these events are reserved for the last act, which opens with the Fiscal freely confiding that he has extracted false testimony from a Japanese soldier with threats of torture and promises of reward. Beamont and another English merchant, Collins, are then led on stage only to be threatened with torture by fire and water:

> *Har.* You shall be muffl'd up like Ladies, with an Oyl'd Cloath put underneath your Chins, then Water pour'd above; which either you must drink or must not breath.
> *1 Dutch.* That's one way, we have others.
> *Har.* Yes, we have two Elements at your Service, Fire, as well as Water; certain things call'd Matches to be ty'd to your Fingers ends, which are as soveraign as Nutmegs, to quicken your short Memories.
>
> $\qquad\qquad\qquad\qquad\qquad\qquad\qquad\qquad\qquad$ (5.1.140–47)

When they refuse to confess, both men are led off to torture. Then two boys and a woman—showing signs that they have "indur'd the Beverage already" (5.1.173–74)—are led on-stage, threatened, and led off to be tortured by fire. The objections that Towerson makes once he appears before the Governor and the Fiscal provide a respite of reasoned discourse that is like the lull before a storm: it gives way to the dramatic spectacle of his fellow countrymen being tortured, revealed when the back scene opens. The back scene closes, in turn, so that Beamont may be tortured at close proximity to Towerson in the hope that the sufferings of the friend may wring a false confession from the Captain. Beamont's determination to die standing up—"they can but burn me naked to my soul that's of a Nobler frame, and will stand Firme, Upright, and Unconsum'd" (5.1.335–37)—marks him as a stoic hero in the tradition of Hercules and brings the play's efforts to depict the English merchants as brave and naturally noble to a climax.

That there is nothing isolated about this incident of cruelty is emphasized not only by another story of Dutch ruthlessness narrated earlier (3.3.64–163), but by the Governor's wish that "your whole *East India* Company were in this room, that we might use them thus," an idea rapturously taken up by the Fiscal with his gloating reference to the Dutch destruction of Pula Run's groves, which had been adjudged to the English: "They shou'd have Fires of Cloves and Cinammon, we wou'd cut down whole Groves to Honour 'em, and be at cost to burn 'em nobly" (5.1.358–62).

In keeping both with Dryden's monarchical and high church politics and with the shifting tides of international power that had occurred during the seventeenth century, the play is concerned to transfer the Black Legend of Spanish cruelty to the Dutch, who now posed the greater threat to England. Dryden not only reused the sets from Sir William Davenant's *Cruelty of the Spaniards in Peru,* he cast Michael Mohun, who had been memorably tortured at the hands of the Spanish in the title role of *The Indian Emperour* (1665), in the role of the tortured Beamont.[13] When he sees his fellow merchants being put to such pains, Towerson laments, "Are you Men or Devils? *D'Alva,* whom you condemn for cruelty did ne're the like" (5.1.310–11). Considering that the duke of Alva butchered whole towns in the Netherlands, the Dutch might be excused for disagreeing, but the play is concerned to show that the Spanish are better than the English think and that the Dutch are worse. That is why Dryden substitutes Julia's husband Perez for the Portuguese captain of slaves who was in reality executed: he wants to contrast the scruples of the Spaniard with the ingratitude of the Dutch, whose failure to be properly thankful for England's intervention in their war of independence against the Habsburgs is suggested by Harman Junior's willingness to kill Towerson despite the captain's having saved his life *twice* in the play.

Because the story of the massacre at Amboyna would have been utterly familiar to Englishmen, the audience could be expected to hear the play's many instances of verbal foreshadowing. Asking for news of the market in the first act, for instance, the Governor exclaims, "Prithee do not torture us, but tell it" (1.1.17). "Captain, very shortly, we must use your Head in a certain business," he later comments to Towerson in the same scene (1.1.252–53). One of the effects of these morbid anticipations—identified only by the audience, for the Governor does not yet know of the plot the Fiscal is hatching—is to make the viewers aware of themselves as a community bound by a common knowledge of Dutch perfidy. The Fiscal's efforts to eliminate survivors who might testify to scenes of Dutch cruelty valorizes both the play's function as testimony and the audience's role, in seeing the cruelties recreated, as witnesses.

In that capacity, the audience is expected not only to see but to *feel.* "Are you yet mov'd?" asks Harman as Towerson watches the scene of torture. "But not as you wou'd have me," the Captain replies. "I could weep tears of Blood to view this usage; but you, as if not made of the same Mould, see with dry eyes the Miseries of Men, as they were Creatures of another kind, not Christians, nor Allies, nor Partners with you, but as if Beasts, transfix'd on Theatres, to make your cruel sport" (5.1.318–24). "Tranfix'd on Theatres" means pierced through in Roman circuses, but it also points to the playhouse itself and thus anticipates what might be delivered by Towerson as an aside to the audience: "We have friends in *England* who wou'd weep to see this acted on a Theatre, which here you make your pastime" (5.1.368–69). By now the play feels like a ritual recreation meant to confirm a communal article of faith.

Cast as scoffers and torturers, the Dutch make plans at the conclusion of the play to divide the greatest wealth of the Englishmen by lot and to "trifle" for the rest, just as the Roman soldiers divided the garments of the crucified Christ and cast lots for his coat (John 19:23–24). As if in compensation for the scenes of torture he must witness, Towerson is granted a prophetic vision of the ironic reversal that later generations of his countrymen will work:

> An Age is coming, when an *English* Monarch with Blood, shall pay that blood which you have shed: to save your Cities from victorious Arms, you shall invite the Waves to hide your Earth, and trembling to the tops of Houses fly, while Deluges invade your lower rooms: Then, as with Waters you have swell'd our Bodies, with damps of Waters shall your heads be swoln;
>
> > Till at the last your sap'd foundations fall,
> > And Universal Ruine swallows all.
>
> (5.1.453–61)

Towerson's prophecy presents history in the future tense: the Netherlands had just flooded their territories in an attempt to forestall the French armies who were advancing as part of the Third Anglo-Dutch War.[14] It has the effect both of confirming the connection between the events of Amboyna and the present war and of making that war seem like the foreordained punishment for an old crime, not the result of a policy hatched in secret negotiations between two monarchs with absolutist ambitions.

Assuming the role of the Spartan poet Tyrtaeus, Dryden professes his desire in the play's epilogue to lead the English people into war by "Showing your tortur'd Fathers in this Play." Affect, in other words, should give rise to resolution. The Dutch republic that had grown through the thriving arts and swollen into a spacious empire in the opening stanzas of *Annus Mirabilis* is here refigured as a watery growth that can be cured, like scrofula, only by that ultimate emblem of sacred kingship, the "royal touch":

> Yet is their Empire no true Growth but Humour,
> And only two Kings Touch can cure the Tumor.

Dryden concludes by referring to that confirmed enemy of Carthage, Cato, whose effort to incite war by holding up a Punic fig in the Roman senate we noticed in our reading of *Paradise Lost:*

> As *Cato* did his *Affricque* Fruits display:
> So we before your Eies their *Indies* lay:
> All Loyal *English* will like him conclude,
> Let *Caesar* live, and *Carthage* be subdu'd.

By placing the name of Caesar on Cato's lips, Dryden is guilty of an anachronism, committed in order to cast England in the role of Imperial rather than republican Rome. If there had been any question in the final act about the article of faith that was being affirmed by this communal ritual, Dryden's final lines leave no room for doubt: *delenda est Carthago.*

In its valorization of the bravery and heroism of the English East India Company, Dryden's play denies the deflationary satire to which Milton had subjected Satan's venture and, by implication, the trading designs of the City and the Crown. In inciting the English people to undertake a war that, while launched in the name of trade grievances, was calculated to advance the twin causes of popery and arbitrary government, *Amboyna* not only does some service for a regime that Milton had fought so hard to resist, it employs dramatic spectacle in a way that could hardly be more different either from Milton's turn *away* from vision at the end of *Paradise Lost* or from his more general poetic practice of "entangling" readers in a complex of interpretive choices that forces them to think twice and thrice.[15] In this sense, *Amboyna* deploys some of the same theatrical techniques that distinguish Dryden's operatic version of *Paradise Lost* (his next work for the stage) from Milton's poem.

In its sympathy with a native Amboyner, however, Dryden's play finds common ground with *Paradise Lost,* for Ysibanda is imagined as a paradise despoiled and Towerson as a "fiery Cherub" placed by Heaven "to guard this Paradice from any second Violation" (4.5.100–101). Buoyed by thoughts of profit, the Dutch Governor Harman Senior may be able to face the death of his own son with equanimity—"I consider, great advantages must with some loss be bought: as this rich Trade which I this day have purchas'd with his death" (5.1.2–4)—but the play is unwilling to accept the death of Ysibanda as a cost of doing business. Her brutal lesson is learned not just from the Dutch but from *"Europe"* (4.5.17).

It is the play's sense of loss at the death of Ysibanda, together with its attempt to model a contractual basis for the relations between England and the native peoples of its trading satellites—one that insists on consent and liking, even if it entails the same submission and indissoluble obligation that English sovereigns expected of their own subjects—that qualifies *Amboyna* as an attempt to register the costs and imagine the responsibilities of a trade empire.

Ironically, the practical lesson that some opposition politicians took away from the Third Anglo-Dutch War was quite the reverse of *Amboyna*'s message. "It is vain," said Sir William Coventry, "to think that the *European* trade can be maintained by us by a war. . . . What probability is there, if we beat the *Hollander,* that we shall get all trade?" The keys to commercial success in Europe were "industry," "parsimony," and "underselling." Campaigns of aggression should be reserved for "*Guinea,* or other barbarous countries."[16]

Toward the Treaty of Westminster

Public opinion may have already been shifting against the war by the time Dryden's play was performed.[17] The United Provinces no longer seemed threatening once Amsterdam and the Hague had been reduced to the necessity of flooding their own suburbs in order to stall the French army. When, in reaction to this reversal, an infuriated mob tore the de Witt brothers to pieces, they extracted another thorn from the side of English monarchists, who found Charles's nephew the Prince of Orange a more amenable leader. If the Netherlands began to seem less threatening, Louis XIV's designs began to seem more so. Reports that the French navy was avoiding engagements led some Englishmen to speculate that it might be in the French king's interest to let the world's two great navies destroy each other. The Prince of Orange encouraged such suspicions with a well-orchestrated propaganda campaign whose most famous pamphlet, *England's Appeal from the Private Cabal at Whitehall to the Great Council of the Nation, the Lords and Commons in Parliament Assembled* (March 1673), sought to drive a wedge between the Court and English people, the king and Parliament. Whether at home or abroad, popery and absolutist government were starting to seem like greater threats than Dutch commerce—especially when, after the passage of the anti-Catholic Test Act, both the duke of York and Lord Clifford resigned their offices rather than take Anglican communion. Sir William Coventry reflected changing opinion when he told Parliament that it was "strange that we and *Holland* should be divided by one, whose interest is destructive to us both."[18] By October 1673 there were few M.P.s prepared to defend an alliance with France that could be characterized as "destructive both to trade and religion."[19] Without the support of Parliament, Charles had to arrive at a separate

27. Gérard de Lairesse's *Allegory of the Prosperity of Amsterdam,* painted after the
Treaty of Westminster. Mercury crowns Lady Amsterdam with laurel as she
accepts tribute from the world. The overland trades and overseas commerce
are represented by the camel and by a woman wearing a maritime crown.
Amsterdams Historisch Museum.

peace with the United Provinces, which was concluded in the Treaty of
Westminster.

Both the English and the Dutch hailed the end of the Third Anglo-
Dutch War in allegorical paintings. Looking forward to the resumption
of normal trade, Gérard de Lairesse painted an *Allegory of the Prosperity of
Amsterdam* (fig. 27).[20] Lady Amsterdam's hand rests on the globe with all
the easy grace of one of van Dyck's aristocrats, but this is still the personification familiar to us from the west pediment of the Town Hall. Mercury
crowns her with a laurel wreath as the goods of the world are piled at her
feet: silks, porcelain, horn, shells, tobacco, teas. If she holds a cornucopia
of gold coins in her left hand, she also kicks another over with her right
foot in an emblem of the mutually enriching circle of trade. The painting

28. Antonio Verrio, *Sea Triumph of Charles II* (c. 1674). Originally placed in
the Second Privy Lodging Room at Whitehall. The Royal Collection © 2001,
Her Majesty Queen Elizabeth II.

thus refutes the claims of England's Anglican Royalists that Amsterdam
showed "an immoderate desire to engross the whole traffic of the universe" and affirms the view of men like Bethel that the "emulation and
example" of Dutch trade was a benefit to other nations too.

Working in a baroque idiom, the Catholic artist Antonio Verrio
painted *The Sea Triumph of Charles II* (fig. 28). The king occupies the place
once held by the personified Republic of England on the title page of the
Commonwealth's *Of Dominion, or Ownership of the Sea* (1652). But whereas
she was seated firmly on a rock, the sea chariot of Charles has a forward
and upward momentum: we behold the advent of a godlike king. While

John Evelyn might opine that "to pretend a *Universal Monarchy* without *Fleets,* was long since looked on, as a Politick *Chymæra,*" these instruments of empire are relegated to the background.[21] At the margin, American or West Indian *putti* hold what was, before Verrio repainted it, a scroll with the motto *regnat pacatum.* The words may mean that Charles rules a friendly or a peaceful realm, but the verb *pacare,* from which the neuter substantive *pacatum* is formed, often means to pacify or subdue with force: the moral ambiguities of England's imperial projects are never far to seek. Realizing, as we saw in Chapters Four and Five, that nothing says "empire of trade" like a map, Verrio replaced the motto with just that.

Peaceful Strife in Pope's *Windsor Forest*

Four decades, three monarchs, and a revolution divide *Amboyna* from *Windsor Forest,* but for all that, Pope's poem provides the natural terminus for Part Three of this study. For in revising and completing the draft of an earlier poem to mark the Peace of Utrecht, with which the Tory Party concluded England's long and costly involvement in the Wars of the Spanish Succession, Alexander Pope looked not only to *Coopers Hill,* as he suggests in his notes to *Windsor Forest* (1713), but to Dryden's *Annus Mirabilis,* a model that Pope does not acknowledge and that critics have therefore largely overlooked.[22] Pope ends *Windsor Forest* not as Denham ends *Coopers Hill* (with a meditation on the balance of power between sovereign and people) but as Dryden ends *Annus Mirabilis* (with a prophetic vision of commercial empire). By applying the terms of Dryden's opening description to London, Pope confirms the reversal that Dryden's poem had prophesied. London now occupies the position once enjoyed by Amsterdam:

> Thy Trees, fair *Windsor!* now shall leave their Woods,
> And half thy Forests rush into my Floods,
> Bear *Britain*'s Thunder, and her Cross display,
> To the bright Regions of the rising Day;
> Tempt Icy Seas, where scarce the Waters roll,
> Where clearer Flames glow round the frozen Pole;
> Or under Southern Skies exalt their Sails,
> Led by new Stars, and born by spicy Gales!
> For me the Balm shall bleed, and Amber flow,
> The Coral redden, and the Ruby glow,
> The Pearly Shell its lucid Globe infold,
> And *Phoebus* warm the ripening Ore to Gold.

(lines 385–96)

Dryden's opening indictment of the Dutch—

> For them alone the Heav'ns had kindly heat,
>   In Eastern Quarries ripening precious Dew;
> For them the *Idumæan* Balm did sweat,
>   And in hot *Ceilon* Spicy Forrests grew
>
> (*AM,* lines 9–12)

—becomes a triumphant prediction once placed in the mouth of the Thames: "For me the Balm shall bleed, and Amber flow." The world's natural processes—reddening, glowing, infolding, warming—now serve England. So too do the spicy gales that helped speed Dryden's ship of state and Milton's Satan.

Pope's conclusion returns to a theme sounded earlier in the poem's sylvan section:

> Let *India* boast her Plants, nor envy we
> The weeping Amber or the balmy Tree,
> While by our Oaks the precious Loads are born,
> And Realms commanded which those Trees adorn.
>
> (lines 29–32)

As Earl Wasserman notes, the "precious loads" borne by the English oaks may refer either to Charles II, who famously hid in an oak tree after the battle of Worcester, or to the foreign commodities carried by English ships.[23] The figure is just one instance of Pope's concern to associate "Peace and Plenty" not with Queen Anne only but with all the Stuarts (line 42). In anticipating a consequent improvement of trade with the return of a Stuart, Pope's personified Thames also recalls the figure of Thames who greeted Charles II at the naval and commercial arch in his entry of 1661.[24] In these ways, Pope's poem reunites the cause of the Stuarts with that of trade.

I say *reunites* because, as we have briefly seen, mismanagement of the Second Anglo-Dutch War, the Stop of the Exchequer in 1672, and the eventual suspicion that he did not really have the interests of merchants at heart in waging the Third Anglo-Dutch War had all damaged the reputation of the Stuart monarchy as a patron of trade late in Charles's reign.[25] While none of these actions had dissevered the partnership between the Stuarts and the Anglican Royalist merchants of the Africa and East India Companies, they had opened the way both for colonial interloping merchants and for old Rumpers like Slingsby Bethel to reemerge, as *Absalom and Achitophel* attests, in support of the Whigs during the Exclusion Crisis of 1678–81. Palpably influenced by the Rump's program through men like

Benjamin Worsley, who had become an economic advisor to the first earl of Shaftesbury and his secretary, John Locke, radical Whigs had resuscitated well-honed arguments about the compatibility of religious toleration, and the incompatibility of absolutism, with commercial growth.[26] The Whigs had won three successive elections in this later struggle for the hearts of merchants, but, unable to achieve anything through the House of Commons alone, they had been forced to bide their time until the Glorious Revolution of 1688. After the Revolution, the established trading interests represented by Sir Josiah Child and the East India Company—whose Toryism had been ensured when James II forced its Whiggish members to resign—had found their credibility so eroded by their previous support of the Stuarts that they had eventually been forced to allow themselves to be absorbed into the reconstituted and predominantly Whig East India Company that was formed in several stages between 1693 and 1709. This is how the cause of trade had been wrested from the Stuart monarchy by its Whig opponents before Pope sat down to write his poem.

For Tories disgruntled with William III's reign, the introduction of a Dutch king had meant the neglect of landed for commercial interests and the involvement of England in costly foreign wars. But Queen Anne and her Tory ministry were determined to represent the Peace of Utrecht not as a way of compensating the Tories' traditional base of support in the Country for its years of trial under William, but as a means of securing Britain's commercial future. In her parliamentary addresses of June 1712, the queen even took the extraordinary step of delivering a detailed report on the progress of the commercial treaty with France, saying that she had used her "utmost endeavors" to set the North American trade on a favorable footing.[27]

Thus, while *Windsor Forest* leaves little doubt of Pope's antipathy to William III—whom the poem associates with Nimrod, hunter of men, and William the Conqueror—it must also be seen as a more positive attempt to bolster support for the commercial treaty that Lords Oxford and Bolingbroke were just concluding when the poem appeared in print.[28] Against pamphlets like *Trade and Tor[y]ism Can Never Agree* (1713), which traced a deep antipathy to trade within Tory ranks all the way back to the Reformation, Pope sets his own historical account, which credits the Stuarts with generating England's peace and prosperity by reconciling its landed and commercial interests. As Maynard Mack asserts, the poem's catalog of rivers related to Windsor (lines 337–48) "shows them uniting their individual currents in the Thames, creating again a conspicuous image of a united commonwealth in which the waters of the Tory countryside contribute significantly, like its oaks, to the Whiggish City's global trade, on which the countryside in turn depends."[29] Pope may even have had the foresight to attempt to disarm the Whigs' predictable criticism that the advantages secured by the treaty were outnumbered by the grievances left unredressed, like French tariffs on woollens and restrictions on British access to French ports. In his note on the lines "The Time shall come, when free as Seas or Wind / Unbounded *Thames* shall flow for all Mankind" (lines 397–98), he expresses his hope that London may one day be turned into a free port, a policy first proposed by the Rump's Council of Trade and long since advocated by Whigs like Slingsby Bethel. He thus sets one traditional plank of the Whigs' platform that was less threatening to the peace against another, the Whigs' insistence that England take a firm line with France, even if that should entail raising tariffs or imposing an embargo on French products in response to France's prejudicial trade policies.

While in his closing vision Dryden had looked forward to a time when London "without a Fleet" might "vindicate her Trade" from all the world (*AM*, lines 1203–04), the analysis of the symbiosis of force and commerce that occupies the greater part of *Annus Mirabilis* could not but make such a hope seem escapist. In *Windsor Forest,* on the other hand, commerce emerges as a means of channeling the passions, as the last of a series of accommodations that replace war with hunting and hunting with trade: at the poem's conclusion, it is not men but balm that bleeds and coral that reddens. If empire demands sacrifice and tribute, commerce is a means of displacing much of the burden onto nature.[30] In the closing books of *Paradise Lost,* Milton had been in no mood to value such gradations, but for Pope they constitute a saving difference. Rather than retreat, like Dryden, from violence to an impossible peace, Pope initially posits what Wasserman calls "the peaceful war" and "well accorded strife" of foreign commerce as a natural emblem of *concordia discors.*[31]

Pope then rises to a high prophetic strain that recalls Isaiah's closing vision of the New Jerusalem, whither all the nations of the world will bring gold, silver, trees, and other tribute (Isa. 60–66). He thus casts London in the role of that great capital that might have been, had only Milton's Adam stood firm, and that will be at the end of time:

> Then Ships of uncouth Form shall stem the Tyde,
> And Feather'd People crowd my wealthy Side,
> And naked Youths and painted Chiefs admire
> Our Speech, our Colour, and our strange Attire!
> Oh stretch thy Reign, fair *Peace!* From Shore to Shore,

> Till Conquest cease, and Slav'ry be no more:
> Till the freed *Indians* in their native Groves
> Reap their own Fruits, and woo their Sable Loves,
> *Peru* once more a Race of Kings behold,
> And other *Mexico's* be roof'd with Gold.
> Exil'd by Thee from Earth to deepest Hell,
> In Brazen Bonds shall barb'rous *Discord* dwell;
> Gigantick *Pride,* pale *Terror,* gloomy *Care,*
> And mad *Ambition,* shall attend her there.
>
> (lines 403–16)

Whereas Adam's vision of the Top of Speculation had suggested that commerce might expand the sway of empire outward and in the process erase the very differences that promised to preserve some vestiges of Christian liberty, Pope imagines the inward attraction of an entrepôt as a force of peace that will promote the community of man even as it preserves the very differences celebrated by the image of Indians wondering at the strange attire of Englishmen—an allusion to an actual embassy of the Iroquois to London in 1710.[32] Since Pope was thoroughly familiar with Adam's vision on the Top of Speculation—and imitated it at length in Book 3 of *The Dunciad*—it is tempting to see the restoration of the Americas' pre-Columbian empires as an act of intertextual reparation.[33] Pope certainly seems to push beyond Dryden's model of a consensual and benign, if unequal and indissoluble, relationship between England and the native inhabitants of its trading satellites, for in Pope's vision, the natives are left to woo each other and reap their own fruits. The reference to *Indians* may denote the Indians of either hemisphere, whether Americans among their wooded groves or East Indians among their spicy groves. Critics have not missed the irony, here, of Pope's looking forward to an end of slavery with the Peace of Utrecht when one of the key provisions of the treaty gave England and the South Sea Company (in which Pope himself invested) the coveted *asiento,* a thirty-year monopoly on the slave trade to the Spanish Americas. Speculation in paradise had hardly come to an end.

It may be, however, that in its seeming self-division—hailing "*Britain's* Thunder" spread to the "bright Regions of the rising Day" even as it anticipates the reign of "fair *Peace*" (lines 387–88, 407)—the end of *Windsor Forest* is not simply an escape into messianism; it may also record a material change in the conduct of England's commercial empire. We have seen briefly that, in contrast to the early resistance of the English to investing in fortifications, a resistance remembered in *Amboyna's* restaging of events from 1623, the Rump and the restored monarchy encouraged a form of trade based on heavy fortifications like those of the Dutch. By the 1680s, Sir Josiah Child had determined that the East India Company must have a fort in every region in which the company had a settled trade. By the end of the century, the company would estimate its expenditures on its infrastructure at a million pounds.[34]

This tremendous investment in forts only a few years after *Amboyna* was performed is just one of many historical ironies, for while it is a sore point of England's colonial history that the East India Company used its position of strength to undermine the authority of local governments and, on occasion, to launch thinly disguised campaigns of plunder, it is perhaps less widely recognized that the strength of these English forts also made them havens from the internecine warfare of the subcontinent and the extortionist rule of some Indian governors. It was, indeed, the safety and freedom that British enclaves afforded the "merchants of all nations," including India, that promoted the growth of settlements in Madras, Bombay, Surat, and Karwar.[35] The company's directors realized as much. As they informed the council at Fort St. George in 1694, "It is undoubtedly our interest to make our garrisoned ports in India marts for nations, which will in a few years aggrandise our revenue, and with that our strength."[36] By providing protection from external military threats and enforcing contracts and property rights through a consistent application of law, the East India Company got into the business of government: its revenue stream depended increasingly on customs, levies, and taxes that it could hope to collect only by maintaining havens for merchandising that could attract traders from all nations, including those in which their forts were located.[37]

In their small way, these settlements proved that the outward projection of force and the inward pull of commercial opportunities, the spread of empire and the maintenance of difference celebrated in Pope's closing vision, were not as utterly incompatible as we might at first imagine. With their dependence on attracting foreign merchants and their consequent responsiveness to the requirements of potential settlers and traders—who could and did vote with their feet and ships—these enclaves bore an ironic resemblance to the "many Commonwealths under one sovrantie" that Milton had advocated for England on the eve of the Restoration. These were commonwealths, however, that subordinated "religion, libertie, honour, safetie, all concernments divine or human" to the dictates of the bottom line: their sole object was to keep up trading.[38] The increasing influence of economic forces and commercial values on the public sphere—so neatly exemplified by the East India Company's provision of government for a fee—did bring with it human liberties and opportunities of a sort, though they were altogether more narrow and secular than Milton could have wished. To a poet like Pope, who was weary of war and did not share Milton's conception of Christian liberty, they seemed like something to celebrate.

PART FOUR

THE MEANING OF WORK

Genesis 2:15 says that God placed Adam in the garden of Eden to dress it and keep it, for "God," says a gloss in the Geneva Bible, "would not haue man idle though as yet there was no neede to labour." "Behold," said the minister Joseph Hall in his *Contemplation* on the passage,

> that which was man's store-house was also his work-house. . . . If happinesse had consisted in doing nothing, man had not been employed; All his delights could not have made him happy in an idle life. Man therefore is no sooner made, then he is set to worke: neither greatnesse nor perfection can priviledge a folded hand; he must labour, because he was happy; how much more we, that we may be?[1]

For many commentators, even postlapserian labor was as much a mercy as a curse. To labor was not only to perform the godly duty enjoined by 2 Thessalonians 3:10 — "if any will not work, neither should he eat" — it was to feel and assert your own identity and agency. "The Lillies which spin not, and are yet so splendidly clad are not in this respect," wrote John Evelyn, "so happy as an Industrious and prudent man, because they have neither knowledge, or sense of their Being and Perfections."[2] One of the perfections that industrious men confirmed while they labored was their very status as freeborn Englishmen. For to be the proprietor of your own body, to exercise your industry and ingenuity as you saw fit, and to know that the product of your labors was your own — that was to enjoy the liberties of the realm.

But for some dissenters after the Restoration, the trial of working in a society in which "evil Governours or Rulers, covetous Merchants and Tradesmen," and "lazie, idle, and negligent Teachers" had brought all under "slavery and Thraldom" could be felt as a form of service in the "yoak of Temporal and Spiritual *Pharaohs,*" one that "wearied" the body with "almost intollerable labour" and barred the soul from "advantage or profit."[3] As lamentable as such personal hardship was, the relationship that monarchists and republicans alike perceived between economic vigor and political power, taxation and warfare, prosperity and governmental stability, presented an even more disturbing prospect. John Locke reported in 1660 that some of his countrymen feared that the king might prove "an Egyptian taskmaster" rather than "a Christian ruler" if he could exercise enough control over the labor of his subjects "and enforce us to make brick without straw to build monuments of his rigour and our slavery."[4] It was not enough, then, for a dissenter to make the effort of devotion and imagination required to experience drudgery as godly labor and labor as an intimation of the native liberty that was otherwise being denied him. He still had to consider the political consequences of his work.

In the following chapter, I read *Samson Agonistes* (1671) as a meditation on the consolations, obligations, and temptations of laboring under a hostile regime. We shall see that in pitting the languages and irreconcilable claims of scripture, the law, and mercantilism against one another, Milton's closet drama makes work into a tragic subject. In order to do so, it undermines the Restoration's politically inflected discourse of work, building, and production, which, flourishing after the Fire of London, looked to the world of goods for things beneath dispute and therefore suitable as the basis for a society otherwise riven by religious and political differences.

CHAPTER SEVEN

Idleness Had Been Worse

W hereas the Book of Judges says only that Samson was bound "with fetters of brass" and "did grind in the prison house" (16:20)—a brief episode in a hectic twenty-year career as a Judge of Israel—Milton's *Samson Agonistes* (1671) can brood on its hero's captivity because it begins with him defeated. In the tragedy's opening speech, Samson announces that his "task" is "servile toyl" enjoined "daily in the common Prison" (lines 5–6). "Eyeless in *Gaza* at the Mill with slaves," clothed in "slavish habit," addressed by the Public Officer of the Philistines as a "Slave enrol'd," he leads a life that has contracted to little more than "these rags, this grinding" (lines 41, 122, 1224, 415). To those around him—Manoa, the Chorus, Harapha of Gath, the Public Officer— his slavery caps a reversal of fortune that is more complete than could be one constituted by mere defeat, imprisonment, and blindness (lines 364– 72, 485–86, 708–09, 1092–93, 1392–95).

Like so much else about the tragedy, Samson's slavery seems to invite, even as it notoriously resists, interpretations informed by its Restoration context.[1] If, as some monarchists maintained, the Stuarts derived their right to rule from William the Bastard's conquest of England, since which time Englishmen had been made to bear the Norman Yoke, and if citizens subject to absolute monarchs were in fact "slaves," as Milton and his fellow republicans insisted in their prose tracts, then Samson, "in bonds under Philistian yoke," is, among other things, a figure of everyman after the Restoration (line 42).[2] Samson himself seems undecided whether his slavery is best understood as God's judgment passed on his sins (as the Old

Testament's logic of slavery would dictate), the natural consequence of his inward slavery to his passions (as the language of Stoicism and republican-ism would suggest), or the result of an impious commercial bargain struck between Dalila and the Philistines.[3] While defeated saints and republicans alike were ready to blame their sin and corruption for the failure of the Good Old Cause, they could also conceive of the Restoration as a bar-gain struck without their consent but committing them, for all that, to slavery. Preferring "bondage with ease" to "strenuous liberty" (line 271), their countrymen had chosen "a captain back for *Egypt*." Their choice could be represented as a sale in which they had traded "religion, libertie, honour, safetie, all concernments Divine or human" for their security be-cause the ability of free men to sell themselves and their progeny into slavery was the key contractual justification that jurists offered for abso-lutist monarchies — a justification that Milton had attempted to refute in his *Defence of the People of England* (1651).[4]

The parallels between Samson's slavery and contemporary experience do more than invite interpretations of the Restoration as a religious and political disaster, a "national" judgment that had destroyed a free Com-monwealth. They press us to consider what it means to labor under a hos-tile regime in "domestic slaverie."[5] In the first section of this chapter, I ask why Samson prefers to "drudge and earn [his] bread" rather than be released from servitude (line 573), why Manoa and the Chorus oppose his wish, and what Samson thinks it means to perform honest and lawful labor for those who have him in their civil power. I suggest that the drama poses these questions in the logically and ethically riven terms provided by scripture, the laws of nature and of nations, and political arithmetic. In the second section, I argue that it is not just the brooding middle of Milton's dramatic poem that is troubled by the moral and political con-sequences of labor but its catastrophe, which I read in dialogue with a different set of texts: the politically inflected poems and pamphlets that were spawned by the Fire of London and that celebrated the values of work, building, and production. If the first sections of *Samson Agonistes* riddle over the moral dilemma of laboring under a hostile regime and thus make work into a tragic subject, its catastrophe attacks, with all the iconoclastic violence of which Milton was capable, the proposition that, because the world of goods was all that Anglicans and dissenters, Royalists and republicans, held in common, it should become the basis of English society. Beyond yielding a fuller appreciation of the resonance that Sam-son's destruction of the Philistine theater must have had for contempo-rary readers, reading the end of the tragedy in the context of poems on the Fire of London should help us see, in the third section, why Milton refuses to reassure readers of a divine authority responsible for Samson's "rouzing motions" (line 1382) and instead thematizes the uncertainty and indecipherability of his own work.

Samson's Labor at the Mill

Although Harapha can claim with some scriptural justification that Samson's slavery should be understood as proof that God no longer "regards" or "owns" his appointed champion and has deserted him as "good for nothing else, no better service" than grinding at a mill among "Slaves and Asses," Samson nevertheless prefers to drudge rather than to be released from servitude because he is able to conceive of his forced labor not as a mere accident of war, or even as the mark of a permanent estrangement from his God, but as a penalty that fits his crime and that means something (lines 1157, 1163, 1162).[6] "Let me here," he says to his father as he resists Manoa's plans to ransom him, "As I deserve, pay on my punishment; / And expiate, if possible, my crime" (lines 488–90). Samson may feel, intuitively, that having like Adam surrendered to the temptation of a woman, he should be punished in a similar manner: now he too can eat bread only in the sweat of his face (Gen. 3:19). To the extent that his labor yields a lesson he can learn, however, it promises to be rehabilitative. Grinding "in Brazen Fetters under task / With this Heav'n-gifted strength . . . / Put to the labour of a Beast, debas't / Lower then bondslave" (lines 35–38) serves as an apposite reminder not only of the thralldom to which he submitted himself in his marriage to Dalila — "servil mind / Rewarded well with servil punishment!" (lines 412–13) — but of the poor use he made of his heaven-gifted strength even when he was free. In return for having figuratively buried his talent like the wicked and slothful servant of Matthew 25:14–30, Samson now finds that he and his locks, his "capital secret" (line 394), are more literally immured in a dark prison.[7] Through his labor, he is offered the equivalent of a true sight of sin, but the lesson comes in the form of its bodily reenactment: straining blindly as he walks in circles about the mill of the Philistines, Samson rehearses his missteps.

If Samson's labor is both the consequence of, and a gloss on, his prior failures to keep faith, it nevertheless implies a continuing relationship with his lord and judge. Just as in Exodus Moses uses the same word to refer to the Israelites' slavery in Egypt and, after their deliverance, to their bondage to Yahweh (2:23; 6:6, 9; 13:3, 4), *Samson Agonistes* uses the words *service* and *servitude* to suggest that the labor that Samson is ostensibly performing for the Philistines may instead be intended for another master,

Yahweh, "Whose ear is ever open; and his eye / Gracious to re-admit the suppliant" (lines 1172–73). With its distinction between "day labour" and "man's work" (on the one hand) and the broader notion of service that may be performed even by those who merely stand and wait (on the other), Milton's nineteenth sonnet should alert us to the possibility that Samson has too quickly leapt to the conclusion that the service he owes Yahweh is to slave at the mill (lines 7, 10). But however misguided that conclusion may be, Samson's insistence on putting his "capital secret" to use now, *despite* being buried in prison, seems to stem from a determination *not* to become the servant who is cast into outer darkness for failing to put his talents to use. By working at the mill, Samson may also mean to signal his acceptance of providence, for in the writings of early Protestants like William Tyndale, to do "whatsoever cometh into thy hands . . . as time, place, and occasion giveth, and as God hath put thee in degree, high or low" is an important gesture of submission to the will of God.[8]

Samson's desire to serve his punishment and submit to providence cannot, however, account for the positive revulsion he feels at the prospect of sitting "idle on the houshold hearth" (line 566). He dreads becoming

> A burdenous drone; to visitants a gaze,
> Or pitied object, these redundant locks
> Robustious to no purpose clustring down,
> Vain monument of strength; till length of years
> And sedentary numness craze my limbs
> To a contemptible old age obscure.
>
> (lines 567–72)

That Genesis identifies labor as a curse did not prevent Milton or his contemporaries from imagining that enforced idleness might be a more dreadful punishment. In *Paradise Lost,* the fallen Adam observes,

> On mee the Curse aslope
> Glanc'd on the ground, with labour I must earne
> My bread; what harm? Idleness had bin worse;
> My labour will sustain me.
>
> (9/10.1053–56)

Milton's readers have noticed that if Samson were to remain idle on the hearth, he would occupy a position normally filled by women.[9] He would be defined in terms of his own passivity and the gaze of others. He would not be permitted to define himself through the dialogue with the world that is labor. That his choice may be conceived in such gendered terms is suggested by John Dryden's version of the lines we have just considered. In *The State of Innocence* (1674), Raphael announces that Adam's lot will be to labor and to "know no plenty, but through painful sweat" (5.4.145), while Eve's will be to "pay obedience to her lawful Lord," to desire "more of love than man can give," and (by implication) *not* to labor (5.4.147–49). "Heav'n is all mercy," answers Adam, "labor I would chuse" when faced with these alternatives (5.4.150). Dryden's Adam, like Milton's, seem to think that labor will "sustain" him not only physically but spiritually, for it is man's "daily work of body or mind," as Milton's unfallen Adam avers, that "declares his Dignitie" (*PL* 4.618–19). I would suggest, conversely, that the "sedentary numbness" that Samson fears is not just a physical degeneration precipitated by inactivity but a debilitated sense of self, an insensate loss of identity. What is true of anyone—that his sense of self-hood depends on activity—must be that much more true of Samson. For it is only by straining at the mill that he can be assured that the strength "summ'd" in his hair, the token of his calling and the secret of his identity, has returned.

Far from affording a purely subjective or symbolic sense of worth, however, Samson's labor also allows him to rate his value as it would be "esteemed by others," to imagine the price that, in Thomas Hobbes's terms, "would be given for the use of his power":[10]

> Much more affliction than already felt
> They cannot well impose, nor I sustain;
> If they intend advantage of my labours
> The work of many hands, which earns my keeping
> With no small profit daily to my owners.
>
> (lines 1257–61)

By the late seventeenth century, the demand for hands to work the labor-intensive crops of the New World, together with the flexible substitution of free, indentured, and slave hands for one another in the Atlantic labor market, must surely have sharpened the awareness of Englishmen that bodies were assets, no matter who held property in them, and that the force they could muster was a key factor of production.[11] One of Samuel Hartlib's papers makes the point neatly: after comparing wind, water, beasts, and men as means of powering engines, it observes that because "in the plantations horses etc are dearer, & shorter lived then Negroes, & more troublesome and chargeable to keep than Negroes," a mill that would permit four to six slaves to do the work of four horses or eight cattle would be "a noble usefull designe, particularly for sugar workes"; the paper's author claims to have invented such an engine and tested it with men.[12] The unwilling participant in a similar impromptu experiment, Samson recognizes his peculiar productive capacity when he measures his exertions against those of his fellow slaves and asses. He seems to realize, at least intuitively, that, thanks to his "capital secret," his body is a valuable asset that yields a profit and requires investment: his complaint over the failure of the Philistines to maintain him properly is not just a way of voicing his grievances but a way of attesting to the value of his body, his secret capital. Thus the very work that threatens to diminish Samson—"I thought / Gyves and the Mill had tam'd thee," exclaims Harapha (lines 1092–93)—simultaneously supplies the terms in which he learns to rate himself highly once again.

Should we assume that Manoa, who is so solicitous of his son's well being in other ways, is merely insensible to the consolations of labor when he laments Samson's "pains and slaveries, worse then death inflicted" (line 485)? His words are a direct contradiction of the logic of slavery as it was explicated by early modern jurists and philosophers like Hugo Grotius, Hobbes, and Samuel Pufendorf. According to the law of nations governing war, a victor had the right to kill the vanquished. If, upon being offered such an alternative by his captor, a prisoner consented to surrender his liberty and his labor in return for the preservation of his life, he expressed his judgment that slavery was *not* worse than death. By not resisting the will of his master and thus drawing death upon himself, a slave regularly reaffirmed that the exchange of his labor for his maintenance and his life was a bargain he was prepared to make.[13]

The drama invites us to understand Samson's slavery in these terms when Harapha calls Samson "a Man condemn'd, a Slave enrol'd, / Due by the Law to capital punishment" (lines 1224–25). Samson is not scheduled for execution. Neither he nor his father ever evinces the least anxiety that he will die of anything but overwork or neglect. Harapha's statement is rather meant to underline the legal basis of Samson's slavery and to remind him, cruelly, of his own consent to the arrangement. "A man condemned as a rebel and an enemy of war, due by the law to capital punishment," Harapha is saying, "you willingly enrolled as a slave." While we might expect Samson to deny any part in his own enslavement, he confirms Harapha's point of view by insisting on the saving remnant of choice that is still his: "Commands are no constraints," he says to the Chorus, waiving their attempts to limit his responsibility for his own actions, "If I obey them, / I do it freely" (lines 1372–73). Samson is as willing as Hobbes to reduce the usual standard by which an agreement may be said to be freely made because only by acknowledging his complicity in his own enslavement can he retain a private sense of agency.[14]

If Samson's conduct proves that *he,* thus far, has not judged the "hard-ship of his Slavery" to "out-weigh the value of his life," however little store he may set in that life, his "pains and slaveries" may nevertheless be worse than his death from the perspective of his nation, which is now subject to a regime sustained partly by his strength.[15] When we consider that Samson is willing to submit himself to the will of heaven as long as doing so requires the labor of a beast, it is remarkable to hear him choos-ing between serving his nation and the work of heaven through inactivity and, alternatively, working at the mill of the Philistines until death—and opting for the latter without regard to the consequences of his choice. His decision amounts to saying, "If serving requires passivity, I will *not* serve":

> To what can I be useful, wherein serve
> My Nation, and the work from Heav'n impos'd,
> But to sit idle on the houshold hearth,
> A burdenous drone.
>
>   *   *   *
>
> Here rather let me drudge and earn my bread,
> Till vermin or the draff of servil food
> Consume me, and oft-invocated death
> Hast'n the welcom end of all my pains.
>
>   (lines 564–67, 573–76)

Manoa responds that Samson's choice is not whether to serve or not to serve but *whom* to serve:

> Wilt thou then serve the *Philistines* with that gift
> Which was expresly giv'n thee to annoy them?
> Better at home lie bed-rid, not only idle,
> Inglorious, unimploy'd, with age out-worn.
>
>   (lines 577–80)

By the Restoration, it was not possible to produce wealth without think-ing about the political consequences of such economic activity, for the relationship between a nation's wealth and its power to wage war abroad, not to mention between a regime's ability to levy funds and its capacity to rule its own subjects, was widely acknowledged. Sir William Petty was so acutely alive to the productive potential of subjects that he insisted on figuring populations into his accounts of national assets; and he eventually did so, in one case, by valuing free citizens at the market price for African slaves.[16] Categorizing subjects as assets led not only to speculations about the sorts of social policies and domestic arrangements that would promote higher birth rates but to proposals for harnessing the productive capacity of compulsory labor.[17] For instance, Petty recommended that criminals be condemned to slavery rather than death, "so as being slaves they may be forced to as much labour, and as cheap fare, as nature will endure, and thereby become as two men added to the Commonwealth, and not one taken away from it." Indeed, such penalties did not have to be reserved for thieves alone, Petty argued, for there was no religious difference, "be it never so small," that was perfectly "consistent with that unity and peace as could be wisht," nor any that was so great that it could not be "muzzled from doing much harm in the State" by keeping any religious dissenter "as a beast," the "proprietor of nothing," and "withall kept to extream bodily labour" for the sake of the "profit" he would yield "to the State."[18] The acts that Parliament passed to suppress Quakers (1662) and Conventicles (1664, 1670) seem to be predicated on a theory like Petty's. They provide for a sequence of punishments beginning with fines and the confiscation of property, graduating (in the case of Quakers) to "hard labour" in the "Common Gaol or House of Correction," and culminating, for repeat offenders, in transportation "to any of his Majesty's Plantations beyond the Seas"—presumably, though the acts are not specific on the point, as indentured servants.[19]

Samson Agonistes never lets us forget that its hero is working at the "common work-house" or "publick Mill" of the Philistines, that his "labours" are "the work of many hands," and that, as Samson himself observes, they bring "no small profit daily" to the enemies of his nation (argument, lines 1327, 1393, 1260–61). The Philistines celebrate the fact when they bring him to the feast day of Dagon "as a public servant . . . , / In thir state Livery clad" (lines 1615–16). While their ability to turn Samson's labors to their advantage is particularly stark, Petty's awareness that the state had many ways, including discriminatory mulcts and taxes, of extracting profits from dissenters, of charging different prices for the privilege of holding different beliefs, meant that dissenters could readily find themselves in the position of Samson—faced with recusing themselves from work or seeing their labors turned to the advantage of the Philistines.

Rather than respond to his son's choice compassionately as the despairing utterance of a man whose genial spirits have drooped, whose hope is lost, and whose nature is weary of itself (lines 594–95), Manoa characteristically suspects that his son is being driven by impulsive and selfish desires, not by any thought of how he might begin delivering his people. His opposition to Samson's desire to keep drudging and earning his bread, together with a vein of imagery that asks us to compare Samson's copulation with Dalila with his exertions at the mill, aligns the son's decision to labor with his earlier, suspect marriage choices, of which Manoa never approved.[20] This has the effect of setting Samson's desire to work on a level with his sexual tastes, guided by motions whose origins may be divine or may be all too human and fallible. The fact that his remaining at the mill, like his first marriage, presents him with an opportunity to annoy his enemies—for he would presumably not have been brought into the theater if he had agreed to go home with Dalila or Manoa—only encourages us to look for the motives of both work and marriage in the wellsprings of desire. The point bears emphasis because John Guillory's influential interpretation of the drama as a contest between "the poem's two fathers, Yahweh and Manoa," with the Hebrew God demanding a "great work" and the earthly father requiring "labor in a calling," has had the effect of distracting our attention from the fact that when Samson willingly labors at the mill, he is *opposing* the authority of his father, the voice of the poem's (earthly) conscience.[21]

It is typical of the drama's dialogue that Samson does not really respond to his father's charge that he is serving the Philistines with his gift. But he seems to think about it. For by the time the Chorus levels a similar charge, he is ready with a moral justification for his labor, one that he still feels compelled to offer, if we may judge from his oblique threat to the Public Officer (line 1347), even *after* he has had a premonition that "This day will be remarkable in my life / By some great act, or of my days the last" (lines 1388–89). That Samson is still eager to justify his labor even though he must suspect that the whole debate is shortly to become moot suggests just how much psychic energy both he and the drama have invested in the question. To the Chorus's anticipation of what "message more imperious" Samson's refusal to entertain the Philistines might bring, Samson offers a sharp retort that the Chorus, for its part, is unwilling to accept untested (line 1352):

> *Sam.* Shall I abuse this Consecrated gift
>   Of strength, again returning with my hair
>   After my great transgression, so requite
>   Favour renew'd, and add a greater sin
>   By prostituting holy things to Idols;
>   A *Nazarite* in place abominable
>   Vaunting my strength in honour to thir *Dagon?*
>   Besides, how vile, contemptible, ridiculous,
>   What act more execrably unclean, prophane?
> *Chor.* Yet with this strength thou serv'st the *Philistines,*
>   Idolatrous, uncircumcis'd, unclean.

> *Sam.* Not in thir Idol-worship, but by labour
> Honest and lawful to deserve my food
> Of those who have me in thir civil power.
>
> (lines 1354–67)

The Chorus appears ready to excuse Samson alike for his participation in the Feast of Dagon and for his work—"Where the heart joins not, outward acts defile not" (line 1368)—but Samson rejoins that the sentence holds only "where outward force constrains," a condition met by neither his contemplated entry into the theater of the Philistines nor his work, which he insists is "labour / Honest and lawful to deserve my food / Of those who have me in thir civil power."

We have already seen that Samson may wish to labor in order to regain a sense of his "being and perfections." With scant opportunity for advancement at Court or in the established Church, denied the freedom to express their political and religious identities as members of a larger national community, many dissenters after the Restoration found that they, like Samson, could assert their personalities and exert their industry *only* through labor. The 1661 Corporation Act might bar dissenters from holding public office, ruled Lord Chief Justice Baron Hales in the Exchequer chamber, but it could not be extended to purge London's livery companies and inferior corporations of dissenters.[22] Dissenters' experience of self-determination in the economic realm, coupled with an assurance of being free in Christ, must have provided them with a sense of enfranchisement and liberty that compensated, in some measure, for their limited political and religious rights and privileges. In Chapter One, we saw that the conceptual and legal relationship between work and liberty was so profound that it was two monopoly cases in which the freedom to work had been at stake that supplied Sir Edward Coke with his gloss on the meaning of the word *libertates* in the Magna Carta.[23] Given the psychological cost of *foregoing* work, it is little wonder that Samson wishes to pronounce his labor honest and lawful.

He does so, first, by drawing a distinction between the spheres of civil power and religious belief—a distinction that Milton himself had advocated in his *Treatise of Civil Power* (1659) but one that could not be maintained, as Petty's proposals for setting dissenters to work for the state suggest, unless the state was itself willing to observe it—and, second, by evading any moral reckoning for the profits he is generating by invoking the legal terms in which Milton's contemporaries defined the respective obligations of master and slave. According to jurists like Grotius and Pufendorf, a master is obliged to provide food and keep for slaves because free men would not voluntarily enter a perpetual state of servitude on any other understanding and because it seems reasonable to extend the same consideration even to slaves who have been taken by force. The very notion that a man would voluntarily enter a state of perpetual servitude presupposes, according to Pufendorf, that he judges the worth of his labor to be worth the cost of the food, lodging, and security that a master can provide him—and no more. Pufendorf is even more explicit about this rule of commensurability when he says that the child of a slave may be considered a slave because, despite the fact that the child has entered slavery through "no fault" of his own, his "subsequent services" to the master will not "much exceed" the cost of maintaining him as a child. According to such formulations, the slave literally labors for his own bread, and his labor is worth little more.[24] We may remember that Samson asks specifically to be left to "earn my bread" (line 573) or "deserve my food / Of those who have me in thir civil power" (line 1366–67). In speaking to the Chorus, he conveniently omits any mention of the residual profits that he is earning for the Philistines.

Unlike Pufendorf, Roman law certainly assumes that a slave will generate profits for his master. By arguing that the service that a slave renders may exceed what can reasonably be expected of a slave—and thus become a benefit conferred on, rather than the service owed to, a master—Seneca even provides the terms of analysis that might permit Samson to see his work of *many* hands not as service owed but as a benefit *conferred* on his enemies.[25] But Samson prefers to pretend that his labor is commensurate with the Philistines' bread: his desire to labor is so strong, in other words, that is he willing to invoke the very fictions about slavery that natural law theorists had employed in order to make the institution seem conformable to reason and to a system of law that could have developed out of a state of nature in which all men were created free.

Samson's sense that he must "deserve" his food of those who have him in their civil power recalls no other moment in Milton's works so much as Eve's troubling assertion that she must divide her labors from Adam's lest "th'hour of Supper [come] unearn'd" (*PL* 8/9.214, 225). We sense that in both cases a desire for self-reliance and self-assertion underlies the appeal to moral duty, a desire that is so deep-seated that both Eve and Samson might be unable fully to articulate or even to recognize it. That both appeals are disingenuous only makes them seem more urgent. Royalist poets like Denham express a similar interest in people who work even when they do not need to, but they tend to look to the hunger of the imagination, the elasticity of the consumer's desires, for their answers.[26] *Paradise Lost* and *Samson Agonistes* recognize that work may be motivated by other and deeper desires than the desire to have, and both texts see that such desires may assume the guise of moral imperatives. They even see that moral injunctions, once internalized, may manifest themselves as subrational drives that cannot be neatly distinguished from desires.[27] With its triad of toil, delight, and reason—"For not to irksom toile, but to delight / He made us, and delight to Reason joyn'd" (*PL* 8/9.242–43)—Adam's response to Eve seeks to prevent the Protestant work *ethic* from degenerating into a *compulsion* to labor. *Samson Agonistes,* in contrast, refuses us any such orienting voice. Like the conversation between Samson and Manoa, the discussion between Samson and the Chorus is left unresolved.

But I do not think we are intended to accept unquestioningly Samson's claim that his labor for the Philistines is unproblematic because working at a mill is, considered narrowly, an "honest and lawful" employment. If Samson's experience has taught him anything, it should be that he lives in a world in which it is impossible to make distinctions between religious, political, and economic acts and obligations. After all, when he tied fire-brands to the tails of foxes for personal and political ends, he destroyed his enemies' means of subsistence, and it was in order to prevent a reprisal in kind that the men of Judah surrounded him: "Meanwhile the men of *Judah* to prevent / The harass of thir Land, beset me round" (lines 256–57). Samson implies that his people decided that by conducting a personal campaign of resistance against insurmountable odds, he was erecting an obstacle to their material well-being: they were willing to put a price on their God or their liberty, and when Samson exceeded it, they handed him over to the enemy. Samson also believes that Dalila betrayed him in the name of gold (lines 829–31), and despite her protests to the contrary (lines 849–50), he will credit no other explanation (lines 958–59). Just as *Samson Agonistes* pits the conflicting moral claims of marriage, nation, and faith against one another, it also dramatizes this less widely recognized contest between varieties of human flourishing: religious, political, and economic. Our sense of the terrible cost of that conflict, particularly as it is waged in the psyche of Samson, must generate much of the drama's tragic force, its sense of unavoidable and terrible waste. But that does not mean that the drama endorses Samson's refusal to recognize that he, like his wife and countrymen, is implicitly and unavoidably attaching a price to competing goods when he makes any choice like the choice to labor at the mill.

While potentially tragic, the coinvolvement of economic, political, and religious actions also holds out a hope of which Samson seems but dimly aware until he draws death on himself. We have seen that if the king could exert sufficient control over the economic and religious lives of dissenters, he might "bring this island to the condition of a galley, where the greater part shall be reduced to the condition of slaves, be forced by blows to row the vessel, but share in none of the lading, nor have any privilege or protection."[28] But it was not clear that the king *would* be able to assert such control, and if he could not, then the labor of dissenters would only strengthen their position in the nation and make them better able to check the absolutist ambitions of a monarch. For any part of the body politic that controls enough economic assets will eventually, as James Harrington understood, make itself heard in political terms.[29] By representing Samson's strength as an attribute of his body, not simply a conduit of God's power, *Samson Agonistes* may finally suggest that its hero's labors at the mill are not, in the end, counterproductive, for whatever profits they yield to the Philistines in the short term are offset by the strength Samson recovers with exercise. "Let divines preach duty as long as they will," said Locke, in counseling Anglican Royalists *not* to treat dissenters like slaves, "'twas never known that men lay down quietly under the oppression and submitted their backs to the blows of others, when they thought they had strength enough to defend themselves."[30]

A Time to Break Down, and a Time to Build Up

We might say that *Samson Agonistes* leaves behind the ethical conundrums of laboring for a hostile regime when Samson enters the theater of the Philistines. If they are never resolved, neither do they seem to matter once the drama shifts from its deliberative to its apocalyptic register. I wish to suggest, however, that even with its brutal conclusion the drama engages, albeit in a new mode, the issues we have been examining. Samson's great act is, as Guillory has insisted, "a deviant *labor of destruction*" that may be viewed as the narrative antithesis of "a specific economic order."[31] But the order that Samson's gesture overturns is not, as Guillory suggests, "the normative vocational narrative of the bourgeois Protestant" so much as an ideology of productivity that was proving an effective means for Anglican Royalists and their allies in the City to counter the iconoclastic rhetoric of their opponents, to consolidate the position of the restored monarchy, and to steer public discourse away from divisive issues of political or church organization toward an ideal of prosperity and productivity that promised to provide a new ground for social consensus.

We examined the genesis of this ideology in Chapters Two, Three, and Four, where we saw how Royalists eventually succeeded in making an acceptance of old political and religious forms seem like a necessary precondition for the resumption of regular commercial activity. Writing in

the midst of a trade depression, the panegyrists of 1660 had naturally celebrated the support, guidance, and protection that a king would be able to
provide England's commercial ventures abroad. It was perhaps in order
to make the same point that the Royal Exchange was selected as the first
site after the Restoration in which to erect statues of Charles II and his
"twice martyred" father, who had been killed not only "in body" but "in
effigy" when Parliament destroyed his statue in the Exchange in 1649.[32]
Such efforts to link the king with the cause of trade did not go untested.
Between 1662 and 1666, opponents of the Crown's system of charters and
monopolies renewed their attacks on such companies as the Merchant Adventurers and the Canary Company.[33] Pamphlets that were presumably
distributed by dissenters blamed the religious intolerance of the Conventicles Act for a widely perceived decay of trade.[34] And as England's initial
naval victories in the Second Anglo-Dutch War were followed by defeats
that culminated in the destruction of the English fleet at Chatham in June
1667, the competence and fiscal responsibility of the government came
under withering scrutiny.

It was essential, therefore, that the king reaffirm the value of London's
trade to the Crown and the nation, and he did so in part by giving top
priority to the rebuilding of the Exchange, which had been destroyed in
the Fire of London in September 1666. In October 1667 he set the first
stone of the first pillar of the new building, while his brother set the first
stone of the pillar opposite. Traders were admitted into the courtyard in
1669, and the shopkeepers returned in 1671.[35] The main entrance of the
second Royal Exchange was flanked by impressive Corinthian pillars and
statues of Charles I and Charles II dressed *all'antica,* the father represented
as a martyred shepherd, the son as an active figure possessing the qualities at once of commander and of architect (see figs. 29–30).[36] For their
part, the poets of the Fire of London found that the king's central role in
the economic life of the nation could be figured most effectively now by
his oversight of the city's—and in particular the Exchange's—reconstruction, an undertaking that would place London in a position once again to
become a bank of world trade. It is against this discursive program that I
propose to set Samson's toppling of the theater of the Philistines.

Of course, this program would not have been effective had its celebration of wealth and social concord not had broad appeal. The Restoration regime's program of naval and commercial expansionism was the
creation not only of a set of Anglican-Royalist courtiers and merchants
who, as Steven Pincus has maintained, acknowledged the nation's interest
in commerce in part so that they might use the claims of trade to advance their own political and religious vision;[37] it was the creation, too,

29. Robert White's engraving of the Cornhill facade of the second Royal Exchange (1671). Between the pillars that flank the entrance may be seen statues of Charles I (left) and Charles II (right). Guildhall Library, Corporation of London.

of former Commonwealthmen and Cromwellians like Benjamin Worsley, Sir George Downing, and Baron Ashley, none of whom was an unthinking or unqualified supporter of Charles II. Indeed, the very popularity of wealth and concord as societal objectives led others, and particularly dissenters, to argue that these good things could be attained only by accepting an entirely different list of policy prescriptions: the restraint of arbitrary power, security of property, freedom from arrest, the opening of monopolized trades, the establishment of free ports, and the extension of religious toleration. The fact that the City could be rebuilt only by throwing open London's building trades to all artificers, laborers, and workmen, whether or not they were freemen of the City, and that many citizens chose to rebuild outside the reach of the Corporation and guilds, with their legal monopolies, must have lent some support to these views. Just to repopulate the square mile of the City, the Corporation had to suspend the prosecution of resident foreigners and extend the freedom

30. John Bushnell's statues of Charles I (*left*) and Charles II (*right*) for the Corn-hill facade of the second Royal Exchange (in situ by 1671). Corporation of London. Photo Courtauld Institute, London.

of the City gratis to anyone who offered to take up permanent residence in a newly built house or shop.[38] Presumably it was because the Council of Trade provided a forum in which these and even more liberal policies could be aired that the duke of York found himself out of humor with it and such members of it as Baron Ashley (later first earl of Shaftesbury).[39] Such "opposition" views were not confined to the halls of power, for they were also circulated in print by men like Slingsby Bethel, Carew Reynel, and Roger Coke.[40] When I refer to the ideology running through much of the poetry on the Fire of London as Royalist, then, I mean neither that writers whose chief priority was trade were inevitably monarchist, nor that Anglican Royalists were the only ones who argued that their po-litical and religious policies must be enacted for the sake of the nation's prosperity. What I do wish to claim is that the greatest part of the verse written on the Fire of London seeks to yoke the commercial future of London to the king and that even if a yoke may be said to chafe its fellows equally, the most important effect of this discursive program—at least in the short term—was to consolidate the position of monarchy in the wake of the Fire of London and the Second Anglo-Dutch War.

Whereas the need to align the monarchy with the cause of trade had forced courtly poets to invent new terms of praise for the king in 1660, the poets of the Fire of London could draw more unproblematically on the verse of Caroline poets like Sir William Davenant and Edmund Waller, who, on the eve of the first Civil War, had made of London's newly restored and erected buildings emblems of the art, prosperity, and political order that the impending strife threatened to destroy.[41] Like the most distinguished model from which they took their cue, Waller's *Upon His Majesties Repairing of Pauls* (1638?), many poems on the Fire find in the labor of rebuilding an instance of, and a metaphor for, the Crown's power to create, government's ability to unite subjects in a great and harmonious design, and the manifest goodness of the flourishing works of peace.[42] According to the logic of these poems, the requirements of the nation can be summed up in the uncontroversial need to *rebuild,* an endeavor that will only be hindered by undue consideration of *what* is being built. Englishmen had already shown themselves incapable of conceiving of any ideal city or New Jerusalem that could win broad assent. Better, then, to focus on the bricks and mortar of London—on the visible and material world shared by sects otherwise divided by politics or religion, a world of goods and commodities so basic as to seem almost beneath dispute. Having thus lowered their sights, the most ambitious of these poems draw more exalted conclusions: they assert that, because the Crown is overseeing the rebuilding of London, *all* its interventions in English society must be equally constructive and that, furthermore, all contributions to the public good, all real work, may be figured as building.

The fact that the Revolution and Restoration had already been dramatized in the Royal Exchange with the destruction and replacement of Charles I's statue may have encouraged some poets to identify the flames that consumed London with the Good Old Cause and thus to use the Great Fire as an occasion to affirm their conviction that the English Revolution had simply destroyed what the monarchy had built before, and rebuilt after, it. The "rebellious" fire becomes "a *Parliament* of flames" in John Crouch's verse as it destroys the statues of England's kings in the Royal Exchange, while in Dryden's, it is like "some dire Usurper Heav'n provides, / To scourge his Country with a lawless sway."[43] Much as Royalists greeted Charles II in 1660 as the phoenix son of his martyred father, poems on the Great Fire anticipate London's "restoration" by describing her (in Dryden's words) as "a *Phœnix* in her ashes, and, as far as Humanity can approach, a great Emblem of the suffering Deity."[44] As "new deifi'd she from her fires does rise," London is "another *PHÆNIX*"; a "*Phœnix* now" with "new-imped Wings" singing "the New City's *Resurrection*"; a "*Phœnix* like" city rising "out of her Ashes, up into the Skies"; "the Phœnix putting off old fate," who "propagates her self, her Midwife womb / Being at once her *Cradle,* and her *Tomb*"; or "the *Bird* that to *himself* is *Heir.*"[45] Conveniently overlooking the phoenix's ability to beget itself, another poem even avers that London's "*Ashes*" can be "hatch'd" only by "a kind *Monarch*'s breath."[46] The image of the phoenix may be applied to the entire city or to individual buildings like St. Paul's, but it is the Royal Exchange that invites the comparison most often. For the spices stored in the basement of the Exchange meant that the building (together with all the monarchs of England whose statues occupied niches in the interior courtyard) really was consumed like the mythical bird in her "spicy nest."[47] In anticipating the reconstruction of the Royal Exchange and its gallery of kings, poems on the Great Fire simultaneously ratify the Restoration and identify the recreation of the metropolis with the rebuilding of the monarchy.

Against the fire's power "to ruinate, / To spoil, consume, destroy, depopulate," many of these poems set the care, labor, or industry of Charles II. One, for instance, praises "The active Prudence, and industrious Cares, / Th'uncessant Labors, and the fervent Pray'rs" of the king.[48] Charles's ability to oversee the reconstruction of London is supposed to be just one specific manifestation of his more general powers as an architect and builder, powers that are also apparent in his political and religious designs. For this reason, praise of the City-building Bill naturally invites an endorsement of the sanctions against religious dissent imposed by the Clarendon Code:

> An *Act;* of *Acts,* which plainly doth impart
> *Conformity* of *Building,* and of *Heart.*[49]

If some poems on the Great Fire seem eager to take up a theme that should be uncontroversial, a number of them find that their subject points to the lesson that there can be no place for dissent in the great work of rebuilding. To build is to do what "*God* commands"; therefore Englishmen must follow the example of "His *Vice-roy,* our dread *Sov'raigne,*" who has already laid "the first Stone of this great structure"—a structure that incorporates, by this time, a good deal more than mere bricks and mortar.[50]

I would like to make the simple observation that, as surely as it appalls revisionist critics, Samson's destruction of the theater of the Philistines would have disturbed many readers in 1671, conditioned by this contemporary strain of verse, with its depiction of ruination as a pure misfortune and building as an unambiguous good. Of course, the frequency with which revolutionaries not only identified themselves with the Israelites and their opponents with the Philistines but claimed Samson as a hero of the Good Old Cause and the Army would have made it natural for readers to suspect that the target of Samson's attack was not confined to Philistea.[51] But I would emphasize that in paying scant attention to Samson's exploits as a warrior and focusing almost exclusively on his destruction of the theater, Milton is reviving a strain of revolutionary discourse that saw in the image of toppling not a call for bloodshed—although it might be prepared to accept carnage as the price of change—so much as an instigation to reform institutions and customs radically.[52] This is the spirit in which the young Milton avers, "Wee shall not doubt to batter, and throw down your *Nebuchadnezzars* Image and crumble it like the chaffe of the Summer threshing floores"; in which Sir Cheney Culpeper anticipates that with the destruction of the monopolies oppressing the commonwealth, Babylon will "tumble, tumble, tumble"; in which the Anabaptist William Goffe explains to the Army, "Now the work of the Spirit is, that we pull down all works [that are not] of the Spirit whatsoever"; and in which John Owen recommends the example of Samson to the Commonwealth Parliament as an exhortation to reform: "Now what are the Pillars of that fatall building? are they not the powers of the world as presently stated and framed?"[53] The vast *difference* between the conception of work that underlies such rhetoric of reform and that which underlies the poetry of the Great Fire, with its simple equation of work with building and building with the public good, is measured by *Samson Agonistes'* inversion of the moral valence attached to fire.

Like the Samson of the Book of Judges, Milton's Samson is repeatedly associated with the destructive force of fire—from the flames in which the angel who announces his birth rides up, to the firing of the foxes' tales, to the shield of fire that the Chorus wishes for Samson. The Semichorus's description of the hero's *virtù* before he takes his terrible revenge—"His fierie vertue rouz'd / From under ashes into sudden flame" (lines 1690–91)—forewarns us that Samson will quit himself like Samson. The image is especially appropriate for one who pulls down destruction on himself because, as one poet of the Great Fire informs us, "of old the Egyptians were perswaded that Fire was an animated Creature, made onely to destroy, and after satiated to dye with the thing devour'd."[54] Even the "ev'ning Dragon" to which Samson is compared reinforces Samson's asso-

ciation with fire, and by extension with the flames of rebellion, for poets
had compared the recent conflagration to a dragon, a ravenous predator,
and an eagle let loose upon chickens (line 1692).[55]

Our sense that Samson's final act depends on a moral recuperation—
and may obliquely prophesy a return of the Good Old Cause—is created
not only by Milton's revival of an apocalyptic strain of rhetoric that flourished during the English Revolution but by his comparison of Samson to
a phoenix:

> So vertue giv'n for lost,
> Deprest, and overthrown, as seem'd,
> Like that self-begott'n bird
> In the *Arabian* woods embost,
> That no second knows nor third,
> And lay e're while a Holocaust,
> From out her ashie womb now teem'd,
> Revives, reflourishes, then vigorous most
> When most unactive deem'd,
> And though her body die, her fame survives,
> A secular bird ages of lives.
>
> (lines 1697–1707)

Whereas for much verse of the 1660s, the Restoration is an outward and
visible event—a triumph over the opposition, a reinstitution of old forms,
a reconstruction of the social and material fabric of the nation—restoration is, at this point of *Samson,* and in the understanding of the Chorus, a
matter of personal regeneration. Restoration and fame alike are thus reserved for an individual and a cause, and their consolations are immaterial.

As critics have noticed, Samson's destruction of the theater recalls
no other moment in Milton's works so much as the Lady's rejection of
Comus in *A Maske* (1634).[56] Hesitant to unfold "the sage / And serious
doctrine of Virginitie" (lines 786–87), she spares Comus to see another
day:

> Yet should I trie, the uncontrouled worth
> Of this pure cause would kindle my rap't spirits
> To such a flame of sacred vehemence,
> That dumb things would be mov'd to sympathize,
> And the brute Earth would lend her nerves, and shake,
> Till all thy magick structures rear'd so high,
> Were shatter'd into heaps ore thy false head.
>
> (lines 793–99)

This Lady—endowed with the "Sun-clad power of Chastitie" (line 782),
fixated on the preservation not just of her virtue but of her virginity,

prone to having her "spirits" kindled to "a flame of sacred vehemence," and confident of her power to topple high-reared structures with obliging earthquakes—must surely remind us of Samson, a biblical hero with his origins in a solar myth, charged with preserving his virginal locks, likewise susceptible to having "His fierie vertue rouz'd / From under ashes into sudden flame" (lines 1690–91), and, at least metaphorically, able to marshal all the powers of nature to produce his own earthquake, for he strains his nerves "As with the force of winds and waters pent, / When Mountains tremble" (lines 1647–48). If Samson's great act is understood to consummate his preliminary victories over Dalila and Harapha, its resemblance to the Lady's last stand is the more striking. For just as she, having resisted the cup of Comus with its "brewd inchantments," shatters his "magick structures rear'd so high" (*A Maske,* lines 696, 798), so Samson resists a "sorceress" who offers a "fair enchanted cup, and warbling charms" (lines 819, 934) and then scorns a warrior whose giant frame is a "pile high-built and proud" (line 1069).

As we noticed in the introduction to Part One, what moves the Lady to eloquence is not so much Comus's attempted seduction as the arguments for circulating and consuming wealth that he introduces in order to expound an economic analogue of his ideal of sexual commerce. Yet if Milton implicitly rejected Comus's views in *A Maske* as "false rules pranckt in reasons garbe" (line 758), he reconciled himself to a subset of economic arguments in the 1640s that similarly emphasized the virtues of circulation and free trade and that promised, in the context of the English Civil Wars, to serve as a force of reform and an ally of Christian liberty. Since 1660, however, economic arguments had been used with greater success by Anglican Royalists than by their opponents. What Royalists and conservatives in the City oligarchy had been particularly effective at arguing was that the nation's trade and industry could prosper only within the familiar and stable context of older political and religious forms. That meant that if economic arguments were given sufficient weight and credence, they might determine the entire structure of English society. Petty was no doubt writing half in jest when he asserted that Englishmen should work until they had accumulated more wealth than any other country and only *then* contemplate God—but he was writing only *half* in jest.[57] It may be no accident, then, that *Samson Agonistes* recalls the moment when the Lady rejects Comus's contention that she could learn something from economic principles, those "false rules pranckt in reason's garbe." For Samson's final labor of destruction is also an agonistic gesture of resistance against a brave new politico-economic order, a gesture that is all the more violent and absolute for the moral and intellectual investment that the younger Milton had made in the century's promising new economic rea-

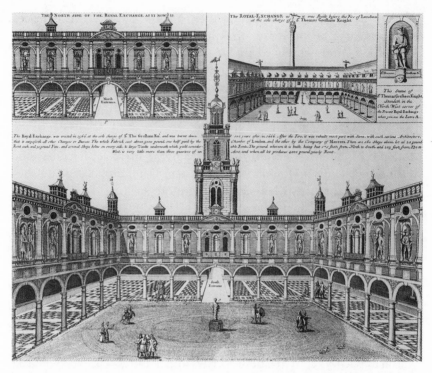

31. Sutton Nichols, *Three Interior Views of the first and second Royal Exchanges,*
showing the gallery of monarchs that, having been destroyed with the first
Exchange, were restored with the second. Engravings of the Exchange that
show it as if it had an open side invite comparison with the theater of the
Philistines in *Samson Agonistes.* Guildhall Library, Corporation of London.

soning. Like the Lady, Milton calls upon his Orphic powers to topple a
high-reared edifice.[58]
    While I do not wish to make undue claims for the architectural simi-
larities between that edifice and the Royal Exchange, I would note that
contemporary engravings of both the first and second Exchanges often
represent them as if, like the theater of the Philistines, they were court-
yards open on one side (fig. 31), while descriptions of the new Exchange
tend to celebrate its role as a gathering place where aristocrats and citizens
may partake in a kind of commercial spectacle as they admire the luxury goods that London imports and are admired for the wealth and taste
displayed in their own dress and pattern of consumption. There are more
similarities between the Exchange and the theater that Samson topples
than we might at first suppose.[59] Even if we suspect some such allusion,

however, we must concede that *Samson Agonistes* does not offer us much guidance if we ask what "false rules" precisely Samson overturns. We might interpret his violent act as a gesture of opposition to the joint commercial program of the Crown and City that we considered in Chapters Three and Four, especially because that program is often restated in poems on the rebuilding of the Exchange.[60] But we would search in vain for the pointed critique of that program that, I have argued, *Paradise Lost* performs.

With its use of the words *labor* and *work, Samson Agonistes* seems instead more concerned not to confine these activities to the economic sphere—as most of the poems on the Fire of London implicitly do—or to let them be dissevered from a conception of what is to be accomplished. The Chorus, for instance, reaffirms a point that Milton had been at pains to make in *Areopagitica* (1644)—that labor can be an activity of the mind as well as the body:

> This Idols day hath been to thee no day of rest,
>   Labouring thy mind
> More than the working day thy hands.
>
> (lines 1297–99)

At this point in the drama, we may suspect that Samson's thoughts have been turning in circles as counterproductive as his circuits about the mill, but the Chorus's application of the word *labor* to mental exertion remains important, for as we saw in Chapter One, it was precisely by describing free religious inquiry as labor that Milton and other reformers represented it as a godly duty with which, according to the logic of "The Case of Monopolies," the Crown had no right to interfere. If these lines and the objections of Manoa and the Chorus to Samson's service for the Philistines suggest that labor need not necessarily be *productive* work, Samson's observation that "laborious works" are forbidden on the feast day of Dagon implies that there *are* works that do not involve labor—works of devotion, perhaps, or service to God (line 14). The Chorus certainly believes that Samson's "great work" is not his labor at the mill but his final act of destruction (line 680). From the text's uses of the words *labor* and *work* a notion of work approaching that of the modern theorist Paul Schrecker emerges. Work, says Schrecker, may include such diverse activities as laboring in a field and praying; it is a "force in action" that "enacts some change in the province of civilization" and that "ought to be done."[61] The frequent appearance of the words *work* and *works* in the tracts of reformers advocating that religious, political, or economic institutions be dismantled suggests, first, that they had a capacious notion of work as a force of change that could operate in any "province of civilization" and, second, that they could readily conceive of tearing down as something that *ought* to be done, a necessary labor. In contrast, the poetry of the Great Fire, with its exclusive focus on the physical fabric of London, not only confines the province of work to the economic realm, it decides its valence. It implies that *all* work must raise up. The simple wonder of one poet when faced with the reconstruction of the city—"What works do I see here?"—is typical.[62] In the face of such claims and against the spectacle of London's reconstruction as the centerpiece of an empire that one poet of the Great Fire boasted would "out-live Time's date, / In lofty Pillars of eternall Brasse," *Samson Agonistes* mounts a work of destruction, "As with amaze shall strike all who behold" (line 1645).[63]

Faith, the World of Goods, and the Public Sphere

Few of *Samson Agonistes'* readers have doubted that Milton identifies with the blind Samson, beset by a vexatious wife and subject to the indignities of his enemies, and many have suspected that the climax of the drama is a projection of his desire, what Kenneth Burke describes colorfully as "a wonder-working spell by a cantankerous old fighter-priest who would slay the enemy in effigy, and whose very translation of political controversy to high theologic terms helps, by such magnification, to sanction the ill-tempered obstinacy of his resistance."[64] Yet as the poem's revisionist critics have ably demonstrated, Milton studiously avoids assuring readers that Samson is regenerate or that his final act of destruction is authorized by God.[65] If Milton had really meant to say not just that Samson *may* be right but that he *is* right, that Samson's action is a prescription for *our* action, should he not, to vary Christopher Hill's complaint, have made himself more clear?[66] I would like to suggest, in closing, that the profound ambiguity of *Samson Agonistes* is not unrelated to its antagonism toward the discourse of work, building, and production that we have been considering.

In order to make this case, I propose to return to what may be the Restoration's boldest poetic attempt to place the king at the center of the productive enterprise of building an empire of trade, Davenant's *To the King's Most Sacred Majestie* (1663). I have already argued that the Restoration's encomia to building and production—which, as we have seen, may include digressions on London as a center of world trade—are as often as not celebrations of the public realm, of a visible and material world held in common by sects otherwise divided by religious or political differences. In celebrating that realm, Davenant goes so far as to insist that even God must be seen through the public light of nature, not the private optic of faith:

> Though Conscience is in others secret shame
> Of doing ill, yet they in publick claim
> Not onely freedom for the ills they do,
> But call for liberty to preach them too.
> They seek out God in cruel Camps, and boast
> They God have found, when they have Nature lost;
> Nature, the publick Light which is held out
> To all dim Minds who do of God-head doubt.
> She openly to all does God-head shew;
> Faith brings him, like a Secret, but to few.
> Sects, who would God by private Opticks reach,
> Invent those Books by which themselves they teach;
> And whilst with Heaven they too familiar grow,
> They to the Gods on earth disdain to bow.
>
> (lines 111–24)

Because Milton and Davenant shared a friendship that transcended their political differences, it seems to me quite likely that Milton knew this poem.[67] My point is not, however, that we must know Davenant's poem in order to read Milton's drama but that Milton chose his words and sharpened the drama's outlines in opposition to the tradition of verse in which Davenant's poem participates.

Against Davenant's God-head who may be perceived by all according to the public light of nature, Milton presents a god who, in the view of the Chorus, often "seems to hide his face" (line 1749) and who reveals himself to Samson precisely, in Davenant's phrase, "like a Secret."[68] To live in a world of common observations as Davenant would have his contemporaries do, is, in the terms of the Chorus again, to be "to sense reprobate, / And with blindness internal stuck" (lines 1685–86). It is to be *condemned*, as John Shawcross glosses the word "reprobate," to and by the sensory world.[69]

As if to emphasize the inadequacy of external observation, Milton establishes a dreadful symmetry between Samson and Dalila, the Israelites and the Philistines, Yahweh and Dagon.[70] Samson says that he married twice to "the same end; still watching to oppress / *Israel*'s oppressours" (lines 232–33; cf. lines 421–23), and he refers to Dalila herself as "my faithless enemy" (line 380). Dalila similarly says that she used her position as Samson's wife "to entrap / A common enemy, who had destroy'd / Such numbers of our Nation" (lines 855–57). The Chorus approvingly tells Samson that

> In seeking just occasion to provoke
> The *Philistine,* thy Countries Enemy,
> Thou never wast remiss.
>
> (lines 237–39)

Their counterparts among the Philistines likewise counsel Dalila that "all bonds of civil Duty / And of Religion" dictate that she entrap a "common enemy" (lines 853–54, 856). Samson takes his most decisive action after feeling "Some rouzing motions in me which dispose / To something extraordinary my thoughts" (lines 1382–83). But Dalila's account of how *she* decided to betray Samson also includes a description of inward persuasion. The "grounded maxim" that "to the public good / Private respects must yield," she says, "*Took full possession of me* and prevail'd" (lines 865, 867–69; my emphasis). Even the monument that Manoa decides to build for Samson is reminiscent of the one that Dalila envisions for herself. Samson's acts will be "enroll'd / In copious Legend, or sweet Lyric Song," and

> The Virgins also shall on feastful days
> Visit his Tomb with flowers, only bewailing
> His unfortunate lot in nuptial choice.
>
> (lines 1736–37, 1741–43)

But Dalila, too, will be

> nam'd among the famousest
> Of Women, sung at solemn festivals,
> Living and dead recorded, who to save
> Her countrey from a fierce destroyer, chose
> Above the faith of wedlock-bands, my tomb
> With odours visited and annual flowers.
>
> (lines 982–87)

She will be to the Philistines what Jael is to Samson's tribe (lines 988–90). Perhaps most disturbing, after having accused Dalila of having cut his hair "to please thy gods" (line 896), Samson argues that

> gods unable
> To acquit themselves and prosecute their foes
> But by ungodly deeds, the contradiction
> Of their own deity, Gods cannot be.
>
> (lines 896–99)

That is a standard to which the Chorus is not eager to hold Yahweh, "Who made our Laws to bind us, not himself" (line 309), and for good reason, for it is not at all apparent that arranging for the locks of a lone man to be shorn is a more nefarious and "ungodly" way for a god to acquit himself than is slaying the choice nobility and flower of an entire nation after sending a "spirit of phrenzie" down among them (line 1675).

This symmetry of external appearances places a tremendous burden of meaning on Samson's divine impulses, which most critics identify as *the* interpretive key to the work. Yet *Samson Agonistes* is candid in admitting that these divine impulses are resistant to discussion and analysis — as Manoa's refusal to speculate on their validity attests (lines 420–24) — and, therefore, an unpromising basis for the sort of public discourse that Davenant has in mind.[71] It even concedes that as guides to private initiatives, they are at best intermittent and ambiguous. For they operate in such close proximity to Samson's sexual drives, violent instincts, and ratiocinations that we, and presumably Samson, can never be certain they are anything *more*.

The real drama of *Samson Agonistes,* in fact, takes place at just this obscure intersection of reason, desire, and the invisible workings of the spirit. Characteristically, the play presents a series of ostensibly reasonable but discontinuous arguments — set in motion by the visits of Manoa, Dalila, and Harapha to the captive Samson — that never really constitute a rational dialogue because they fail to respond to one another. We might contrast the rhetorical texture of *Samson Agonistes* with (on the one hand) that of Restoration heroic drama, with its grandly declamatory style and externalized "inner" debates, burlesqued so brilliantly in the duke of Buckingham's *The Rehearsal* (1671), and with (on the other hand) that of Restoration comedy, with its characters rationally pursuing irrational but transparent appetites in a contest whose artistic design is ultimately a calculus of so many selfish designs. If, as I have asserted, the public sphere was increasingly being conceived as a space in which so many private interests had to compete and might be accommodated, we can see how some such conception underlies, and may in turn have been reinforced by, the conventions of Restoration comedy. With its "irrational design," *Samson Agonistes,* in contrast, hews closer to the form of biblical narratives, whose truth seems to subsist, as one critic has observed, "in [their] ambiguity and inconsistency," not "in spite" of it.[72]

I thus find myself in agreement with Joseph Wittreich's claim that Milton's is an "order of art, the meaning of which completes itself outside the poem — in history — although some would say within the experience of the audience that receives the poem."[73] *Samson Agonistes* itself seems to endorse this model of reading by repeatedly asking what others will make of the story of Samson and Dalila, to "Ages an example" that must be understood (line 765).[74] Samson and Manoa assume that the champion's victories should be "Acknowledg'd" and "consider'd / Deliverance offer'd," that they should be recognized as "freedom," if only Israel will "lay hold on this occasion," but the text itself certainly leaves open the possibility that they are mistaken (lines 245–46, 1715–16). Milton's drama asks to be read, finally, as Milton thought scripture should be read, and as the reader of the volume of 1671 has already watched the Jesus of *Paradise Regained* read—in a spirit of charity, not according to the public light of nature. If Milton ever really hoped to evolve a notion of rational Christian liberty as Mary Ann Radzinowicz has argued, he found that after the Restoration rational liberty had degenerated into license.[75] By reinserting desire, tragic conflict, the claims of conscience, and iconoclastic violence into the realm of public discourse, he attempted to prevent the public sphere from being reduced to the world of goods. He made a paradoxical plea for responsible attention to interior lights. The real meaning of *Samson Agonistes* subsists not in a call to action but in the interpretive labor of the private reader, in the *experience* of that labor, which is calculated to unsettle assumptions and to activate our critical and moral faculties. That is the "new acquist / Of true experience" with which the poem dismisses us (lines 1755–56).[76]

From the perspective of this chapter, which has confined itself to the engagement of *Samson Agonistes* with the Royalist discourse of work and productivity after the Restoration, Milton's effort to defend the province of individual conscience may be seen to react against the particular tendency of economic analysis to abstain from the moral evaluation of internal states (something that Milton himself was never prepared to do) and to remove a spectrum of decisions from the moral sphere by focusing on the ability of notional agents acting on the margin, and obeying rational incentives, to force the hands of *all* individuals participating in the same market—in short, to deprive men and women of moral authorship.[77] Some of Milton's contemporaries were already beginning to suggest that it was no more feasible or laudable to fight the laws of the market than to resist the winds and the tides.[78] As if in a concession to the power of their claims, Samson dies "tangl'd in the fold / Of dire necessity," but not before he makes himself felt as an unbound will and uncontrolled passion, a holdover from another time (lines 1665–66).

Conclusion

In Part One, we considered several sermons that, responding to the commercial language of Proverbs 23:23 and Matthew 13:45–46, enjoined men to buy the truth and sell it not. For the Milton of the 1640s, alive to the possibility of a universal reformation, these texts suggested that initiative and industry in one sphere—religious, political, or economic—might promote liberty and understanding in the others. For the John Bunyan of the late 1670s, the same texts measured the distance between men who lived as pilgrims on earth and citizens of heaven and men who lived solely for the world. Determined to *"buy the Truth,"* Bunyan's pilgrims "set very light" by all the "Wares" of Vanity Fair, put their fingers in their ears, and look upwards, "signifying that their Trade and Traffic [is] in Heaven." For their part, the merchants of the Fair scorn the pilgrims as "Outlandish-men."[1] The gulf between *Areopagitica* and *Pilgrim's Progress* is not simply one of authorial temperament; it is one of changed circumstances. Milton's *Samson Agonistes* (1671) is, in some ways, less like his own early pamphlet than it is like Bunyan's Restoration allegory. Did Milton finally conclude, then, that all the ideas he had acquired from economic discourse were specious trifles, or did he find that some of them were the genuine article?

We have seen that in *A Maske Presented at Ludlow Castle* (1634) Milton endorsed the Lady's denunciation of luxury and her call for distributive justice. He never left her voice behind. In his antiprelatical tracts of the early 1640s, he attacked the prelates of the Anglican Church for "revell[ing] like *Belshazzar* with their full carouses in *Goblets,* and *vessels* of *gold"* when they should be building schools and churches "where they cry out for want" and distributing a "moderate maintenance" to "every painfull Minister."[2] Even in *Paradise Regained* (1671), Milton's Jesus insists that "majestic show / Of luxury"—such as "gorgeous feasts / On *Cittron* tables" or Falernian wine quaffed in gold cups—"to me should'st tell who thirst / And hunger still" (4.110-21). But starting in the early 1640s, Milton also began to demonstrate a countervailing interest in arguments like Comus's, which insisted on the benefits of circulation and of a freer commerce among men. If Milton denounced the luxury of the prelates in tracts like *Of Reformation* (May 1641), he proposed not only that they live more virtuously but that there be a systematic *"unmonopolizing* the rewards of *learning* and *industry."* This was a matter not just of charity but, more crucially, of liberty. For "Liberty consist[ed] in manly and honest labours" and could not flourish when monopolists used their "cruel authority" to oppress other men who were attempting to "labour in the word."[3] Free trade pamphlets advanced the same line of argument. Moreover, their denunciation of economic oppression accorded with Milton's own opposition to political and religious tyranny, and their emphasis on the elastic, communal, and generative attributes of trade fit with his own ideas of free spiritual inquiring and continuing revelation. He therefore came to believe that economic principles might be set in action to promote the cause of truth and liberty. It was his faith in the efficacy of a free marketplace of ideas that enabled Milton, in his regicide tracts and defenses of the English people, to apologize for the actions of a militant minority in the name of a free people who would learn to be worthy of that appellation. For a time, he believed that when commonwealths flourished, they did so in all ways, enjoying wealth, displaying civic virtue, and supporting a culture of letters that, far from being impoverished by commerce, might be enriched by it.[4] For as tracts on trade observed, when the merchants of nations converged on a city, they brought not only goods but language, learning, and culture.

By the eve of the Restoration, however, Milton found the voice of the people, and more specifically the voice of economic complaint, not opposed to tyranny but aligned with it in a desire to bring back the Stuart monarchy for the sake of trade. Rather than turn away from the principles of economic reasoning, he bravely proposed a federal system of government that, by making the polity subject to the forces of choice and competition, might rescue Christian liberty *from* popular sovereignty and kingship alike. *The Readie and Easie Way* thus marks Milton's high-water mark as a political economist. But it also records his painful realization that if economic discourse could serve as an instrument of liberation and a source of intellectual inspiration, short-term material grievances could lead men to surrender civic and religious freedoms. In this way, both economic discourse and the claims of trade could serve the ends of absolutism and empire—an insight that *Paradise Lost* (1667) brilliantly elaborates. It may seem that, with the iconoclastic violence of *Samson Agonistes* (1671) and its opposition to the false rules of the Restoration regime's ideology of work and production, Milton returns to his beginnings, rejecting *Areopagitica*'s hope that economic processes might spread the light of God and reassuming the position of the Lady in *A Maske* (1634). If we see Samson's toppling of the theater as a type of the apocalyptic destruction of that other "great city," Babylon—bewept by the merchants of the earth who trade in luxuries, slaves, and the "souls of men" (Rev. 18:9–19)—then Milton may seem to us, in the end, to have given up on making fine distinctions between commercial relations that might promote and preserve Christian liberty and those that would enslave and corrupt the spirit.

I think it would be wrong, however, to conclude that Milton finally rejected all the economic positions that he had assumed between 1634 and 1671. We must remember that while the economic discourse to which Milton was attracted in the 1640s had deep resonances with popular beliefs about rights and freedoms, especially among townsmen, its foremost proponents were a minority of men who were interested in entering foreign trade but who had to overcome an entrenched and exclusive merchant elite in order to do so. While the faction opposed to London's established trading companies seemed to be gaining ground in the 1640s, they had suffered important reversals even before 1660, when the chartered companies secured their relationship with the Crown and commerce was valued as an instrument of empire. To be sure, Elizabethan works promoting voyages of discovery had not failed to appeal to the imperial ambitions of the queen and her subjects, but it was not until the 1650s and 1660s that celebrations of trade as a means of extending freedom and community—so long a part of London's civic pageants—were clearly reduced to secondary importance by works like Dryden's *Annus Mirabilis*. It may not be Milton who changed after the 1640s, in other words, so much as circumstances that changed around him. *Paradise Lost*'s withering analysis of trade and *Samson Agonistes'* dark meditation on the trials of labor under a hostile regime represent not a turn against commerce of all types, I would suggest, but a rejection of a particular vision that Royalists in particular, though not Royalists alone, expounded. The Jesus of *Paradise Regained* has no patience for "Worthies" who do nothing "But rob and spoil, burn, slaughter, and enslave / Peaceable Nations, neighbouring, or remote" (3.74–76), but he can still lament their destruction of "all the flourishing works of peace" (3.80), works that are presumably not *limited* to the daily routines of industry and commerce (for in our reading of *Samson Agonistes* we saw that Milton wants men to labor at *all* things) but that surely must comprise them.

It is true that in Raphael's injunction "Dream not of other Worlds" (7.812/8.175) *Paradise Lost* entertains an even darker possibility: that, on the margin, commerce among men may not be productive but destructive because it may simply afford opportunities for force and guile, not to mention selfishness and greed, to extinguish liberty and virtue. But this is perhaps to be expected. Milton's final years coincided with the Second and Third Anglo-Dutch Wars, the Crown's attempt to extend its control over the American trade and the colony with which we can expect Milton to have sympathized most, Massachusetts Bay, and Sir William Petty's earliest suggestions to the Crown about how it might make more efficient use of its citizens—as if they were just so many resources. As it turned out, the American colonial trade was resistant to regulation, despite the Navigation Acts, and thus remained accessible and attractive to small traders and merchants who had long histories of resisting state regulation of their economic activities or religious beliefs. And in the longer term, classical economics would embrace not a vision of imperial entrepôts sustained by force and directed by worldly sovereigns but a model of individuals freely participating in a market ordered by an "invisible hand." But Milton, who doubtless would have had his own reservations about classical economics, could hardly have predicted when, if ever, the vision of his contemporary opponents would lose its sway.[5] He may have felt with some reason that to distinguish between commerce and production in toto and the Restoration regime's vision of them would be to draw a distinction without a difference.

That Milton was never tempted by the vision of Petty—and remained true, instead, to an economic ideal that prized individual autonomy and that sought to avoid state direction—is evident in his writings for the republic. As we might suppose, he was more tolerant of republicans than of Royalists pursuing an empire of trade: "If you long for wealth, freedom, peace, and [empire], would it not be much better, much more in accord with your own deserts, to strive resolutely for those ends through your own virtue, industry, prudence, and courage than to hope for them in vain under a king's control?" Yet even here in *A Defence of the People of England* (1651), during a high point of his enthusiasm for a model of empire inspired by republican Rome, Milton withholds full assent from such ambitions by placing them in the conditional—emphasized by the *si* [if] that precedes each objective in his Latin text—and focuses, instead, on the conduct of citizens acting autonomously.[6] After the dissolution of the Rump in 1653, Milton became far less tolerant of the statists in his own party. In *A Second Defence of the English People* (1654), he worried aloud that, with its interest in raising taxes and strengthening the state, the new government he was defending might forget that the state existed not to aggrandize itself but to distribute justice and to ensure that men were able to live in a state of Christian liberty:

> If you begin to slip into the same vices, to imitate those men, to seek the same goals, to clutch at the same vanities, you actually are royalists yourselves, at the mercy either of the same men who up to now have been your enemies, or of others in turn, who, depending on the same prayers to God, the same patience, integrity, and shrewdness which were at first your strength, will justly subdue you, who have now become so base and slipped into royalist excess and folly. (*CPW* 4:681)

Royalism, Milton is saying, is not just a party standard; it is a theory of government's role in the polity and economy that is made even worse in practice by the transgressions of those in power. When Milton framed his own proposals for a commonwealth, he remembered that it would not be able to survive without a strong navy and flourishing trade; but when he came to think about funding such national priorities, he tellingly made provisions for the people to inspect the government's books and thus make it accountable to them. His objection to the economic vision of Royalist poets cannot, I would argue, be reduced to that vision's mere association with monarchy: it is aimed at an economic program that prizes power over empowerment, accumulation over distribution, empire over community, nations over individuals.

From beginning to end, Milton opposed the "great Marchants of this world," whether they took the form of monopolistic churchmen or chartered companies.[7] He consistently attacked fixed forms and visible powers, and, in doing so, he made various uses of that strain of economic analysis that sought to describe the power of independent initiatives and invisible processes. Milton's faith that this strain of analysis would be bought as truth by his own countrymen, so recently gulled by false trifles and glittering wares, was no doubt shaken or destroyed by 1671. But there remained a place for it in his moral vision.

Assuming I am right in all this, what correction does this book ask us to make to the versions of Milton that are more current today in scholarly circles? In contrast with the work of critics who stress Milton's commitment to the rule of the saints, it asks us to see him attempting to frame a polity in blueprint that would not only accommodate but seek to preserve the secular rights and opportunities of an unregenerate majority.[8] In contrast with the views of critics who try to explain Milton's work as the expression of an author actuated by the Protestant work ethic first described by Max Weber, it asks us (in Chapter Seven) to see him as someone who was well aware that the search for assurances of individual salvation could—albeit unintentionally—lead to unreflecting habits of thrift and labor. In other words, while the arch-ironist Weber assumes that the Protestants he describes are unaware of the connection between Protestant spirituality and capitalist behavior that he uncovers, this book holds that Milton is conscious of how readily a work ethic can degenerate into a compulsion to labor. He warns of the phenomenon in the figures of Eve and Samson, both of whom labor in misguided attempts to affirm their merit. But Milton's interest in economic questions is hardly limited to labor. It extends to topics like trade, which Milton shows himself able to address in a sophisticated and creative manner. He thus emerges from these pages as more broadly interested in economic questions, and yet also more critical and suspicious of economic relations, than most critics who view him through the lens of Weber's theory are wont to assume.[9]

In contrast to a common view of Milton's republicanism as conservative, agrarian, and anticommercial, this book asks us to see it (and that of many of his contemporaries) as reformist, fungible, deeply informed by the contemporary example of the United Provinces, and committed to an ideal of active citizenship that can and should include production and market exchange.[10] While a fuller understanding of Milton's economic thought asks us to resist flattening out his career into an unwavering commitment to radicalism, it yields readings of *Paradise Lost* and *Samson Agonistes* that complement the findings of critics who have pointed to evidence of his continued political engagement after the Restoration. It reveals that if Milton's late verse shows a drive toward the personal, it does not represent a *quietist* retreat in terms of economics any more than it does in terms of politics.[11]

This book also asks us to recognize that Milton's literary response to the commercial revolution differs from that of his contemporaries in ways that cannot be explained simply in terms of political allegiances. More able and more creative as an abstract economic thinker than any of the other major writers we have considered, Milton nevertheless chose to apply his mastery of economic logic as often as not to problems (like intellectual exchange or the preservation of choice in the polity) that were not on the face of it economic. He thus made a contribution not just to the literary representation of trade but, just as crucially, to the rise of economic analysis as a tool for thought, a way of looking at things. Had it not been for the pioneering efforts of men like Milton and Lilburne to analyze the political and religious spheres in terms of economic analogies, a political economist like Bernard Mandeville would not have found it so easy to attribute the diligence of some clergymen to their need to compete with dissenters once their church did not enjoy a state-sanctioned monopoly.[12]

Yet Milton did not wear his modernity on his shirtsleeve. While many of his contemporaries, from Hobbes to the Royal Society's Committee for Improving the English Language, attempted to cultivate a restrained and transparent prose style that would be serviceable in an increasingly commercial and scientific society, he preferred to write in Ciceronian periods; and while poets like Davenant and Dryden showed a willingness to reimagine poetic inspiration in terms of commerce or to let their verse take its cue from the formal properties of trade, Milton associated his poetry with prophecy and perfected a grand style that was deeply informed by biblical and classical poetics.[13] To be sure, the swelling periods of Milton's prose and the enjambed free verse of *Paradise Lost* (intended to recover an "ancient liberty" from "the troublesom and modern bondage of Rimeing") evince their own formal compatibility with his belief in a free and unconstrained commerce. Milton's willingness to construct one of his epic's two main plots out of the Restoration regime's discourse of trade and to devote so much imaginative energy to the problem of Samson's labor under a hostile regime also reveals how much he thought was at stake in economic relations. It nevertheless remains important to acknowledge that when Milton makes use of economic analysis in his prose tracts, it is often to preserve or promote values that we might call humanist or millenarian; and that when he sets out to find a literary style, it is a classical and scriptural tradition of letters, not the commercial revolution, that supplies it. We might say, then, that while Milton was willing to reconfigure the polity in economic terms that were ultimately far more radical than those presented, say, in the opening stanzas of *Annus Mirabilis,* he was ultimately less eager than Dryden to let his poetic enterprise be identified with the new discourse of trade and productivity. Such differences suggest that if Milton and his contemporaries could not escape the economic transformation through which they lived or the new discourse of trade and production that sprang from and sustained it, they could, as conscious artists and deliberating agents, take it on their own terms.

In the preceding chapters, we viewed the response of Milton and his contemporaries to England's mid-seventeenth-century commercial transformation through the lens of four particular controversies that did not

play themselves out to tentative conclusions until about 1720 at the earliest. I would now like to turn to those conclusions in the hope of clarifying
the significance of the conflicts that we considered at mid century.

In Part One, we saw that for some reformers in the 1640s, economic
defenses of free trade not only provided a model argument for the free circulation of ideas and the consequent production of truth; they suggested
that the exchange of ideas and information might at once make the economic realm more open and equitable and spur economic diversification
and growth. Seen in this light, free trade, free expression, and the toleration of religious diversity might be conceived as equal contributors to a
dynamic and progressive polity. These ideas started to gain currency after
the Third Anglo-Dutch War, when many Englishmen began to fear that
France, a Catholic and absolutist monarchy with restrictive trade policies
and considerable influence in the Stuart Court, might be able to remake
England in its own image. During the Exclusion Crisis (1679–81), opponents of the Licensing Act revived Milton's language to avert the renewal
of "one of the most dangerous and mischievous Monopolies and Oppressions our Government is subject to." Drawing on *Areopagitica* verbatim,
they emphasized the "Labour of Book-writing," which entailed "working
at the hardest Labour in the deep Mines of Knowledge." They revived
the charge that the licensor, as a monopolist, was *vir sanguinis,* or a man
of blood: "You had almost as good kill a Man, as a good Book." And they
objected to the regulation of truth as if it were any other commodity:
"Truth and Understanding are not such Wares as to be Monopolized and
Traded in Tickets, Statutes, and Standards. We must not think to make a
Staple Commodity of all the knowledge in the Land, to Mark, and License it like our Broadcloath and Wool-packs: What is it but a servitude,
like that imposed by the *Philistines,* not to be allow'd the Sharpning of
our own Axes, but we must repair from all quarters to twenty Licensing
Forges?"[14] It seems likely that such arguments-by-economic-analogy met
with a more receptive and sophisticated audience in 1681 than they had in
1644, for London now *looked* like a bank of world trade, and the language
and interests of trade now played a larger part in its public discourse.

But it was not until the 1690s that the major premises of the program we considered in Chapter One really won popular assent. By that
time, at least in part because religious toleration was considered one of
the keys to Amsterdam's great economic success, dissenters were accorded
greater freedom: the penalties for dissent had been suspended; tests, while
technically in force to exclude non-Anglicans from office, were only laxly
enforced; and the acceptance of occasional conformity meant that some
dissenters could behave as if fully enfranchised. The same decade saw

an unprecedented number of pamphlets calling for the unrestricted exchange of goods in marketplaces like Billingsgate and Smithfield and for the opening of the trades to foreign destinations like Russia, Africa, and the East Indies. Most of these free trade pamphlets were directly or indirectly addressed to Parliament, which was now more important as a source of commercial regulation than the Crown. It is a measure of the success of these lobbying efforts that only the Levant and East India Companies survived the decade with any real monopoly power, and even these companies were modified so as to make them more national, less exclusive, concerns.[15] By 1707, Englishmen and Scotsmen alike could appeal to the Articles of Union for protection from "the Encroachments of any private Companies, or Societies" that might hinder "the free Intercourse of Trade and Navigation to and from any Part of the united Kingdom, and the Plantations thereunto belonging."[16] By 1711, the courts affirmed not only that monopolies were void because they were "against the policy of the common law, and contrary to *Magna Charta*" but that "grants and charters from the Crown and by-laws" were "generally void" because they were contrary to "the encouragement which the law gives to trade and honest industry" and to "the liberty of the subject."[17] Because Parliament was unable to agree on an act to replace the Printing Act of 1662, it also allowed pre-publication licensing, which had been briefly revived in 1693, to lapse once and for all in 1695. The three-pronged monopoly denounced by John Lilburne—the Anglican clergy, chartered companies, and licensors—was thus dealt a major blow some fifty years after he attacked it.

It was not, however, destroyed. William III, his propagandists, and their successors continued to support the Anglican Church. Not only did Parliament permit some monopolies like the East India Company to escape its net, it generated a new body of trade regulations, which may have been intended to promote the commerce and navigation of the realm but was susceptible to the manipulation and corrupting influence of "combinations" of men. What is more, the assembly repeatedly raised tariffs on foreign trade in an effort to finance the nation's expensive wars. What began as a fiscal policy was gradually transformed by the parliamentary lobbying of manufacturing interests and popular hostility to France into the protectionist program that was codified by Robert Walpole's customs reform of 1722. This was the system that drew Adam Smith's ire in 1776 and that would not be dismantled until the nineteenth century.[18] Even freedom of the press cannot be said to have arrived in 1695. For if Parliament gave up on licensing because it was unable to agree "where to fix the Power of Restraint," it was still able to control the press through specific prosecutions and a new instrument created by the Stamp Act of

1712, which not only restricted the supply of paper by taxing it but made party subsidies more essential to the business of political publishing.[19] In short, there were still actual and metaphorical monopolies for the essayists John Trenchard and Thomas Gordon to denounce in 1722: "monopolies are equally dangerous in trade, in politicks, in religion: A free trade, a free government, and a free liberty of conscience, are the rights and blessings of mankind."[20] And there was still work for *Areopagitica* itself to perform even in 1738, when the poet James Thomson prefaced a new edition of it with a timely warning against the reintroduction of licensing.

With the vast expansion of the stock and insurance markets, an explosion of new patents, the foundation of the Bank of England, and the creation of a National Debt in the same decade, the contiguity between information and commodities became more obvious than ever.[21] This not only led to the creation of private express services by men like Sir Josiah Child and the directors of the Bank of England, which in bringing market information to them before it was generally known created opportunities for profit; it also led to reforms aimed at ensuring public accounting and publicity so that the expanding opportunities for government corruption created by new financial instruments might be kept in check.[22] For two generations of writers that included Defoe, Swift, Pope, Addison, Steele, and the key journalists during the South Sea crisis, Trenchard and Gordon, to write for the public meant, among other things, to render judgment on trade policies, government finance, and public credit.[23] Because (as Charles Davenant observed) citizens in a commercial society had to translate their evaluations of the public good into future speculations, it became a responsibility of the man of letters to ensure that his readers were informed consumers, investors, and creditors.[24] A contemporary engraving of a jumble of newspapers, ephemera, and stock-jobbing cards seems to acknowledge precisely this coinvolvement of the popular press and investment (fig. 32).

In Chapter Two, I suggested that the future of the federalist principles of *A Readie and Easie Way* lay not in England but in America. The simpler debate between republicans and Royalists that we followed did, however, find its resolution in the motherland. The Glorious Revolution affirmed that both sides were right: trade loathed absolutism *and* craved stability. This dual requirement could best be met, it was widely agreed, by "Kings, that could not wrong, because / Their Power was circumscrib'd by Laws."[25] For Nicholas Barbon, the Settlement of 1688 had established such a limited monarchy. There were no longer grounds, he argued in 1690, to think that "a Publick Bank" could not "be safe in a Monarchy." To be sure, the prince of "a Government wholly Dispotical," in which trade

32. *The Bubblers Medley* (1720). A synoptic engraving occasioned by the South
Sea Bubble, this satire depicts a jumble of writing, from stock-jobbing cards
to the *London Gazette*. Guildhall Library, Corporation of London.

had "no Concern in the Affaires of State," might be tempted to seize it; but in England, where "the Government is not Dispotical; But the People Free . . . ; where the Customs makes great Figures, in the Kings Exchequer; where the Ships are the Bullworks of the Kingdom; and where the Flourish of Trade is as much the Interest of the King as of the People, There can be no such Cause of Fear."[26]

The creation of the Bank of England in 1694 meant that polemics about the government's economic virtues began to focus not directly on trade but on the intervening *speculation* of investing citizens about the government's future economic behavior; they focused, in other words, on the state of the public credit market. Writing in 1711, Addison said that after visiting the Bank of England, he dreamed that he returned to the Bank's hall, where he saw a "beautiful Virgin, seated on a Throne of Gold," whose name was *"Publick Credit."* On either wall hung Magna Carta, the Acts of Uniformity, Toleration, and Settlement, and the various acts made for the establishment of public funds. "The Lady seemed to set an unspeakable Value upon these several Pieces of Furniture, insomuch that she often refreshed her eye with them . . . but at the same time showed a very particular Uneasiness, if she saw anything approach them." When the Stuart pretender to the throne and a republican burst into the hall— thus neatly representing the two economic cases we saw mounted in Part Two—the Lady fainted, and the bags of gold that had been piled up behind her throne turned into wind.[27] The requirements of commerce had long exercised some control over the shape of government—early in the violent revolution of 1648–49 that cost Charles I his head, General Fairfax had attempted to forestall a flight of capital by publishing a guarantee that the freedom and security of property would be preserved in England and the nation's trade promoted—but the ability of the new credit and stock markets of the 1690s to quantify public faith in the government made that shaping influence more visible and effective.[28]

These markets also gave rise to visions of uncoercive social organization that, while bearing a real similarity to some of those we considered in the previous pages, placed a new emphasis on the importance of such intangibles as trust and faith in defining the national community. As Charles Davenant wrote,

> no trading nation ever did subsist, and carry on its business by real stock; that trust and confidence in each other, are as necessary to link and hold a people together, as obedience, love, friendship, or the intercourse of speech. And when experience has taught each man how weak he is, depending only upon himself, he will be willing to help others, and call

upon the assistance of his neighbours, which of course, by degrees must set credit afloat.[29]

"There are the beginnings here of a civic morality of investment and exchange," J. G. A. Pocock comments on this passage, "and indeed an equation of the commercial ethic with the Christian."[30] That investment could produce communities that transcended the barriers between nobles and commoners, Whigs and Tories, rich and poor is acknowledged with greater irony by an engraving satirizing the South Sea Bubble (fig. 33). Anne Finch's charming "Song of the South Sea" (1720) similarly depicts "young tender virgins" leaving aside their games, pawning their jewels, mixing undismayed with whiskered Jews and gentiles at the Exchange, and (because they are controlled by "avarice" rather than the "gayer passions of the mind") dividing all their hours with brokers rather than lovers.[31] Finch's perception that older customs for affirming communal bonds were being transfigured (though not exalted) by the market is suggested by the engraving as well, for with their outstretched arms, the investors seem to dance around a list of bubbles that resembles a Maypole.

It was against various models of uncoercive organization that we considered another possibility in Part Three: that force and commerce might not be substitutes but complements for each other. Beginning in the 1690s, these opposed propositions became aligned with a distinction between center and periphery. At the center of it all, Addison could wonder at the way in which private English subjects convening at the Exchange seemed to have all the power and liberty of another age's nobility:

> When I have been upon the 'Change, I have often fancied one of our old Kings standing in Person, where he is represented in Effigy, and looking down upon the wealthy Concourse of People with which that Place is every Day filled. In this Case, how would he be surprized to hear all the Languages of Europe spoken in this little Spot of his former Dominions, and to see so many private Men, who in his Time would have been the Vassals of some powerful Baron, Negotiating like Princes for greater sums of Mony that were formerly to be met with in the Royal Treasury! Trade, without enlarging the British Territories, has given us a kind of additional Empire.[32]

Addison was right to associate English liberty with that "additional Empire," however little he explored the connection. It was, in fact, precisely by making force and commerce substitutes at home, and thus preserving an uncoercive politico-economic system in the motherland, that England was able to project its power abroad, where force and commerce con-

33. *The Bubblers Bubbl'd, or the Devil Take the Hindmost* (1720). Fortune rules in the Stock Exchange, and the ability of commerce to erase differences between Whig and Tory, rich and poor, duke and commoner is ironically celebrated. Guildhall Library, Corporation of London.

tinued to complement each other.[33] The ability of England's credit markets to "waft an Army o'er" to the Continent provided one instance of this rule, but the "opening" of the African trade provided a more striking and tragic one. For in disabling a monopoly, it increased the economic freedoms of Englishmen, quickened trade, and in consequence doubled the rate at which black Africans were enslaved and supplied to colonies like Jamaica.[34]

In this context, I would like to return to the suggestion I made in my reading of *Windsor Forest* that if the coinvolvement of force and commerce could lead to conflicts like the Second Anglo-Dutch War, it could also serve as an instrument of peace. I cited as an example the ability of the East India Company to charge a fee for the provision of an institutional framework within which trade might be conducted on a safe and regular basis. I observed that the company's trading forts bore an ironic resemblance to Milton's blueprint for the English polity, for their limited reach made them subject to the disciplinary force of the merchants of all nations, who could choose whether or not to settle and trade there. This precarious balance was disturbed in the 1750s, when, as Adam Smith said, "the spirit of war and conquest" took possession of the company's "servants in India," who ceased to be "traders" and became "sovereigns" instead.[35] Once the East India Company acquired the ability to found an empire of dominion, not merely of trade, it was felt (by Smith, among others) that the company must cede that sovereignty to the state, whose interests as sovereign would not be at odds with an opposing set of commercial interests. This takes us well beyond the ken of our study to a chapter of colonial history when the distinction between empire and trade that Dryden and Milton had deliberately erased in *Annus Mirabilis* and *Paradise Lost* was reasserted. Some time after Smith published *The Wealth of Nations,* in other words, the state emerged as the monopolist of force and representative of empire, and trade relations were again conceived as properly peaceful and voluntary, even if they did not always conform to that model.

In Part Four, we considered *Samson Agonistes* as a meditation on the problem of work after the Restoration, one in which the competing notions of slavery found in scripture, the law, and the writings of such state-building political economists as Sir William Petty are invoked in an effort to examine the dangers, consolations, and obligations of laboring for a hostile regime. While dissenters were not slow to use the language of slavery in the 1670s and 1680s to denounce the encroachments of the Crown on their liberties and property, and while they may occasionally have felt like Samson at the public mill, their worst fears proved unwarranted. For in the Glorious Revolution, they showed themselves able, in

no small part because of their economic exertions in the previous decades, to topple high-reared structures. We have already noted that, as in
the case of the "opening" of the slave trade, liberties won at home were
not necessarily communicated abroad. The same Charles Davenant whom
we have seen opposing absolutist governments and working toward a
civic morality of investment and exchange that prized love and friendship
could staunchly support the Africa Company's trade in slaves.[36] It would
be inaccurate to say that dissenters and interloping merchants who complained of their own "slavery" refused to participate in the Atlantic's triangular trade. Perhaps we should not be surprised. For slavery had always
been a part of Western culture, sanctioned by the law of nations and consistent with natural law if seen as a contractual relationship. Slavers justified the institution in both ways: slaves were either "captives" taken in
war or servants who implicitly contracted to labor for their entire lives
in return for food and lodging.[37] If such claims failed to convince, the
trade's advocates—and, indeed, even its unwilling supporters—could fall
back on necessity, the tyrant's plea: slavery's contribution to the wealth of
England and the strength of its navy was too great for humanitarian considerations to be permitted to direct policy.[38] There could scarcely be a
better illustration of the tendency, which Milton understood all too well,
for politicians to determine that if trade was the means for "one Nation
or State . . . to straighten and pinch another," then in such matters private respects, especially those of an unenfranchised group, must yield to
public policy.[39]

It was Milton's fear that as a consequence of the rise of economic reasoning and its exclusive concern for the light of nature, appeals to inward persuasion might be debarred from public debate. The prominence
of evangelists and Quakers in the antislavery movement suggests that the
promptings of the spirit could not be so easily dismissed as a force of social
change.[40] By denouncing slavery as the "Practice of the Beast" pursued in
the name of *"carnal Interest"* and as a human sacrifice to that "great idol, the
god of gain," moralists like George Wither (in the seventeenth century)
and Bishop Warburton (in the eighteenth) deployed apocalyptic rhetoric in the belief that, as *Samson Agonistes* insisted, tearing down could be
useful work.[41] Many of London's livery companies and corporations even
provided a forum for such interventions in the public sphere by renting
their halls to dissenting congregations when they were permitted to do
so by measures like the Declaration of Indulgence (1672).[42]

Yet it was by no means Christians alone who attacked the institution of slavery. Besides those champions of political liberty like Thomas
Paine who recognized the indecency of colonists' complaining "loudly"
of the British government's "attempts to enslave them" while they them-

selves held "so many hundred thousand in slavery," there arose a new class of economic critics who held that the labor of free men paid wages must be more efficient.[43] The argument may be traced back to Aristotle's claim that free men who are holders of property will always make better soldiers than men who are not fighting for their own. It was enunciated by Thomas Hedley in 1610 when he said that if citizens were treated like the "king's bondsmen," they would "use little care or industry to get that which they cannot keep and so will grow both poor and base minded."[44] It was repeated as a commonplace toward the end of the century by Charles Davenant: "Industry has its first foundation in liberty: They who are either slaves, or who believe their freedom precarious, can neither succeed in trade nor meliorate a country."[45] But it was not until the next century that this lesson, so often invoked to defend the liberty and property of freeborn Englishmen, was used by Adam Smith to attack Negro slavery. If slavery persisted, it was because "the pride of man makes him love to domineer, and nothing mortifies him so much as to be obliged to condescend to persuade his inferiors."[46] If he could dispense with that pride, he would find that even highly paid wage laborers are ultimately less costly than slaves because men who stand to profit by their own exertions will be more industrious and efficient. In Smith's terms, the economic system that Milton opposed—a system that saw a role for force in trade relations, that looked to the strength of the state before it consulted the liberty of the individual, and that found its most perfect expression in the Atlantic slave trade—was an all too predictable expression of man's natural disposition to tyranny, of his desire to lord it over other men. But he might have to choose between glory and prosperity: an economic system predicated on autonomy, choice, and the invisible discipline of the market would, in the end, produce greater wealth. We need not believe that Smith or the English industrialists who praised wage labor and criticized slavery were acting from disinterested motives to recognize that the *effects* of their arguments were liberating for an army of slaves.[47] Ironically, it was the very worldliness of such worldly philosophers that made them unwilling, like George Wither or John Locke, to contemplate the possibility that being free in Christ might be an adequate substitute for slaves' being free to dispose of their labors as they saw fit.[48]

That such an ancient institution as slavery was not abolished until the rise of capitalism has encouraged one historian to make a bolder claim. The expansion of markets and the rise of economics as a discipline in the eighteenth century led, says Thomas Haskell, to a "change in cognitive style—specifically, a change in the perception of causal connection and consequently a shift in the conventions of moral responsibility—that underlay the new constellations of attitudes and activities that we now call humanitarianism."[49] That shift, argues Haskell, made the general population receptive to the arguments of abolitionists: capitalism may not be an inherently humane system, but it *enabled* eighteenth-century Englishmen to conceive of their own powers and responsibilities more expansively. If there is any truth in this argument, and I suspect there is, then it is the crowning proof of just how difficult it is to predict which economic forces and principles will enslave and corrupt citizens and which ones will enlarge and improve them.

I hope that in pursuing into the eighteenth century the debates that gave shape to this book, I have suggested how consequential they were for the long-term development of English culture. I certainly would not like to leave the impression, however, that the utterly transformative effects of England's commercial and financial revolutions were not really felt until a century after Milton's death.

Already by 1700, a man of business in London could bank at one of fifty establishments, settle his accounts with virtually any region of the world without shipping specie abroad, and find the price of stocks listed in periodicals like *The Course of the Exchange*. The port of London, employing perhaps a quarter of the city's workforce, was an entrepôt of world trade: one-third of its imports came from such distant regions as India, Africa, America, and the West Indies. The world's goods were offered for sale not only in the New Exchange, "the richest piece of ground, perhaps, in the whole world," but in sixteen new suburban markets. But vast improvements to the isle's coastal harbors, navigable rivers, and roads meant that tobacco from Virginia, calico from India, and porcelain from China were not confined to the metropolis.[50] All this persuaded Daniel Defoe to "lay down the Fact" in 1705 that

> *England* is a Trading Nation, that the Wealth and Oppulence of the Nation, is owing to Trade, that the Influence of Trade is felt in every Branch of its Government, in the Value of its Land, and the Blood of Trade is mix'd and blended with the Blood of Gallantry, so that Trade is the Life of the Nation, the Soul of its Felicity, the Spring of its Wealth, the Support of its Greatness, and the Staff on which both King and People lean, and which (if it should sink) the whole Fabrick must fall, the Body Politick would sicken and languish, its Power decline, and the Figure it makes in the World, grow by degrees, most Contemptibly Mean.[51]

Perhaps none of the authors we have considered would have been entirely happy with Defoe's unreserved identification of the nation with commerce, but, as we have seen, they all conceded the increasing importance of trade and production to the English polity and to English culture.

If one of my aims in reading economic reformers against chartered company apologists, republicans against Royalists, and Milton against Dryden has been to show that divergent economic interests and convictions could lead men to support opposed political programs (and that different political values could, conversely, produce sharply opposed economic models), another has been to suggest some of the ways that economic assumptions, arguments, and *topoi* could be shared or appropriated across political, cultural, and even national boundaries as writers searched for adequate responses to a widely perceived and very real economic transformation that changed the patterns of everyday life, the way human relations were ordered, and the meanings with which they were invested.

For many literary historians, the chief importance of the commercial and financial revolutions was, in retrospect, their contribution to the rise of a new literary form, the novel.[52] It would be tempting to see this new genre as the eighteenth century's answer to the texts we have considered at length. In many of its formal characteristics—such as its plain prose style and its turn away from a ceremonial calendar to an ethic of daily accounting—the novel does indeed look like a child of the commercial and financial revolutions. Yet, with spectacular exceptions like Charles Johnstone's *Chrysalis; or, the Adventures of a Guinea* (1760), eighteenth-century novels often accord less prominence to abstract economic forces than, say, *Annus Mirabilis* does. I would suggest this is so for two reasons. The first is the success with which poets like Dryden and economists like Peter Paxton (who tellingly complained that economic regulations did "a violence against nature") were able to convince readers that economic forces operated with an abstract inevitability that made them akin to natural forces and similarly resistant to moral analysis.[53] Once this notion was widely accepted, authors could let such forces recede, like nature itself, into the background of literary representations, to be called forward only when they were required to impinge on the private life of individuals. The second reason is that the commercial and financial revolutions also contributed to the creation of an articulate and affluent audience of middle-class readers who attached a new ethical and aesthetic value to the domestic sphere, which, constructed in part as a sanctuary from the pressure and anonymity of the marketplace, became the primary subject of the new genre. The novel did not forget the discoveries of the commercial revolution and the writers who lived through it: that trade and credit could pocket states, fetch or carry kings, and waft whole armies to a distant shore.[54] It was just mindful of another lesson: that such great things, whether they be Mammon's or Adam's, are accomplished by small.

Abbreviations

Bacon, *Works*	*The Works of Francis Bacon,* ed. James Spedding, Robert Leslie Ellis, and Douglas Denim Heath, 14 vols. (London: Longman, 1858–74).
CJ	*Journals of the House of Commons.*
Coke, *2 Institutes*	Sir Edward Coke, *The Second Part of the Institutes of the Laws of England* (1642).
Coke, *3 Institutes*	Sir Edward Coke, *The Third Part of the Institutes of the Laws of England* (1644).
CPW	*The Complete Prose Works of John Milton,* gen. ed. Don M. Wolfe, 8 vols. (New Haven: Yale University Press, 1953–82).
CSP Domestic	*Calendar of State Papers, Domestic Series,* ed. Mary Anne Everett Green (London: Her Majesty's Stationary Office, 1858).
CSP Venetian	*Calendar of State Papers, Venetian,* ed. Allen B. Hinds (London: Public Records Office, 1927).
D'Ewes	Sir Simonds D'Ewes, *A Complete Journal of the Votes, Speeches, and Debates, Both of the House of Lords and House Commons Throughout the Reign of Queen Elizabeth* (1693).
Dryden, *Works*	*The Works of John Dryden,* ed. Edward Niles Hooker and H. T. Swedenberg, Jr., 20 vols. (Berkeley: University of California Press, 1956–89).
DNB	*Dictionary of National Biography.*
Economic Docs.	Joan Thirsk and J. P. Copper, eds. *Seventeenth-Century Economic Documents* (Oxford: Oxford University Press, 1972).
Eng. Rep.	*English Reports,* 178 vols. (reprint, Edinburgh: W. Green, 1900–32).

French, *Records*	J. Milton French, *Life Records of John Milton*, 5 vols. (New Brunswick: Rutgers University Press, 1949–58).
Grey, *Debates*	Anchitell Grey, *Debates of the House of Commons from the Year 1667 to the Year 1694*, 10 vols. (1763).
Harl. Misc.	*Harleian Miscellany*, ed. J. Malham, 12 vols. (London: Dutton, 1808–11).
Hartlib Papers	*The Hartlib Papers.* Computer file: a complete text and image data base of the papers of Samuel Hartlib held in Sheffield University Library, prepared by Judith Crawford et al. (Ann Arbor, Mich.: UMI, 1995).
LJ	*Journals of the House of Lords.*
Middleton, *Works*	*The Works of Thomas Middleton*, ed. A. H. Bullen, 8 vols. (London: John C. Nimmo, 1886).
PP1610	*Proceedings in Parliament, 1610*, ed. Elizabeth Read Foster, 2 vols. (New Haven: Yale University Press, 1966).
Rushworth	J. Rushworth, *Historical Collection of Private Passages of State* (1659–1701).

Notes

Introduction

1. Historians apply the term *commercial revolution* to different decades, but I use it like C. G. A. Clay to refer to 1630–1700; see his *Economic Expansion and Social Change: England, 1500–1700*, 2 vols. (Cambridge: Cambridge University Press, 1984), 2:181.

2. Keith Wrightson, *Earthly Necessities: Economic Lives in Early Modern Britain* (New Haven: Yale University Press, 2000), pp. 30–50, 70–82, 110, 159; Clay, *Economic Expansion*, 1:2, 122–23, 2:100–102; Donald C. Coleman, *Economy of England, 1450–1750* (Oxford: Oxford University Press, 1977), pp. 8–12, 72–75.

3. See Astrid Friis, *Alderman Cockayne's Project and the Cloth Trade* (London: Humphrey Milford, 1927); and B. E. Supple, *Commercial Crisis and Change in England, 1600–1642* (Cambridge: Cambridge University Press, 1959), chap. 2.

4. J. D. Gould, "The Trade Depression of the Early 1620s," *Economic History Review*, 2d ser., 7 (1954): 81–90.

5. On the intellectual response to the trade crisis of the early 1620s, see Supple, *Commercial Crisis;* Joyce Appleby, *Economic Thought and Ideology in Seventeenth-Century England* (Princeton: Princeton University Press, 1978), chap. 2; and Andrea Finklestein, *Harmony and the Balance: An Intellectual History of Seventeenth-Century English Economic Thought* (Ann Arbor: University of Michigan Press, 2000), chaps. 2–4.

6. See Thomas Mun, *A Discovrse of Trade, from England vnto the East Indies* (1621) and *England's Treasure by Forraign Trade* (written c. 1623; published 1664).

7. Edward Misselden, *The Circle of Commerce; or, the Balance of Trade, in Defence of Free Trade* (1623), pp. 93, 17.

8. Clay, *Economic Expansion*, 2:13–21, 154–82, 240–41; Wrightson, *Earthly Necessities*, pp. 166–67, 209–12; Coleman, *Economy of England*, pp. 113, 175; Supple, *Commercial Crisis*, pp. 152–62.

9. Robert Ashton, *The City and the Court, 1603–1643* (Cambridge: Cambridge

University Press, 1979), chaps. 4−7; Kevin Sharpe, *The Personal Rule of Charles I* (New Haven: Yale University Press, 1992), esp. chaps. 3, 9; Clay, *Economic Expansion*, 2:256.

10. Rushworth, pt. 3, vol. 1, pp. 21−34.

11. *Areopagitica* (Nov. 1644), in *CPW* 2:559.

12. Henry Robinson, *England's Safety, in Trade's Encrease* (1641), p. 56.

13. On the "economics of diversification," see Supple, *Commercial Crisis*, pp. 221−24.

14. Aristotle, *Politics*, bk. 1, chap. 11, 1259a. On the scholastic tradition of treating commerce as a problem of justice, which owed a debt to Aristotle and continued to exercise an influence on Adam Smith, who still classed political economy as a branch of jurisprudence, see Odd Langholm, *Economics in the Medieval Schools: Wealth, Exchange, Value, Money, and Usury According to the Paris Theological Tradition, 1200−1350* (Leiden: E. J. Brill, 1992); and Langholm, *The Legacy of Scholasticism in Economic Thought* (Cambridge: Cambridge University Press, 1998).

15. William Letwin stresses the importance of the accrual of a literature of trade whose scope slowly defined the purview of what he terms "scientific economics"; see his *The Origins of Scientific Economics* (New York: Doubleday, 1964), pp. 230−38. We can see that the process is well underway by the mid-seventeenth century. S. E., the author of *The Toutch-Stone of Mony and Commerce; or, an Expedient for Increase of Trade, Mony, and Shiping in England* (1654), admits that he has "extracted the principal parts of this composure from other Authors" whom he duly names and whose proposals he summarizes and evaluates (p. 12). In *Britannia Languens* (1680), William Petyt likewise acknowledges that he has relied on other authorities, nevertheless complains that his subject is "so *Copious,* and so little laboured by other Writers" that he has had "no common Places or beaten Tracks to follow, as in other Studies," but trusts that his own inadequate efforts will "awaken and spur on the *virtuous emulation* of others to a more compleat disquisition into the several branches of our Trade" (p. 154).

16. John Cary, *A Discourse on Trade* (1717), p. 1. For the importance of the concepts of agency and organization to the period's political and scientific debates, see Otto Mayr, *Authority, Liberty, and Automatic Machinery in Early Modern Europe* (Baltimore: Johns Hopkins University Press, 1986). John Rogers has made them central to his own analysis of the intersection of politics and science in the writings of Milton and his contemporaries; see his *The Matter of Revolution: Science, Poetry, and Politics in the Age of Milton* (Ithaca: Cornell University Press, 1996).

17. For a reading of the period's literature that emphasizes its open and unstable qualities, see Nigel Smith, *Literature and Revolution in England, 1640−1660* (New Haven: Yale University Press, 1994).

18. William Goffe, *How to Advance the Trade of the Nation and Employ the Poor* (1641).

19. See Alan Craig Houston, "A Way of Settlement: the Levellers, Monopolies, and the Public Interest," *History of Political Thought* 14 (1993): 381−420.

20. Gerrard Winstanley, *The Law of Reason in a Platform, or True Magistracy Restored* (1652), in *The Works of Gerrard Winstanley*, ed. George H. Sabine (Ithaca: Cornell University Press, 1941), p. 531.

21. Benjamin Worsley, *The Advocate* (1652), sig. Br.

22. On this point, see Letwin, *Origin*, pp. 140−41.

23. For some interesting remarks on the way groups within a society can try to

change the dominant ideology by changing the meaning or application of words, see Quentin Skinner, *Meaning and Context: Quentin Skinner and His Critics,* ed. James Tully (Princeton: Princeton University Press, 1988), pp. 107–32, esp. p. 128, where he discusses the word *commodity.*

24. For this argument about the eighteenth century, see Donald Davie, *Purity of Diction in English Verse* (London: Chatto and Windus, 1952).

25. Literary critics who write in terms of "libidinal economies" or "symbolic capital" draw on the work of François Lyotard, *Libidinal Economy,* trans. Iain Hamilton Grant (London: Athlone Press, 1993); and Pierre Bourdieu, some of whose key essays are gathered in *Fields of Cultural Production: Essays on Art and Literature,* ed. Randal Johnson (Cambridge: Polity Press, 1993).

26. For attempts to accord greater autonomy to the superstructure of society as a means of developing a more viable Marxist literary criticism, see Louis Althusser, "Contradiction and Overdetermination," in his *For Marx,* trans. Ben Brewster (London: NLB, 1977); Raymond Williams, "Base and Superstructure in Marxist Cultural Theory," in his *Problems in Materialism and Culture: Selected Essays* (London: NLB, 1980); and James Holstun, "Ranting at the New Historicism," *ELR* 19 (1989): 189–225. Because Marx read both seventeenth- and eighteenth-century English economic writers and duly appropriated some of their ideas, critics should have no trouble remapping some of my arguments in Marxist terms. I have not done so myself because, while I believe that literary criticism owes a considerable debt to Marxists for long insisting on the importance of "real history" to the study of "culture," and while I share with Marxists an interest in long-term structural changes in society, I fear that now that a wider audience is interested in the sort of questions that Marxists have long posed, the dominance of their analytical terms is doing more to hinder than to help the search for instructive answers.

27. Notable examples include Marc Shell, *The Economy of Literature* (Baltimore: Johns Hopkins University Press, 1978); Shell, *Money, Language, Thought: Literary and Philosophic Economies from the Medieval to the Modern Era* (Baltimore: Johns Hopkins University Press, 1982); Shell, *Art & Money* (Chicago: University of Chicago Press, 1995); Sandra Sherman, *Finance and Fictionality in the Early Eighteenth Century: Accounting for Defoe* (Cambridge: Cambridge University Press, 1996); and James Thompson, *Models of Value: Eighteenth Century Political Economy and the Novel* (Durham: Duke University Press, 1996).

28. Shell, *Economy,* p. 38.

29. Michael Drayton, "Pæan Triumphal" (1604), lines 113–16.

30. Shell, *Economy,* p. 152.

31. Louis Montrose, "New Historicisms," in *Redrawing the Boundaries: The Transformation of English and American Literary Studies,* ed. Stephen Greenblatt and Giles Gunn (New York: MLA, 1992), p. 410. On literature as a mirror, see Jean Howard, "The New Historicism in Renaissance Studies," *ELR* 16 (1986): 18.

32. Montrose, "New Historicisms," p. 410. An instance is Alan Liu's reading of Wordsworth: "That such figuration denies history is indisputable. But surely such denial is also the strongest kind of engagement with history"; see his *Wordsworth: The Sense of History* (Stanford: Stanford University Press, 1989), p. 35.

33. Oscar Kenshur, *Dilemmas of Enlightenment: Studies in the Rhetoric and Logic of*

Ideology (Berkeley: University of California Press, 1993), p. 11. For one such argument, see Stephen Greenblatt, *Shakespearean Negotiations: The Circulation of Social Energy in Renaissance England* (Berkeley: University of California Press, 1988), pp. 21–65. For a defense of New Historicists against charges like Kenshur's, see Montrose, "New Historicisms," pp. 402–03.

34. Both these techniques have been widely criticized. See Dominick LaCapra, *Soundings in Critical Theory* (Ithaca: Cornell University Press, 1989), p. 193; Holstun, "Ranting"; Howard, "The New Historicism," p. 39; Alan Liu, "The Power of Formalism: The New Historicism," *ELH* 56 (1989): 721–30; and Montrose, "New Historicisms," pp. 400–402.

35. See J. G. A. Pocock, *Politics, Language, and Time: Essays on Political Thought and History* (New York: Atheneum, 1960), pp. 3–41; and Skinner, *Meaning and Context*. Defining a context in this second sense is fraught with perils, but I have asked myself whether an informed contemporary reader would have felt the omission as palpable. When Dryden published a heroic poem on the Second Anglo-Dutch War in 1667 after popular satires on the same subject had enjoyed wide circulation, he must have anticipated that readers would interpret his poem in the context of those satires, even if he disregarded them.

36. This is to recognize that speech and texts may not only *mean* but *do*. On the promise and limitations of speech-act theory for literary interpretation, see J. L. Austin, *How to Do Things with Words* (Cambridge: Harvard University Press, 1962); Jacques Derrida, "Signature Event Context," in his *Limited Inc.* (Evanston: Northwestern University Press, 1988); Skinner, *Meaning and Context;* and Sandy Petrey, *Speech Acts and Literary Theory* (New York: Routledge, 1990).

37. Perry Anderson, *In the Tracks of Historical Materialism* (Chicago: University of Chicago Press, 1984), chap. 2.

38. *The Readie and Easie Way* (Feb. 23–29, 1660), in *CPW* 7:385–86.

39. John Locke, *First Tract on Government* (1660), in *Political Essays,* ed. Mark Goldie (Cambridge: Cambridge University Press, 1997), p. 38.

40. Hugh R. Trevor-Roper, "The Elitist Politics of Milton," *TLS,* June 1, 1973: 601.

Introduction to Part One

1. See Cedric Brown, *John Milton's Aristocratic Entertainments* (Cambridge: Cambridge University Press, 1985).

2. For the texts and designs of Stuart masques, see Stephen Orgel and Roy Strong, *Inigo Jones: The Theatre of the Stuart Court,* 2 vols. (Berkeley: University of California Press, 1973). On the court masque in general, see David Bevington and Peter Holbrook, eds., *The Politics of the Stuart Court Masque* (Cambridge: Cambridge University Press, 1998); Erica Veevers, *Images of Love and Religion: Queen Henrietta Maria and Court Entertainments* (Cambridge: Cambridge University Press, 1989); Kevin Sharpe, *Criticism and Compliment: The Politics of Literature in the England of Charles I* (Cambridge: Cambridge University Press, 1987); David Lindley, ed., *The Court Masque* (Manchester: Manchester University Press, 1984); Graham Parry, *The Golden Age Restor'd: The Culture of the Stuart Court, 1603–42* (Manchester: Manchester University Press, 1981); Stephen

Orgel, *The Illusion of Power: Political Theater in the English Renaissance* (Berkeley: University of California Press, 1975); and John G. Demaray, *The Masque Tradition: The Early Poems, "Arcades," and "Comus"* (Cambridge: Harvard University Press, 1968).

3. For readings of *A Maske* that stress the way it reforms the genre, see Barbara Lewalski, "Milton's *Comus* and the Politics of Masquing," in *Politics of the Stuart Court Masque*, ed. Bevington and Holbrook; Leah Marcus, *The Politics of Mirth: Jonson, Herrick, Milton, Marvell, and the Defense of Old Holiday Pastimes* (Chicago: University of Chicago Press, 1986), chap. 6; David Norbrook, "The Reformation of the Masque," and John Creaser, "'The Present Aid of this Occasion': The Setting of *Comus*," both in *Court Masque*, ed. Lindley; and Maryann Cale McGuire, *Milton's Puritan Masque* (Athens: University of Georgia Press, 1983).

4. For a reading that interprets Comus as a representative of the rising bourgeoisie and looks for topical references to local industries, see Michael Wilding, *Dragon's Teeth: Literature in the English Revolution* (Oxford: Clarendon Press, 1987), pp. 69–77. For the Lady as a representative of the bourgeoisie, see Christopher Kendrick, "Milton and Sexuality: A Symptomatic Reading of *Comus*," in *Re-Membering Milton: Essays on the Texts and Traditions*, ed. Mary Nyquist and Margaret W. Ferguson (New York: Methuen, 1987). On beauty and chastity as forms of currency, see Julie H. Kim, "The Lady's Unladylike Struggle: Redefining Patriarchal Boundaries in Milton's *Comus*," *Milton Studies* 35 (1997): 1–20. Also see William Kerrigan, *The Sacred Complex: On the Psychogenesis of "Paradise Lost"* (Cambridge: Harvard University Press, 1983), p. 46.

5. On the Council of the Marches, see Penry Williams, *The Council of the Marches in Wales under Elizabeth I* (Cardiff: University of Wales Press, 1958) and "The Activity of the Council in the Marches under the Early Stuarts," *Welsh Historical Review* 1 (1961): 133–60; and Kevin Sharpe, *The Personal Rule of Charles I* (New Haven: Yale University Press, 1992), pp. 448–56. On the earl of Bridgewater's investigation of the rape of Marjorie Evans, see Leah Marcus, "The Milieu of Milton's *Comus*: Judicial Reform at Ludlow and the Problem of Sexual Assault," *Criticism* 25 (1983): 293–327. For readings of *A Maske* that stress its relationship with other aspects of the Lord President's office and duties, see Philip Schwyzer, "Purity and Danger on the West Bank of the Severn: The Cultural Geography of *A Masque Presented at Ludlow Castle, 1634*," *Representations* 60 (1997): 22–48; and Creaser, "'Present Aid.'"

6. Compare the arguments that Christopher Marlowe gives to Leander in his attempted seduction of Hero:

> Vessels of brass oft handled brightly shine;
> What difference betwixt richest mine
> And basest mould but use? For both, not us'd,
> Are of like worth. Then treasure is abus'd
> When misers keep it; being put to loan,
> In time it will return us two for one.
>
> (*Hero and Leander*, 1.231–36)

I cite Christopher Marlowe, *Complete Plays and Poems*, ed. E. D. Pendry and J. C. Maxwell (London: Everyman, 1976).

7. Of particular interest are Thomas Mun's *A Discovrse of Trade, from England vnto the East Indies* (1621), *England's Treasure by Forraign Trade* (written c. 1623; published

1664), and *The Petition and Remonstrance of the Governor and Company of Merchants of London Trading to the East-Indies* (1628); and Edward Misselden's *Free Trade; or, the Meanes to Make Trade Florish* (1622) and *The Circle of Commerce; or, the Balance of Trade, in Defence of Free Trade* (1623).

8. Aristotle, *Politics*, bk. 1, chap. 10, 1258b. "Dante says that usury is a sin against nature and against art: against nature because it makes money beget money, which is an unnatural begetting," writes Milton in his commonplace book before recording the places where arguments in favor of usury may be found (*CPW* 1:418–19).

9. Erasmus, *The Education of a Christian Prince*, trans. Lester K. Born (New York: Columbia University Press, 1936), p. 218.

10. For a study of these themes in early modern England, see Craig Muldrew, *The Economy of Obligation: The Culture of Credit and Social Relations in Early Modern England* (New York: St. Martin's Press, 1998).

11. John Calvin, *Institutes of the Christian Religion*, trans. John Allen (Philadelphia: Presbyterian Board of Education, 1936), bk. 3, chap. 10, sec. 5. Georgia Christopher quotes the same passage; see her *Milton and the Science of the Saints* (Princeton: Princeton University Press, 1982), pp. 49–50.

12. See *Christian Doctrine*'s comments on temperance, contentment, avarice, frugality, and industry in *CPW* 6:724, 728–33.

13. I cite the text in Orgel and Strong, *Inigo Jones*.

14. Calvin, *Institutes*, bk. 3, chap. 10, sec. 5.

15. Bulstrode Whitelocke, *Memorials of the English Affairs*, 4 vols. (Oxford: Oxford University Press, 1853), 1:58.

16. Christopher Hill, *Milton and the English Revolution* (London: Faber and Faber, 1977), p. 47.

17. For the charge that the Lady must feel incontinent desires, see Kerrigan, *Sacred Complex*, pp. 28–29. For a rebuttal, see John Leonard, "Saying 'No' to Freud: Milton's *A Mask* and Sexual Assault," *Milton Quarterly* 25 (1991): 129–40. Also see Deborah Shuger, "'Gums of Glutinous Heat' and the Stream of Consciousness: The Theology of Milton's *Maske*," *Representations* 60 (1997): 1–21.

Chapter One

1. On *Areopagitica*'s position amid other pleadings for free speech and liberty of conscience, see William Haller, ed. with comm., *Tracts on Liberty in the Puritan Revolution*, 3 vols. (New York: Columbia University Press, 1934); and Ernest Sirluck, introduction and notes, in *CPW* 2:1–216, 480–570. The most suggestive efforts to account for *Areopagitica*'s trade imagery are Kevin Dunn, "Milton among the Monopolists: *Areopagitica*, Intellectual Property, and the Hartlib Circle," in *Samuel Hartlib and Universal Reformation: Studies in Intellectual Communication*, ed. Mark Greengrass, Michael Leslie, and Timothy Raylor (Cambridge: Cambridge University Press, 1994); and Lawrence Manley, *Literature and Culture in Early Modern London* (Cambridge: Cambridge University Press, 1995), pp. 552–54. On licensors as engrossing middlemen, see Sandra Sherman, "Printing the Mind: The Economics of Authorship in *Areopagitica*," *ELH* 60 (1993): 323–47. For a Marxist interpretation, see Christopher Kendrick, "Ethics and the Orator in *Areopagitica*," *ELH* 50 (1983): 655–91. On the context of such imagery,

see Nigel Smith, "*Areopagitica:* Voicing Contexts, 1643–5," in *Politics, Poetics, and Hermeneutics in Milton's Prose,* ed. David Lowenstein and James Grantham Turner (Cambridge: Cambridge University Press, 1990), p. 115; and Sharon Achinstein, *Milton and the Revolutionary Reader* (Princeton: Princeton University Press, 1994), pp. 34–35.

2. On the lost petition against Milton that the Stationers presented to the Commons, see Sirluck, introduction, in *CPW* 2:142. The petition was preceded by Herbert Palmer's sermon before Parliament (Aug. 13, 1644), which attacked Milton. For Milton's complaints against intellectual restrictions in the divorce tracts, see *The Doctrine and Discipline of Divorce* (Aug. 1, 1643) and *The Judgement of Martin Bucer* (July 15, 1644), in *CPW* 2:223–26, 479.

3. Like Jürgen Habermas, I apply the phrase *public sphere* to a space of negotiation between the private and the governmental; see his *The Structural Transformation of the Public Sphere: An Inquiry into a Category of Bourgeois Society,* trans. Thomas Burger (Cambridge: MIT Press, 1991). Unlike Habermas, I argue that the new ideal of the public sphere that emerged in England did not simply coincide with the economic transformations of the seventeenth century but owed a specifiable intellectual debt to the economic discourse of the period. In focusing on the 1640s as a key period in the genesis of this new ideal, I reach behind Habermas's favored originary moment of 1694–95. More crucially, I contend that many reformers recognized that the public sphere was not simply political or literary but economic and that the realms of civilization and culture, necessity and freedom, need not be sharply distinguished. For an insightful critique of Habermas's ideas in the context of the English Civil Wars, see David Zaret, *Origins of Democratic Culture: Printing, Petitions, and the Public Sphere in Early Modern England* (Princeton: Princeton University Press, 2000).

4. On the theory and practice of monopoly patents, see William Hyde Price, *The English Patents of Monopoly* (Cambridge: Harvard University Press, 1913); E. Wyndam Hulme, "The History of the Patent System under the Prerogative and the Common Law," *Law Quarterly Review* 12 (1896): 141–54; Hulme, "The History of the Patent System under the Prerogative and the Common Law: A Sequel," *Law Quarterly Review* 16 (1900): 44–56; Joan Thirsk, *Economic Policy and Projects: The Development of a Consumer Society in Early Modern England* (Oxford: Clarendon Press, 1978), chaps. 1–3; and David Harris Sacks, "The Countervailing of Benefits: Monopoly, Liberty, and Benevolence in Elizabethan England," in *The Tudor Monarchy,* ed. John Guy (London: Arnold, 1997). On the legal and ethical significance of the concept of monopoly, see Sacks, "Parliament, Liberty, and the Commonwealth," in *Parliament and Liberty from the Reign of Elizabeth to the English Civil War,* ed. J. H. Hexter (Stanford: Stanford University Press, 1992) and "The Greed of Judas: Avarice, Monopoly, and the Moral Economy in England, ca. 1350–ca. 1600," *Journal of Medieval and Early Modern Studies* 28 (1998): 263–307.

5. D'Ewes, pp. 649, 644, 645. For the parliamentary debate on monopolies in 1601, see J. E. Neale, *Elizabeth I and Her Parliaments, 1584–1601* (London: J. Cape, 1957), pp. 376–93; and Sacks, "Countervailing of Benefits."

6. The case is reported in 11 Co. Rep. 84b, 77 Eng. Rep. 1260 (1603); Moore 671, 72 Eng. Rep. 830 (1603); and Noy 173, 74 Eng. Rep. 1131 (1603). See Jacob I. Corré, "The Argument, Decision, and Report of *Darcy v. Allen,*" *Emory Law Journal* 45 (1996): 1261–1327.

7. Noy 180, 74 Eng. Rep. 1137 (1603).

8. *PP1610*, 2:160.

9. Noy 181, 74 Eng. Rep. 1138 (1603); 11 Co. Rep. 86b, 77 Eng. Rep. 1263 (1603). Coke explains the logic of this claim in *3 Institutes*: "And the law of the Realm in this point is grounded upon the law of God, which saith *Non accipies loco pignoris inferiorem & superiorem molam, quia animam suam apposuit tibi* [Deut. 24:6]. Thou shalt not take the nether or upper milstone to pledge, for he taketh a mans life to pledge. Whereby it appeareth that a mans trade is accounted his life, because it maintaineth his life" (p. 181).

10. Coke, *3 Institutes*, p. 181.

11. John Lilburne, *Innocency and Truth Justified* (1645), p. 61. He refers to the passage again in *London's Liberties in Chains Discovered* (1646), p. 56. The frontispiece of *The Trial of Lieut. John Lilburne* (1649) depicts him defending himself with Coke's *Institutes* in hand.

12. 11 Co. Rep. 86b, 77 Eng. Rep. 1263 (1603); Noy 180, 74 Eng. Rep. 1137 (1603).

13. D'Ewes, p. 646.

14. Noy 178, 74 Eng. Rep. 1135 (1603).

15. Sir Francis Bacon assumed in the parliamentary debates of 1601 that a grant to a company of men could not be a monopoly (D'Ewes, p. 645). Fuller also exempted corporations from his attack on Darcy's grant; see Noy 183, 74 Eng. Rep. 1139 (1603).

16. In 1601, the lawyer Richard Martin called monopolists, "Bloodsuckers of the Common-Wealth" (D'Ewes, p. 646). James I's charter is reproduced in *Economic Docs.*, p. 462. I quote *A Discourse Consisting of Motives for the Enlargement and Freedome of Trade* (Apr. 11, 1645), p. 4. Cf. Thomas Hobbes: "there is sometimes in a commonwealth a disease which resembleth the pleurisy; and that is when the treasure of the commonwealth, flowing out of its due course, is gathered together in too much abundance in one or a few private men, by monopolies or by farms of the public revenues, in the same manner as blood in a pleurisy, getting into the membrane of the breast, breedeth there an inflammation, accompanied with a fever and painful stitches" (*Leviathan* [1651], ed. Edwin Curley [Indianapolis: Hackett, 1994], pt. 2, chap. 29, par. 19). On the political uses of the image of bodily circulation in early Stuart and Interregnum England, see Annabel Patterson, *Fables of Power: Aesopian Writing and Political History* (Durham: Duke University Press, 1991), pp. 111–37; John Rogers, *The Matter of Revolution: Science, Poetry, and Politics in the Age of Milton* (Ithaca: Cornell University Press, 1996), pp. 16–38; and Quentin Skinner, *Liberty before Liberalism* (Cambridge: Cambridge University Press, 1998), pp. 24–36.

17. *A Discourse Consisting of Motives*, p. 3.

18. *Economic Docs.*, p. 20. Such claims had been made as early as the 1580s; see R. H. Tawney and Eileen Power, eds., *Tudor Economic Documents: Being Select Documents Illustrating the Economic and Social History of Tudor England*, 3 vols. (London: Longman, 1924), 3:266–67. They were forcefully reenunciated by the Leveller William Walwyn in "W Walwins Conceptions; For a Free Trade, 1652," in *The Writings of William Walwyn*, ed. Jack R. McMichael and Barbara Taft (Athens: University of Georgia Press, 1989), pp. 446–52.

19. John Wheeler, *A Treatise of Commerce* (1601), ed. with intro. George Burton Hotchkiss (New York: New York University Press, 1931), pp. 338, 373; *Economic Docs.*, p. 59; Wheeler, *A Treatise of Commerce*, p. 333.

20. *A Discourse Consisting of Motives*, pp. 6, 22, 27–28.

21. 11 Co. Rep. 86b, 77 Eng. Rep. 1263 (1603).

22. William Walwyn claims that "the numerousness of Merchants will occasion a strife & emulation among them, who shall produce the best ordered goods . . . whereas Merchants in Companyes have noe need of such diligence, none being at the places of their sale, but themselves" ("W Walwyns Conceptions," in *Writings*, p. 449).

23. *CJ*, 1:218. Sandys's distinction between an inheritable right and a purchased liberty presented itself conveniently to free trade advocates in Acts 22:27–28: "Then the chief captain came, and said unto him, Tell me, art thou a Roman? He said, Yea. And the chief captain answered, With a great sum I obtained this freedom. And Paul said, But I was free-*born*." For a citation of the passage, see Thomas Johnson, *A Plea for Free-Men's Liberties; or the Monopoly of the Eastland Merchants Anatomized* (1646).

24. David Harris Sacks drew my attention to this point; see Sacks, "Parliament," pp. 95–96.

25. Lilburne, *Innocency and Truth Justified*, p. 61.

26. *A Discourse Consisting of Motives*, p. 3.

27. Thomas Johnson cites Revelation 13:16–17 as the parting salvo of *A Plea*, sig. A4v. John Lilburne reproduces Johnson's tract in his own *The Charters of London; or, the Second Part of Londons Liberty in Chaines Discovered* (1646).

28. *The Triumphs of Truth* (1613) and *The Triumphs of Honour and Virtue* (1622), in Middleton, *Works*, 7:248, 358.

29. Bacon, *Works*, 3:164. The engravings share these basic features, but they are different works.

30. Gabriel Plattes, *Macaria* (1641) in Charles Webster, *Samuel Hartlib and the Advancement of Learning* (Cambridge: Cambridge University Press, 1970), p. 80. On its authorship, see Webster, "The Authorship and Significance of *Macaria*," *Past and Present*, no. 56 (1972): 34–48. On Mede, Twisse, the Hartlib circle, and Bacon's importance to them, see Webster, *The Great Instauration: Science, Medicine, and Reform, 1626–1660* (New York: Holmes and Meier, 1976). In their personal correspondence, members of the Hartlib circle often depict themselves as merchants of truth. For example, in a letter to Hartlib, Sir Cheney Culpeper says that he will willingly become a "merchant venturer in the business" of sending Benjamin Worsley as a factor to the scholar Johannes Rudolphes Glauberus to "purchase his ingenuities of him." See Hartlib Papers 13/196A (Letter, Sir Cheney Culpeper to Hartlib, Oct. 20, 1647).

31. Nicholas Fuller, *The Argvment of Master Nicholas Fvller, in the Case of Thomas Lad, and Richard Mavnsell, his Clients* ([Holland?], 1607). This pamphlet was reprinted in London in 1640.

32. This sermon is gathered but separately paginated in Jeremiah Dyke, *Divers Select Sermons on Several Tracts* (1640).

33. There is no doubt that Dyke was a staunch Puritan, but many other facts about his life are in question; see *DNB*, s.v. "Dyke, Jeremiah."

34. Manley, *Literature and Culture*, pp. 552–54, discusses the sermons of Hill and Goodwin together with *Areopagitica* in the context of the Puritan Revolution's antisedentarist ideology.

35. See *DNB*, s.v. "Hill, Thomas"; and James Winn, *John Dryden and His World* (New Haven: Yale University Press, 1987), pp. 8, 11, 17, 36–38, 57, 59–62, 66, 70, 129, 131, 373, 556 n. 43, 577 n. 38.

36. *PP1610*, 2:152–66, esp. 2:160.

37. *The Works of Thomas Goodwin*, 12 vols. (Edinburgh: James Nichol, 1861–63), 4:246–48.

38. I quote [Henry Parker], *To the High Court of Parliament: The Humble Petition of the Company of Stationers* (1643), sig. A2v. For the charge of monopoly, see Michael Sparke, *Scintilla; or a Light Broken into Darke Warehouses* (1641), pp. 3, 6. On passage of the Licensing Act, see Michael Mendle, "De Facto Freedom, De Facto Authority: Press and Parliament, 1640–43," *Historical Journal* 38 (1995): 307–32.

39. On the petition, see Valerie Pearl, *London and the Outbreak of the Puritan Revolution: City Government and National Politics, 1625–43* (Oxford: Oxford University Press, 1961), p. 175. Since quite a number of aldermen were themselves monopolists or members of corporations that some opponents called monopolies, it need hardly be said that not *all* Londoners were opposed to monopolies. For a sense of the diverse opinions and interests that coexisted in London, see Keith Lindley, *Popular Politics and Religion in Civil War London* (Aldershot: Scolar Press, 1997). I quote Lord Digby's speech in Rushworth, pt. 3, chap. 1, p. 31.

40. Rushworth, pt. 3, chap. 1, p. 33.

41. *A Dialogue or Accidental Discourse Betwixt Mr. Alderman Abell, and Richard Kilvert* (1641), p. 8.

42. *Bishops, Iudges, Monopolists* (1641), p. 5.

43. Wilson H. Coates, Anne Steele Young, and Vernon F. Snow, eds., *The Private Journals of the Long Parliament, 3 January to 5 March 1642* (New Haven: Yale University Press, 1992), pp. 284, 287.

44. Hyde, *English Patents of Monopoly*, pp. 126–28.

45. Robert Ashton, *The City and the Court, 1603–1643* (Cambridge: Cambridge University Press, 1979), p. 156.

46. 11 Co. Rep. 86b, 77 Eng. Rep. 1263; Coke, *2 Institutes*, p. 47; Coke, *3 Institutes*, p. 181.

47. On Parker's three pamphlets on behalf of commercial interests (the Vintners, the Stationers, and the Merchant Adventurers), see Michael Mendle, *Henry Parker and the English Civil War* (Cambridge: Cambridge University Press, 1995), chap. 7.

48. [Parker], *Humble Remonstrance*, sigs. A1v, A1r, A1v, A2r, A3r.

49. D'Ewes, p. 648. John Lilburne thought the remark too good not to make it his own: "the next *Monopoly*, it is to be feared will be upon *Bread* and *Beer* . . . Oh *Englishmen!* Where is your freedoms." See his *Englands Birth-Right Justified* (1645), p. 11.

50. 11 Co. Rep. 85b–86a, 77 Eng. Rep. 1261–62 (1603).

51. [Parker], *Humble Remonstrance*, sigs. A3r-v.

52. Sparke, *Scintilla;* [Parker], *Humble Remonstrance*, sigs. A3v–A4r.

53. *An Abstract of the Generall Grieuances of the Poore Free-men and Iourney-men Printers Oppressed, and Kept in Servile Bondage All Their Lives by the Unlawful Ordinances of the Master and Wardens of the Company* (1614?), in Edward Arber, *Transcripts of the Registers of the Company of Stationers of London, 1554–1640,* 5 vols. (London, 1875–84), 4:526; George Wither, *The Schollers Purgatory, Discouered in the Stationers Common-wealth* (1625?), p. 10.

54. Wither, *Schollers Purgatory*, p. 5. Wither says that the Stationers have "vsurped vpon the labours of all writers" and "do peremptorily challenge an unjust interest in

euery mans labour of this kind"; but "vnless [they] can proue, the Author hath sould them his birthright . . . he being the elder brother, the right first . . . falleth vnto him" (pp. 5, 31).

55. Michael Wilding remarks on *Areopagitica*'s structural contrast between the dignity of labor and its opposite, a lazy, loitering life, the former associated with the sects and the latter with beneficed clergy and priests; see his "Milton's *Areopagitica: Liberty for the Sects*," in *The Literature of Controversy*, ed. Thomas Corns (London: Frank Cass, 1987), pp. 16–18.

56. Jeremiah Dyke also observes that truth is a "necessary and usefull commodity" like bread or clothing; see *The Pvrchase and Possession of the Truth*, pp. 312–13.

57. Aristotle, *Nichomachean Ethics*, bk. 3, chap. 2, 1112a. My emphasis.

58. [Richard Overton], *A Sacred Decretal, Or Hue and Cry* (May 1645), p. 388; Lilburne, *London's Liberty in Chains Discovered*, p. 40. For a brilliant analysis of the Levellers' concept of monopoly, see Alan Craig Houston, "A Way of Settlement: The Levellers, Monopolies, and the Public Interest," *History of Political Thought* 14 (1993): 381–420.

59. Kendrick, "Ethics and the Orator"; Stanley Fish, "Driving from the Letter: Truth and Indeterminacy in Milton's *Areopagitica*," in *Re-Membering Milton*, ed. Mary Nyquist and Margaret W. Ferguson (New York: Methuen, 1987).

60. Sirluck, introduction, in *CPW* 2:164.

61. Goodwin, *Works*, 4:248.

62. Such a positive valuation of circulation had recently had divine authority ascribed to it in *The Commons Petition of Long Afflicted England*, a populist poem of 1642. In response to the commons' bitter denunciation of "Monopoly-mongers" in the poem, a heavenly voice rules, "The common-wealth should alwayes be in motion, / Seas flow to brooks, and brooks should fall to th'ocean" (sigs. A3r, A4r).

63. Largely on the basis of this passage, critics have argued that Milton felt a disgust for tradesmen. J. F. Camé refers to Milton's "contempt of commerce" ("Images in Milton's *Areopagitica*," *Cahiers Elisabethains* 6 [1974]: 24). Alan F. Price says that the passage "clearly implies a loathing of commercialized religion and a disdain of traders" ("Incidental Imagery in *Areopagitica*," *Modern Philology* 49 [1952]: 219 n. 9). Kevin Dunn remarks, "Yet [Milton] consistently represents the merchant as a figure of contempt" ("Milton among the Monopolists," p. 187). For a more interesting reading of this passage, see Lana Cable, *Carnal Rhetoric: Milton's Iconoclasm and the Poetics of Desire* (Durham: Duke University Press, 1995), pp. 140–43.

64. Roger Edgeworth, "The Fourth Sermon, Treatyng of the Fift Gift of the Holy Ghost, Called the Spirite of Science," in his *Sermons Very Fruitful, Godly and Learned* (1557), ed. Janet Wilson (Cambridge, U.K.: D. S. Brewer, 1993), p. 146. For a discussion of Edgeworth's views in the context of Bristol's religious and economic controversies, see David Harris Sacks, "Bristol's 'Wars of Religion,'" in *Town and Countryside in the English Revolution*, ed. R. C. Richardson (Manchester: Manchester University Press, 1992), esp. pp. 114–15.

65. Brian Manning, *The English People and the English Revolution, 1640–1649* (London: Heinemann, 1976) pp. 15, 106; quotation on pp. 12–13.

66. John Millar, "The Advancement of Manufactures, Commerce, and the Arts," in William C. Lehman, *John Millar of Glasgow, 1735–1801: His Life and Thought and His*

Contribution to Sociological Analysis (Cambridge: Cambridge University Press, 1960), p. 339.

67. *Animadversions upon the Remonstrants Defence* (1641) and *The Likeliest Means to Remove Hirelings* (1659), in *CPW* 1:676-77 and 7:306-07.

68. Adam Smith writes: "In the progress of the division of labour, the employment of the far greater part of those who live by labour, that is, of the great body of the people, comes to be confined to a few very simple operations. . . . But the understandings of the greater part of men are necessarily formed by their ordinary employments. The man whose whole life is spent in performing a few simple operations . . . has no occasion to exert his understanding, or to exercise his invention in finding out expedients for removing difficulties which never occur. He naturally loses, therefore, the habit of such exertion, and generally becomes as stupid and ignorant as it is possible for a human creature to become. The torpor of his mind renders him, not only incapable of relishing or bearing a part in any rational conversation, but of conceiving any generous, noble, or tender sentiment, and consequently of forming any just judgment concerning many even of the ordinary duties of private life. Of the great and extensive interests of his country, he is altogether incapable of judging" (*An Inquiry into the Nature and Causes of the Wealth of Nations* [1776], ed. R. H. Cambell and A. S. Skinner, 2 vols. [Indianapolis: Liberty Classics, 1981], pp. 781-82).

69. On Puritan ideas of the Golden Age and Millennium, see Webster, *Great Instauration,* pp. 15-27.

70. *The Great Instauration* and *The New Organon,* in Bacon, *Works,* 4:15 (the same view is expressed at 3:291-92); 4:77, 91-92.

71. *Preparative towards a Natural and Experimental History* and *The New Organon,* in Bacon, *Works,* 4:251-52, 114.

72. See, for instance, Henry Parker, *Observations upon Some of His Majesties Late Answers and Expresses* (1642), pp. 1-2.

73. William Walwyn, *The Compassionate Samaritane* (1644): "He that bade us to try all things, and hold fast that which was good, did suppose that men have faculties and abilities wherewithal to try all things, or else the counsell had beene given in vaine" (*Writings,* p. 108). Cf. [Henry Robinson], *Liberty of Conscience; or the Sole Meanes to Obtaine Peace and Truth* (Mar. 24, 1644), p. 41.

74. *The Reason of Church Government* (1642), in *CPW* 1:802. The great Marchants of this world" seem to be the merchants of Revelation 18:10-20, who set themselves against the impending apocalypse.

75. Lilburne, *Englands Birth-Right Justified,* pp. 8-10. In the same passage, Lilburne summarizes *A Discourse Consisting of Motives* and says where it can be bought.

76. On the Merchant Adventurers' regulations, see Hotchkiss's introduction, in Wheeler, *A Treatise of Commerce,* p. 32. On the Levant and East India Companies' reliance on informal barriers to entry, see Robert Brenner, *Merchants and Revolution: Commercial Change, Political Conflict, and London's Overseas Traders, 1550-1653* (Princeton: Princeton University Press, 1993), pp. 54-55, 67-73, 87-88.

77. *A Discourse Consisting of Motives,* p. 12; *The Commons Petition of Long Afflicted England,* sig. A3r; Johnson, *A Plea,* sig. A4v.

78. See, for example, *A Discourse Consisting of Motives,* pp. 17-18. In 1621 the House of Commons had attempted to examine the patents and rule books of the Merchant

Adventurers and had been prevented only by James I's admonition: "there have been diverse things between them [the Merchant Adventurers] and me not so fitt for yow to see and deale in. Medle not with those things that belong to me and the state." Presumably the author of *A Discourse* gained access to the Adventurers' minutes and accounts because the House of Commons finally got hold of their court book, register book, and accounts in 1624. For James's warning, see Ashton, *City and the Court,* pp. 109–10. Also see Brenner, *Merchants and Revolution,* pp. 214–15.

79. Along with a whole series of complementary proposals, the Levellers called for "General Accomptants of the Kingdom, who shal publish their Accompts every moneth to the publick view, and that henceforth there be only one Common Treasury where the books of Accompts may be kept by several persons, open to the view of all men" (Don M. Wolfe, ed., *Leveller Manifestoes of the Puritan Revolution* [New York: Thomas Nelson & Sons, 1944], p. 269). In *A Plea,* Thomas Johnson begins with the premise that "this Kingdom is a corporation or society of men" (sig. A2v).

80. *The Readie and Easie Way* (1660), in *CPW* 7:433; cf. *A Second Defence of the English People* (1654) and *Digression on the Long Parliament,* in *CPW* 4:682–83; 5:445.

81. Supple, *Commercial Crisis,* pp. 221–24. Also see *A Discourse Consisting of Motives;* William Goffe, *How to Advance the Trade of the Nation and Employ the Poor* (1641); Lewes Roberts, *The Treasure of Traffike; or, a Discourse of Forraign Trade* (1641); *Sir Thomas Roe his Speech in Parliament* (1641); Henry Robinson, *Englands Safety, in Trades Encrease* (1641); Robinson, *Briefe Considerations Concerning the Advancement of Trade* (1649); Walwyn, "W Walwins Conceptions," in *Writings,* pp. 449–50.

82. John Hall, *The Advancement of Learning,* ed. A. K. Croston (Liverpool: Liverpool University Press, 1953), pp. 28, 5–6, 19, 30, 33, 14. Croston notes the references to Milton. He adds that shortly after *Areopagitica* appeared, Hall wrote to Hartlib that he was "most ambitious of the acquaintance of Mr. Milton" (p. xi n. 2). Various academies were established in the hope that lectures on science, commerce, foreign laws, and the like would promote new industries and trade routes. One such was formed by Sir Balthazar Gerbier (whom we shall meet again in Chapter Three) with the assistance of Hartlib.

83. See John Dury, *Considerations Tending to the Happy Accomplishment of Englands Reformation in Church and State* (1647); and Samuel Hartlib, *A Further Discoverie of the Office of Publick Addresse for Accommodations* (1648). For a discussion of *Areopagitica,* Hartlib's project, and the notion of knowledge as a commodity or as property, see Dunn, "Milton among the Monopolists."

84. Hartlib, *A Further Discoverie,* pp. 4–6.

85. Henry Robinson, *The Office of Addresses and Encounters: Where All People of Each Ranke and Quality May Receive Direction and Advice* (Sept. 7, 1650). Also see Haller, *Tracts on Liberty,* 1:64–67; and Wilbur K. Jordan, *Men of Substance: A Study of the Thought of Two English Revolutionaries, Henry Parker and Henry Robinson* (Chicago: University of Chicago Press, 1942), pp. 250–53. Robinson's office attracted imitators and competitors, some as well meaning, others less scrupulous; see Webster, *Great Instauration,* pp. 69, 76.

86. On Milton's connections with the Hartlib circle, see Sirluck's introduction in *CPW* 2:206–12. For many other direct and indirect contacts between Milton and Robert Boyle, Sir Cheney Culpeper, John Dury, Theodore Haak, John Hall, and

Benjamin Worsley, see Christopher Hill, *Milton and the English Revolution* (London: Faber and Faber, 1977); and Barbara Lewalksi, *The Life of John Milton: A Critical Biography* (Oxford: Blackwell, 2000).

87. Hartlib Papers 30/4/89A (Hartlib, *Ephemerides*, 1643); Timothy Raylor, "New Light on Milton and Hartlib," *Milton Quarterly* 27 (1993): 19–30.

88. Montaigne, *Les Essais*, bk. 1, chap. 35; for a response to Hartlib's inquiries about Renaudot's *Bureau d'Adresse*, see Hartlib Papers 58/3A–4B (Letter, Arnold Boate to Hartlib, July 26, 1648).

89. Hartlib Papers 13/136A (Letter, Sir Cheney Culpeper to Hartlib, March 4, 1646).

90. Aristotle, *Politics*, bk. 1, chap. 11, 1259a; on this story, also see Sacks, "Greed of Judas," pp. 273–75.

91. See *The Character of the Rump* (1659); and Ernest Sirluck, "Milton's Political Thought: The First Cycle," *Modern Philology* 61 (1964): 209–24.

92. See Victoria Kahn, "The Metaphorical Contract in Milton's *Tenure of Kings and Magistrates*," in *Milton and Republicanism*, ed. David Armitage, Armand Himy, and Quentin Skinner (Cambridge: Cambridge University Press, 1995).

93. *Eikonoklastes* (1649), *Tenure of Kings and Magistrates* (1649), *A Defence of the English People* (1651), in *CPW* 3:356, 206; 4:459–60.

94. Johnson, *A Plea*, sig. A2v.

95. Houston, "Way of Settlement," p. 386.

Introduction to Part Two

1. See the commentary in Dryden, *Works*, 1:257–58.

2. John Evelyn, *Navigation and Commerce, Their Original and Progress. Containing a Succinct Account of Traffick in General* (1674), pp. 11–14.

3. "Of the True Greatness of the Kingdom of Britain. To King James" (1607–08?), in Bacon, *Works*, 7:61. Bacon later used this incomplete manuscript as the basis of his more general essay "Of the True Greatness of Kingdoms and Estates" (in *Works*, 6:444–52). It is not clear that the letter was actually delivered to James I.

4. See James Knowles, "Cecil's Shopping Centre: The Rediscovery of a Ben Jonson Masque in Praise of Trade," *TLS*, Feb. 7, 1997: 14–15. In connection with his cloth finishing scheme, Sir William Cockayne presented James I with valuable gifts and a (lost) entertainment in which dyers, cloth dressers, and merchants from Hamburg were presented to the king and "spake such language as Ben Jonson putt in theyre mouthes" (*CSP Domestic, 1611–18*, p. 373). On *The Triumph of Peace*, see Stephen Orgel and Roy Strong, *Inigo Jones: The Theatre of the Stuart Court*, 2 vols. (Berkeley: University of California Press, 1973), 2:537–61; Martin Butler, "Politics and the Masque: The Triumph of Peace," *The Seventeenth Century* 2 (1987): 117–41; and Kevin Sharpe, *Criticism and Compliment: The Politics of Literature in the England of Charles I* (Cambridge: Cambridge University Press, 1987), pp. 214–23. Patricia Fumerton argues that *Neptune's Triumph for the Return of Albion* (1624) gestures toward the East India trade, but even in her own terms the masque's oblique fictions differ markedly from contemporary civic entertainments or the Restoration literature we will consider; see her *Cultural Aesthetics: Renaissance Literature and the Practice of Social Ornament* (Chicago: University

of Chicago Press, 1991), chap. 5. It is possible that Prince Henry would have sponsored a rival tradition of courtly art with more direct and heroic representations of
trade had death not intervened in 1612. That event left works like Samuel Daniel's
Tethys' Festivall (1610) associated with an aborted future rather than the mainstream
of the early Stuart monarchy. See John Pitcher, "'In those figures which they seeme':
Samuel Daniel's Tethys' Festival," in *The Court Masque,* ed. David Lindley (Manchester:
Manchester University Press, 1984); Christopher Hill, *Intellectual Origins of the English
Revolution* (Oxford: Clarendon Press, 1965), pp. 213–19; David Norbrook, *Poetry and
Politics in the English Renaissance* (London: Routledge and Kegan Paul, 1984), pp. 203–
05; and Roy Strong, *Henry, Prince of Wales, and England's Lost Renaissance* (London:
Thames and Hudson, 1986).

   5. Lewes Roberts, *The Treasure of Traffike, or a Discourse of Forraigne Trade* (1641),
p. 55/sig. H4r (irregular pagination). On the financial basis of Charles I's monarchy,
see Kevin Sharpe, *The Personal Rule of Charles I* (New Haven: Yale University Press,
1992), p. 128. Charles I and his poets did address the trade grievances of 1640–41 in
minor ways. The frieze of the proscenium arch for Sir William Davenant's *Salmacida
Spolia* (1640) included riches and commerce among the benefits of a well-ordered
polity, and in an address during his entry into London in 1641, Charles I briefly acknowledged the City's interest in trade and pledged to better it. When we remember
that Charles's seizure of the bullion deposits at the mint in 1640 had crippled the capital market and brought the City's trade to a halt, however, his words seem like slight
consolation. On the proscenium arch, see Sharpe, *Criticism and Compliment,* p. 252.
For Charles's speech, see *Ovatio Carolina, The Triumph of King Charles* (1641), pp. 11–13,
esp. p. 12.

   6. *LJ,* 4:541.

Chapter Two

   1. Gerrard Winstanley, *Fire in the Bush* (1649–50?), in *The Works of Gerrard Winstanley,* ed. George H. Sabine (Ithaca: Cornell University Press, 1941), p. 465.

   2. A core of republican M.P.s, including Thomas Chaloner, Thomas Scot, and
Sir Arthur Haselrig, formulated commercial policy. They worked closely with M.P.s
from the Cinque Ports, Sussex, and the colonial trades, and they consulted economic
theorists from the Hartlib circle like Benjamin Worsley, Henry Robinson, Sir Cheny
Culpeper, and Robert Honeywood.

   3. For an account of Milton's official duties under the Commonwealth and Protectorate, see Robert T. Fallon, *Milton in Government* (University Park: Pennsylvania
State University Press, 1993).

   4. On the Rump's naval and commercial policies, see J. C. Farnell, "The Navigation Act of 1651, the First Dutch War, and the London Merchant Community,"
Economic History Review, 2d ser., 16 (1964): 439–54; Blair Worden, *The Rump Parliament,
1648–1653* (Cambridge: Cambridge University Press, 1974), pp. 40–41, 58, 254–62; J. P.
Cooper, "Social and Economic Policies under the Commonwealth," in *The Interregnum: The Quest for Settlement, 1646–1660,* ed. G. E. Aylmer (London: Macmillan, 1982);
Derek Massarella, "'A World Elsewhere': Aspects of the Overseas Expansionist Mood
in the 1650s," in *Politics and People in Revolutionary England: Essays in Honour of Ivan Roots,*

ed. Colin Jones, Malyn Newitt, and Stephen Roberts (Oxford: Blackwell, 1986), esp. pp. 141–48; and Robert Brenner, *Merchants and Revolution: Commercial Change, Political Conflict, and London's Overseas Traders, 1550–1653* (Princeton: Princeton University Press, 1993), pp. 577–637. For an account that places those policies in a slightly wider perspective, see Richard Conquest, "The State and Commercial Expansion: England in the Years 1642–1688," *Journal of European Economic History* 14 (1985): 155–72.

5. Benjamin Worsley, *The Advocate* (1652), pp. 1–2. Cf. Samuel Lambe, *Seasonable Observations* (1657).

6. On the Dutch as an economic example, see Joyce Appleby, *Economic Thought and Ideology in Seventeenth-Century England* (Princeton: Princeton University Press, 1978), pp. 73–97. It is noteworthy that a number of the men who published economic programs at this time based on the Dutch example (such as Henry Robinson, Benjamin Worsley, Thomas Violet, and Hugh Peters) had lived in the Netherlands. On the early Stuart distaste for the Dutch, see Christopher Hill, *Intellectual Origins of the English Revolution* (Oxford: Clarendon Press, 1965), p. 161; Simon Adams, "Spain or the Netherlands? The Dilemmas of Early Stuart Foreign Policy," in *Before the English Civil War: Essays in Early Stuart Politics and Government,* ed. Howard Tomlinson (London: Macmillan, 1983), pp. 79–101; and Kevin Sharpe, *The Personal Rule of Charles I* (New Haven: Yale University Press, 1992), pp. 76, 217.

7. Hugh Peter, "Prefatory Epistle to J. T.," *Good Work for a Good Magistrate* (1651).

8. Brenner, *Merchants and Revolution,* p. 607.

9. Francis Osborne, *A Perswasive to a Mutuall Compliance under the Present Government. Together with a Plea for a Free State Compared with Monarchy* (Oxford, 1652), p. 20.

10. *CSP Venetian, 1647–52,* pp. 188.

11. This paragraph draws heavily on Steven Pincus, *Protestantism and Patriotism: Ideologies and the Making of English Foreign Policy, 1650–1668* (Cambridge: Cambridge University Press, 1996), chap. 3.

12. *The Troubles of Amsterdam; or, the Disturbed or Disquieted Amsterdammer,* trans. L. W., reprinted by William Du-Gard, printer to the Council of State (1650), p. 13.

13. L. A. Harper, *The English Navigation Laws: A Seventeenth-Century Experiment in Social Engineering* (New York: Columbia University Press, 1939), pp. 39–45; Charles Wilson, *Profit and Power: A Study of England and the Dutch Wars* (The Hague: M. Nijhoff, 1957), pp. 48–60; R. W. K. Hinton, *The Eastland Trade and the Common Weal in the Seventeenth Century* (Cambridge: Cambridge University Press, 1959), pp. 84–94; Farnell, "Navigation Act"; Worden, *Rump Parliament,* pp. 290–91; Pincus, *Protestantism and Patriotism,* pp. 40–75.

14. More generally, see Leo Miller, *John Milton's Writings in the Anglo-Dutch Negotiations, 1651–1654* (Pittsburgh: Duquesne University Press, 1992).

15. Charles Wilson, *England's Apprenticeship, 1603–1763,* 2d ed. (London: Longman, 1984), p. 63.

16. On the First Anglo-Dutch War, see Wilson, *Profit and Power,* pp. 48–77; Simon Groenveld, "The English Civil Wars as a Cause of the First Anglo-Dutch War, 1640–1652," *Historical Journal* 30 (1987): 541–66; Jonathan Israel, "Competing Cousins: Anglo-Dutch Trade Rivalry," *History Today* 38 (July 1988): 17–22; Israel, *Dutch Primacy in World Trade, 1585–1740* (Oxford: Clarendon Press, 1995), pp. 713–26; J. R. Jones, *The Anglo-*

Dutch Wars of the Seventeenth Century (London: Longman, 1996), pp. 107–44; and Pincus, *Protestantism and Patriotism,* pp. 11–191.

17. Joost van den Vondel, *Inwydinge van het Stadthuis 't Amsterdam* (Amsterdam, 1655), line 242.

18. Pincus, *Protestantism and Patriotism,* esp. pp. 37, 130. The identification of the United Provinces with Tyre was not a new one. Vondel makes it in the closing lines of his poem on the Amsterdam Exchange, "Aen de Beurs van Amsterdam" (1643).

19. Brenner, *Merchants and Revolution,* p. 629.

20. Pincus, *Protestantism and Patriotism,* pp. 115–19; Worden, *Rump Parliament,* p. 86.

21. The epithets appear in Guibon Goddard's notes on the parliamentary debate of September 7, 1654, printed in *The Diary of Thomas Burton,* ed. John Towill Rutt, 4 vols. (1828; reprint, New York: Johnson Reprint Corp., 1974), 1:xxv. Writing at the end of the century, Roger Coke could still remember Cromwell's dissolution of the Rump with all the pathos of a tragedy: "Thus, by their own mercenary Servants, and not a Sword drawn in their Defence, fell the Haughty and Victorious *Rump,* whose mighty Actions will scarcely find Belief in future Generations; and to say the Truth, they were a Race of Men most indefatigably industrious in Business, always seeking Men fit for it, and never preferring any for Favour, nor by Importunity" (*A Detection of the Court and State of England,* 3d ed. [1697], p. 363).

22. The Nominated Assembly is sometimes called Barebones' Parliament or the Little Parliament. See Austin Woolrych, *Commonwealth to Protectorate* (Oxford: Clarendon Press, 1982). For a brief review of the governments established in the 1650s, see David L. Smith, "The Struggle for New Constitutional Forms," in *Revolution and Restoration: England in the 1650s,* ed. John Morrill (London: Collins and Brown, 1992).

23. Menna Prestwich, "Diplomacy and Trade in the Protectorate," *Journal of Modern History* 22 (1950): 103–21; M. P. Ashley, *Financial and Commercial Policy under the Cromwellian Protectorate* (Oxford: Oxford University Press, 1934), p. 99 et passim; Massarella, "'World Elsewhere,'" pp. 146–47; Pincus, *Protestantism and Patriotism,* chaps. 9–10.

24. I cite the text supplied in *Expans'd Hieroglyphicks: A Critical Edition of Sir John Denham's "Cooper's Hill,"* ed. Brendan O Hehir (Berkeley: University of California Press, 1969), app. C.

25. "Of the True Greatness of Kingdoms and Estates," in Bacon, *Works,* 6:451. Cicero's apothegm also appears (though with slight variations) on the title pages of [Henry Stubbe], *A Justification of the Present War against the United Netherlands* (1672) and John Evelyn, *Navigation and Commerce, Their Progress and Original. Containing a Succinct Account of Traffick in General* (1674).

26. Thomas Hobbes, *Leviathan* (1651), ed. Edwin Curley (Indianapolis: Hackett, 1994), pt. 2, chap. 22, pars. 18–20. Waller knew and admired Hobbes's works. He considered translating *De Cive* into English in 1645, and he thanked Hobbes for the gift of a volume containing *Of Body* and *Six Lessons* in a letter of 1656 that displays his familiarity with recent criticisms of *Leviathan.* See *The Correspondence of Thomas Hobbes,* ed. Noel Malcolm, 2 vols. (Oxford: Clarendon Press, 1994), 1:124-25, 294-96; and *"Brief Lives," Chiefly of Contemporaries, Set Down by John Aubrey, Between the Years 1669 and 1696,* ed. A. Clark, 2 vols. (Oxford: Oxford University Press, 1898), 2:297.

27. David Armitage, "The Cromwellian Protectorate and the Languages of Empire," *Historical Journal* 35 (1992): 531–55.

28. For a contemporary comment on this process, see *Diary of Burton*, 1:xlix.

29. On these negotiations, see *A Collection of the State Papers of John Thurloe*, 7 vols. (1742), 2:125–26; S. R. Gardner, *History of the Commonwealth and Protectorate, 1649–56*, 4 vols. (1894–1901; reprint, New York: AMS Press, 1965), 3:49–51.

30. Pincus, *Protestantism and Patriotism*, pp. 184–85.

31. Ashley, *Financial and Commercial*, pp. 107, 141–44; Godfrey Davies, *The Restoration of Charles II, 1658–1660* (San Marino, Calif.: Huntington Library, 1955), pp. 71, 190, 198; Armitage, "Cromwellian Protectorate."

32. *To Mr. Waller vpon His Panegyrique to the Lord Protector.* For the text of the previously unpublished poem and its attribution to Lucy Hutchinson, see David Norbrook, "Lucy Hutchinson versus Edmund Waller: An Unpublished Reply to Waller's *A Panegyrick to My Lord Protector*," *The Seventeenth Century* 11 (1996): 61–86.

33. Henry Fletcher's sympathetic biography of 1660 was typical in its silence on Cromwell's economic record. He seemed to feel that credit for England's naval and mercantile expansion was properly reserved for the Rump, which had "acted in their Infancy like *Hercules* in the Cradle, stifling all those Serpents that offered to *hiss* against their authority" until "the Authority of thir Power being thus miraculously extended, it grew at length dreadful to the neighbouring Nations, especially the Dutch," who feared that the "current of Traffick would be stopped which they had so long enjoyed." See Fletcher, *The Perfect Politician; or, a Full View of the Life and Actions (Military and Civil) of O. Cromwell* (1660), pp. 212, 215; Cf. Andrew Marvell's poem occasioned by the First Anglo-Dutch War, "The Character of *Holland* " (1651): "And now the *Hydra of seven Provinces* / Is strangled by our *Infant Hercules*" (lines 137–38). Marvell's reference to the infant Hercules extends his description of the new republic, established after the beheading of Charles I, as "Our sore new circumcised *Common wealth*" (line 118). By 1660, tactful silence about Cromwell's record on trade had degenerated into abuse. "The oil and honey, promised us by Oliver, is turned into gall and bitterness," lamented one pamphlet. Another had Cromwell cite his destruction of English trade among the other accomplishments that made him deserve precedence over his rival in hell, the Borgia Pope Alexander VI. See *Awake, O England; or, the People's Invitation to King Charles. Being a Recital of the Ruins Overrunning the People and their Trades* (1660) and *Cromwell's Complaint of Injustice; or, His Dispute with Pope Alexander the Sixth, for Precedency in Hell*, both in *Harl. Misc.*, 1:276 and 7:375–76.

34. *Diary of Burton*, 3:102, 97, 112.

35. Bethel insisted that at the dissolution of the first Rump, "the Kingdome was arrived at the highest pitch of Trade, Wealth, and Honour, that it, in any Age, ever yet knew." See his *The World's Mistake in Oliver Cromwell; or, A Short Political Discourse, Shewing, that Cromwell's Mal-Administration, (during His Four Years, and Nine Moneths Pretended Protectorship,) Layed the Foundation of Our Present Condition, in the Decay of Trade* (1668), p. 3.

36. *The Grand Concernments of England Ensured* (1659), pp. 15–17, 32–35.

37. J. S., *The Continuation of This Session of Parliament, Justified* (May 16, 1659), p. 11.

38. *PP1610*, 2:194. For two discussions of Hedley's famous speech, see J. G. A. Pocock, *The Ancient Constitution and the Feudal Law: A Study of English Historical Thought*

in the Seventeenth Century, 2d ed. (Cambridge: Cambridge University Press, 1987), pp. 270–79; and David Harris Sacks, "The Paradox of Taxation: Fiscal Crises, Parliament, and Liberty in England, 1450–1640," in *Fiscal Crises, Liberty, and Representative Government, 1450–1789,* ed. Philip T. Hoffman and Kathryn Norberg (Stanford: Stanford University Press, 1994), pp. 58–64.

39. *A Discourse of the Invention of Ships . . . Together with Five Manifest Causes of the Sudden Appearing of the Hollanders* and *Observations Touching Trade and Commerce with the Hollander, and Other Nations; Presented to King James,* both in *The Works of Sir Walter Ralegh,* 8 vols. (Oxford University Press, 1829), 8:332, 357, 374–75; "Of Seditions and Troubles," "Of the True Greatness of Kingdoms and Estates," "Of the True Greatness of the Kingdom of Britain. To King James," *Apothegms,* and "Considerations Touching a War with Spain. To the Prince," all in Bacon, *Works,* 6:410, 446, 7:60–61, 177, 14:497; Sir Fulke Greville, "A Treatise of Monarchy," in *The Remains, Being Poems of Monarchy and Religion,* ed. G. A. Wilkes (Oxford: Oxford University Press, 1965), stanzas 376, 395, 414–15; Greville, *The Life of the Renowned Sir Philip Sidney* (written 1610–14; published 1652), p. 143; Thomas Mun, *A Discovrse of Trade, from England vnto the East Indies* (1621), p. 49; Mun, *England's Treasure by Forraign Trade* (written c. 1623; published 1664), pp. 8–9; Lewes Roberts, *The Treasure of Traffike* (1641), pp. 43–44/sigs. G2r–v, pp. 49–61/sigs. H1r–I3r, pp. 77–78/sigs. L4r–M2r, pp. 99–101/sigs. O3r–O4r (irregular pagination).

40. Thomas Hobbes, *Behemoth,* ed. Ferdinand Tonnies, 2d ed. (New York: Frank Cass, 1969), pp. 3–4. Hobbes completed his manuscript in 1668, but Charles II suppressed its publication until a pirated edition was published in 1679.

41. *A Declaration of the Parliament of England* (1649). Milton translated this text into Latin. Also see Osborne, *A Perswasive,* p. 35.

42. *Parliamentary or Constitutional History of England* (often called *Old Parliamentary History*), 24 vols. (1751–66), 21:59, 22:141–42.

43. On the Rump's hardening secularism, see Worden, *Rump Parliament,* pp. 260–61.

44. Hobbes, *Behemoth,* p. 126.

45. George Wither, *A Cordial Confection . . . Written to Mr. Ro. Hamon, Merchant* (Oct. 24, 1659), pp. 29–30; quotation on p. 30.

46. John Evelyn, *An Apology for the Royalist Party.*

47. C. Culpepper, *A Message Sent from the King of Scots . . . to the Lord Douglas* (Nov. 6, 1659).

48. *The Remonstrance of the Apprentices in and about London* (1659).

49. Milton to Henry Oldenberg, October 20, 1659. See French, *Records,* 4:287–88.

50. This appears in the long title of *Awake O England* (1660).

51. Arthur Barker, *Milton and the Puritan Dilemma, 1641–1660* (Toronto: University of Toronto Press, 1942), p. 277. Barker refers to Milton's proposals as "a crazy structure hastily raised from the debris of the crumbling republic, weakly supported by appeals to the past and the future." He adds that Milton was "never at ease with details of organization" and that Milton's ideas "are made the more inconsistent and disordered" by his frustration (p. 260). Austin Woolrych confirms Barker's low estimate of Milton's polity: "It would be otiose to dwell at length on the impracticability of Milton's proposals"; see his "Historical Introduction," in *CPW* 7:1–228; quotation on p. 186. More recently Thomas Corns has described Milton's model as characterized

by "the absence of a viable theoretical component" (*Uncloistered Virtue: English Political Literature, 1640–1660* [Oxford: Clarendon Press, 1992], p. 282). Also stressing Milton's increasing conservatism and largely endorsing Barker is John Rogers, *Matter of Revolution: Science, Poetry, and Politics in the Age of Milton* (Ithaca: Cornell University Press, 1996), pp. 109–10. Steven Pincus argues that Milton could be classed as a conservative by 1660 because he was always anticommercial; I firmly disagree with the picture of Milton that he presents in "Neither Machiavellian Moment nor Possessive Individualism: Commercial Society and the Defenders of the English Commonwealth," *American Historical Review* 103 (1998): 705–36. Readings of the pamphlet as a jeremiad whose rhetoric of lamentation is more important than its proposals have made the work more sympathetic, perhaps, but they have only confirmed a tendency to find the significance of *The Readie and Easie Way* in anything but the model of government it advances. See James Holstun, *A Rational Millennium: Puritan Utopias of Seventeenth-Century England and America* (New York: Oxford University Press, 1987), pp. 247–65; and Laura Lunger Knoppers, "Milton's *Readie and Easie Way* and the English Jeremiad," in *Politics, Poetics, and Hermeneutics in Milton's Prose,* ed. David Loewenstein and James Grantham Turner (Cambridge: Cambridge University Press, 1990). Joad Raymond adds nuance to the reading of the tract as a jeremiad: "the distinctiveness of the tract in large part lies in Milton's desire to speak the language of a recognizable community of readers at the same time as he distances himself from that community by assuming, not for the first time, the voice of Jeremiah" ("The Cracking of the Republican Spokes," *Prose Studies* 19 [1996]: 269). Samuel Beer makes a welcome departure. He accords Milton a significant place in the history of federalism, though he does so largely for the idea of a national republic expressed in *Areopagitica.* His discussion of *The Readie and Easie Way* is brief but does recognize that Milton advocates a federal division of powers. See his *To Make a Nation: The Rediscovery of American Federalism* (Cambridge: Belknap Press, 1993), pp. 66–83, 125–28.

52. For readings that stress this point, see Don M. Wolfe, *Milton and the Puritan Revolution* (New York: Thomas Nelson and Sons, 1941), pp. 297–310; and Barbara Lewalski, "Milton: Political Beliefs and Polemical Methods, 1659–1660," *PMLA* 74 (1959): 191–202.

53. Milton's state papers may be found in *CPW,* vol. 5. For his writings on trade matters, see pp. 480, 482, 491, 500, 502–05, 517, 530, 544, 554–61, 566–67, 574, 579, 592–94, 605–06, 617, 629, 639, 656–57, 711–12, 716, 760–69, 784, 788–92, 801, 812–13, and 867–70. Also see Leo Miller, *John Milton and the Oldenburg Safeguard* (New York: Loewenthal Press, 1985); and Fallon, *Milton in Government.*

54. On Milton's involvement in these negotiations, see Miller, *Milton's Writings in the Anglo-Dutch Negotiations.*

55. On the precarious stability of the Dutch government during the First Anglo-Dutch War, see Jonathan Israel, *The Dutch Republic: Its Rise, Greatness, and Fall, 1477–1806* (Oxford: Clarendon Press, 1995), pp. 717–22.

56. Israel, *Dutch Republic,* p. 276.

57. See esp. "No. 11 — The Utility of the Union in Respect to Commercial Relations and a Navy," in Alexander Hamilton, John Jay, and James Madison, *The Federalist Papers* (New York: Modern Library, 1937), pp. 62–69.

58. George Starkey, *The Dignity of Kingship Asserted* (1660), p. 113.

59. David Quint, *Epic and Empire: Politics and Generic Form from Virgil to Milton* (Princeton: Princeton University Press, 1993), pp. 334–40.

60. For more on this passage, see John Rogers, *Matter of Revolution,* pp. 138–39.

61. Writers like the author of "An Apologie of the Citie of London," which John Stow attached to *A Survay of London* (1603), had used the figure of shearing to defend the usefulness of merchants to the sovereign: "for the prince and realme are both enriched by their riches: the realme winneth treasure, if their trade be so moderated by authority, that it breake not proportion, and they besides beare a good fleece, which the prince may Sheare when Hee seeth good" (p. 562). At the Restoration, Royalists revived the traditional figure of the king as good shepherd. They contrasted Cromwell's high taxes in a time of depression with the behavior of a good shepherd (like Charles II), who would not shear his flock in winter.

62. On Milton's reading of Machiavelli, see David Armitage, "John Milton: Poet against Empire," in *Milton and Republicanism,* ed. David Armitage, Armand Himy, and Quentin Skinner (Cambridge: Cambridge University Press), pp. 206–14.

63. Aristotle, *Politics,* bk. 2, chap. 4, 1262b; bk. 7, chap. 4, 1326b.

64. Niccolò Machiavelli, *Discourses on Livy,* bk. 1, chap. 6; Harvey C. Mansfield, Jr., *Machiavelli's New Modes and Orders: A Study of the "Discourses on Livy"* (Ithaca: Cornell University Press, 1979), p. 50.

65. For a succinct description of Venice's elaborate election process, which involved a series of nominating committees and selections by lottery, see Frederic C. Lane, *Venice: A Maritime Republic* (Baltimore: Johns Hopkins University Press, 1973), pp. 109–11. The crucial feature of the Venetian system, the one that really limited the possibility of factions forming, was the use of lotteries. Milton probably does not include lotteries in his system because he wishes to imagine the citizenry "each in thir several active Sphears assignd" (*PL* 5.477)—with the most worthy raised by merit, not lot. See John Rogers, *Matter of Revolution,* pp. 110–11. Milton's system would permit voters bent on faction to determine the outcome of elections from the first round. But he may have felt that the voters in a series of nominating committees would at least know one another's characters, as Aristotle prescribed.

66. Israel, *Dutch Republic,* p. 276.

67. On this point, also see Woolrych, "Historical Introduction," in *CPW* 7:183. Also see *The Second Agreement of the People* (1648), in *Puritanism and Liberty: Being the Army Debates (1647–49),* ed. A. S. P. Woodhouse, 3d ed. (London: J. M. Dent, 1992), p. 367.

68. Starkey, *Dignity of Kingship,* pp. 107–11.

69. George Wither was also troubled by this irony. "What would be the effects," he asked on October 24, 1659, "of giving Liberty at this present (as it is by the greatest number desired) for any man to chuse, or to be chosen a Member of Parliament, but the destroying of *Propriety, Morality,* and *Piety,* together with all the just Liberties of the people, which they have so dearly paid for, and were likely to recover when almost quite lost? For the worst men are most numerous, and the greater part of them consisting of those, who by conniving at, or complying with Tyrants and Oppressours (under whom they shall enjoy most Licentiousness) were the chief Causers and Continuers of our late and present Troubles" (*A Cordial Confection,* pp. 9–10).

70. R[oger] W[illiams], *The Fourth Paper Presented by Major Butler, with Other Papers*

Published and Edited by Roger Williams in London, 1652, facs. repr. with intro. and notes by Clarence Saunders Brigham (Providence: Club for Colonial Reprints, 1903), p. 17.

71. Raymond Phineas Stearns, *The Strenuous Puritan: Hugh Peter, 1598–1660* (Urbana: University of Illinois, 1954), p. 401. Milton and Williams even found themselves fighting shoulder to shoulder when Milton's licensing of a Racovian Catechism caused a scandal and Parliament responded by forming a committee to set the limits of toleration. When questioned by Parliament, Milton admitted that he had licensed the Socinian treatise. Ironically, in his *Humble Remonstrance* (1643), Henry Parker had specifically cited the threat of Socinian works among the reasons that a Licensing Act was needed (sig. A1v). But Milton simply told Parliament that "men should refrain from forbidding books; that in approving of that book he had done no more than what his opinion was" (French, *Records*, 3:206). Milton protested against Parliament's efforts to limit toleration in his sonnet "To the Lord General Cromwell, May 1652. On the proposals of certain ministers 'at the Committee' for Propagation of the Gospel," which warns against foes "threatning to bind our Souls with Secular chains" (line 12). Williams similarly published *The Fourth Paper Presented by Major Butler* (1652) in reaction to the committee. It reiterates and defends a paper presented by William Butler, a soldier in Cromwell's army and a proponent of extreme toleration. See Barbara Lewalski, *The Life of John Milton: A Critical Biography* (Oxford: Blackwell, 2000), pp. 283–87.

72. For a recent analysis of mobility in New England, much of which consisted of corporations making a determined move for reasons of conscience or opportunity, see Roger Thompson, *Mobility and Migration: East Anglian Founders of New England, 1629–1640* (Amherst: University of Massachusetts Press, 1994). Providence, Portsmouth, Newport, and Exeter were founded by settlers who were expelled from Boston or Salem because of their religious views. When Massachusetts annexed Exeter in 1642, the antinomian followers of John Wheelwright were forced to move again to Wells, Maine. It was over land policies that a group of Sudbury residents founded Marlborough. Occasionally, a few residents of one colonial town might declare themselves and their lands part of the neighboring town because they preferred its church or its taxes.

73. On the surprising degree of mobility in early modern England, see Peter Clark and David Souden, eds., *Migration and Society in Early Modern England* (London: Hutchinson, 1987).

74. Robinson realized that the government might have to extend commercial concessions or civic immunities like the freedom of worship in order to attract productive citizens. See, for example, his *Liberty of Conscience; or the Sole Means to Obtaine Peace and Truth* (Mar. 24, 1644), preface, p. 7. For a similar view, see Francis Osborne, *Historical Memoirs on the Reigns of Elizabeth and King James* (1651), in *The Secret History of the Court of James I*, 2 vols. (Edinburgh: James Ballantyne, 1811), 1:97. Milton's observation that the United Provinces had begun to live in greater "concord and prosperitie" since they stopped persecuting the Arminians seems to refer to arguments like Robinson's and Osborne's (*CPW* 7:380).

75. Henry Roseveare, "Prejudice and Policy: Sir George Downing as Parliamentary Entrepreneur," in *Enterprise and History: Essays in Honour of Charles Wilson*, ed.

D. C. Coleman and Peter Mathias (Cambridge: Cambridge University Press, 1984), pp. 142–43.

76. Conquest, "State and Commercial Expansion," pp. 164–66; *His Majesties Gracious Declaration, for the Incouraging the Subjects of the Low-Countries of the United Provinces, to Transport Themselves with Their Estates, and to Settle in This His Majesties Kingdom of England* (Edinburgh, 1672). Another declaration printed at the same time invited Dutchmen to settle in Scotland. The declarations were also printed on the Continent.

77. The General Court of Massachusetts formally defined the extensive powers of the town in 1635 (*Records of the Governor and Company of Massachusetts Bay in New England*, 5 vols. [Boston: W. White, 1853], 1:172). These powers were periodically reaffirmed and redefined in the seventeenth century. On the subsequent evolution of town government, see Kenneth A. Lockridge and Alan Kreider, "The Evolution of Massachusetts Town Government, 1640 to 1740," *William and Mary Quarterly*, 3d ser., 23 (1966): 549–74. On the importance of conformity within towns, see Michael Zuckerman, "The Social Context of Democracy in Massachusetts," *William and Mary Quarterly*, 3d ser., 25 (1968): 523–44. Even today, New England remains the only region of the United States in which the town is the basic unit of General Purpose government (as defined by the Bureau of the Census). New England towns control activities that are delegated to other governmental units in most states: schools, civil justice, utilities, roads, safety, and public health. For instance, New England is the only region in which school districts are town-based, rather than independent jurisdictions. There are 2.9 times as many General Purpose governments per square mile in New England as in the rest of the United States. See Bureau of the Census, United States Department of Commerce, *Government Organization*, vol. 1 of *The 1997 Census of Governments* (Washington, D.C.: United States Government Printing Office, 1999), pp. v–ix, 4–5, 9–12, app. A-1.

78. Holstun, *Rational Millennium*, p. 250.

79. The development of that state may be followed in John Brewer, *The Sinews of Power: War, Money, and the English State, 1688-1783* (New York: Alfred Knopf, 1969); and D. W. Jones, *War and Economy in the Age of William III and Marlborough* (London: Basil Blackwell, 1988).

80. Nedham, *Interest Will Not Lie*, p. 48. The idea that kings seek to keep their subjects low is not a new one. Its locus classicus is Sallust, *Bellum Catilinae*, sec. 7. The author of "An Apologie of the Citie of London" writes: "Cities and great Townes, are a continuall briole against tyranny, which was the cause that *Targuin, Nero, Dionisius*, and such others have always sought to weaken them" (in Stow, *Survay of London*, p. 550). He adds that cities are, however, bulwarks of the aristocracy and "just royalty."

81. On Nedham's and Milton's arguments from interest against the king, also see Raymond, "Cracking of the Republican Spokes," pp. 262–63.

82. *The Censure of the Rota upon Mr. Milton's Book, Entitled, The Ready and Easie Way to Establish a Free Common-Wealth* (1660), p. 13.

83. Osborne, *A Perswasive*, pp. 19–20, 35, 41.

84. *The Likeliest Means to Remove Hirelings* (1659), in *CPW* 7:306–07.

85. David Hume, "Of Commerce," in *Essays, Moral, Political, and Literary*, ed. Eugene F. Miller (Indianapolis: Liberty Classics, 1985), pp. 262–63.

86. Leslie Brisman, *Milton's Poetry of Choice* (Ithaca: Cornell University Press, 1973), p. 175.

87. Plato, *Laws*, bk. 4, 704–05; Jean Bodin, *The Six Bookes of a Commonweale*, ed. Kenneth Douglas McRae (Cambridge: Cambridge University Press, 1962), p. 564. Both are cited in *CPW* 7:372 n. 70.

Chapter Three

1. Earl of Clarendon (Edward Hyde), *The Life of Edward Earl of Clarendon*, 3 vols. (Oxford: Clarendon Press, 1827), 2:231.

2. John Evelyn, *A Panegyric to Charles the Second* (1661), p. 11.

3. For an overview of the uses of pageantry and theater in Charles II's London, see Paula R. Backscheider, *Spectacular Politics: Theatrical Power and Mass Culture in Early Modern England* (Baltimore: Johns Hopkins University Press, 1993), pp. 1–66, esp. (on commercial themes) pp. 16–18, 25, 34, 36, 39–40, 43, 46–47, 51.

4. John Tatham, *The Royal Oake* (1660), pp. 6, 15.

5. *A Poem upon His Majesties Coronation* (Apr. 23, 1661), p. 9.

6. On the panegyric tradition, see James D. Garrison, *Dryden and the Tradition of Panegyric* (Berkeley: University of California Press, 1975). On Caroline panegyrics, see M. L. Donnelly, "Caroline Royalist Panegyric and the Disintegration of a Symbolic Mode," in *"The Muses Common-weale": Poetry and Politics in the Seventeenth Century*, ed. Claude J. Summers and Ted-Larry Pebworth (Columbia: University of Missouri Press, 1988).

7. Besides the poems discussed below, see Thomas Higgons, *A Panegyrick to the King* (June 20, 1660), pp. 6–7; and Thomas Mayhew, *Upon the Joyfull and Welcome Return of His Sacred Majestie, Charls the Second* (May 24, 1660), pp. 7, 9. Among more humble productions, see *Quesumus te* (Mar. 9, 1660), p. 4; *News from the Royall Exchange: Gold Turnd into Mourning* (Mar. 16, 1660); and *Good Newes from the Netherlands; or, a Congratulatory Panegyrick* (May 31, 1660).

8. Edmund Waller, *To the King, upon His Majesty's Happy Return* (1660), line 111; John Crouch, *A Mixt Poem, Partly Historicall, Partly Panegyricall* (1660), pp. 14–15.

9. Benjamin Worsley, *The Advocate* (1652), p. 11; Waller, *To the King, upon His Majesty's Happy Return*, lines 79–80. Contrast Waller's lines with Francis Osborne's earlier defense of the Commonwealth: "the *sword* in all ages, during the stormes of War, hath pretended to a *priviledge* of *cutting* such *knots*, as under a more serene Heaven might have puzled not only *Reason* but *Religion to untie*" (*A Perswasive to a Mutuall Compliance* [Oxford, 1652], p. 2).

10. Clarendon, *Life*, 1:320–21.

11. Arthur Brett, *The Restauration* (June 5, 1660), p. 21.

12. Neither is mentioned among the virtues of princely government reviewed by Quentin Skinner, *The Foundations of Modern Political Thought*, 2 vols. (Cambridge: Cambridge University Press, 1978), 1:113–28. Although Erasmus does not mention care or industry in his main list of the virtues that a sovereign should display, he does enjoin care elsewhere; see his *The Education of a Christian Prince*, trans. Lester K. Born (New York: Columbia University Press, 1936), esp. pp. 180, 189, 208–09. A rare example of Industry appearing in an early Stuart entertainment is Samuel Daniel's

Tethys' Festivall (1610), performed for the investiture of Henry as Prince of Wales. Henry was a known sympathizer of economic reformers like Ralegh. The figure of Industry recommends the fishing industry (one obsession of reformers who took their lead from the Dutch) as a consolation for England's lack of a western empire. It thus plays one aspect of the reformers' program off another (and more dangerous) one that would mean a confrontation with the Habsburgs. As courtiers frustrated with the Stuarts' faint interest in trade were well aware, general recommendations to princes to favor merchants are not alien to courtesy literature. For instance, Baldesar Castiglione has Ottaviano recommend that princes "favor merchants and even aid them with money"; see his *Book of the Courtier,* trans. Charles Singleton (New York: Anchor Books, 1959), bk. 4, sec. 41.

13. *The Triumphs of Love and Antiquity* (1619) and *The Triumphs of Honour and Industry* (1617), both in Middleton, *Works,* 7:330 (cf. 7:349); 7:298. On royal entries and mayoral pageants, see Lawrence Manley, *Literature and Culture in Early Modern London* (Cambridge: Cambridge University Press, 1995), chap. 5.

14. "vobis iam Mulciber arma / praeparat et Sicula Cyclops incude laborat" [even now Vulcan prepares the arms for their subjection and Cyclops labors on the Sicilian anvil] (Claudian, *Panegyric on the Third Consulship of the Emperor Honorius* [lines 191–92]).

15. The best discussion of the entry is Ronald Knowles's introduction to John Ogilby, *The Entertainment of His Most Excellent Majestie Charles II* (1662; facs. reprint, Binghamton, N.Y.: Medieval and Renaissance Texts and Studies, 1988). Knowles briefly notices some of the entry's mercantilist themes, but he suggests that the second arch was "probably seen in a more religiously sublimated way" (p. 10). The entry is discussed in the context of other contemporary entertainments in Backscheider, *Spectacular Politics,* pp. 1–66. Unless otherwise stated, references to the entry cite Ogilby's *Entertainment,* henceforth abbreviated *Ent.* and cited parenthetically in the text.

16. Clarendon, *Life,* 2:10.

17. *CSP Domestic, 1660–61,* p. 553. On Ogilby, see the *DNB,* s.v. "Ogilby, John"; Katherine S. Van Erde, *John Ogilby and the Taste of His Times* (London: Dawson, 1976); and Annabel Patterson, *Pastoral and Ideology: Virgil to Valery* (Berkeley: University of California Press, 1987), pp. 169–80.

18. On Gerbier, see the *DNB,* s.v. "Gerbier, Balthazar"; and Hugh Ross Williamson, *Four Stuart Portraits* (London: Evan Brothers, 1949), pp. 26–60, 143–46.

19. *The None-such Charles His Character* (1651). The pamphlet has also been attributed to Silas Taylor.

20. Ogilby omitted the pageant of the East India Company from his later *Entertainment* (1662). All citations referring to it are from his *Relation of His Majesties Entertainment* (1661), henceforth abbreviated *Rel.* and cited parenthetically in the text.

21. See Basil D. Henning, *The House of Commons, 1660–1690,* 3 vols. (London: History of Parliamentary Trust, 1983), s.v. "Ford, Sir Richard." Ford's activities on behalf of the East India Company after the Restoration, which included casual conversations with the Lord Chancellor or the king about trade policies, may be followed in *A Calendar of the Court Minutes, Etc., of the East India Company, 1660-1663,* ed. Ethel Bruce Sainsbury (Oxford: Clarendon Press, 1922).

22. Quoted in Steven Pincus, "Popery, Trade and Universal Monarchy: The Ideological Context of the Outbreak of the Second Anglo-Dutch War," *English Historical Review*, no. 422 (1992): 13.

23. See the chronological list of aldermen printed in Alfred B. Beaven, *The Aldermen of the City of London* (London: Corporation of the City of London, 1908–13).

24. For examples, see *The Subjects Desire to See Our Gracious King Charles the Second His Safe Arrival* (May 26, 1660); *To the King upon His Majesties Happy Return* (June 3, 1660, an anonymous poem not to be confused with Waller's poem of the same title), p. 3; and Samuel Willes, *To the Kings Most Sacred Majesty* (June 25, 1660).

25. Samuel Purchas, "A Large Treatise of King Salomons Navie Sent from Eziongeber to Ophir," in his *Hakluytus Posthumus* (1625), vol. 1 (Glasgow: James MacLehose and Sons, 1905), chap. 1.

26. Henry Parker, *Of a Free Trade* (1648), p. 35.

27. *Advice of His Majesty's Council of Trade, Concerning the Exportation of Gold and Silver,* in *A Select Collection of Scarce and Valuable Tracts on Money,* ed. J. R. McCulloch (London: Political Economy Club, 1856), pp. 145–53; K. N. Chaudhuri, "The East India Company and the Export of Treasure in the Early Seventeenth Century," *Economic History Review,* 2d ser., 16 (1963): 23–38; Patricia Fumerton, *Cultural Aesthetics: Renaissance Literature and the Practice of Social Ornament* (Chicago: University of Chicago Press, 1991), chap. 5.

28. For the later involvement of the Crown's and the East India Company's interests that this entertainment may be seen to inaugurate symbolically, see Arnold A. Sherman, "Pressure from Leadenhall: The East India Company Lobby, 1660–1678," *Business History Review* 50 (1976): 329–55.

29. Jean Gaspard Gavaerts, *Pompa Introitus Honori Serenissimi Principis Ferdinandi Austriaci Hispaniarum Infantis* (Antwerp, 1641), p. 150.

30. Ronald Knowles, introduction, in Ogilby, *Entertainment,* p. 36.

31. Claudian, *Panegyric on the Third Consulship of the Emperor Honorius,* lines 210–11.

32. On Rubens's arches on economic themes, see Roy Strong, *Art and Power, Renaissance Festivals, 1450–1650* (Woodbridge, Suffolk, U.K.: Boydell Press, 1984), pp. 49–50.

33. Gavaerts, *Pompa Introitus,* p. 150.

34. Sir Balthazar Gerbier, *A Brief Discourse Concerning the Three Chief Principles of Magnificent Building* (1662), p. 16. Also see Katharine Fremantle, *The Baroque Town Hall of Amsterdam* (Utrecht: Haentjens Dekker & Gumbert, 1959); and Eymert-Jan Goossens, *Schat van beitel en penseel: Het Amsterdamse stadhuis uit de Gouden Eeuw* [Treasure Wrought by Chisel and Brush: The Town Hall of Amsterdam in the Golden Age] (Amsterdam: Zwolle, 1996).

35. Thomas Dekker, *The Magnificent Entertainment* (1604), sigs. D4r–E2r; and Stephen Harrison, *The Arches of Triumph Erected in Honor of the High and Mighty Prince James* (1604), sig. Er.

36. While in Charles I's service, Gerbier himself had distributed bribes in the Netherlands in an embarrassing and failed attempt to ease the sale of fishing licenses.

37. Sir William Temple, *Observations upon the United Provinces of the Netherlands* (1668), ed. Sir George Clark (Oxford: Clarendon Press, 1972), pp. 123–24.

38. Crouch, *A Mixt Poem, Partly Historicall, Partly Panegyricall,* p. 15.

39. Ronald Knowles notes this in his introduction to Ogilby, *Entertainment,* p. 37.

40. Clarendon MS 109, f. 41, Bodleian Library, Oxford, printed in *The Restoration,* ed. Joan Thirsk (London: Longman, 1976), p. 115.

41. Samuel Pordage, *Heroick Stanzas on His Majesties Coronation* (1661), p. 8.

42. Samuel Sorbiere, *Relation d'vn voyage en Angleterre* (Paris, 1664), pp. 130–31. I follow the translation that Thomas Sprat provides in his running commentary, *Observations on Monsieur de Sorbiere's Voyage into England* (1665), pp. 159, 168.

43. Backscheider, *Spectacular Politics,* pp. 43, 46–47.

44. *London's Triumph: Presented in Several Delightful Scenes* (1662), p. 18.

45. Letter, Francesco Giavarina, Venetian Resident in England, to the Doge and Senate, *CSP Venetian, 1661–64,* p. 205. On these "years of trial," see Ronald Hutton, *The Restoration: A Political and Religious History of England and Wales, 1658–1667* (Oxford: Clarendon Press, 1985), pp 185–219.

46. Algernon Sidney, *Court Maxims* (c. 1662–64), ed. Hans W. Blom, Eco Haitsma Mulier, and Ronald Janse (Cambridge: Cambridge University Press, 1996), pp. 73–77, 80.

47. Sprat, *Observations,* pp. 163–65. This paragraph owes several facts about the Africa Company to Michael McKeon, *Politics and Poetry in Restoration England: The Case of Dryden's "Annus Mirabilis"* (Cambridge: Harvard University Press, 1975), pp. 105–16. Also see K. C. Davies, *The Royal African Company* (London: Longman, 1957), esp. pp. 63-66 on the company's aristocratic investors.

48. Ogilby, *Entertainment,* p. 104.

49. Charles Davenant's works are collected in his *Political and Commercial Works . . . Relating to the Trade and Revenue of England,* ed. Sir C. Whitworth, 5 vols. (London, 1771). Joseph Schumpeter lists him among the five or so earlier economic writers who "might have taught" Adam Smith "a lot"; see his *History of Economic Analysis,* ed. Elizabeth B. Schumpeter (Oxford: Oxford University Press, 1954), p. 184.

50. Cf. Henry Robinson, *Briefe Considerations Concerning the Advancement of Trade and Navigation* (1649), p. 1.

51. In "Nature's *Traffick,*" Margaret Cavendish makes a similar comparison between trade and the imagination:

> The Mind's a Merchant, Trafficking about
> The Brain, as th'Ocean, t'find Opinions out;
> Remembrance is the Ware-house, where are laid
> Goods, by Imaginations Ships conveigh'd,
> Which every Tradesman of belief still Buys,
> Gaining by Truth, but Losing by all Lies;
> Thoughts as the Journey-men and Prentice Boys,
> Do help to Sort the Wares, and Sell the Toys.

See her *Poems and Phancies* (1664), p. 175.

52. Arthur Nethercot, *Sir William D'Avenant* (Chicago: University of Chicago Press, 1938), p. 256.

53. William Hazlitt, *Characters in Shakespeare's Plays* (New York: Wiley and Put-

nam, 1845), pp. 48–49. On the applicability of Hazlitt's words to epic, see David Quint, *Epic and Empire: Politics and Generic Form from Virgil to Milton* (Princeton: Princeton University Press, 1993), pp. 207–09.

54. On the connections between Milton and Davenant, see French, *Records,* 5:1–3, 436, 460–61.

55. Charles Davenant's thought is discussed in J. G. A. Pocock, *The Machiavellian Moment: Florentine Political Thought and the Atlantic Republican Tradition* (Princeton: Princeton University Press, 1975), pp. 436–46, esp. pp. 437–38, which I follow closely. Also see Davenant, *Political and Commercial Works,* 1:348–49; 4:33–41.

56. Dryden, *Works,* 1:48–49. On the poem as a panegyric to London, see Edward N. Hooker, "The Purpose of Dryden's *Annus Mirabilis,*" *Huntington Library Quarterly* 10 (1946–47): 49–67.

57. On some of the ways the poem masks the nation's factionalism, see McKeon, *Politics and Poetry.*

58. Sherman, "Pressure from Leadenhall," p. 336.

Introduction to Part Three

1. Richard Mather, *An Apologie of the Churches of New-England for Church-Covenant* (1643), pp. 21–22; quotation on p. 22.

2. Simon Ford, *The Lords Wonders in the Deep,* preached in Northampton July 4, 1665 (Oxford, 1665), p. 7.

3. Sir Thomas Roe, *The Embassy of Sir Thomas Roe to India, 1615–19, As Narrated in His Journal and Correspondence,* ed. Sir William Foster, rev. ed. (Oxford: Oxford University Press, 1926), p. 457. For many similar quotations, see Bruce I. Watson, "Fortifications and the 'Idea' of Force in Early English East India Company Relations with India," *Past and Present,* no. 88 (1980): 70–87. For a compatible analysis of the use of force in the East Indian trade, see K. N. Chaudhuri, *The Trading World of Asia and the English East India Company, 1660–1760* (Cambridge: Cambridge University Press, 1978), pp. 109–29.

4. For the charter, see *Charters Granted to the East-India Company, from 1601* ([London], n.d.), pp. 54–79.

Chapter Four

1. See Henry Roseveare, *The Treasury, 1660–1870: The Foundations of Control* (New York: Barnes and Noble, 1973), pp. 19–45; Roseveare, "Prejudice and Policy: Sir George Downing as Parliamentary Entrepreneur," in *Enterprise and History: Essays in Honour of Charles Wilson,* ed. D. C. Coleman and Peter Mathias (Cambridge: Cambridge University Press, 1984), pp. 135–50; Charles Wilson, *Profit and Power: A Study of England and the Dutch Wars* (The Hague: M. Nijhoff, 1957), pp. 94–103; and J. R. Jones, *The Anglo-Dutch Wars of the Seventeenth Century* (London: Longman, 1996), p. 153.

2. Earl of Clarendon (Edward Hyde), *The Life of Edward Earl of Clarendon,* 3 vols., new ed. (Oxford: Clarendon Press, 1827), 3:29. For more on such ideological divisions between Downing and Clarendon, see J.R. Jones, *Anglo-Dutch Wars,* pp. 92–96. For a nearly contemporary analysis of the cumulative advantages of primacy in world

trade—because of economies of scale and specialization—see *The Economic Writings of Sir William Petty,* ed. Charles Henry Hull, 2 vols. (1889; reprint, Fairfield, N.J.: A. M. Kelley, 1986), 1:257–61. Although not published until 1690, Petty's *Political Arithmetic* was already circulating in manuscript in 1676.

3. Steven Pincus, *Protestantism and Patriotism: Ideologies and the Making of English Foreign Policy, 1650–1668* (Cambridge: Cambridge University Press, 1996), p. 246.

4. *The Newes, Published for Satisfaction and Information of the People,* May 5, 1664, p. 290.

5. The classic account of the war as a merchants' war is Wilson, *Profit and Power,* pp. 111–42. Wilson's interpretation has been criticized for undervaluing the importance of national honor, Court politics, the private financial interests of courtiers within the Royal Africa Company, and the strategic foreign policy objectives of Anglican Royalists. On the importance of these factors, see Paul Seaward, *The Cavalier Parliament and the Reconstruction of the Old Regime, 1661–1667* (Cambridge: Cambridge University Press, 1989); J. R. Jones, *Britain and the World, 1649–1815* (Brighton: Harvester Press, 1980), pp. 52–80, and his *Anglo-Dutch Wars,* pp. 145–78; Michael McKeon, *Politics and Poetry in Restoration England: The Case of Dryden's "Annus Mirabilis"* (Cambridge: Harvard University Press, 1975), pp. 99–131; and Pincus, *Protestantism and Patriotism,* pp. 195–452. The most significant points to take away from these studies are that the war was not universally supported, that our earlier understanding of the conflict as a simple "trade war" was influenced by Court propaganda, and that some of the war's proponents were prepared to take short-term losses in the hope of achieving long-term policy objectives. There is nevertheless a tendency in some of these accounts to lose Wilson's forest for the trees.

6. This crucial point is stressed by Jonathan Israel; see his "Competing Cousins: Anglo-Dutch Trade Rivalry," *History Today* 38 (July 1988): 17–22; "England's Mercantilist Response to Dutch World Trade Primacy, 1647–1674," in *State and Trade: Government and the Economy in Britain and the Netherlands since the Middle Ages,* ed. Simon Groenveld and Michael Wintle (Zutphen: Walburg Press, 1988); and *Dutch Primacy in World Trade, 1585–1740* (Oxford: Clarendon Press, 1989).

Given the tremendous cost of the Anglo-Dutch Wars and their usual result in something very near the status quo before hostilities began, it is difficult to believe that they were wise in practice. It nevertheless bears emphasizing that armed conflict with the Dutch, particularly if it could be kept from escalating to total war, could be justified not just according to the fallacious tenets often imputed to seventeenth-century mercantilism but according to economic principles that are still held valid. Preventing the Dutch from settling in Africa could be justified, first, in terms of option value: even if England could not establish viable trading forts, it might be cost-effective to keep Africa open for future occupation. The conviction of English observers that England's ports were naturally superior to the United Provinces', together with their strong sense that a hub-structure of trade, once established, tended to reinforce itself—both because it provided economies of scale in the bulk-carrying trade and because financial and commodities markets will naturally converge on a focal point—also made some of them think, quite reasonably, that if only Dutch trade could be sufficiently disrupted, then London might be able to assert itself as a more natural entrepôt of world trade. Finally, it is necessary to remember that trade was important as a source both of wealth and of strength. Thus the *relative* proportion of trade remained significant in calculating England's position in foreign affairs.

7. *Of Dramatick Poesie,* in Dryden, *Works,* 17:8.

8. J. R. Jones, *Anglo-Dutch Wars,* pp. 64, 66, 51–62.

9. On the *Painter* poems, see Annabel Patterson, *Marvell and the Civic Crown* (Princeton: Princeton University Press, 1978), pp. 111–74.

10. For a useful survey of the poetry of the Second Anglo-Dutch War, see Nicholas Jose, *Ideas of Restoration in English Literature, 1660–71* (Cambridge: Harvard University Press, 1984), pp. 97–119. To the authors whom Jose discusses, we might add the duchess of Newcastle (Margaret Cavendish), *The Blazing World* (1666), in *"The Description of a New World Called the Blazing World" and Other Writings,* ed. Kate Lilley (London: William Pickering, 1992), esp. pp. 204–18. For a bibliography of relevant pamphlet literature, see Pincus, *Protestantism and Patriotism,* pp. 463–85.

11. Epistle Dedicatory to *The Rival Ladies* (1664), in Dryden, *Works,* 8:100.

12. Samuel Johnson, *Lives of the English Poets,* ed. George Birkbeck Hill, 3 vols. (Oxford: Clarendon Press, 1905), 1:77.

13. In the last chapter, we noticed the imitation of *Coopers Hill* that William Godolphin presented to Oliver Cromwell just after the successful conclusion of the First Anglo-Dutch War in 1654. During the Second Anglo-Dutch War, Robert Fage published his own imitation, *St. Leonard's Hill* (1666). This passage also seems to have served as a model for William Smith's description of the Thames in another poem on the war, *Ingratitude Reveng'd* (1665). Smith's closing vision clumsily anticipates that of *Annus Mirabilis:*

> And thou, oh stately *City,* whose fair face
> *Minerva, Mercury,* Bellona grace
> Whose *Arms,* and *Arts* astonish'd *Europe* owns,
> Whose *Trade* the frigid and the torrid *Zones,*
> Whose double-named River kindly brings
> As Tribute useful, and all precious things,
> Rich *Indian* Harvests, what is rare or strange,
> Whilest his transparent Stream's the *Worlds Exchange,*
> Oh may thou flourish still secure from Foes,
> Whilest lucid *Thames* in his Meander goes
> Through reedy Banks, but slowly hast'ning thus,
> To the embraces of *Oceanus.*

$$\text{(p. 8).}$$

14. Jacob Viner, *The Role of Providence in the Social Order: An Essay in Intellectual History* (Philadelphia: American Philosophical Society, 1972), pp. 36ff. Viner cites the pagan author Libanius as the source of the idea, which early Church fathers like St. Basil, St. John Chrysostom, Theodoretus, and St. Ambrose repeated.

15. Albert O. Hirschman, *The Passions and the Interests: Political Arguments for Capitalism before Its Triumph* (Princeton: Princeton University Press, 1977), pp. 56–63.

16. Johnson, *Lives,* 1:430. He is referring to Dryden's depiction of modern naval techniques in *Annus Mirabilis.*

17. See especially the commentary in Dryden, *Works,* 1:257–58. Michael McKeon

argues that Dryden's poem represents the war as being in the national interest in order to mask the conflicting domestic interests at stake (*Politics and Poetry*, chap. 3). McKeon's chapter contains much useful historical information but does not express great interest in the way Dryden actually represents trade in verse.

18. The clearest expression of this ethos in the *Aeneid* is given to the dead Polydorus, who exclaims to Aeneas, "quid non mortalia pectora cogis, / auri sacra fames!" [To what dost thou not drive the hearts of men, O accursed hunger for gold!] (3.56–57). Greed may have brought about the death of Polydorus, but Rome is built on *pietas* and *labor*. On the anti-acquisitive ethos in later epics, see David Quint, *Epic and Empire: Politics and Generic Form from Virgil to Milton* (Princeton: Princeton University Press, 1993), pp. 256–66.

19. The opening formula of the *Aeneid* may be seen to combine the subjects of the *Iliad* (arms) and the *Odyssey* (a man). Subsequent epics tend to announce either arms, a man, or a joint subject like the *Aeneid*'s as their theme. Consider the "bella" [war] of Lucan's *Civil War;* the "fraternas acies" [strife of brethren] of Statius's *Thebaid* and "magnanimum Aeciden" [great-hearted Aecides] of his *Achilleid;* the "arma" [arms] of Silius Italicus's *Punica;* "Le donne, i cavallier, l'arme, gli amori" [knights and ladies, arms and loves], in the case of Ariosto's *Orlando Furioso;* and "l'armi pietose e 'l capitano" [reverent armies and the captain], in the case of Tasso's *Gerusalemme Liberata*. On the *Aeneid*'s opening, see A. D. Nuttall, *Openings: Narrative Beginnings from the Epic to the Novel* (Oxford: Clarendon Press, 1992), pp. 1–32. On opening formulas in the epic, see Alastair Fowler, *Kinds of Literature: An Introduction to the Theory of Genres and Modes* (Oxford: Clarendon Press, 1992), pp. 92, 102.

20. Francesco Robortello, *In librum Aristotelis, De Arte poetica explicationes* (Florence, 1548), p. 268.

21. Henry Parker, *Of a Free Trade* (1648), p. 34.

22. Petronius, *Satyricon,* 119.

23. See *A True Relation of the Vnjust, Cruell, and Barbarous Proceedings against the English at Amboyna in the East-Indies* (1624); *A True Declaration of the News That Came of the East-Indies, with the Pinace Called the Hare* (1624); *Answer vnto the Dutch Pamphlet, Made in Defence of the Vnjust and Barbarous Proceedings against the English at Amboyna* (1624); and *An Authentick Copy of the Confession and Sentences, against M. Towerson, and Complices* (1632). These pamphlets, or similar ones, were often reprinted during the Anglo-Dutch Wars. On the Dutch bribing James I, see *The None-such Charles His Character* (1651), pp. 86–87.

24. This appears in the long title of *Dr. Dorislaw's Ghost, Presented by Time to Unmask the Vizards of the Hollanders* (1652).

25. Both quoted in Steven Pincus, "Popery, Trade and Universal Monarchy: The Ideological Context of the Outbreak of the Second Anglo-Dutch War," *English Historical Review,* no. 422 (1992): 23–24.

26. Even works like Silius Italicus's *Punica* and Luís de Camões's *Os Lusíadas* — which, in recounting the Second Punic War and the Portugese voyages of discovery, require no recourse to the immortals — trace the origin of their actions back to councils of the gods.

27. Simone Weil, *"The Iliad"; or, the Poem of Force,* trans. Mary McCarthy (Wallingford, Pa.: Pendle Hill, 1957), p. 3.

28. Johnson, *Lives*, 1:432.

29. Euryalus and Turnus, for instance, are killed in part because of the booty they are wearing (*Aen.* 9.357–66, 371–78; 12.938–52). As Michael Murrin writes of these deaths, "Value loci in the poem are always internal, and anyone who turns to outside objects dies. . . . All external things are finally either rejected or lost in the *Aeneid*" (*The Allegorical Epic: Essays in Its Rise and Decline* [Chicago: University of Chicago Press, 1980], p. 48).

30. On the properties of chorographic poetry, see Richard Helgerson, *Forms of Nationhood: The Elizabethan Writing of England* (Chicago: University of Chicago Press, 1992), pp. 131–39.

31. John Ogilby, *The Entertainment of His Most Excellent Majestie Charles II*, ed. with intro. Ronald Knowles (1662; facs. reprint, Binghamton, N.Y.: Medieval and Renaissance Texts and Studies, 1988), pp. 96–101.

32. Ogilby, *Entertainment*, p. 104.

33. In what could serve as a gloss on Dryden's lines, J. R. Jones writes: "Indeed, it can be said that the factors that contributed directly and crucially to the commercial ascendency which the Dutch established before 1652 turned into serious disadvantages during the wars against England—as de la Court and De Witt themselves recognized. Their entrepôt trade could not be maintained beyond the capacity of their warehouses to store commodities imported from, and re-exported to, distant regions in the Baltic, the Mediterranean, Biscay, America, and Asia. The disruption of Dutch trade during periods of effective English control of the seas, which proved to be relatively brief—the summers of 1653, 1665 and 1672—severely damaged Dutch business confidence and threatened to provoke a flight of venture capital. Shipowners became alarmed that the carrying trade would be taken over by vessels based on Hamburg and other neutral ports, many of them financed by Dutch money, and they were adversely affected by higher insurance premiums and taxes. The advanced nature of the Dutch economy, with a higher degree of economic specialization and a heavier concentration of entrepreneurs, artisans and casual labour in the Holland towns than anywhere else in Europe, made it more vulnerable than the less developed economy of even south-east England. Equally Holland's society, which was predominantly urban, with a significant proportion of immigrants from abroad and from the landward provinces, in which traditional relationships or conventions had been weakened or effaced by virtually unrestricted market forces, could not have stood the strain of prolonged disruption of the economy" (*Anglo-Dutch Wars*, p. 220).

34. A ship entering port was such a common figure for sexual intercourse that Charles Sackville, Lord Buckhurst, could not employ it without first wryly acknowledging what a tired metaphor it had become. See *Complete Poems of George Etherege*, ed. James Thorpe (Princeton: Princeton University Press, 1963), p. 36.

35. Maps of Amsterdam commonly featured the title *Amsteldami Celeberrimi Hollandiae Emporii Delineatio Nova*. In his gloss on the word "emporium" in *The Poems of John Dryden*, ed. Paul Hammond (London: Longman, 1995), Hammond notes that Bede appears to have used the word, and Camden did use it, in Latin references to London. The economic stakes of the Second Anglo-Dutch War may have encouraged its wider usage in English. As Hammond also notes, William Smith refers to London as "the great / *Emporeum* of our Kings, and royal Seat" (*A Poem on the Famous*

Ship Called the Loyal London [1666], p. 10). By 1667, Edward Waterhouse would even import the word into Tacitus's reference to London in *The Annals*.

Chapter Five

1. Because I stress the context of *Paradise Lost*'s initial appearance, I quote from the first edition of 1667, silently incorporating corrections that appeared in later issues of the first edition. Line numbers for the second, twelve-book, edition of 1674 follow references to the first, ten-book edition when there is a difference between the two.

2. Quint argues that by associating Satan with actual and literary trading ventures, Milton invokes a long-standing connection between mercantilism and romance. As a merchant adventurer, Satan must depend on fortune to direct his course and further his aims, but he is destined to be frustrated by God's plan, which unfolds with the certainty of a Virgilian epic. Thus their mercantile spirit betrays the fallen angels' disaccord with providence. At the same time, the association of trade with romance serves as a reading of the epic tradition: it demotes Luís de Camões's subject matter to the stuff of romance. For Quint, Milton's generic manipulations not only imply "an indictment of European expansion and colonialism that includes his own countrymen and contemporaries," they also yield, in the split between epic and romance, "an ideology of class distinction that begins to suggest the historical demise of epic itself." See Quint, *Epic and Empire: Politics and Generic Form from Virgil to Milton* (Princeton: Princeton University Press, 1993), pp. 248–67; quotations on pp. 265, 249. Quint builds on suggestions made by J. Martin Evans in his edition of *Paradise Lost: Books 9–10* (Cambridge: Cambridge University Press, 1973), pp. 46–47, and since developed in his *Milton's Imperial Epic: "Paradise Lost" and the Discourse of Colonialism* (Ithaca: Cornell University Press, 1996). For some cavils with Quint's reading, see Paul Stevens, "*Paradise Lost* and the Colonial Imperative," *Milton Studies* 34 (1996): 3–21.

3. David Armitage, "John Milton: Poet against Empire," in *Milton and Republicanism*, ed. David Armitage, Armand Himy, and Quentin Skinner (Cambridge: Cambridge University Press, 1995), pp. 206–25. As we have seen, there is no call to make absolute distinctions between the Commonwealth, Protectorate, and Restoration ideals of naval and commercial expansion: each succeeding regime took over and revised the ideals of its predecessors in complex ways. I nevertheless believe that Milton would be more concerned to oppose an active Royalist threat than to conduct a postmortem examination of the Protectorate. However much he may have come to regret Cromwell's actions, he had supported Cromwell for a time as he had not the Stuarts. Armitage's reading pushes us into a logical corner: Are we really rooting for a republic of fallen angels who would have thriven if only they had lived unto themselves in hell?

4. I agree with Barbara Lewalski that "Milton probably had someone read to him Dryden's *Annus Mirabilis*" when it appeared in print in January 1667 and that he probably continued to work on his own epic up to the time he gave it to the printer— well after Ellwood saw it (*The Life of John Milton: A Critical Biography* [Oxford: Blackwell, 2000], pp. 452, 444). We are not sure when precisely that was. *Paradise Lost* was

probably licensed shortly before Milton signed his contract with the publisher Samuel Simmons on April 27, 1667. It was registered with the Stationers on August 20. Thus, while Milton would have had neither the time nor the inclination to revise the design of his epic in response to *Annus Mirabilis,* he would have had four months to sharpen the differences between his poem and Dryden's. For a recent argument that it was "contestation, perhaps envy and denial" that "determined Milton's response to Dryden" (an argument that I hope this chapter will buttress), see Steven Zwicker, "Milton, Dryden, and the Politics of Literary Controversy," in *Culture and Society in the Stuart Restoration: Literature, Drama, History,* ed. Gerald MacLean (Cambridge: Cambridge University Press, 1995); quotation on p. 137. A few echoes in Andrew Marvell's *Last Instructions to a Painter* (Sept. 4, 1667) suggest that he, at least, may have been privy to Milton's poem in manuscript, but it has generally been supposed that Dryden did not read *Paradise Lost* until roughly the winter of 1668–69.

On the date of *Paradise Lost,* see Helen Darbishire, ed., *The Early Lives of Milton* (London: Constable, 1932), p. 13; Thomas Ellwood, *The History of the Life of Thomas Ellwood* (1714), ed. C. G. Crump (London: Methuen, 1900), p. 145; French, *Records,* 4:417; William R. Parker, *Milton: A Biography,* 2 vols. (Oxford: Clarendon Press, 1968), pp. 595–96, 1004, 1079, 1100, 1119; John T. Shawcross, *John Milton: The Self and the World* (Lexington: University Press of Kentucky, 1993), pp. 145–49; Nicholas von Maltzahn, "The First Reception of *Paradise Lost* (1667)," *Review of English Studies* 47 (1996): 479–99; and Lewalski, *Life of John Milton,* pp. 443–60. On the date of *Annus Mirabilis* and Dryden's reading of *Paradise Lost,* see Dryden, *Works,* 1:256; and James Winn, *John Dryden and His World* (New Haven: Yale University Press, 1987), p. 577 n. 28.

5. We saw in Chapter Three the prominence of Atlas on the western pediment of Amsterdam's Town Hall and on the naval and commercial arch of Charles II's royal entry of 1661. In 1666, at the end of a chapter that discusses the importance of trade not just to Maryland but to the English and other European monarchies, the ardent Royalist George Aslop could declare: "Trafique is Earth's great *Atlas,* that supports / The pay of Armies and the height of Courts" (*The Character of the Province of Maryland* [London, 1666], p. 70). Gerard Mercator applied the name *Atlas* to his book of maps not in honor of the Titan Atlas but in honor of an eponymous king of Libya who was supposed to have constructed the first terrestrial globe. But whether knowingly or through a misapprehension, the Titan Atlas became associated with maps and commerce alike. The frontispiece of the most lavish sea atlas published in the Netherlands in the seventeenth century—Romeyn de Hooghe's *Cartes Marine* (Amsterdam, 1693)—tellingly features the Titan Atlas supporting the globe.

6. *Paradise Lost* 2.636–42, 891, 1011, 1042–44, 4.159–66.

7. On representations of the city in *Paradise Lost,* see Lawrence Manley, *Literature and Culture in Early Modern London* (Cambridge: Cambridge University Press, 1995), pp. 566–82.

8. Guillame de Salluste du Bartas, *Bartas His Devine Weekes and Works,* trans. Joshua Sylvester, with intro. by Francis C. Haber (1605; facs. reprint, Gainesville, Fla.: Scholars' Facsimiles and Reprints, 1965), p. 445. As Armitage notes, the "adventrous Song" of Milton's opening invocation (*PL* 1.13) alludes to Sylvester's description of his own verse as an "adventurous Rime" in the invocation to "The Colonies" (p. 438); see Armitage, "Poet against Empire," p. 216.

9. At 2.402–29, Satan volunteers like the young scouts in the stories of Dolon in the *Iliad* (10.313–464) and of Nisus and Euryalus in the *Aeneid* (9.176–316). He appears like a merchant at 2.632–42.

10. For a reading of Milton's depiction of the debate and activities in hell as a critique of Protestant meliorism, see Catherine Gimelli Martin, "Self-Raised Sinners and the Spirit of Capitalism: *Paradise Lost* and the Critique of Protestant Meliorism," *Milton Studies* 30 (1993): 109–34.

11. *The Moderate Publisher of Every Daies Intelligence from the Parliaments Army,* April 8–15, 1653, p. 804.

12. Dryden, *State of Innocence,* 1.1.85, 89. Dryden's "States-General" may have been further suggested by Milton's "The bold design / Pleas'd highly those infernal States" (*PL* 2.386–87).

13. For another reading of this instability, see Quint, *Epic and Empire,* pp. 263–66.

14. Milton's comparison of Satan to a fleet returning from Bengal (where the English had a foothold) or Ternate or Tidore (both monopolies of the Dutch by 1663) seems calculated to implicate the English and Dutch East India Companies alike in Satan's design. For this reason I think Robert Markley is wrong to associate Satan only with the Dutch and to see in that identification Milton's frustration that the English are being kept out of the eastern trades ("'The destin'd Walls / Of Cambalu': Milton, China, and the Ambiguities of the East," in *Milton's Imperial Vision,* ed. Balachandra Rajan and Elizabeth Sauer [Pittsburgh: Duquesne University Press, 1999], pp. 205–06). The comparison of Satan to a Dutch merchant is, however, an apt one. It reverses the tenor and vehicle of some of the anti-Dutch literature of the East India trade, which declared of Dutch merchants that "from Hell they came, and thither without doubts they must return again" (*The Dutch-mens Pedigree,* a broad-side of 1653). The comparison of Satan to such a trader is appropriate to the events of Books 1 and 2, for according to another pamphlet, "The Majores . . . vse the Indies as the *Tucht-house* or Bridewell, to manage their vnruly & vnthrifty children & kindred; whom they cannot rule and order at home, they wend to the Indies, where they are preferred to offices and places of gouernment" (*An Answer vnto the Dutch Pamphlet* [1624], p. 30). We have just seen the angels whom heaven could not rule and order at home cast out to a prisonlike world where they promptly established offices and places of government. Such accounts of the massacre at Amboyna were revived before each of the Anglo-Dutch Wars. Milton would almost certainly have been acquainted with them because of his role in Anglo-Dutch negotiations. Dryden studied them carefully in preparation for writing *Amboyna,* the play that preceded his rewriting of *Paradise Lost* as an opera.

15. For a fascinating account of aristocratic involvement in the Royal Africa Company, see Clarendon's *Life,* where he describes the duke of York's eagerness for war with the Dutch and the threat that the company might be "broken or disordered by the jealousy that the gentlemen adventurers have of the merchants, and their opinion that they understand the mysteries of trade as well as the other, by which they refuse to concur in the necessary expedients proposed by the other, and interpose unskillful overtures of their own with pertinacy" (*The Life of Edward Earl of Clarendon,* 3 vols., new ed. [Oxford: Clarendon Press, 1827], 2:233–34).

16. In the prefatory verse to Marchamont Nedham's translation of *Mare Clau-*

sum (1652), Neptune says to the Commonwealth, "Thy great endeavors to encreas / The Marine power, do confess / thou act'st som great design" (stanza 3). William Godolphin's imitation of *Coopers Hill* also refers to England's "design" of becoming the entrepôt of world trade:

> Far now our Ships their Canvas Wings shall stretch,
> And the World's Wealth to richer *England* fetch,
> Till greater Treasures over-spread our Coast,
> Than *Tagis* or *Pactolus* Sands can boast.
>   With this Design our busy Vessels range
> About, to make our Isle the World's Exchange.

(lines 17–22)

Milton's description of Satan's wings as sails reverses this more common comparison of sails to wings. I would suggest, of course, that Milton has rather specific sails in mind: those of a merchant empire. Some ten years later, Thomas Sprat lauded Charles II's "Designe, which will infallibly make the *English* the Masters of the Trade of the world; and that is the bringing in of our *Gentry,* and *Nobility,* to contribute towards it" (*Observations on Monsieur de Sorbier's Voyage into England* [1665], p. 165). Objecting to the Second Anglo-Dutch War, George Wither complained, "We are so much inclined to rely / Upon the trustless and bewitching Charms / Of *State-designs*" (*Sighs for the Pitchers* [1666], p. 14). In the *Black Prince*'s "Epilogue to the King," (spoken on October 19, 1667), Roger Boyle, earl of Orrery, uses the word more heroically, but again associates it with the empire of trade that Charles is attempting to found:

> As when the Universe was made,
> The Vast Design was on the Waters laid;
> So you, in Conquering it, like Method keep,
> Laying your first foundations in the Deep.

(lines 13–16)

For the argument that Milton intends a more narrow, veiled allusion to Cromwell's Western Design, see Armitage, "Poet against Empire." For a different view of the Western Design, see Robert Fallon, "Cromwell, Milton, and the Western Design," in *Milton and the Imperial Vision,* ed. Rajan and Sauer.

17. *Paradise Lost* 2.arg, 403, 410, 867; 3.565; 4.34, 113, 159–65, 391; 5.340–41; 8/9. 1099–1118; 9/10.arg, 257, 293, 377.

18. For another discussion of Satan in Paradise that touches on mercantile themes, see Linda Gregerson, *The Reformation of the Subject: Spenser, Milton, and the English Protestant Epic* (Cambridge: Cambridge University Press, 1995), pp. 217–24.

19. See the note to 5.339–41 in *Paradise Lost,* ed. Alastair Fowler, 2d ed. (London: Longman, 1998). During the First Anglo-Dutch War, Marchamont Nedham commented, "methinks I see the Old game betwixt *Rome* and *Carthage* (the two great Commonwealths of the elder Times) revived again." The Carthaginians (and by implication the Dutch) were "base and sordid, such as steered all their Counsels by the Card of Profit" (*Mercurius Politicus,* Nov. 25–Dec. 2, 1652, p. 2053). Andrew Marvell expected that "their *Carthage* overcome / Would render fain unto our better *Rome*" ("The Character of Holland," lines 141–42). And Joost van den Vondel wrote,

"Karthage en Rome zien elckandre grimmigh aen" [Carthage and Rome eye each other angrily] (*Inwydinge van het Stadthuis 't Amsterdam* [Amsterdam, 1655], line 243). During the Second Anglo-Dutch War, the analogy was given extended treatment in the anonymous poem *Bellum Belgicum Secundum* (1665). In *A Poem on the Famous Ship Called the Loyal London* (1666), William Smith wrote: "With equal folly, and with equal fate / Mistaken *Carthage* urg'd the *Romane* State." We have already seen that Dryden makes a similar comparison in *Annus Mirabilis*, lines 17–20.

20. We might think of this as the flip side of the process by which merchants compared their own achievements to those of the martial aristocracy and thus ennobled themselves. See Quint, *Epic and Empire*, pp. 264–66.

21. *The Reason of Church-Government* (1642), in *CPW* 1:801–02.

22. For similar remarks on this passage, see J. Martin Evans, *Milton's Imperial Epic*, p. 70.

23. Sir William Davenant, *Poem to the Kings Most Sacred Majesty*, lines 306, 349–54; cf. Dryden, *Annus Mirabilis*, lines 561–64.

24. *The Readie and Easie Way* (1660), in *CPW* 7:386–87.

25. On geography more generally in *Paradise Lost*, see Bruce McLeod, "The 'Lordly eye': Milton and the Strategic Geography of Empire," in *Milton and the Imperial Vision*, ed. Rajan and Sauer.

26. On the parallels to Deuteronomy, see Jason P. Rosenblatt, "Adam's Pisgah Vision: *Paradise Lost*, Books XI and XII," *ELH* 39 (1972): 66–86. For various connections between Satan's voyage and the voyages of discovery in Luís de Camões's *Os Lusíadas*, see the pioneering studies of James H. Sims: "Camoens' *Lusiads* and Milton's *Paradise Lost*: Satan's Voyage to Eden," in *Papers on Milton*, ed. Philip M. Griffith and Lester F. Zimmerman (Tulsa, Okla.: University of Tulsa Press, 1969); " 'Delicious Paradise' in *Os Lusíadas* and in *Paradise Lost*," *Ocidente*, special no. (Nov. 1972): 163–72; and "*Os Lusíadas*: A Structural Prototype of *Paradise Lost*," *Explorations in Renaissance Culture* 4 (1978): 70–75. Also see Louis Martz, *Poet of Exile: A Study of Milton's Poetry* (New Haven: Yale University Press, 1980), pp. 155–68; and Quint, *Epic and Empire*, pp. 248–67.

27. Rosenblatt, "Adam's Pisgah Vision," pp. 68–70.

28. Milton's language shows him to have used the 1655 translation of the Royalist Sir Richard Fanshawe. Fanshawe's translation was printed by Humphrey Moseley, the well-known publisher who issued Milton's *Poems* of 1645. I follow Luís de Camões, *The Lusiad*, trans. Richard Fanshawe, ed. Jeremiah D. M. Ford (Cambridge: Harvard University Press, 1940).

29. Eliot, "Milton I," in *Selected Prose of T. S. Eliot*, ed. Frank Kermode (New York: Harcourt Brace Jovanovich, 1975), pp. 263–64. For a general discussion of Milton's use of maps, see George Wesley Whiting, *Milton's Literary Milieu* (Chapel Hill: University of North Carolina Press, 1939), pp. 94–128. Also see Markley, " 'Destined Walls,' " pp. 212–13.

30. "You say that they ask one hundred and thirty florins. I think it must be the Mauritanian Mount Atlas, not the book, that you say is to be bought at such a steep price. Such now is the extravagance of typographers in printing books that the furnishing of a library seems to have become no less costly than that of a villa. Since to me, blind, pictured maps could hardly be useful, surveying as I do the actual globe

with unseeing eyes, I fear that the more I paid for the book, the more I should mourn my loss. I beg you to do me the further favor to find out, so that you can tell me when you return, how many volumes there are in the whole work and which of the two editions, Blaeu's or Jansen's, is the fuller and more accurate" (*CPW* 7:494–95).

31. Most of these were ultimately derived from the charts of the Blaeu family, the official cartographers of the Dutch East India Company.

32. This is not the only place in which Milton evinces his interest in maps in *Paradise Lost*. He cannot refrain from using a figure from cartography even in Book 5, where it presumably cannot much help Adam understand the distances involved in Raphael's story of the war in Heaven:

> Regions to which
> All thy Dominion, *Adam,* is no more
> Than what this Garden is to all the Earth,
> And all the Sea, from one entire globose
> Stretcht into Longitude.

> (5.747–51/5.750–54)

"Stretcht into Longitude" means shown in flat projection, and that is precisely the way Adam seems to see here in Book 10 (Book 11 of the 1674 edition).

33. This identification is also made in the literature of the East India trade, e.g., Samuel Purchas, *Hakluytus Posthumus* (1625), vol. 1 (Glasgow: James MacLehose and Sons, 1905), pp. 35, 74. Under the heading "Soffala," *The East-India Trade: A True Narration of Divers Ports in East-India* [1641?] remarks: "this is the true Ophir whence *Salomo[n]* fetched Gold and other riches, as by tradition and ancient monuments there to this day appeares" (p. 3).

34. See the note to 11.396–407 in *Paradise Lost,* ed. Fowler, which analyzes the significance of the passage's numerological patterning and supplies biblical references to the gold of Ophir.

35. Henry Parker, *Of a Free Trade* (1648), p. 34; John Ogilby, *Relation of His Majesties Entertainment* (1661), p. 10.

36. See Bernard Bailyn, *The New England Merchants in the Seventeenth Century* (Cambridge: Harvard University Press, 1955), pp. 112–42; and J. M. Sosin, *English America and the Restoration Monarchy of Charles II: Transatlantic Politics, Commerce, and Kinship* (Lincoln: University of Nebraska Press, 1980), esp. pp. 1–10, 31–42, 74, 94, 108, 122.

37. For an optimistic reading of Adam's vision, see Armitage, "Poet against Empire," p. 222.

38. Dryden, *Works,* 4:14–15; cf. 3:17; Joseph Addison, no. 363 (Apr. 26, 1712) and no. 369 (May 3, 1712) in *The Spectator,* ed. Donald F. Bond, 5 vols. (Oxford: Clarendon Press, 1965), 3:357–66, 385–92, esp. 385–86. Dryden's complaint is less targeted than Addison's, but his disappointment with Milton when he gets into a "Track of Scripture" seems best applied to the verse that follows Adam's vision (in Book 10 of the first edition, Books 11 and 12 of the second). Louis Martz notes the reactions of both men in the course of arguing that Milton's "lowered style" may be intended to "create a number of ironical contrasts" with the endings of the *Aeneid,* the *Metamorphoses,* and *Os Lusíadas* (*Poet of Exile,* pp. 155–84; quotations on p. 156). On interpretations

of the "lust of the eyes" in 1 John 2:16 as ambition, see Barbara Lewalski, "Structure and the Symbolism of Vision in Michael's Prophecy, *Paradise Lost*, XI–XII," *Philological Quarterly* 42 (1963): 27–28.

39. For some other ways in which Carlo's voyage in *Gerusalemme Liberata* is relevant to *Paradise Lost*, see Quint, *Epic and Empire*, pp. 249–67.

40. I quote the Italian from Torquato Tasso, *Gerusalemme Liberata*, ed. Fredi Chiappelli (Milan: Rusconi, 1982). The English is from *Jerusalem Delivered*, trans. Ralph Nash (Detroit: Wayne State University Press, 1987).

41. Thomas Traherne, "Shadows in the Water," lines 49–56, in his *Centuries, Poems, and Thanksgivings*, ed. H. M. Margoliouth, 2 vols. (Oxford: Clarendon Press, 1958).

42. Stanley Fish, *Surprised by Sin: The Reader in "Paradise Lost*,*"* (1967; reprint, Berkeley: University of California Press, 1971), pp. 296–300; Manley, *Literature and Culture*, pp. 574–82.

43. Many biblical commentators asserted that Tubal-cain, whom Milton represents "at the Forge / Labouring" and draining ore "Into fit moulds prepar'd; from which he formd / First his own Tooles; then, what might else be wrought / Fusil or grav'n in mettle" (10.560–61, 567–69/11.564–65, 571–73), was the same as Mulciber or Vulcan. (See, for instance, the remarks on Genesis 4:22 in H[enry] A[insworth], *Annotations upon the First Book of Moses, Called Genesis* [1616].) Thus Milton's reference to his apparent invention of artillery ties Tubal-cain both to the fiends of Books 1, 2, and 6 and to the Charles II of Restoration panegyrics, whose purported care for the artillery of the British navy encouraged comparisons to Vulcan.

44. This last phrase is reminiscent of the terms in which Royalist poets had celebrated the capture of Dutch merchant vessels in England's trade wars—described by Waller as "wealthy prey" (*Instructions to a Painter*, line 40) and by Dryden as "perfum'd prey" betrayed by its "rich scent" (*Annus Mirabilis*, line 101)—but Milton's more pressing concern seems to lie with the effect of empire even on the victorious.

45. E. H. Gombrich writes: "One explanation became standard in the glosses and paraphrases, from the *Glossa Ordinaria* of the ninth century to Petrus Comester's *Historia Scholastica* of the twelfth, a book which enjoyed such popularity that it almost eclipsed the Bible itself: what God had meant was that He would destroy the *fertility* of the earth." For more on this commentary tradition and the consequent proposal that Hieronymus Bosch's *Garden of Earthly Delights*, with its giant fruits, actually represents the earth before the deluge, see Gombrich, *Heritage of Apelles: Studies in the Art of the Renaissance* (Ithaca: Cornell University Press, 1976), pp. 83–90; quotation on p. 85. Milton's yoking together of luxury and violence as alternative forms of consumption finds an analogue in a curious detail of Bosch's painting: near the left-hand corner of the central panel, a monk holds a giant bunch of grapes composed partly of human heads.

46. Laura Knoppers remarks on the political significance of Milton's reference to Bacchic revelries in his invocation to Book 7 (*Historicizing Milton: Spectacle, Power, and Poetry in Restoration England* [Athens: University of Georgia Press, 1994], pp. 87–91). Although it treats only Book 4 of *Paradise Lost*, Steven Zwicker's discussion of the "politics of pleasure" in *Annus Mirabilis, The Last Instructions to a Painter*, and *Paradise Lost* is also relevant here (*Lines of Authority: Politics and English Literary Culture, 1649–1689* [Ithaca: Cornell University Press, 1993], pp. 90–129).

47. In a curious incident, Milton was given the opportunity to prove his ethical consistency in 1667 when he rejected the Royal Society's invitation to write on their behalf. See von Maltzahn, "First Reception," pp. 495–96.

48. For the argument that *Paradise Lost* ultimately displaces dominion from empire to the household, see Janel Mueller, "Dominion as Domesticity: Milton's Imperial God and the Experience of History," in *Milton's Imperial Vision,* ed. Rajan and Sauer.

49. See Neil Keeble, *The Literary Culture of Nonconformity in Later Seventeenth-Century England* (Leicester: Leicester University Press, 1987), pp. 187–214; and Manley, *Literature and Culture,* pp. 533–82.

50. Thomas Gouge, quoted in Keeble, *Literary Culture,* p. 221; on nonconformist notions of pursuing worldly business more generally, see pp. 220–29.

51. [George Fox], *The Line of Righteousness and Justice Stretched Forth over All Merchants* (1661), p. 1. Also see Paul H. Eden, *Quakers in Commerce: A Record of Business Achievement* (London: S. Low Marston, 1940); David Burns Windsor, *The Quaker Enterprise: Friends in Business* (London: Methuen, 1980); and David Harris Sacks, *The Widening Gate: Bristol and the Atlantic Economy, 1450–1700* (Berkeley: University of California Press, 1991), pp. 312–26.

52. Another way of expressing this idea is to say that the practice of "fair dealing" espoused by the Quakers, and fairly generally practiced in the English economy, leads to low "transactions costs," which Douglas C. North defines as "the costs of specifying and enforcing the contracts that underlie all exchange. . . . They are the costs involved in capturing the gains of trade. They include a specification of what is exchanged or of the performance of agents and an analysis of the costs of enforcement. The costs of contracting are in general those of searching who has rights with respect to what is being traded, what rights they have, and what are the attributes of the rights; those of searching for prices associated with the transaction and the predictability of those prices; and those of stipulating contracts and contract performance" ("Transactions Costs in History," *European Economic History Journal* 14 [1985]: 558).

Chapter Six

1. For a contemporary dialogue purporting to record the Court's privy debates about which alliance would be in England's interest, see *A Free Conference Touching the Present State of England Both at Home and Abroad, in Order to the Designs of France* (1668).

2. [Slingsby Bethel], *The Present Interest of England Stated* (1671), pp. 34, 30–31, 33.

3. J. R. Jones, *The Anglo-Dutch Wars of the Seventeenth Century* (London: Longman, 1996), pp. 179–216; C. L. Grose, "Louis XIV's Financial Relations with Charles II and the English Parliament," *Journal of Modern History* 1 (1929): 177–204.

4. Grey, *Debates,* Feb. 7, 1672, 2:10.

5. *LJ,* 12:525.

6. On the date of *Amboyna,* see James Winn, *John Dryden and His World* (New Haven: Yale University Press, 1987), p. 239–41; Dryden, *Works,* 12:257–58.

7. *A True Relation of the Vnjust, Cruell, and Barbarous Proceedings of the English at Amboyna* (1624), "To the Readers," pp. [vii-viii]. The play's editors cite this passage in their note to 1.1.72–76, in Dryden, *Works,* 12:288. For a complementary account of the way the Dutch East India Company had managed its affairs "like a Commonwealth

rather than a Trade," with a substantial dependence on force that had increased its costs, see Sir William Temple, *Observations upon the United Provinces of the Netherlands* (1668), ed. Sir George Clark (Oxford: Clarendon Press, 1972), pp. 117, 124–25.

8. In a similar vein, Joseph Hill criticized Dutch and Englishmen who advocated war in the name of commerce, crying, "We are competitors for trade! It's our interest! Our interest! Down with the English!" even though "the world is wide enough, and the sea large enough for both nations to exercise their skill and industry." See his *The Interest of These United Provinces* (Amsterdam, 1673), sig. G2.

9. On the play's sensationalism, see Louis I. Bredvold, "Political Aspects of Dryden's *Amboyna* and *The Spanish Fryer*," *University of Michigan Publications in Language and Literature* 8 (1932): 120–23.

10. For a reading of the play that examines themes of national identity, see Robert Markley, "Violence and Profits on the Restoration Stage: Trade, Nationalism, and Insecurity in Dryden's *Amboyna*," *Eighteenth-Century Life* 22 (1988): 2–17.

11. Robert Codrington, *His Majesties Propriety, and Dominion of the British Seas Asserted; Together with a True Account of the Neatherlanders Insupportable Insolencies, and Injuries, They Have Committed* (1665), preface.

12. For the major pamphlet accounts of these events, see Chapter Four, n. 23.

13. On such details of staging and casting, see Colin Visser, "John Dryden's *Amboyna* at Lincoln's Inn Fields, 1673," *Restoration and Eighteenth-Century Theatre Research* 15 (1976): 1–11; Winn, *Dryden*, p. 239; and Dryden, *Works*, 12:269–71.

14. Mary Caroline Trevelyan, *William the Third and the Defence of Holland, 1672–1674* (London: Longman, 1930), pp. 183, 187–96.

15. On Milton's "entangling" verse, see Stanley Fish, *Surprised by Sin: The Reader in "Paradise Lost"* (1967; reprint, Berkeley: University of California Press, 1971).

16. Grey, *Debates*, Oct. 31, 1673, 2:203.

17. On this shift of public opinion, see K. H. D. Haley, *William of Orange and the English Opposition, 1672–4* (Oxford: Clarendon Press, 1953); Steven Pincus, "From Butter Boxes to Wooden Shoes: The Shift in English Popular Sentiment from Anti-Dutch to Anti-French in the 1670s," *Historical Journal* 38 (1995): 333–61; and J. R. Jones, *Anglo-Dutch Wars*, pp. 205–16.

18. Grey, *Debates*, Oct. 31, 1673, 2:204.

19. Grey, *Debates*, Oct. 31, 1673, 2:203.

20. See Alain Roy, *Gérard de Lairesse (1640–1711)* (Paris: Arthena, 1992), pp. 258–60.

21. John Evelyn, *Navigation and Commerce, Their Original and Progress* (1674), p. 16.

22. An exception is Pat Rogers, "Trade and Empire: *Annus Mirabilis* and *Windsor Forest*," *Durham University Journal* 64 (1976): 14–20.

23. Earl Wasserman, *The Subtler Language: Critical Readings of Neoclassical and Romantic Poems* (Baltimore: Johns Hopkins University Press, 1959), pp. 109–10.

24. John Ogilby, *The Entertainment of His Most Excellent Majestie Charles II,* ed. with intro., Ronald Knowles (1662; facs. reprint, Binghamton, N.Y.: Medieval and Renaissance Texts and Studies, 1988), pp. 103–04.

25. On the involvement of (vigorously Protestant) merchants in the opposition to Charles II from 1670 to 1683, see Margaret Priestley, "London Merchants and Opposition Politics in Charles II's Reign," *Bulletin of the Institute for Historical Research* 29 (1956): 205–19. Also see Gary Stuart DeKrey, *A Fractured Society: The Politics of London*

in the First Age of Party, 1688–1715 (Oxford: Clarendon Press, 1985), pp. 22–34, 99–112, 121–76.

26. On the events and controversies of the Exclusion Crisis, a term that some historians now eschew, see K. H. D. Haley, *The First Earl of Shaftesbury* (Oxford: Clarendon Press, 1968); Richard Ashcraft, *Revolutionary Politics and Locke's "Two Treatises of Government"* (Princeton: Princeton University Press, 1986); Jonathan Scott, *Algernon Sidney and the Restoration Crisis, 1677–1683* (Cambridge: Cambridge University Press, 1991); and Mark Knights, *Politics and Opinion in Crisis, 1678–81* (Cambridge: Cambridge University Press, 1994).

27. *CJ,* 17:258, 275. On the Anglo-French Trade Treaty of 1713, which was hotly debated and eventually defeated in the House of Commons by nine votes on June 13, 1713, thanks to the defection of some seventy Tories, see D. C. Coleman, "Politics and Economics in the Age of Anne: The Case of the Anglo-French Treaty of 1713," in *Trade, Government, and Economy in Pre-Industrial England: Essays Presented to F. J. Fisher* (London: Weidenfeld and Nicolson, 1976); and Perry Gauci, *The Politics of Trade: The Overseas Merchant in State and Society, 1660–1720* (Oxford: Oxford University Press, 2001), chap. 6.

28. *Windsor Forest,* lines 42, 61–64; Wasserman, *Subtler Language,* pp. 117–23.

29. Maynard Mack, *Alexander Pope: A Life* (New York: Norton, 1985), p. 201.

30. David B. Morris, "Virgilian Attitudes in Pope's *Windsor Forest,*" in *Pope: Recent Essays by Several Hands,* ed. Maynard Mack and James Winn (Hamden, Conn.: Archon, 1980), esp. pp. 156–58; Wallace Jackson, *Vision and Re-Vision in Alexander Pope* (Detroit: Wayne State University Press, 1983), pp. 26–27. On the more general history of the idea that violent passions might be controlled by commercial interests, see Albert O. Hirschman, *The Passions and the Interests: Political Arguments for Capitalism before Its Triumph* (Princeton: Princeton University Press, 1977).

31. Wasserman, *Subtler Language,* p. 163.

32. On this embassy and its appearance in *Windsor Forest,* see Joseph Roach, *Cities of the Dead: Circum-Atlantic Performance* (New York: Columbia University Press, 1996), pp. 119–78.

33. On Pope's thorough knowledge of Milton's verse from an early age, see Barbara Lewalski, "On Looking into Pope's Milton," *Milton Studies* 11 (1978): 29–50.

34. Bruce I. Watson, "Fortifications and the 'Idea' of Force in Early English East India Company Relations with India," *Past and Present,* no. 88 (1980): 72–73.

35. Niccolao Manucci, *Storia do Mogor,* quoted in Watson, "Fortifications," p. 82.

36. Dispatch to Fort St. George, Jan. 3, 1694, quoted in Watson, "Fortifications," p. 86.

37. K. N. Chaudhuri, *The Trading World of Asia and the English East India Company, 1660–1760* (Cambridge: Cambridge University Press, 1978), pp. 109–29; Watson, "Fortifications," pp. 83–87.

38. *The Readie and Easie Way* (1660), in *CPW* 7:385–86.

Introduction to Part Four

1. Joseph Hall, *Contemplations,* bk. 1, in *The Works of Joseph Hall of Exeter* (1634), p. 777.

2. John Evelyn, *Navigation and Commerce, Their Original and Progress* (1674), p. 5.

3. Pieter Corneliszon Plockhoy, *A Way Propounded to Make the Poor in These and Other Nations Happy* (1660), sigs. A1r, A3r, A3v.

4. John Locke, *First Tract on Government* (1660), in *Political Essays,* ed. Mark Goldie (Cambridge: Cambridge University Press, 1997), p. 38.

Chapter Seven

1. Attempts to read *Samson Agonistes* in the context of the Restoration include David Masson, *The Life of John Milton* (London: Macmillan, 1877), 6:670–78; Christopher Hill, *Milton and the English Revolution* (London: Faber and Faber, 1977), pp. 428–48, 481–86, *The Experience of Defeat: Milton and Some Contemporaries* (New York: Penguin, 1984), pp. 310–19, and "*Samson Agonistes* Again," *Literature and History,* ser. 2, 1 (1990): 24–39; Nicholas Jose, *Ideas of Restoration in English Literature, 1660–71* (Cambridge: Harvard University Press, 1984), chap. 8; Laura Knoppers, *Historicizing Milton: Spectacle, Power, and Poetry in Restoration England* (Athens: University of Georgia Press, 1994), chap. 6; Blair Worden, "Milton, *Samson Agonistes,* and the Restoration," in *Culture and Society in the Stuart Restoration,* ed. Gerald MacClean (Cambridge: Cambridge University Press, 1995); and David Loewenstein, *Representing Revolution in Milton and His Contemporaries: Religion, Politics, and Polemics in Radical Puritanism* (Cambridge: Cambridge University Press, 2001), chap. 9.

2. On the notion of a Norman Yoke (which was variously interpreted), see Christopher Hill, *Intellectual Origins of the English Revolution* (Oxford: Clarendon Press, 1965), pp. 50–106; and R. B. Seaberg, "The Norman Conquest and the Common Law: The Levellers and the Argument from Continuity," *Historical Journal* 24 (1981): 791–806. Among many other instances, see Milton's references to the subjects of tyrants or hereditary monarchs as slaves in *The Tenure of Kings and Magistrates* (1649), *Eikonoklastes* (1649), and *A Defence of the People in England* (1651), in *CPW* 3:244, 462, 580; 4:303, 338, 367, 374, 387, 399, 401–02, 532. Also see Algernon Sidney, *Court Maxims,* ed. Hans W. Blom, Eco Haitsma Mulier, and Ronald Janse (Cambridge: Cambridge University Press, 1996), pp. 28, 41, 65, 78, 94, 154, 200–201. On the meaning of slavery in republican (or neo-Roman) thought, see Alan Craig Houston, *Algernon Sidney and the Republican Heritage in England and America* (Princeton: Princeton University Press, 1991), chap. 3; and Quentin Skinner, *Liberty before Liberalism* (Cambridge: Cambridge University Press, 1998), pp. 36–44. On Milton and slavery, see Sharon Achinstein, "Imperial Dialectic: Milton and Conquered Peoples," in *Milton and the Imperial Vision,* ed. Balachandra Rajan and Elizabeth Sauer (Pittsburgh: Duquesne University Press, 1999).

3. On the notion that inward slavery to one's passions can lead to outward slavery, see Milton's *Second Defence of the English People* (1654): "it happens that a nation which cannot rule and govern itself, but has delivered itself into slavery to its own lusts, is enslaved also to other masters whom it does not choose, and serves not only voluntarily but also against its will. Such is the decree of law and of nature herself" (*CPW* 4:684).

4. I quote *The Readie and Easie Way* (1660), in *CPW* 7:463, 462. For the justification of monarchy in terms of slave-sales, see Hugo Grotius, *De Jure Belli ac Pacis,* 2 vols., facs. reprint of the 1646 edition with trans. by Francis W. Kelsey (Buffalo:

William S. Hein, 1995), bk. 1, chap. 3, sec. 8. *De Jure Belli* first appeared in 1625. Milton attempted to refute Salmasius's use of this argument (*Regia* [1649], p. 142) in *A Defence of the People in England* (1651): "But, you say, 'Just as of old many individuals would sell themselves to another as slaves, so can a whole people.' You knight of the lash, concealer of slavery's blemishes, eternal shame even to your own land, you are so foul a procurer and hireling pimp of slavery that even the lowest slaves on any auction block should hate and despise you. If a people could thus yield itself to a king, he might equally yield that same people to some other master or put them up for sale, while in fact it is well-known that a king cannot alienate even his crown property! Shall he then who enjoys only the usufruct of the crown, as it is said, and of crown property by the grant of the people, be able to claim title to that people itself?" (*CPW* 4:460–61).

5. *The Readie and Easie Way*, in *CPW* 7:387, 359.

6. Those whom the Israelites defeated with the assistance of Yahweh were subject to slavery: Isa. 14:2, 1 Ki. 9:21. Conversely, the Lord's special relationship with the Israelites is suggested by his freeing them from bondage: Ex. 20:2, Deut. 5:6, 6:2, 8:14, 13:15, 13:8, Judg. 6:8.

7. On the importance of the parable of the talents to *Samson Agonistes*, see John Guillory, "The Father's House: *Samson Agonistes* in Its Historical Moment," in *Re-Membering Milton: Essays on the Texts and Traditions*, ed. Mary Nyquist and Margaret W. Ferguson (New York: Methuen, 1987), pp. 156–59.

8. William Tyndale, *The Parable of the Wicked Mammon* (1527), in *Doctrinal Treatises and Introductions to Different Portions of Holy Scriptures*, ed. Rev. Henry Walter (Cambridge: Parker Society, 1847), p. 100 and (on working as submission to God's will) p. 101.

9. Mary Beth Rose, "'Vigorous Most / When Most Unactive Deemed': Gender and the Heroics of Endurance in Milton's *Samson Agonistes*, Aphra Behn's *Oroonoko*, and Mary Astell's *Some Reflections upon Marriage*," *Milton Studies* 33 (1996): 88.

10. Thomas Hobbes, *Leviathan* (1651), ed. Edwin Curley (Indianapolis: Hackett, 1994), pt. 1, chap. 10, par. 16.

11. Between 1580 and 1640 it was commonly, though by no means universally, argued that England's population was excessive and that one use of colonies would be to absorb that excess; see K. E. Knorr, *British Colonial Theories, 1570–1880* (Toronto: University of Toronto Press, 1944), pp. 41–48. But settlement of the New World, with all its arable land and natural resources, so radically changed Europe's labor-to-capital ratio that labor soon became a newly scarce resource. Demand for labor was extremely high in the New World, and even in England real wages began to rise as the population leveled off at mid century. That scarcity of labor led to higher wages was well understood by writers on trade. It is not surprising that, just as they wrote about currency when there were shortages of coin, they should think about the contribution of labor to the economy when it was in short supply. In the second half of the century, authors like Sir William Petty, Carew Reynel, and Josiah Child closely equated the wealth of a nation with its population; as Reynel said in *The True English Interest* (1674), "the more populous, the more Trade; the more Trade, the more populous, and the more Trade and populacy, the more Money" (p. 18). Others criticized colonies because they drained the mother country of laborers. On theories of

labor in England, see Donald C. Coleman, "Labour in the English Economy of the Seventeenth Century," *Economic History Review,* 2d ser., 8 (1956): 280–95. For useful overviews of the Atlantic labor market, see Edwin E. Rich and C. H. Wilson, eds., *The Cambridge Economic History of Europe* (Cambridge: Cambridge University Press, 1966–67), 4:345–64; and Richard S. Dunn, "Servants and Slaves: The Recruitment and Employment of Labor," in *Colonial British America: Essays in the New History of the Early Modern Era,* ed. Jack P. Greene and J. R. Poole (Baltimore: Johns Hopkins University Press, 1984).

12. Hartlib Papers, 67/8/1A-2B (Anon., Memo on Types of Mills, n.d.).

13. Grotius, *De Jure Belli,* bk. 3, chap. 7, secs. 1–8; Hobbes, *Leviathan,* pt. 2, chap. 20, pars. 10–14; Samuel Pufendorf, *On the Duty of Man and Citizen According to Natural Law* (1673), ed. James Tully, trans. Michael Silverthorne (Cambridge: Cambridge University Press, 1991), pp. 129–31; John Locke, *Two Treatises of Government,* ed. Peter Laslett (Cambridge: Cambridge University Press, 1988), p. 284. It could be argued that a Christian, barred from suicide, could not freely choose the alternative of death, but this quibble did not prevent jurists from viewing slavery in contractual terms. Jurists and theologians seem to have been slow to label a death that was courted, but not self-administered, a suicide. For another reading of Samson's story in terms of Grotius's discussion of slavery, see Leonard Tennenhouse, "The Case of the Resistant Captive," *South Atlantic Quarterly* 95 (1996): 930–36. Also see Achinstein, "Imperial Dialectic."

14. See esp. Hobbes, *Leviathan,* pt. 2, chap. 21, pars. 1–4; and Skinner, *Liberty before Liberalism,* pp. 6–10.

15. Locke, *Two Treatises,* p. 284. Samson expresses a distaste for life at lines 521–22 and 1262–64.

16. Sir William Petty, *Two Essays in Political Arithmetic* (1687), in *The Economic Writings of Sir William Petty,* ed. Charles Henry Hull (1899; reprint, Fairfield, N.J.: A. M. Kelley, 1986), p. 512.

17. That population may pose political and economic problems is assumed in *Paradise Lost;* see David Glimp, "Paradisal Arithmetic: *Paradise Lost* and the Genesis of Populations," *Modern Language Quarterly* 60 (1999): 1–31. A concern with population similarly informs the utopian fiction of the republican Henry Neville, *The Isle of Pines* (1668).

18. Sir William Petty, *A Treatise of Taxes and Contributions* (1662), in *Economic Writings,* pp. 68, 71–72.

19. 13–14 Car. 2. c. 1, whence the quotations are drawn, 16 Car. 2. c. 4, and 22 Car. 2. c. 1. See *Statutes at Large, from the First Year of King James I to the Tenth Year of the Reign of King William the Third* (1770), pp. 217–18, 290, 322–25.

20. The similarity between Samson's sexual relationship with Dalila and his labor at the mill is particularly obvious to readers who recall Milton's contention in *The Doctrine and Discipline of Divorce* (1643) that a husband should not be compelled to "grind in the mill of an undelighted and servil copulation" (*CPW* 2:258). But Samson's depiction of his relationship with Dalila as true slavery (lines 410–19) and his admission that he betrayed his secret to Dalila "at times when men seek most repose and rest" (line 406) also establishes a parallel between copulation and his labor. On Manoa's disapproval of Samson's marriages, see lines 420–33, 1742–44.

21. Guillory, "The Father's House," p. 152. In some places, Guillory thinks of Manoa (rightly, in my view) as someone who wants Samson to lead a life that is narratable and that is explicable in terms of his vocation to deliver Israel (pp. 151, 156). But elsewhere Guillory allows his alignment of the Hebrew God with a "great work" and of the earthly father with "labor in a calling" to slide into a distinction between a God who demands "destruction" and a father who demands "production" (p. 164). Both fathers demand destruction. Manoa simply cannot understand why Samson will not kill Philistines during regular business hours. It is Samson's compulsive urge to *produce*, even if for an enemy nation, that worries Manoa.

22. 13 Car. 2, stat. 2, c. 1, in *Statutes at Large, from the First Year of King James I*, pp. 213–15; Mark Knights, "A City Revolution: The Remodelling of the London Livery Companies in the 1680s," *English Historical Review* 112 (1997): 1144–45.

23. Coke, *2 Institutes*, chap. 29. I owe this point to David Harris Sacks.

24. Grotius, *De Jure Belli*, bk. 2, chap. 5, sec. 27; Pufendorf, *Duty of Man*, pp. 129–31. Grotius concedes that *if* the child's upkeep and his service to his master were commensurable, then his continuing enslavement would be just, but he assumes that the child's labor will eventually exceed the charge of his maintenance, at which point the civil law binding him to remain a slave is "more generous than just" to his master (*De Jure Belli*, bk. 3, chap. 14, sec. 8).

25. See *The Digest of Justinian*, Latin ed. Theodor Mommsen with Paul Krueger, trans. and ed. Alan Watson, 4 vols. (Philadelphia: University of Pennsylvania Press, 1985), bk. 7, chap. 7. Also see Seneca, *De Beneficiis*, bk. 3, secs. 20–22, esp. 22, where he cites Chrisippus's dictum that a bondman (*servus*) is a perpetual hireling (*perpetuus mercennarius*). In his translation of 1614, Thomas Lodge translates *ministerium* and *beneficium* as "service" and "benefit." For a useful discussion of Seneca's conception of slavery, see Paul Veyne's introduction to *Sénèque: Entretiens, lettres à Lucilius* (Paris: Robert Laffont, 1993), pp. cxxxvii–cxliii.

26. In *Coopers Hill*, Denham writes:

> I see the City in a thicker cloud
> Of business, then of smoake; where men like Ants
> Toyle to prevent imaginarie wants;
> Yet all in vaine, increasing with their store,
> Their vast desires, but make their wants the more.
> As food to unsound bodies, though it please
> The Appetite, feeds onely the disease.
>
> (The "A" Text, Draft 3, lines 28–34)

27. Some such theory seems to motivate the period's many advocates of child labor and make-work schemes predicated on the belief that indoctrination is essential to make work a life-long habit. See Joyce Appleby, *Economic Thought and Ideology in Seventeenth-Century England* (Princeton: Princeton University Press, 1978), pp. 141–44.

28. John Locke, *An Essay on Toleration* (1667), in *Political Essays*, ed. Mark Goldie (Cambridge: Cambridge University Press, 1997), pp. 154–55.

29. See James Harrington, *The Commonwealth of Oceana* (1656), in *The Political Works of James Harrington*, ed. J. G. A. Pocock (Cambridge: Cambridge University Press, 1977), pp. 163–64 et passim.

30. Locke, *An Essay on Toleration*, in *Political Essays*, p. 155.

31. Guillory, "House of the Father," p. 152.

32. Katherine Gibson, "'The Kingdom's Marble Chronicle': The Embellishment of the First and Second Buildings, 1600–1690," in *The Royal Exchange*, ed. Ann Saunders (London: London Topographical Society, 1977), pp. 144–45. The quotations translate a Latin inscription placed under the new statue of Charles I after the Great Fire.

33. Michael McKeon, *Politics and Poetry in Restoration England: The Case of Dryden's "Annus Mirabilis"* (Cambridge: Harvard University Press, 1975), pp. 105–10.

34. Steven Pincus, *Protestantism and Patriotism: Ideologies and the Making of English Foreign Policy, 1650–1668* (Cambridge: Cambridge University Press, 1996), p. 253.

35. Ann Saunders, "The Second Exchange," in *Royal Exchange*, ed. Saunders, p. 131–34.

36. Gibson, "'The Kingdom's Marble Chronicle,'" in *Royal Exchange*, ed. Saunders, pp. 148–49.

37. Pincus, *Protestantism and Patriotism*, chaps. 11–25.

38. See T. F. Reddaway, *The Rebuilding of London after the Great Fire* (London: Edward Arnold, 1940), esp. chap. 5; and John R. Kellet, "The Breakdown of Guild and Corporation Control over the Handicraft and Retail Trade in England," *Economic History Review*, 2d ser., 10 (1958): 381–94.

39. On the sympathies of many of the Council of Trade's members with dissenters, and later with the Whigs, see William Letwin, *The Origins of Scientific Economics* (New York: Doubleday, 1964), pp. 24–27.

40. See Slingsby Bethel, *The World's Mistake in Oliver Cromwell* (1668) and *The Interest of England Stated* (1671). For a response to the latter work that accepts the idea that trade may require religious toleration, see George Villiers, second duke of Buckingham, *A Letter to Sir Thomas Osborne, One of His Majesties Privy Council, upon the Reading of a Book, Called, The Present Interest of England Stated* (1672). Also see Carew Reynel, *The True English Interest*, esp. p. 6; and Roger Coke, *A Discourse of Trade* (1670) and *A Treatise Wherein Is Demonstrated That the Church and State of England Are in Equal Danger with the Trade of It* (1671).

41. The work of Sir William Davenant that I have in mind is *Salmacida Spolia* (1640). Much relevant information on this strain of Caroline verse may be found in Lawrence Manley, *Literature and Culture in Early Modern London* (Cambridge: Cambridge University Press, 1995), chap. 9. Also see David Norbrook, *Writing the English Revolution: Poetry, Rhetoric, and Politics, 1627–1660* (Cambridge: Cambridge University Press, 1999), pp. 71–79.

42. Most of this poetry, and (with the exception of *Annus Mirabilis*) all the poetry that I cite, is gathered in Robert Arnold Aubin, ed., *London in Flames, London in Glory: Poems on the Fire and Rebuilding of London, 1666–1709* (New Brunswick: Rutgers University Press, 1943). Other relevant poetry that appeared before 1671 includes Simon Ford, *Conflagratio Londinensis* (1667), *Londini quod reliquum* (1667), *Actio in Londini incendiarios* (1667), and *Londini renascentis imago poetica* (1668); William Smith, *De urbis Londini incendio elegia* (1667); and [Jeremiah Wells], "In Londini incendium," in his *Poems upon Divers Occasions* (1667). Also important is Samuel Rolls's lengthy prose work, *Londons Resurrection; or, The Rebuilding of London Encouraged, Directed, and Improved, in Fifty Discourses* (1668). For a recent analysis of the writings occasioned by London's destruction,

see Cynthia Wall, *The Literary and Cultural Spaces of Restoration London* (Cambridge: Cambridge University Press, 1998), chaps. 1–2.

43. John Crouch, *Londons Second Tears* (1666), lines 121, 136; Dryden, *Annus Mirabilis* (1667), lines 849–50.

44. Dryden, preface to *Annus Mirabilis*, in *Works*, 1:49.

45. Dryden, *Annus Mirabilis*, line 1178, and *London's Epitaph* (1666), line 10, printed in the collection *Rome Rhym'd to Death* (1683); Simon Ford, *London's Resurrection* (1669), lines 7–8; George Eliott, *Great Brittains Beauty; or, Londons Delight. Being a Poem, in the Commendation of the Famous Incomparable City of London, and the Royal Exchange* (1671), lines 29–30; W[illiam?] F[enne?], *London Surveyed* (167[0?]), lines 148, 152–53; Simon Ford, *Londons Remains*(1667), line 8. Additional examples include E.C., *London Undone* (1666), lines 85–86; and *The Burning of London* (1667), line 15. Examples of the phoenix in poems appearing after 1671 include *Londons Stately New Buildings* (1672), lines 5–12; *A Brief Description of the Royal Exchange* (1672), lines 487–88; *The Glories of London* (1674), lines 11–17; *London's Index* (1676), lines 21–24; and James Wright, *Phœnix Paulina* (1709), lines 13–16.

46. Crouch, *Londons Second Tears*, lines 233–34. Cf. Dryden, *Annus Mirabilis*, lines 1151–52.

47. *Upon the Rebuilding of the City, The Right Honourable the Lord Mayor and the Noble Company of Batchelors Dining with Him, May 5th 1669*, line 41.

48. Samuel Wiseman, *A Short and Serious Narrative of Londons Fatal Fire* (1667), lines 337–38, 305–06.

49. *The Citizens Joy for the Rebuilding of London* (1667), lines 37–38. For another instance of religious policy being counseled in terms of architectural and building principles, see *Upon the Rebuilding of the City* (1669), lines 167–86. Some poems on the Great Fire, in contrast, counsel religious toleration, for there was a theoretical connection between toleration and vigorous trade.

50. *The Citizens Joy*, lines 17, 19–20.

51. Jackie DiSalvo, "'The Lord's Battells': *Samson Agonistes* and the Puritan Revolution," *Milton Studies* 4 (1972): 36–62; Christopher Hill, *Milton*, pp. 429–30, 435–36; Joseph Wittreich, *Interpreting "Samson Agonistes"* (Princeton: Princeton University Press, 1986), pp. 192–200; Worden, "Milton, *Samson Agonistes*, and the Restoration," pp. 116–17.

52. Nicholas Jose similarly argues that "in overturning this building Samson is overturning an accumulation of Restoration panegyrical claims and by extension rejecting the Restoration settlement itself" (*Ideas of Restoration*, p. 157).

53. *Animadversions* (1641), in *CPW* 1:700; Hartlib Papers, 13/136A (Letter, Sir Cheney Culpeper to Hartlib, March 4, 1646); A. S. P. Woodhouse, ed., *Puritanism and Liberty: Being the Army Debates (1647–49)*, 3d ed. (London: Dent, 1992), p. 41; John Owen, *OYPANΩN. OYPANIA. The Shaking and Translating of Heaven and Earth. A Sermon Preached to the Honourable House of Commons in Parliament Assembled* (Apr. 19, 1649), p. 27. On the iconoclasm of *Samson*, see David A. Loewenstein, *Milton and the Drama of History: Historical Vision, Iconoclasm, and the Literary Imagination* (Cambridge: Cambridge University Press, 1990), pp. 128–51; and Lana Cable, *Carnal Rhetoric: Milton's Iconoclasm and the Poetics of Desire* (Durham: Duke University Press, 1995), pp. 171–96.

54. Joseph Guillim, prefatory epistle to "The Dreadful Burning" (1667).

55. Crouch, *Londons Second Tears*, lines 83–84; William Sancroft, *Lex Ignea, or the School of Righteousness. Preached before the King. Octob. 10, 1666*, p. 34.

56. William Kerrigan, "The Irrational Coherence of *Samson Agonistes*," *Milton Studies* 22 (1986): 227–28.

57. Petty, *Verbum Sapienti* (1664), in his *Economic Writings*, p. 119.

58. For an opposed interpretation, see Christopher Kendrick's claim that "Milton comes to terms with the Revolution's overt failure by symptomatically recognizing its underground success, i.e., the political entrenchment of capitalism." See his "Typology and the Ethics of Tragedy in *Samson Agonistes*," *Criticism* 33 (1989): 118 (for the quotation) and 145–46 (for the explanation).

59. For the argument that the theater of the Philistines bears a resemblance to Sir Christopher Wren's Sheldonian Theatre (1664–69), see Jose, *Ideas of Restoration*, p. 156.

60. Far from forgetting or rejecting the aspirations of those poets at the Restoration who had looked forward to London becoming the capital of an extensive empire of trade, the poets of the Great Fire continue to celebrate the city as "the great *Emporeum* of the world," "the Granary of the World, and Mine / Of golden Oare," a "Storehouse of men, and armes; who hast a Mass / Of wealth to-boot," and "the Worlds *Chief Mart*," whither "Gold, Silver, Pearl, Wine, Oyl" come swimming on the back of the Thames. They celebrate the convergence of the world's fleets bringing needed building materials up the Thames and even see in this *"floating Town,"* a foreshadowing of "a City Statelier than a Fleet," a "nobler Navy on the Land" that, rebuilt in part of prefabricated houses sent from the United Provinces, may "prove Amsterdam." See W[illiam?] F[enne?], *London Surveyed*, lines 18, 30–31, 72–74; Eliott, *Great Brittains Beauty*, line 61, 53; Jeremiah Wells, *On the Rebuilding of London* (1667), lines 217–20; and Ford, *Londons Resurrection*, lines 220, 224.

61. Paul Schrecker, *Work and History: An Essay on the Structure of Civilization* (Princeton: Princeton University Press, 1948), pp. 13, 15.

62. F[enne?], *London Surveyed*, line 162.

63. Wells, *On the Rebuilding of London*, lines 247–48.

64. Kenneth Burke, "The Imagery of Killing," *Hudson Review* 1 (1948): 153. For another reading emphasizing the motive of revenge behind the work, see Kendrick, "Typology and the Ethics of Tragedy."

65. For discussions that emphasize the uncertain authority for Samson's actions, see Stanley Fish, "Question and Answer in *Samson Agonistes*," in *"Comus" and "Samson Agonistes": A Casebook*, ed. Julia Lovelock (London: Macmillan, 1975); Wittreich, *Interpreting "Samson Agonistes,"* pp. 345–46 et passim; Guillory, "House of the Father," pp. 159–66; and Dayton Haskin, *Milton's Burden of Interpretation* (Philadelphia: University of Pennsylvania Press, 1994), pp. 179–80.

66. Christopher Hill, *Experience of Defeat*, p. 316.

67. French, *Records*, 5:1–3, 436, 460–61.

68. On the importance of secrecy in the poem, see Haskin, *Milton's Burden*, pp. 162–82; and John Rogers, "The Secret of *Samson Agonistes*," *Milton Studies* 33 (1996): 111–32. Samson represents his infidelity to God as a betrayal of a secret at lines 201, 377–78, 497–98, 879, and 1000–1002.

69. *The Complete Poetry of John Milton*, ed. John T. Shawcross (New York: Anchor Books, 1971).

70. So Christopher Hill: "Milton often seems deliberately to blur the external distinctions between good and evil in order to emphasize the all-importance of the internal spirit" (*Milton*, p. 444).

71. Even George Wither found himself silenced by appeals to the secret passages of the spirit. He says that he will neither defend nor condemn the recent actions of the Army in dissolving Parliament because "I know there have been heretofore, and that possibly there may be now and hereafter, (when the people of GOD are in extraordinary streights) such impulses of spirit inducing other men at some times, to extraordinary Executions, that I dare not judge them to be performed with an *evil conscience,* or without Divine approbation; because I am not privy to the *secret passages* which are or may be betwixt GOD and the *Prosecutors;* and because also, I finde, that the *Holy Ghost* hath justified many in undertakings of that nature; as *Phineas, Rahab, Jael,* and others remembered in *Holy Scripture;* who were active, so repugnantly to common Rules of just proceeding, and to the literal sence of Laws morally and ordinarily obliging; that, *I* should have thought them worthy to have been condemned for *Murther, Treason, Truce-breaking,* and barbarously *infringing the Law of Hospitality,* if the Spirit of GOD had not by *Sacred Writ,* informed me, that those Prosecutions, were effects of their *Faith.*" See his *A Cordial Confection* (1659), p. 3. Harapha describes Samson in similar terms as a "League-breaker," murderer, and "Robber" (lines 1184, 1186, 1188).

72. See Kerrigan, "Irrational Design." On biblical narratives, I quote Herbert Schneidau, *Sacred Discontents: The Bible and Western Literature* (Baton Rouge: Louisiana State University Press, 1976), p. 279. In this spirit, Wittreich writes: "*Samson* may be seen as a poem about the interpretive conflicts it has spawned, about the ideological rifts they have opened; it does not proselytize or propagandize but instead exposes ideological differences and mediates the space between them" (*Interpreting "Samson Agonistes,"* p. 52).

73. Wittreich, *Interpreting "Samson Agonistes,"* p. xvii.

74. Singly, or as a pair, Samson and Dalila are depicted as exemplary figures at lines 241-46, 290-92, 765, 955-57, 971-96, 1714-17, 1733-40.

75. Mary Ann Radzinowicz, *Towards "Samson Agonistes": The Growth of Milton's Mind* (Princeton: Princeton University Press, 1978).

76. On this phrase, see Barbara Lewalski, "Milton's *Samson* and the 'New Acquist of True [Political] Experience,'" *Milton Studies* 24 (1988): 233-51.

77. Milton consistently insists on drawing distinctions between acts on the basis of inner states that seem to defy articulation. "ELEGANCE is the discriminating enjoyment of food, clothing and all the civilized refinements of life, purchased with our honest earnings," we are told in *Christian Doctrine,* while "luxury" is "opposed to this," but the opposition seems to depend on the spirit in which these two modes of consumption are undertaken (*CPW* 6:732-33).

78. Alfred F. Chalk, "Natural Law and the Rise of Economic Individualism in England," *Journal of Political Economy* 59 (1951): 332-47; Appleby, *Economic Thought,* pp. 242-79.

Conclusion

1. John Bunyan, *Pilgrims Progress* (Part 1, 1678; Part 2, 1684), ed. N. H. Keeble (Oxford: Oxford University Press, 1984), pp. 74-75.

2. *Of Reformation* (May 1641), *CPW* 1:590.

3. *Of Reformation* and *The Reason of Church Government* (Jan.-Feb. 1642), in *CPW* 1:613, 588, 856.

4. See "To Benedetto Buonmattei the Florentine" (Sept. 10, 1638) and *The History of Britain*, in *CPW* 1:328-32, 5:39-41.

5. The extent to which Adam Smith's economic vision is informed by a moral conception of the individual is sometimes underestimated. Consider his denunciation of monopolies in terms reminiscent of the free trade pamphlets of the 1640s: "Like the laws of Draco, these laws may be said to be all written in blood." See his *An Inquiry into the Nature and Causes of the Wealth of Nations* (1776), ed. R. H. Campbell and A. S. Skinner (Indianapolis: Liberty Classics, 1981), p. 648. Like Milton, figures of the Scottish Enlightenment were still willing to consider the possibility that modern ideas of wealth, justice, and liberty might not be perfectly compatible with virtue. See Richard B. Sher, "From Troglodytes to Americans: Montesquieu and the Scottish Enlightenment on Liberty, Virtue, and Commerce," in *Republicanism, Liberty, and Commercial Society, 1649-1776,* ed. David Wootton (Stanford: Stanford University Press, 1994), pp. 371-74.

6. *CPW* 4:532. Milton's Latin reads: "Quanto præstabilius esset, vobísque dignius, si opes, si libertatem, si pacem, si imperium vultis, à virtute, industria, prudentia, fortitudine vestra non dubitare petere hæc omnia, quàm su regio dominatu necquicquam sperare?" (*The Works of John Milton,* ed. Frank Allen Patterson et al., 20 vols. [New York: Columbia University Press, 1931-38], 7:542).

7. *The Reason of Church Government,* in *CPW* 1:802.

8. See Arthur Barker, *Milton and the Puritan Dilemma, 1641-1660* (Toronto: University of Toronto Press, 1942). For Barker, Milton was "an impractical idealist rather than a political thinker; and his theory of society was essentially religious and ethical, not secular and economic" (p. xiv). But, says Barker, "it is of illogicality rather than insincerity that he should be accused" (p. xx).

9. See Max Weber, *The Protestant Ethic and the Spirit of Capitalism,* trans. Talcott Parsons (New York: Charles Scribner's Sons, 1930); and R. H. Tawney, *Religion and the Rise of Capitalism: A Historical Study* (1929; reprint, Gloucester, Mass.: Peter Smith, 1962). Weber's "Protestant Ethic" informs, for instance, Jackie DiSalvo, *War of Titans: Blake's Critique of Milton and the Politics of Religion* (Pittsburgh: Pittsburgh University Press, 1981), pp. 261-67; and John Guillory, "The Father's House: *Samson Agonistes* in Its Historical Moment," in *Re-Membering Milton: Essays on the Texts and Traditions,* ed. Mary Nyquist and Margaret W. Ferguson (New York: Methuen, 1987). For a critique of this tradition on theological grounds, see Catherine Gimelli Martin, "Self-Raised Sinners and the Spirit of Capitalism: *Paradise Lost* and the Critique of Protestant Meliorism," *Milton Studies* 30 (1993): 109-34.

10. An influential interpretation of republicanism that has stressed its conservative and anticommercial qualities is J. G. A. Pocock, *The Machiavellian Moment: Florentine Political Thought and the Atlantic Republican Tradition* (Princeton: Princeton Uni-

versity Press, 1975). Despite sprinkling his pages with interesting references to the economic ideas of republicans, Pocock stresses republicanism's "basically hostile perception of early modern capitalism" (p. ix). More recently Pocock has contended that "the appeal to commercial individualism was always conducted by English and Scottish writers as a vindication of established, and usually traditional, forms of authority" ("*The Machiavellian Moment* Revisited: A Study in History and Ideology," *Journal of Modern History* 53 [1981]: 58). For a criticism of Pocock, see Joyce Appleby, "Republicanism and Ideology," *American Quarterly* 37 (1985): 463-71. On the context and significance of Pocock's book, see Daniel T. Rodgers, "Republicanism: The Career of a Concept," *Journal of American History* 79 (1992): 11-38; and David Wootton, "Introduction: The Republican Tradition: From Commonwealth to Common Sense," in *Republicanism,* ed. Wootton, pp. 8-26. For an essay that often takes issue with Pocock but still represents Milton's republicanism as anticommercial, see Steven Pincus, "Neither Machiavellian Moment nor Possessive Individualism: Commercial Society and the Defenders of the English Commonwealth," *American Historical Review* 103 (1998): 705-36. One aim of my study has been to show that to speak in terms of an enthusiasm for or hostility toward commerce is to employ standards that are too imprecise, for as Milton and his contemporaries well knew, not all forms of commerce are created equal.

11. On the quietist readings of Milton's late verse against which more recent criticism has reacted, see Mary Ann Radzinowicz, "The Politics of *Paradise Lost,*" in *Politics of Discourse: The Literature and History of Seventeenth Century England,* ed. Kevin Sharpe and Steven N. Zwicker (Berkeley: University of California Press, 1987).

12. Bernard Mandeville, *Fable of the Bees; or, Private Vices, Public Benefits* (1704-24), ed. F. B. Kaye, 2 vols. (Oxford University Press, 1924), 1:94-95.

13. On the Royal Society's attempts to reform English prose, see George Williamson, *The Senecan Amble: A Study in Prose from Bacon to Collier* (Chicago: University of Chicago Press, 1951), chap. 9. The theory of poetic language advanced in Sir William Davenant's letter to Thomas Hobbes and Hobbes's answer, both of which preface *Gondibert* (1651), contrasts markedly with Milton's practice in *Paradise Lost.*

14. [Charles Blount,] *A Just Vindication of Learning: or, An Humble Address to the High Court of Parliament in Behalf of the Liberty of the Press* (1679), pp. 11, 6, 14, 3, 9. *An Apology for the Liberty of the Press,* printed at the end of William Denton's *Jus cæsaris et ecclesiæ vere dictæ* (1681), likewise attacks the "holy *Inquisition*" of licensing, by which some men seek to "appropriate and monopolize unto themselves the whole power of the Press" (p. 2), and argues that "to stifle and mortifie Reason and Truths is the worst of all Murders" (p. 4). The main part of Denton's treatise begins with a consideration of Milton's *Treatise of Civil Power* (Feb. 16, 1659), and his *Apology for the Liberty of the Press* borrows many turns of phrase from *Areopagitica.*

15. George L. Cherry, "The Development of the English Free-Trade Movement in Parliament, 1689-1702," *Journal of Modern History* 25 (1953): 103-19; Tim Keirn, "Monopoly, Economic Thought, and the Royal Africa Company," in *Early Modern Conceptions of Property,* ed. John Brewer and Susan Staves (London: Routledge, 1995); Henry Horowitz, "The East India Trade, the Politicians, and the Constitution: 1689-1702," *Journal of British Studies* 27 (spring 1978): 1-18; Christopher Hill, *The Century of Revolution, 1603-1714* (New York: Norton, 1966), pp. 263-64; Perry Gauci, *The Politics of*

Trade: The Overseas Merchant in State and Society, 1660-1720 (Oxford: Oxford University Press, 2001), esp. chap. 5.

16. *CJ,* 16:308.

17. *Mitchel v Reynolds,* 1 Peere Williams 183-86, 24 Eng. Rep. 348-49 (1711).

18. Ralph Davis, "The Rise of Protectionism in England, 1689-1786," *Economic History Review,* 2d ser., 29 (1966): 306-17.

19. *The History and Proceedings of the House of Commons from the Restoration to the Present Time,* 14 vols. (1742), Feb. 29, 1697, 3:72-73.

20. [John Trenchard and Thomas Gordon,] no. 91 (Aug. 25, 1722), in *Cato's Letters: Or, Essays on Liberty, Civil and Religious, and Other Important Subjects,* a reprinting of the 6th ed. of 1755, ed. Ronald Hamowy (Indianapolis: Liberty Fund, 1995), 2:653.

21. See William Robert Scott, *The Constitution and Finance of English, Scottish and Irish Joint-Stock Companies to 1720,* 3 vols. (1910-12; reprint, New York: P. Smith, 1951), 1:326-471; Kenneth G. Davies, "Joint-Stock Investment in the Later Seventeenth Century," *Economic History Review,* 2d ser., 4 (1952): 283-301; P. G. M. Dickson, *The Financial Revolution in England: A Study of the Development of Public Credit, 1688-1756* (London: Macmillan, 1967); and John Clapham, *The Bank of England: A History,* 2 vols. (Cambridge: Cambridge University Press, 1944).

22. William Robert Scott, *Constitution and Finance,* 1:358; John Brewer, *The Sinews of Power: War, Money, and the English State, 1688-1783* (New York: Alfred Knopf, 1969), pp. 139, 221; Tony Claydon, *William III and the Godly Revolution* (Cambridge: Cambridge University Press, 1996), chap. 6. Bernard Mandeville offers an illustration of the importance of information to trade with his story of two sugar merchants whose strategies shift during a protracted bargaining process with each bit of private intelligence; see his *Fable of the Bees,* 1:61-63.

23. Guides to the period's polemical literature include W. T. Laprade, *Public Opinion and Politics in Eighteenth Century England to the Fall of Walpole* (New York: Macmillan, 1936); Michael Foot, *The Pen and the Sword* (London: Macgibbon and Kee, 1957); Dickson, *Financial Revolution,* pp. 15-35; and James O. Richards, *Party Propaganda under Queen Anne: The General Elections of 1702-13* (Athens: University of Georgia Press, 1972).

24. See Charles Davenant, *Political and Commercial Works . . . Relating to the Trade and Revenue of England,* ed. C. Whitworth, 5 vols. (1771), 1:151-52; and Pocock, *Machiavellian Moment,* p. 440, whose summary of Davenant I follow.

25. Bernard Mandeville, "The Grumbling Hive: or, Knaves Turn'd Honest," lines 11-12, in *Fable of the Bees,* 1:17. Milton's federalism may be seen to meet this dual requirement rather differently in the tension between local authority and a strong central government. In the American version of federalism, the central government is, in addition to being checked by local authority, modeled on the English constitution's balance of powers.

26. Nicholas Barbon, *A Discourse of Trade* (1690), pp. 30-31. Steven Pincus argues that many of the innovations of the 1690s, including the establishment of a National Bank, may be understood as the triumph of a commercial vision long propounded by such radicals as Nedham, Bethel, Robinson, and Worsley; see his "The Making of a Great Power? Universal Monarchy, Political Economy, and the Transformation of English Political Culture," *European Legacy* 5 (2000): 531-45. For a recent economic

analysis that supports Barbon's implication that it was the absolutism of the Stuarts that prevented the creation of a bank during their reigns, see Douglass C. North and Barry R. Weingast, "Constitutions and Commitment: The Evolution of Institutions Governing Public Choice in Seventeenth-Century England," *Journal of Economic History* 49 (1989): 803–32.

27. Joseph Addison, no. 3 (Mar. 3, 1711), in *The Spectator*, ed. Donald F. Bond, 5 vols. (Oxford: Clarendon Press), 1:15.

28. *A Declaration of His Excellency the Lord Fairfax, Lord General, and His Council of War, Concerning Their Resolution to Preserve and Protect the Freedom of Trade and Commerce* (Dec. 15, 1648).

29. Charles Davenant, *Works*, 1:152.

30. Pocock, *Machiavellian Moment*, p. 440.

31. I follow the text in Countess of Wichilsea (Anne Finch), *Selected Poems*, ed. Denys Thompson (Manchester: Fyfield Books, 1987).

32. Addison, no. 69 (May 19, 1711), in *The Spectator*, ed. Bond, 1:296.

33. See Brewer, *Sinews of Power*.

34. *CJ*, 16:297; Christopher Hill, *Century of Revolution*, p. 262–63.

35. Adam Smith, *Wealth of Nations*, pp. 749, 638; cf. pp. 91, 631–38, 819, 945–46. For a recent reassessment of these events, see Patrick Tuck, ed., *Warfare, Expansion, and Resistance*, vol. 5 of *The East India Company: 1600–1858*, ed. Tuck (London: Routledge, 1998).

36. See esp. "Reflections upon the Constitution and Management of the African Trade," in Charles Davenant, *Works*, 5:247–353.

37. David Brion Davis, *The Problem of Slavery in Western Culture* (Oxford: Oxford University Press, 1966), p. 183; Thomas Paine, *African Slavery in America*, in *The Writings of Thomas Paine*, ed. Moncure Daniel Conway, 4 vols. (1894; reprint, New York: AMS, 1967), 1:5; Samuel Seabury, *American Slavery Distinguished from the Slavery of English Theorists and Justified by the Law of Nature* (New York, 1861), p. 201–02.

38. Reginald Coupland, *The British Anti-Slavery Movement* (Oxford: Oxford University Press, 1933), p. 37, referring to *The African Slave Trade the Great Pillar and Support of the British Plantations in America* (1709) and another pamphlet of 1764.

39. Benjamin Worsley, *The Advocate* (1652), p. 12. Henry Wadsworth Longfellow eventually revived the figure of Samson to admonish his countrymen that if they did not liberate their slaves, their slaves might well liberate themselves—and in the process jeopardize the very "liberties" that Americans held so dear. He ends "The Warning" thus:

> There is a poor, blind Samson in this land,
> > Shorn of his strength and bound in bonds of steel,
> Who may, in some grim revel, raise his hand,
> > And shake the pillars of this Commonweal,
> Till the vast Temple of our liberties
> A shapeless mass of wreck and rubbish lies.

I quote from *The Poetical Works of Longfellow* (Boston: Houghton Mifflin, 1975).

40. Coupland, *British Anti-Slavery*; Roger Anstey, *The Atlantic Slave Trade and British Abolition, 1760–1810* (Atlantic Highlands, N.J.: Humanities Press, 1975).

41. George Wither, *Sighs for the Pitchers* (1666), pp. 29–30; Bishop Warburton is quoted in Coupland, *British Anti-Slavery*, pp. 41–42.

42. Mark Knights, "A City Revolution: The Remodelling of the London Livery Companies in the 1680s," *English Historical Review* 112 (1997): 1145.

43. Paine, *African Slavery in America*, in *Works*, 1:7.

44. *PP1610*, 2:224.

45. Charles Davenant, "On the Plantation Trade," in *Works*, 2:35.

46. Adam Smith, *Wealth of Nations*, p. 388.

47. See David Brion Davis, *Problem of Slavery*; Thomas Bender, ed., *The Antislavery Debate: Capitalism and Abolitionism as a Problem in Historical Interpretation* (Berkeley: University of California Press, 1992).

48. Although Wither denounces the physical abuses of slavery feelingly in *Sighs for the Pitcher* (1666), pp. 29–30, he adds that by preaching the Word to Negro slaves, Englishmen may lessen their own culpability. In *The Fundamental Constitutions of Carolina*, Locke writes, "Since charity obliges us to wish well to the souls of all men, and religion ought to alter nothing in a man's civil estate or right, it shall be lawful for slaves, as all others, to enter themselves and be of what church any of them shall think best, and thereof be as fully members as any freemen. But yet, no slave shall hereby be exempted from that civil dominion his master has over him" (*Political Essays*, ed. Mark Goldie [Cambridge: Cambridge University Press, 1997], pp. 179–80).

49. Thomas Haskell, "Capitalism and the Origins of Humanitarian Sensibility, Part I," in *Antislavery Debate*, ed. Bender, p. 111.

50. I quote Richard Chamberlayne, *Angliæ Notitia*, 3d ed., part 2 (1671), p. 209. On financial innovations, see Dickson, *Financial Revolution*. On England's foreign trade, see C. G. A. Clay, *Economic Expansion and Social Change: England, 1500–1700*, 2 vols. (Cambridge: Cambridge University Press, 1984), pp. 154–82. On the workforce of London's port, see Ralph Davis, *The Rise of the English Shipping Industry in the Seventeenth and Eighteenth Centuries* (London: Macmillan, 1962), pp. 15–19, 390. On England's internal trade, see J. A. Chartres, *Internal Trade in England, 1500–1700* (London: Macmillan, 1977); and D. C. Coleman, *Economy of England, 1450–1750* (Oxford: Oxford University Press, 1977), pp. 146–47.

51. Daniel Defoe, *The Review* 2, no. 3 (Mar. 6, 1705): 9.

52. See Ian Watt, *The Rise of the Novel: Studies in Defoe, Richardson, and Fielding* (Berkeley: University of California Press, 1965); and Michael McKeon, *The Origins of the English Novel, 1600-1740* (Baltimore: Johns Hopkins University Press, 1987). Studies of the financial revolution and the novel include Sandra Sherman, *Finance and Fictionality in the Early Eighteenth Century: Accounting for Defoe* (Cambridge: Cambridge University Press, 1996); and James Thompson, *Models of Value: Eighteenth Century Political Economy and the Novel* (Durham: Duke University Press, 1996).

53. Peter Paxton, *A Discourse Concerning the Nature, Advantage and Improvement of Trade* (1704), p. 16.

54. Alexander Pope, *Moral Essays: Epistle to Bathhurst*, lines 72–74.

Index